W9-CDO-937

THE IRISH

Portrait of a People

THE IRISH

Portrait of a People

RICHARD O'CONNOR

G. P. PUTNAM'S SONS
New York

 Published on the same day in Canada by Longmans Canada Limited, Toronto.

Library of Congress Catalog
Card Number: 75-161540

Printed in the United States of America

Foreword

To an unavoidable extent this book deals in generalizations, which are often both unfair and dangerous as well as glittering with temptation when attempting to describe a whole people. They are even more meretricious in trying to define and differentiate the Irish, who are notoriously individualistic and resent being dumped into categories. Ireland is a small island, smaller than the state of Indiana, but to the Irish the national character varies greatly from province to province, from county to county, and especially from urban centers to rural areas.

There is an old Irish nursery rhyme which runs, "Ulster for a soldier,/ Connaught for a thief,/ Munster for learning,/ and Leinster for beef." This is both inaccurate and libelous, but it indicates the extent of Irish sectionalism as well as the "dwarf-like mischievousness" which one writer has identified as the worst of Irish traits. It is true enough, however, that a man from Kerry will eye a Wexford man, for instance, with the same parochial suspicion as a Croat surveying a Montenegrin, as though they were separated by a continent rather than the width of an island.

One of the most perceptive observers of the Irish character, the sympathetic Anglo-Irish writer Robert Lynd, warned against the temptation to generalize about the Irish in 1910, and his admonition is no less valid today: "Almost all generalizations, I suppose, were in the beginning born of one seed of truth. Nearly all generalizations about Ireland, however, have grown up into perverted and lying shapes, like monstrous light-hiding trees, and in their branches the parrots of the nations chatter innumerable foolish things."

Lynd, however, couldn't resist a generalization of his own:

"The 'real Irishman' is neither essentially a Celt nor essentially a Catholic. He is merely a man who has had the good or bad fortune to be born in Ireland of Irish parents, and who is interested in Ireland more than any other country in the world." It is quite true that the Irish are notably self-engrossed. When World War I broke out, the Skibbereen *Eagle,* published in a small West Cork market town, warned in boxcar type across its front page: THE SKIBBEREEN EAGLE HAS ITS EYE ON THE KAISER.

Fascinated though they are by themselves, the Irish strongly resent anyone writing about them, particularly anyone from the "outside world," because they are convinced that no one can understand them without at least a half century's intense study on the ground. And they are right. The Irish are a whirlwind of contradictions; for any general statement you make about them, they can find a dozen opinions to the contrary, complete with scholarly citations. They also hate to be quoted because they know how awkward and foolish things can look in cold print; toward this they have the same attitude of certain other peoples who will not permit themselves to be photographed out of fear that the camera will snatch away their souls. For this reason I have avoided quoting anyone but public figures who presumably have grown protective calluses.

It is only fair to add that the Irish are as fascinating as their reputation and their country as beautiful as its propaganda makes it out to be.

R. O'C.

Contents

THE IRISH
Portrait of a People

ATLANTIC OCEAN
IRISH SEA
ST. GEORGE'S CHANNEL
ULSTER
CONNAUGHT
LEINSTER
MUNSTER
DONEGAL
LONDONDERRY
ANTRIM
TYRONE
Belfast
FERMANAGH
ARMAGH
DOWN
LEITRIM
SLIGO
MONAGHAN
CAVAN
MAYO
LOUTH
ROSCOMMON
LONGFORD
MEATH
WESTMEATH
DUBLIN
Dublin
GALWAY
OFFALY
KILDARE
LEIX
WICKLOW
CLARE
CARLOW
KILKENNY
TIPPERARY
LIMERICK
WEXFORD
WATERFORD
KERRY
CORK

1.

The Quality of Irishness

I found them to be good-humored, clever . . . economical and hospitable.

—ANTHONY TROLLOPE.

Preconceptions fade fast, almost from the moment the big Aer Lingus jet from Boston or New York swoops down from the cloud cover and the lush wet greenness of the island comes into view, the industrialized Shannon estuary, the bustling international airport at Shannon with a Bulgarian airliner on the tarmac, finally the growing sprawl of Dublin itself from the mountains to the sea. The Englishman and the European may think of Ireland as the Continent's western outpost, but to the American, particularly the Irish-American, the island is a lot more than a geographic entity; he comes looking for a clue to himself as a Jewish-American goes to Israel, as on a pilgrimage.

He may have read or heard that Ireland in the past decade has been modernizing itself, has become accustomed to relative prosperity, has succumbed in part to television, the automobile, the miniskirt, student rebellions and youthful radicalism, but in the back of his mind is an indelible picture of thatched cottages and saintly old ladies dozing before open turf fires and rural Voltaires spouting wit and wisdom in every crossroads pub. But he is about to suffer from something akin to culture shock—a brisk shaking down of his expectations. Dublin traffic roars and sputters, with hardly a donkey cart to be seen. Huge signboards block the view of the deplaning passenger. What is visible mainly are thickets of towering television aerials designed to pluck the signals of BBC and ITV from across the Irish Sea and allow the Dubliner a spicier variety of entertainment than Telefis Eireann offers. Driving in from the airport along the Upper Drumcondra Road, the visitor finds himself in shoals of cars, motorcycles, motor scooters, bicycles—not a few of the cars being gleaming Mercedes assembled in a plant outside Dublin—speeding past the sprawling northern suburbs, thousands of new houses without turf sheds or whitewashed stone walls.

Once in the city center he will find many of the Georgian houses being destroyed and replaced by blocks of flats and offices, without the fanlights, the stoops, and the brass fittings which have made Dublin an architectural glory—but also without the broken windows, the splintered doors, the tenement litter of battered prams and dented garbage cans, the old women in shawls and the young ones with a scrap of scarf around their heads waiting in the doorways for husbands, fathers, brothers, and sons to return from the pub on the corner.

On O'Connell Street he will be engulfed by the roar of double-deck buses and other vehicular traffic down a thoroughfare as wide and bustling as San Francisco's Market Street or New Orleans' Canal Street, with several skyscrapers looming over but not quite dominating the older landmarks, the General Post Office with the Irish tricolor whipped by the steady breeze off the Irish Sea, or the green copper domes of the Four Courts and the Customs House. There is the immemorial leaden flow of the Liffey under the O'Connell Bridge; the mercantile activity along the quays of the river which neatly bisects Dublin Town; the student atmosphere—more like the Sorbonne than the Harvard Yard—around College Green.

Once he reaches Grafton Street and his hotel, with American Express and Cook's comfortingly close by, the visitor will quickly learn that tourism is one of Ireland's most lucrative industries, all efficiently packaged and as briskly managed as a sausage-making machine. He will be shown the sights of Dublin and whisked out into the countryside on a bus to be shown a carefully preserved thatched cottage or two, a glimpse of Galway

Bay, a kiss at the Blarney Stone, a "medieval" dinner at a restored castle, probably Bunratty near the Shannon Airport, the lakes of Killarney and the Ring of Kerry. No doubt he will be suitably stuffed with touristic sights and sounds, impressions of a wet green land with vistas that change color and shape with every shading of light and mist, from emerald to amethyst, of mist-covered lakes and fuchsia-starred hedgerows, of a land in which everything seems tilted, physically and perhaps psychologically, of hundreds of villages whose façades have not changed in a century, of long empty roads that stretch seemingly from nowhere to nowhere, of the curious but deceptive openness and innocence of country faces.

If he is an Irish-American, he may backtrack through a hundred or more years of family history—the famine, the escape to America, the dim and wrenched memories of his antecedents—and find his ancestral home and the distant kinfolk who stayed behind, smaller and more gnarled than he would have imagined, perhaps a trifle resentful of his visible affluence and suspicious of his American ways. If he has the time to get off the well-defined tourist triangle between Dublin and Galway and Limerick, he may gain an impression of what seems a creeping anti-Americanism—the fear and resentment of a big power endemic in so many parts of the world, but also a more personal contempt for certain American attributes. He may find himself representing a caricature of the American abroad, though a modest little fellow himself, as a potbellied, loud-spoken, liquored-up barbarian with an oversize cigar between his teeth, festooned with photographic equipment, and driving a car much too big and powerful for the narrow Irish roads.

He may find himself caught up in strange, semihallucinatory experiences—odd meetings and encounters by the roadside—or being suddenly caught up in a swirl of social activity, with hospitality striking like forked lightning, and himself speeding through the night in a car full of strangers headed for the back room of a pub over the mountains and forty miles away. Unaware of the sly potency of Irish whiskey—though it is only seventy proof—and the black beer of the countryside, he may well find himself in the backroom of a dimmed-out pub, with the proprietor keeping an eye out for the Garda, talking deep into the night with a chance-met drinking companion about deeply significant matters which he will forget entirely in the grip of a ferocious hangover.

Unless he is unusually perceptive and has more time to spend in Ireland than the average visitor, he will sense only the outer edges of the Irish quality, the elusive traits, the slippings and slidings of a national temperament that sometimes seems as unpredictable as the weather, the power of rumor, and the elliptical meanings of Irish-English with all its indirect approaches. John D. Sheridan, whose penetrating humor enlivens the *Irish Press,* has defined this devious use of the language:

> We have intricate conventions when we are merely looking for information. Less sophisticated peoples go straight to the point and say: "Did you see Johnny Mac?" but to our minds this brutal directness smacks of insensitivity and bad breeding. What we say is: "You didn't happen to see Johnny Mac anywhere about?" "Anywhere about" has prepositional force but only in a very vague and general way. It merely cuts down the area under investigation and implies that the person who is being questioned may confine his self-examination to his own immediate neighborhood, and need not consider the possibility of his having seen Johnny Mac in Greenland, Buenos Aires, or Wagga Wagga.

Communicating with the Irish is always tricky for literal-minded persons of Saxon descent or upbringing in Britain or America. It is subject to mind-bending switchbacks and paralyzing short circuits. It causes people who think along what they conceive to be a straight line, and do not speak with forked tongue, to attribute their misunderstanding of the Irish form of communication to poetic license, or Celtic mysticism, or something fuzzy in the atmosphere. One wet night in Dublin I met a prosperous-looking businessman, with a diffident young English associate in tow, who was sinking doubles of Powers Gold Label in preparation for his annual three-day sabbatical to take in the Punchestown races. Somehow the conversation turned to President Eamon De Valera, the towering grand totem of the Irish Republic, in and out of power for half a century, a superannuated George Washington. Like many Irishmen, my newfound friend would like to tear that totem down with his bare hands or says he would when, as the quaint Irish police court phrase describes it, "in drink taken." The pub was well populated, but he denounced De Valera for a catalogue of political and personal crimes that would have made Caligula hang his head in shame. And he spoke loud enough to be heard in every nook of the establishment and possibly out in the President's stately residence in Phoenix Park. The secret police, or Special Branch, were everywhere, he roared, listening and taking down the names of dissidents. At the end of his recital, he tapped the side of his rubicund nose with a forefinger and murmured, "But mind you, I've said nothing." That is the standard cautionary, uttered after an astonishing outpour of confidences, after in fact *everything* has been said. It is also true that if someone from abroad had denounced President De Valera, the same man would have risen thunderously to his defense.

The Irish are winningly full of self-criticism. They are notorious for it. Who has flayed them so mercilessly as their own writers and politicians and professional moralists? Self-deprecation, in Irish hands, can attain the proportions of an art form. From head hanging of the most pitiful kind, however, the Irishman can turn swiftly to the offensive and lay waste to anyone who agrees with him too readily in his moment of self-abnegation. It is far better to take the other side when an Irishman is running Ireland down, much safer to insist on his excellence when he is deploring his own failings.

Thus, when an American tourist's letter to the editor was published in one of the Dublin newspapers in the spring of 1970 complaining of the dirt and disorder of the capital's streets, the presence of beggars, and other unseemly sights (the man must have come from a very small tidy town to be shocked by Dublin), there was an answering barrage from the Irish readership. The unofficial critic was advised, in effect, to get out of the country or keep a civil tongue in his head. Yet there was only a minimal response to a much more definitive assault on Irish public hygiene by Gay Byrne, who is presiding magistrate of Irish television's weekly *Late Show,* on which shocking things are said. "I think the Irish are basically a lazy people. I also think we are untidy, unhygienic and dirty," Mr. Byrne said. "Generally speaking, you only have to walk down O'Connell street and see the sloppy clothes, heavy and crumpled suits on people. The Irish are not particularly soap-and-water conscious. Look at the public toilets . . . usually desperately untidy and unhygienic." Since every Irishman is licensed to belabor other Irishmen, Mr. Byrne's remarks drew only mild reproofs from the Irish Tourist Board, the Irish Hotels Federation, and other image-conscious groups.

There is something in the Irish climate that seems disorienting to the visitor and may contribute to the Irishman's attitude toward work and personal effort of all kinds, not to mention a time sense almost as elastic as a Mexican's. It is wet or threatening to be wet much of the time. There is a constant unreality of haze and mist, a lack of definition. No doubt this has contributed toward a lackadaisical approach to keeping appointments, to starting and finishing a job with dispatch. In Ireland no one bounds out of bed in the morning and rushes off to punch a time clock or makes a tigerish spring at the work to be done. The start of every day is approached with cautious deliberation, and lashings of tea, and a slow revving up of the metabolism. Once under way, however, the Irishman is anything but lazy; he works long hours, and his energy seems to reach a peak long after the rest of the world has quit work for the day. And if his time sense seems out of whack, it may be because of that tilting of the natural order, which ordains that in summer the light stays on the hills until eleven o'clock at night, that a little lamb of a cloud can drift over the sky and drench you to the skin, that the atmosphere is pervaded by an almost semitropical languor.

All that affects only the physical movement of the Irishman. Mentally he operates on a coiled-spring mechanism. It has often been remarked that Ireland is a slow country full of quick-witted people. The Irish are masters of the put-down, often administered so deftly that a man can be utterly deflated, stripped of pretense, and not realize it until he collapses halfway home. They are artists indeed of the spoken word, able to sum up in a flashing image, puncture pomposity with a short sentence, leave you for dead on the bare boards of a pub floor if you venture (with leaden phrases out of a television jokebook) to enliven the conversation.

The art of keeping the invader, or tourist, in his place has been cultivated through centuries of dealing with the outsider, who in the past usually came with more disciplined battalions and heavier firepower than the Irish, always disorganized and ready to quarrel over matters of procedure, could muster against them. Their quick wits have always been the Irishmen's last line of defense, making certain that while the invader might occupy the last bog and village in the island, he would never be comfortable with his conquests.

A young Dublin taxi driver I know recently picked up a fare at the airport, an Englishman whose family had once (he said) owned vast estates in County Cork. The Englishman was bemoaning how his family had come down in the world since the Irish decided half a century ago that they could dispense with any further guidance from Westminster. "Why," he said, "it used to take us three and a half minutes to drive from the gate to the great house." The Dublin cabby was unimpressed. "Sure," he replied, "I had the same trouble until I traded in my old car."

An American can also be sharply reduced in size if he is not mindful that while Irish hospitality is quite as warm and openhanded as it is reputed to be, the native tenderness toward the stranger cannot always subdue the urge to take a jab at his sensibilities. A gregarious Irish-American from Colorado whom I met on an Aer Lingus flight back to the States was still shaking his head ruefully over an encounter in County Clare.

His name was O'Connor, and he was strolling down a country road when he came across a farmer baling hay in a field. The American genially summoned the farmer from his labors, said his name was O'Connor, and asked if there were any O'Connors in the district.

The farmer, a little edgy over having been disturbed at his labors, replied, "It depends on which branch of the family you mean."

"I didn't know the O'Connors were divided up into clans," the American said.

"Oh, yes," the farmer told him, "you'd have to know whether you belonged to the sheep-stealing O'Connors or the well-poisoning O'Connors or the barn-burning O'Connors."

Another Irish practice of which the visitor should be wary is the local version of the put-on. It is called codding, which is kidding, or ribbing, or leg pulling, with Celtic variations. One form is to stuff the gullible stranger with the most outrageous tales, which he is expecting to hear anyway, about Little Men and fairy rings and hyperactive ghosts. Another is the more subtle gambit of the excessive compliment, a wholesale puffing up of a man's ego to the point where he is ready to soar over the rooftops. It must be done with style and grace, of course, or the intended victim may suffer a sudden attack of overinflation. As the evening waxes, the compliments became more exaggerated, progressing from the generalized "Ah, what a lovely class of man you are" to specific flattery of the victim's eyelashes or the way he lights a cigarette or the immense wisdom of his outlook. The trick is to make the victim swallow the most outrageous compliments without realizing that he is being codded. If he catches on, of course, the game is over.

The way to an Irishman's heart is through his risibilities. If you can make him laugh, you can bring him down quicker than if you struck him with the thickest blackthorn stick on the island. Though he may wear a long gloomy face, with eyes as melancholy as one of Poe's lost tarns, he is always on the lookout for whatever comedy he can find in life. His humor is indigenous, rooted to the life around him, and the metronomic humor of films and television has little appeal for him. And he has the ultimate grace of being able to laugh at himself.

Like the gallows humor of the Jews, the Irishman's has served as his buffer against a history of oppression and adversity. It is often a mocking humor; "it is as if the very spirit of Ireland," wrote Oliver St. John Gogarty, "mocked and revelled in vicissitude, deriding death."

Despite much propaganda to the effect that all Irishmen are reckless, swashbuckling, impractical and sentimental, they are more likely to be sober-minded and down-to-earth when money, land, and possessions are at stake. There are no laughing boys when the shillings and pence are counted out. For many years, the dowry was as essential to a proper Irish marriage as the white veil. The observation of Anthony Trollope after a long stay in Ireland is still true: "I found them to be good-humored, clever—the working classes much more intelligent than those of England

—economical and hospitable. We hear much of their spendthrift nature; but extravagance is not the nature of an Irishman. He will count the shillings in a pound much more accurately than an Englishman and will with much more certainty get twelve pennyworth from each."

The Irishman's folk wisdom is acerb, all illusion and sentimentality leached out: "Death is the poor man's doctor. . . . A borrowed saw cuts anything. . . . If you want praise, die; if you want blame, marry."

Sentimentality is a luxury, from the Irish viewpoint, to be afforded by the historically successful, the affluent, the winners in the game that destiny plays with men and nations. "Mother Machree" and other tushery set to treacly music came out of Tin Pan Alley. More in keeping with the Irish spirit of jeering at fate was the street ballad popular just after World War I, "Johnny, I Hardly Knew Ye," which some have suggested should be the Irish national anthem. Supposedly sung by a young woman whose husband deserted her to run away to war and returned a wreck, its verses include:

> Ye haven't an arm and ye haven't a leg,
> Huroo! Huroo!
> Ye eyeless, noseless, chickenless egg;
> Ye'll have to be put in a bowl to beg,
> Johnny, I hardly knew ye.
>
> Where are the legs with which you run?
> Huroo! Huroo!
> Where are the legs with which you run
> When you went to shoulder the gun?
> Begob, your dancing days are done.
> Johnny, I hardly knew ye.
>
> Where are the eyes which were so mild?
> Huroo! Huroo!
> Where are the eyes which were so mild
> When of my love you were beguiled?
> Why did you skedaddle from me and the child?
> Johnny, I hardly knew ye!

As those mocking verses suggest, the Irishman looks upon life without any illusions about love, martial glory, or the pursuit of happiness on earth. He may be fanciful and whimsical, he may play the traditional, wayward Celt at times, but for the most part he is in close touch with the realities. With the flush of prosperity that began about ten years ago, he discovered the formerly scarce uses and pleasures of materialism. To many old republicans who had fought and bled to establish an independent Ireland, there was cause for head shaking over the condition of the Irish psyche on the occasion of the fiftieth anniversary of the Easter Rising in 1966. A few weeks before the official celebration a band of activists, identity still unknown, but widely suspected, blew up Nelson's Pillar, which for more than a century and a half had stood in the middle of O'Connell Street as a symbol of the old English dominion over Ireland. As a whole, however, the Irish were rather tepid in their enthusiasm for the brave and bloody old days when a trench-coated and cloth-capped underground army fought for their liberty; official celebrations, the requirement of turning out to wave flags and listen to windy speeches about dead martyrs, are liable to bore them. ("Johnny, I Hardly Knew Ye" sounds its bitter counterpoint to talk of past glory.) The feeling of noninvolvement was particularly noticeable among the younger people, who feel that the ancients have profited too long and too well from their participation in the Rising and the Troubles and have kept their grip on the levers of power with inordinate tenacity.

Sean O'Faolain, the preeminent Irish writer and an old freedom fighter himself, wondered aloud whether the modern Irish were worthy of all the sacrifices made on their behalf, whether he and his old comrades hadn't hoped for too much, hadn't "idealized" the prospects for an Ireland that could combine the Celtic precept of total equality with a prosperity in which all could share. Like many others, he had the feeling that the revolution, somehow, had been betrayed in many of its aspirations. He wrote:

> What we have got "is a modern version of the kind of society that James Joyce described so contemptuously, as he saw it, in the Dublin of 1902, a society from which this modern thing dif-

> fers only in that Irish names have been plastered over English names. . . . We have set up a society of urbanised peasants, whose mentality, whose whole image of life is, like that antiquated society, based on privilege; a society run by a similar small minority of ambitious businessmen, "rugged individualists" looking down at, fearing, even hating "the men and women of no property," thriving on the same theory of God-made inequality, welcoming and abetting, by the same self-interested silence, the repression of every sign of individual criticism or reconsideration of the social and moral results of history.

It would seem that the present Irish fixation on materialism (as the idealists see it), on efficiency and modernization, on catching up with the rest of the world, on chasing the tourist dollar, even on gazing wistfully across the Irish Sea at England's brand of hedonism/materialism, would negate the outsiders' general belief that the slothful Irish aren't making the best of what they've got. Prince Bismarck once suggested that the Irish and Dutch should trade places; the energetic Dutch would soon make Ireland a paradise (at least from the Prussian viewpoint, for which the Irish have little respect), while the Irish in Holland would let the dikes collapse and drown themselves—good riddance.

The Irish today, whatever the degree of their past infatuation with decay and procrastination, are beginning to hustle. There are signs of impatience with quaintness, with charming eccentricity, with mooning over or in the "Celtic twilight." There is an atmosphere of creeping Rotarianism, a spreading of the gospel of the entrepreneur. And there is a solemn nodding of agreement when the sales manager of an import-export firm dealing largely with West Germany returns to Dublin and is quoted in the press as warning that Irish businessmen will have to "pull up their socks and get cracking," acquire the aggressive outlook of a Düsseldorf executive, because "in the Common Market either Irish industry will be taken over by German industry or it will be put out of business." The prospect of joining the Common Market has whetted appetites for sharing in the head-turning affluence of Western Europe. Certain visionaries, with computers at their elbows, catch a glimmering of smokestacks, oil-transfer depots, refineries, assembly lines, and high-tension lines rising against the old green horizons, no matter that it can take an hour to complete a telephone call from Dublin to the countryside or that cattle are still driven down the main streets of fair-sized towns.

The businessman, the bureaucrat, the professional planner with his schemes for knocking down Georgian houses and replacing them with glass and steel skyscrapers, the politician with his eye on the main chance, the revved-up gombeen-man who is the microscopic tycoon of the Irish villages—all are forming what is called elsewhere the power structure, and the social establishment as well, in which the pecking order is rigidly maintained.

The progress of such schemes, the fruition of plans for modernization, will be impeded not so much by inertia as by a much more positive force. It is rather difficult to isolate, but it is a sort of perversity which delights in bringing down schemes and schemers of anything regarded as grandiose; it is a diffuse and subconscious desire, seemingly, to see things *not* work, a part of the Celtic psyche that holds all earthly projects of any magnitude in deep contempt. The workings of that indefinable force can be witnessed in the temper tantrum of a German businessman, fresh from the well-ordered life of the Ruhr, exploding at the Cork City Airport when he is unable to complete a telephone call to Dublin, can find no one who will drive him where he wants to go, and learns that the Irish version of the English language is something else again. The brisk planners of the Common Market are going to find Ireland and its resistance to well-laid plans a refreshing change from nations which worship graphs, charts, and blueprints.

The Irish simply have their own way of doing things, an oblique approach to problems which other peoples would meet head on. In the twelfth century a vexed English scholar named Giraldus Cambrensis noted that "on making signs either with the hands or the head, they beckon when they mean that you should go away, and nod backward as often as they wish to be rid of you."

They have an astonishing ability to separate abstraction from reality, a quality which is much misunderstood and underestimated by the non-Irish. This trait, which sometimes strikes outsiders as hilariously disconnected from the natural order of things, is illustrated by the story of two Irishmen slogging through the rain on a country road on their way to ambush a much-hated English landlord. They waited for hours, drenched to their skins, at the site chosen for the ambush without their intended victim's showing up. Finally one of the would-be assassins remarked to the other, "I hope the dear man hasn't caught a cold." This sounds like a joke but isn't. The man wasn't trying to be funny. Killing the landlord would have been an act of justice. His health was another matter. It was possible to hate the landlord for his sins but to wish him well as a human being.

Only an Irishman will sob while trying to knock your head off in a pub during a misunderstanding. Not that he isn't capable of unmixed loathing. His pursuit of a feud would wring admiration from a Corsican and reminds one that one of the parties to the most celebrated American vendetta was named McCoy. A nineteenth-century observer perhaps delved to the core of such matters when she wrote that feuds were "a great solace to ennui" and were the "mainstay of society in West Cork . . . thoroughly made, solid, and without a crack into which any importunate dove could insert so much as an olive leaf." The Irish will do almost anything to ward off ennui.

They like to "hang loose," as an American would say. Choking up over trivialities is the surest way to lose face with an Irishman. There is a certain joyful resilience, an amiable adjustability about Irish society. The Irish may be renowned individually for their explosive tempers and volatile spirits, but collectively they can exhibit a coolness and unflappability that should be the envy of nations with a greater reputation for phlegm.

One indication of this amazing adaptability is the Irish attitude toward labor strikes. The most unlikely unionized groups—bank executives, for instance—suddenly storm out of their places of employment en masse. They set about rectifying their grievances with the same dogged determination that characterized the revolution against Great Britain. Any other modern nation would probably have been brought to the verge of economic and social collapse by the two paralyzing bank strikes which have afflicted Ireland in the past several years. The first, by lower-echelon employees, took place in 1966 and lasted thirteen weeks.

In any other modern economy a general bank closure of even a week would have caused, at least, a mass nervous breakdown. There was no place where sizable checks could be cashed, none where they could be exchanged. The larger business establishments, department stores, and hotels had no place to deposit their cash. The credit system was completely ensnarled. Naturally enough, the continental economists, to whom such a situation was unthinkable, predicted a national disaster, not having reckoned with the Irish ability to work things out on a personal basis, in the same spirit as deals are made, merely on a man's word, in all the village cattle markets. At first checks were accepted and stored away against the day the banks reopened. Then everyone ran out of checks. It was common enough to see checks being written on the back of old envelopes. An informal barter system was quickly developed. Everyone lived out of each other's pockets, and there were some check writers who hoped the strike would never end. It was a fiscal comedy, unseemly to the gnomes of Zurich, perhaps, but a tribute to the Irish genius for improvisation and accommodation.

In the late spring of 1970, around the first of June, the bank executives decided it was time to brandish their spears and demand a measure of affluence to match the dignity of their positions. Shrewdly enough they struck just when the tourist season was beginning, and despite government intervention, they stayed out on strike until the last bewildered and confounded tourist had left the island after the September bank holiday—a rather hollow occasion in Ireland. The country survived with a considerable loss of face and an alarming loss of tourist revenue, with foreigners hard put to cash their traveler's checks and even harder put to understand how the Irish could endure such a wrenching inconvenience without taking stern reprisals against the bank executives. Aside from rather pompous statements from government officials on the "damage to the Irish image with other nations," the loss of national dignity, the embarrassment of having such an economic stricture occur just when Ireland was putting in her bid for membership in the Common Market—ignoring the hardship caused every individual Irishman—the country took it all in stride.

With the same general lack of outrage the Irish were accepting a government scheme by which a small exclusive group would be exempted from paying any income tax—foreigners at that—a proposal that in most other countries would have called forth demands for impeachment, if not something more violent. Shortly before his dismissal from Prime Minister Jack Lynch's Cabinet, in the spring of 1970, on charges of being implicated in the guns-for-Ulster conspiracy, Finance Minister Charles Haughey pushed through his plan for luring artists, writers, and musicians to Ireland. The bait was exemption from paying any income tax in Ireland. A number of famous or notorious American writers soon appeared on the scene to find out whether such a unique patronage would really be bestowed upon them. In their own country, after all, the depletion of their creative resources, unlike the production of oil wells, was given no consideration whatever.

There were a couple of wrinkles in the Haughey Plan which have yet to be ironed out. One of the larger ones is who would decide whether a certain artist was producing works of certifiable cultural value, because that was one of the provisos of the plan. What bureaucrat is competent to sort out the hacks and pretenders from the genuine creative artist? Would a writer be eligible if his works were proscribed by the Irish censorship? Another catch is that the tax refugee would have to give up his original citizenship and become an Irish national, or his income would be taxed at the source. And what would happen if another government decided to revoke the Haughey Plan?

Strangely enough the Irish people accepted the plan without much of an outcry, partly, perhaps, out of remembered pride in the tradition of Ireland as the sanctuary of "saints and scholars." There was some indignation expressed in the letters columns of the national newspapers over the creation of a privileged class in their midst, but it was less passionate than several other controversies then engaging the letter writers. Transplanted to the United States or most other countries, the Haughey Plan would have kicked up an uproar no major political party could have survived. The Irish, however, do not generate an excess of passion over matters which do not directly touch their lives.

They may be inflamed to riot over the outcome of a hurley match, but for the time being, to the intense irritation of those laboring to bring about a radical social and political change, they draw on one of the last sizable reservoirs of placidity available in the modern world.

There is an eternal Ireland existing beneath the surface of modern life, untouched by jackhammers or the increasing roar of tourist buses or the clatter of industrialization, that can be glimpsed occasionally out of the corner of your eye, that can be sensed in the reflection that no other small island, nor many a larger one, has made such a stir in the world.

2.

A Hundred Thousand Welcomes

Lord, how doth that country alter men.
—EDMUND SPENSER

The Irishman relatively is an ascetic character whose attitude toward creature comforts, dating back to the Firbolgs and Fomorians of the pre-Celtic past, is that of the nomadic herdsman. A religious oleograph, a color photograph of John F. Kennedy, and possibly one of Michael Collins or some other hero will do nicely for interior decoration. Generally he seems to have dressed in the dark or to have slept in his clothing, and a necktie is not much better than a noose. A deodorant is an offense in the nostrils of a decent man. Food is something to be taken in quantity, with no great amount of discourse during or between courses and without any ululating over the delicacy of a sauce. Plain food without any esoteric additions from the herb shelf is what he favors. His drink is stout or beer or whiskey, or whiskey with a stout or beer chaser, and any variations on the alcoholic theme are left to those of dubious and effete habits.

All this is unfair and insulting generalization, of course, because there are Irish gourmets and connoisseurs, there are glossily tailored Irishmen (and many more well-turned-out Irishwomen), there are those members of expense-account society in Dublin and the larger cities who make appreciative or critical noises over the quality of the hollandaise, and there may even be some who quaff vintage champagne in trusted company and behind drawn draperies.

Nevertheless, you can take the word of Monica Sheridan, who writes cookbooks and presides over a delightfully haphazard session on cooking over Irish television, when she affirms that there is "no tradition of elaborate cooking" in Ireland. The Irishman looks with the utmost suspicion on any dish that he doesn't recognize at a glance—steak and chips, for preference—and that his mother hasn't cooked for him.

The menu in most Irish restaurants, Dublin and a few other places always excepted, consists of sirloin steak with chips, grilled salmon or plaice, roast chicken on a slice of ham—and that's about it. As far as I am concerned, Irish cuisine is more than tolerable, but I have often heard persons with more refined tastes and sensitive palates complain that the cooking of Ireland is only a cut above the English, which ranks somewhere below the Eskimo, the Bedouin, and the Patagonian. Tradition is very deep-rooted in Ireland, and the attitude toward the culinary arts, as well as interior and exterior decoration, design and personal adornment, goes back to antiquity and a time when a cookfire and a few pots were all that was needed. Nomads to begin with, forcibly uprooted so many times since then by various conquerors, the Irish have not had the time or inclination to cultivate sybaritic tastes: Food is for nourishment, clothing for warmth, four walls and a roof for shelter, and besides they have a truly aristocratic disdain for the external, for fripperies and niceties.

All of which makes it difficult for those trying to lead the nation into an era of gracious living. Monica Sheridan recalls the pioneering days of her campaign to make the Irish, particularly the men, more conscious of the possibilities of civilized dining. She started in the right place, at home, but with an unwilling subject, her husband. She spent a whole afternoon preparing a French pudding called *croque-en-bouche* to round off a dinner party. "When the time came to serve it," she recalls, "I proudly planted this complicated confection right in the middle of the dining-room table expecting it to call forth squeaks of admiration from the assembled guests. Nobody even noticed it except my husband, who glowered at me, obviously furious at the intrusion. He was momentarily distracted in the middle of a very funny story he was telling about Brendan Behan, stark naked, in some hospital in Dublin. I had heard the story maybe a dozen times before and felt that my own labours deserved more attention."

Since then Mrs. Sheridan has concentrated on cooking simple dishes without embellishment, because the meat and vegetables grown in Ireland, and the fish caught off her shores, are so good in themselves that they don't require a culinary disguise. Educating the palate of the Irish male, in Mrs. Sheridan's expert opinion, is a lost cause. "A black sole grilled on the bone is acceptable but a *sole bonne femme* will cause grave doubts about whether you are trying to palm them off with whiting, or trying to poison them and get your hands on their life insurance. A duck is a duck and must come to the table with the two fat thighs sticking out of it. A *canard à la presse* is, to most Irishmen, a piece of newspaper speculation or possibly an instrument of torture invented by the Spanish Inquisition. My younger sister, fresh from her honeymoon, made an omelette for her new husband. He looked at her coldly across the table, turning the omelette over with a searching fork. 'If I must have eggs I'd rather have them boiled,' he said with finality. That clipped *her* culinary wings."

There must have been many similar brides firmly discouraged from frivolous experiment and subversion by French cookbooks. The women's magazines, as well as Mrs. Sheridan in her television appearances, have been crusading for a more venturesome atmosphere in Irish kitchens, but the Irish male will probably never be a devotee of Brillat-Savarin or recognize the supremacy of the Cordon Bleu.

Actually the raw materials of the Irish diet are the best available anywhere, and only the most jaded palate requires much fiddling with spices, herbs, and sauces. The lobsters caught off the west coast are so highly rated that most of them are snatched up by the French the moment they reach shore and consigned to French tables. The beef, lamb, pork, milk, and dairy products are superlative; so are the fish which the Irish, like Catholics anywhere who still observe the church's rule for abstaining from meat on Friday, will eat only when they have to. The smoked salmon, however, is regarded as a delicacy and is as popular as lox in New York City. The brown bread and white soda bread, of course, are one of the few natural glories left to Western civilization. Irish sausages are also highly regarded, so much so by James Joyce that anyone visiting him from Ireland was expected to smuggle in a few pounds of them. Barmback, a rich cake laced with fruit and spread with butter, is something to make high tea live up to its name.

There are a number of regional dishes which, to the outlander, testify more to mother wit than an instinct for refined noshing. Almost unknown outside Dublin, but highly favored by men returning from a Saturday night's tour of the pubs, is something called Dublin coddle—a stew made of sausages, bacon and onions. On the word of Monica Sheridan it was the favorite dish of Dubliners from Dean Swift to Sean O'Casey to Brendan Behan, and its homely ingredients are therefore not to be denigrated.

Stouter hearts and stronger stomachs are required for something called drisheen which is held to be a delicacy in County Cork but which would make even a Scotsman capable of ingesting haggis (oatmeal stuffed in a sheep's intestine) blanch in dismay. You won't find it in any restaurant; more likely in a backcountry cooking pot suspended over a peat fire.

The basic ingredient of drisheen is a quart of sheep's blood, which makes it a cousin to the blood pudding favored by the British and blood sausage highly regarded by the Germans, and which also makes it not at all unseemly that the author of *Dracula* was an Irishman. To the sheep's blood are added a quart of milk and a quart of cream, mutton suet, bread crumbs, salt, pepper, thyme, sage, tansey, and mace. After all this is mixed and strained and warmed up, it is poured into the intestines of a pig, baked, and allowed to congeal. According to Tony Butler, the Dublin columnist and (a cautionary note) the author of *The Art of Blarney,* drisheen is what makes Corkmen so formidable in business, the civil service, and police work that they are known as the Prussians of Ireland. Obviously it will never appear on the menu of the tourist hotels or the castles serving "medieval" dinners, desperate though their search for authenticated quaintness.

Aside from such culinary ventures as drisheen and a tasty mixture of potato, onion, and cabbage called colcannon, the inner Irishman is sustained on a monotonous traditional diet. Boiled potatoes and buttermilk, in amazing quantity, make up the noonday meal in many farmhouses. The Irishman likes only what he was raised on; the cooker, or bottled-gas stove, has taken over most kitchens, but until recently most cooking was done in pots over a turf fire, which did not allow for much variation. What goes into his stomach is vastly less important than what goes on in his head; the imagination and ritual which the French and Italians devote to the pleasures of the table are a waste of thinking time to him. His feeding habits are those of his ancestors, who were hard pressed by the exigencies of making a living off the Irish soil and by coping with their enemies and who never had the leisure to cultivate a taste for the graces.

The Irishman at drink like the Irishman at table has a utilitarian approach. Most pubs are dingy, comfortless as a bail bondsman's office, and apparently designed to make the transaction between man and alcohol as direct and uncomplicated as possible. Soft lighting, padded stools, television, jukebox? Not in an Irish pub in the countryside. In the cities and on the tourist beat a number of cocktail lounge types of places have sprung up caparisoned in the usual plastic upholstery, chrome fittings, neon lighting, and other excrescences which most tourists are fleeing from. The real pub is an institution worthy of national pride, a refuge and sanctuary where the drinking man and his moods are thoroughly understood. It bears a considerable resemblance to the old pre-Prohibition American saloon, which is not surprising since many of the saloons were operated by Irish-Americans. It may be going a little too far, though, to maintain, as Tony Butler does, that "everything is soluble" in Irish booze, including "genius, troubles, joys, talent, bankruptcy and anything else you like to contemplate."

In the main the pub is still a male institution, which adds to its value in the Irishman's eyes and which may also account for its determined dinginess. Even now few Irishwomen will venture into a pub, outside the cities, without a male escort. There's no law against it, but tradition has marked off the pub as a male preserve. In the countryside you rarely find a woman at the bar, and if so, she's probably a foreigner.

The pub, like the Englishman's local, is one of the pillars of daily life, a place not only for drinking, as most American bars are, with their nervous downing of drinks, but for relaxation, cashing a check or borrowing money, tapping the grapevine for the latest gossip, meeting friends. The drinking is often incidental and inconsiderable—a pint or two to last the evening while talking and playing the dartboard. A stop at the pub is simply part of the daily routine; even nondrinkers call in for an orange squash, which can be ordered without prejudice. To many it is really a second home, if not a first. A Dubliner I know spends every night at his favorite pub; his wife and children see him only at mealtimes and on Sunday afternoons, when he takes them on an outing, and he is not a rarity. An Irishman regards his association with the boys as a continuing and inalienable privilege, just as Latins spend their evenings in a neighborhood café without being accused of neglecting their domestic duties.

On the subject of drink the Irish are, typically, of two minds. (If Hamlet had been an Irishman he would have phrased it, "To be and not to be, that is the answer.") There are those who regard alcohol as the national curse, and others who believe the legendary Irish tosspot is a creation of self-advertising. An Irishman with a few pints of stout in him can act out the part of the stouthearted tankard man with more credibility than any other nationality; it is part of his instinct for the theater, no matter how small the stage or how sparse the audience. Then, too, part of his notoriety as an inveterate sot was gained abroad by migrating Irishmen who may have resorted to drink as a specific against homesickness, against the unfamiliar squalor of shantytowns all over the world. The Irish drunk just stands out a little more because Paddy is expected to behave like that and is not averse to living up to his reputation.

The Irish drunkard may not be entirely mythic; his feats with the bottle may not be completely a product of the unofficial Irish propaganda machine, in consideration of the fact that there is supposed to be one public house for every sixty drinkers on the island and that on many of the main streets the pubs outnumber all other business establishments combined. Yet it is true that you see fewer drunks in Ireland than in any other Western country. This isn't because the Irishman is so experienced a toper that he holds his liquor better; he is more likely to exaggerate his condition than attempt to conceal it. The English and Americans statistically are more determined drinkers, and in alcoholic content the Irishman doesn't come close to the Frenchman with his doggedly maintained daily intake of wine or the German with his vast absorption of beer and schnapps. It's just that every so often a heroic public drinker like the late Brendan Behan comes along to enhance the image of the Irishman on an eternal bender.

Another factor affecting the Irish drinking man is a slightly puritanical attitude toward "the creature." Many tend to ride the water wagon for long periods, with a rather sanctimonious, purse-mouthed air about them, and then fall off with a mighty splash. Single-mindedly they will embark on a bender of brief duration but violent dedication and be all the more noticeable than the steady drinker who always has a flame on the back burner but looks as sober as a bank manager. Another indication of this shamed attitude toward drinking is that many Irishmen appear to have wandered into a pub more or less by accident, perhaps to buy a packet of cigarettes, and will be hurrying on home momentarily. They will sit for hours with their hats and coats on, collars turned up, as though in transit. People with a touch of the puritan, in fact, are more likely to be susceptible to alcohol as a release from sexual repressions, according to some psychologists. The Irish reputation for heavy drinking, according to the same experts, also derived from a temperamental affinity for an alcoholic solution to their problems. "If unsteady emotions hasten a man to a glass," as George Potter wrote in his study of the immigrant Irish, *To the Golden Door,* "then the Irishman fulfilled the specification outlined by psychologists as the root causes of excessive drinking. . . . The temporary victory in drink over frustration, insecurity and a sense of inferiority which constantly dogged him, probably accounted as much for the Irishman's intemperance as any of a score of other factors."

The drunken Irishman, however, is a figure from the past, along with the stage Irishman exploding with begorras and the fighting Irishman battering skulls with his shillelagh.

Ireland, proportionately, has more teetotalers than any other nation outside the Moslem world. One-sixth of the population, roughly 500,000 out of 3,000,000, never have and never will touch the stuff: They wear the shieldlike emblem of the Sacred Heart which signifies the total abstainer.

The unlikely founder of the abstinence movement was a young priest who liked a drop himself. Father Theobald Mathew was, in fact, expelled from the seminary at Maynooth for throwing a party in his room. Eventually he was ordained despite a strong affection for whiskey punch; the clergy included some of the heaviest drinkers this side of the Liffey quays. In 1838, a Quaker, in what must have been one of the earliest essays in ecumenism, convinced Father Mathew that the Irish were ruining themselves with drink. They initiated the pledge system, whereby the pledger swore off the stuff forevermore. Father Mathew himself was the first to sign up. Within a few months 150,000 Irishmen had been persuaded to sign pledges not to drink.

The movement was formalized by a Jesuit, Father James Cullen, in 1898, when he founded the Pioneer Total Abstinence Association of the Sacred Heart. And while the Women's Christian Temperance Union in the United States and similar organizations elsewhere have tended to wither in the past fifty years, the Pioneers of Ireland are stronger and more numerous than ever. They take the pledge as children, and surprisingly few ever break that pledge as adults. They often serve liquor in their homes and abstain not only from liquor but—much more difficult—from frowning on, deploring or proselytizing those who are unenlightened. Nor is there any jeering at Pioneers from the other camp. The situation of the boozers and the pledged nondrinkers—instead of turning rancorous as it did in the United States through an excess of zeal—is still another monument to Irish tolerance.

There are other Irish attitudes which set them apart, which, like that open-armed institution the pub, make an outlander feel that he has stumbled into some sort of paradise where the suspicions and standoffishness that divide people elsewhere have been swept out of existence. The Nordic temperament, in particular, can thaw out at remarkable speed on immersion in the Celtic bath of instant friendship. A chance encounter—an inquiry regarding a street address, for instance—can lead precipitously to an exchange of confidences and oaths of undying fealty. The Celtic phrase "a hundred thousand welcomes" takes on a deep personal significance. Disillusionment may follow, and the Irish themselves will warn you that their society must be entered with all the caution of an early spring bather testing the temperature of the water with his big toe. The tale is told of the English visitor—and there must be many who have suffered similar experiences, because the Saxon is touchingly susceptible to wild Irish charm, so susceptible it's a wonder the Irish didn't con the British out of their empire—who tumbled into disaster a few minutes after landing at Dublin Airport. He was swept up by a crowd of wassailers, carried along on a tour of the pubs, apparently became engaged to and bitterly estranged from an Irishwoman within the space of two hours, and was found the next morning coated with detergent and within seconds of being plunged into the hotel laundry's washing machine. This may be more parable than sober fact, but it points up the dangers of being swept off your feet by the magic of Irish friendship.

The speed and intensity of such relationships, which might lead to operatic consequences elsewhere, usually result in nothing more disastrous than a misspent evening or an aching skull. They help the stranger to understand that it is silly to take himself too seriously; that the Irish door opens and closes with bewildering rapidity and usually at a whim; that if you're taken for a great fellow one moment and a bloody nuisance the next, it has very little intrinsically to do with you yourself but very much to do with the quick-shifting mood of the Celt. You will learn to invest cautiously in the face value of a hundred thousand welcomes; after all, you'll still come out a winner even if the hundred thousand in reality are a dozen. More than fifty years ago Edith Somerville, the Anglo-Irish writer, made some wise observations on this score:

> The Irish man or woman does not open his or her "whole heart" to strangers. Hardly do we open them to each other. We are, unlike the English, a silent people about the things that affect us most deeply; which is, perhaps, the reason that we are, on the whole, considered to be good company. It is in keeping with the contradictiousness of Ireland that the most inherently ro-

> mantic race in the British Isles is the least sentimental, the most conversational, the most reserved, and also that Irish people, without distinction of sex or class, are pessimists about their future . . . lighthearted, humorous, cheerful on the whole, and quite confident that nothing will ever succeed.

The cheerful custom known as blarney is part of the Irishman's attitude toward the outside world. Presumably it will not work on a born-and-bred Irishman, who is too sophisticated in the ways of his race to be taken in for more than a split second; nor will it work any harm on anyone else if taken in moderate doses, with a psychological emetic close at hand. It is enshrined at Blarney Castle, County Cork, where a chunk of limestone allegedly bestows magical powers of persuasion on whoever kisses it, surely one of the few places in the world where a habit—once a sort of defense mechanism, no doubt—has been turned into a tourist attraction.

Blarneying, as a native art form, is so indelibly an Irish characteristic that it seems entirely fitting that Rudolf Erich Raspe, the author of *The Adventures of Baron Munchausen,* is buried in Ireland, not too far from the Blarney Stone. Raspe was employed as keeper of the gems by the Landgrave of Hesse until it was discovered that some of the gems were missing and Raspe had to flee. He ended up in Ireland, where his tales of the swivel-tongued baron were regarded as inferior to the standards set by Irish liars, and is buried near Killarney.

Blarney is dourly defined by Webster as "smooth, wheedling talk," an anti-Irish declaration if ever there was one. It misses entirely the artistry, the imagination, the intuition, and the insight required of the successful blarneyer. Generally there is no object in view except to make the subject feel better, and no harm done if the purveyor feels self-congratulatory over having stuffed his victim with arrant nonsense.

It's not simply a matter of deception, as Tony Butler, the resident expert, points out. "It's words, gesture and atmosphere; it's verbal psychiatry when the subject is stretched on the couch of conversation and environment. One thing—it's no illusion, it's for real. It will seep into the marrow of your bones like a drug and whether we look for love, life or the pounds and dollars falling from your wallet like aged leaves in the gentle breeze of a moon-bronzed Autumn night—it will work."

Mr. Butler admits that blarney, in a sense, is part of the Irish arsenal designed as a protective measure against all sorts of adversities. "Blarney is the secret weapon of the Irish. We have stockpiled to last beyond the Day of Judgment and we'll dance into Heaven and take no excuse to keep us out. Indeed we are told by the saints of the past that all Irishmen will be judged by St. Patrick on the last day and the country, it is said, will be spared the horrors of Doomsday by a gentle wave inundating it a week before."

The only defense against blarney is counterblarney, but all suggestions of parody must be avoided. It would be a shame, after all, to have the flatterer round on *you* with an invective which is quite as potent in its own way as blarney. The switchbacks of the Irish temper, the unpredictable changes in mood from unalloyed admiration to caustic denunciation, are not something to be lightly invoked. And while the blarneyer will be speaking confidentially, in a low soothing murmur, the denouncer—one and the same man—is likely to raise a thunderous voice. It's better to reflect that there's something flattering about being considered worthy of flattery and not examine unsolicited compliments with too critical or literal a mind. A modest, uninfatuated smile will do nicely.

As a conservative people, on the whole, the Irish are entitled to a few excesses. They also tend to go overboard in the matter of hospitality, which to the more skeptical outlander appears to be compulsive. Ireland is literally the Land of the Open Door. A Frenchman may have to know you for twenty years before he invites you to his home, but an Irishman is likely to have you over after a whirlwind acquaintance of twenty minutes. An Englishman's home is his castle; an Irishman's is everybody else's castle.

In the matter of hospitality the Irish really need to be protected against themselves. They are almost neurotic about lavishing it even on strangers. You can stop at the poorest farmhouse to ask directions and a few minutes later find yourself with a cup of tea in your hand and a small feast spread out before you; it's quite possible the larder has been emptied to provide it, even though your face will never be seen there again. "A cup of tea" is a very loose phrase in Ireland. In the first place, it's a succession of cups, and to keep it all down, you are stuffed with slices of ham and chicken, scones, biscuits, cake, and assorted pastries.

Outside his home an Irishman can be as mean or sharp about money matters as anyone else, but once you set foot over his threshold, you have him in your power. The poor fellow is helpless, caught up in a rather self-destructive tradition that the guest is not only always right but must be cozened in every way possible.

This isn't a form of exhibitionism; he isn't trying to prove anything with his lavish hospitality. It stems from terror at the thought of being considered ungenerous in his own home. Furthermore, the Irish practice this openhandedness on each other, on people they've known all their lives.

The worst thing that can be said of a housewife, as John D. Sheridan noted in one of the essays in *The Right Time,* which examines national foibles with a kindly but knowing eye, is the complaint "She never asked me had I a mouth on me." Ireland, he maintains, is being impoverished by the custom of brewing tea at the slightest provocation. There is a certain ritual that must be observed by both parties; on the hostess' part that she is really doing nothing at all, while making elaborate preparations, and on the guest's that he or she is completely unaware that the hostess is hurriedly whipping up a tea that would nourish a squad of infantry. "The ceremonial that goes with our tea-drinking," Mr. Sheridan says, "is based on the pretence that the hostess can be in two places at once. When she goes to the sideboard to get out the 'good' china, or to the kitchen to put on the kettle (the technical term being to 'stick' on the kettle) she pretends that she is still in the facing armchair, throws her voice from the hall like a ventriloquist, and comes back to resume conversations that haven't even begun. This elaborate buildup would be a strain on her but for the fact the guest lends a hand —it is the height of bad manners to withhold cooperation, and you are expected to be as blind as a bat and as stupid as a mule." When the overburdened tea tray arrives, the guest is supposed to register amazement. "The traditional opening is 'Good gracious —surely this isn't for me?'—as if it could be for Joe Louis, or the

Sultan of Turkey. You say too that had you known she was making tea you would have stopped her—though both of you know that Joe Louis couldn't have stopped her."

The hospitality syndrome, apparently, has afflicted the Irish for centuries. It has nothing to do with the comparative affluence of the present. The tradition of the countryside, dating back to medieval times, has always been that the traveler must be fed and sheltered with whatever resources are at hand. The Irish home reaches out and encompasses, as open-ended as when it was a herdsman's campfire. Domestic privacy, except in times of strife, is not highly prized. The Irish are too interested in people—and in each other's affairs, to be candid—to let any scrap of human activity escape them. They are rarely indifferent to you; they may rake you over the coals on matters personal or impersonal, but they are intensely interested in what makes you tick. The greatest bore will not be suffered gladly or spared the sharp edge of an Irish tongue, but he will not be ignored or frozen out.

It is possible to overdo the nest-of-kindly-folk view of the Irish, of course, and there is a corrective readily available. You have only to watch them, 90,000 strong and in full cry, at Croke Park in Dublin during the All-Ireland hurling or Gaelic football finals. When it comes to sports of any kind, the Irish are bare-knuckled and ferocious: a warrior race sprung back to life.

Whatever is aggressive and warlike about the Irish is expended, except for an odd pub brawl or two and the subterranean activities of the IRA, on the country's playing fields. Ireland has not fought a war against anybody but the British for a millennium. No one could call the Irish pacifists, but en masse they have no thirst for organized slaughter or combat on the grand scale. Even if the British army dwindled to a senile field marshal and a corporal's guard, England would be safe from Ireland. It is tempting to speculate that if Britain's wars were won on the playing fields of Eton, Ireland's peaceful posture conversely has been maintained through expending its primeval instincts in the sporting arena. It is a country of weekend gladiators, and on Monday morning the streets are filled with the walking wounded with battered faces, sprung muscles, blackened eyes, and wrenched knees suffered on the field of athletic battle. There are few professional athletes, but almost every able-bodied man below the age of forty is a violent partisan of some sort or other, which probably accounts for the large number of casualties.

Sports may not be the most reliable index to national character, but they can't be ignored by any but the most pedantic investigator. You can tell a lot about the American ethos from watching a professional football game with its severe disciplines, its precise patterns, its almost computerized sequence of plays, its emphasis on split-second teamwork; it can easily be translated into terms of a military blitzkrieg. The wild individualism of a Latin American soccer team is also instructive, or the white-flanneled Britisher sedately swishing a cricket bat at Lord's, or a Central European turning into a demon on an Alpine ski slope.

When the Irish take the field at one of their games of regulated mayhem, you witness a rebirth of tribal warfare, in the course of which you would not be greatly surprised to learn that hostilities have broken out between Wexford and Kilkenny and the brawniest youth on both sides have been appointed to settle the issue with an armament limited to curved sticks.

As in any intensely Irish sphere of activity, athletics are permeated with nationalistic politics and a brooding sense of history. Gaelic football and hurling, both exclusively Irish games seen abroad only when Irish teams go overseas to take on those of Irish emigrants in England or America, are the province of the Gaelic Athletic Association, which started as an arm of the Irish revolutionary movement. Gaelic games were promoted by the association as an extension of the national pride, a symbol of the struggle for liberation from British rule. The number one rule of the GAA is that any member caught playing a "foreign" game, such as rugby, cricket, hockey, or maybe even baseball, or even watching others play it is drummed off the field. To outsiders this seems not only harsh but excessively chauvinistic. The Irish, however, accept the "GAA ban" as necessary to preserving the purity of Irish sports. One of its founders, Dr. Douglas Hyde, attended an international rugby match in his ceremonial capacity as the President of the Irish Republic and was excommunicated by the association.

Hurling is a fast, rough sport which pits fifteen young bravos on each side against each other, all armed with something that looks like a hockey stick, only heavier at the base, and belaboring a small leather-bound ball. The idea is to whack the ball either into the net at the opposite end of the field for a goal (three points) or between the goalposts above (one point). It is possibly the oldest game in the world, one account of the First Battle of Moytura (1272 B.C.) referring to a hurling match which the warriors may have used as a warmup for the real thing, though it is difficult to believe that armed combat could have been much bloodier. Cuchullain, the golden boy of Celtic antiquity, is supposed to have defended a goal against the combined efforts of 150 other players, but hyperbole often enters into accounts of his career. The Norman conquerors studied the game and sensibly decided to prohibit it under the Statutes of Kilkenny, but hurling survived.

The casual brutalities of the sport make American football seem tame by comparison. Since the hurley is brandished above the player's head (unlike a hockey stick) and is employed with a reckless abandon in riotous sweeps up and down the field, it seems miraculous that more players aren't carried off the field with fractured skulls; there is no finer testimonal to the Irish cranium than the sight of a player felled by a hurley or struck by the hard leather ball, shaking himself, staggering around for a moment, and then returning to the struggle.

Recently there have been increasing protests that hurling is hardly the sport for a civilized nation; but the GAA has both political and sentimental power, and any governmental curb on the game (unlikely as long as Prime Minister Jack Lynch is in power; he was an All-Ireland hurling star for Cork, and a sizable number of politicians have graduated from the hurling pitch to the floor of the Dail) would be regarded as unseemly as turning over six more counties to Northern Ireland. Yet even a hurling enthusiast like Raymond Smith, the author of two books on the sport, was appalled recently after visiting the locker rooms of the Tipperary and Clare teams following a hard-fought match. Wounded athletes were lying all over the place, and surgeons were patching them up for the ambulance ride to the city hospital. One Tipperary man was spilling blood from three gashes on his face, and another had a cut on the face that took eight stitches. A Clare man had a broken finger. There were others who had to be stitched or otherwise mended. "I do not know, really, if any man came out of this brutal Munster Championship tussle unscathed," Smith concluded his article in a Sunday newspaper. It was titled "Is Hurling Doomed?"

In spite of such hazards, more then 100,000 Irishmen participate in the Gaelic sports. Only a few reach semipro status, receiving a few pounds a week for expense money and working at regular jobs for a living. The reward for most of the weekend warriors is a little local fame and the privilege of demonstrating the Irish form of *machismo*.

Gaelic football is only slightly less lethal than hurling and to the uninitiated looks like a cross between rugby and soccer with a few touches of American football. The ball is round, as in soccer, but unlike soccer, it can be handled, bounced, or punched as well as kicked toward the goal. From the viewpoint of an American accustomed to the finicky rules of college and professional football, the Gaelic variety looks like an exercise in anarchy.

In addition to the Gaelic games, the sports-mad Irish are devotees of golf, dog and horse racing, bowling, sailing, and GAA members "desert" every year to play soccer, it is said, because it offers the possibility of international competition. The number of soccer teams is also growing, particularly since the 1970 international soccer finals were televised via satellite in Ireland as well as the Continent. What really unites the country, however, is anything to do with horses, from breeding them for racing or jumping to betting on them in the ubiquitous legalized bookmaking establishments known as turf accountants. "In Ireland," as Niall Sheridan has observed, "what used to be called the sport of kings is the bond which cements a vast, colourful and heterogeneous democracy—the vivid world of owners, trainers, jockeys, punters, tipsters and the racing public. The breeding, training and racing of horses is an important industry, an endless topic of conversation, almost a national obsession. Among a race of fervent individualists, hippomania is a great unifying force cutting clean across all social, cultural and economic barriers. It may be significant that while thousands of punters regularly put a half-crown on a horse, Ireland is the only country which, in designing its official currency, has put a horse on a half-crown."

Only slightly less obsessive is the fascination with greyhound racing. A common sight along Irish roads is a man out trotting along with a pair of greyhounds, or whippets, that are being trained for the dog track. Greyhounds are also deployed in a bloody sport called coursing, with live rabbits instead of the electric ones used to stimulate the competition at a dog track. In coursing, the hares are released in a field with the greyhounds in hot pursuit; they have a sporting chance to escape, but to the tender-minded it is appallingly apparent that it is always the rabbits, not the greyhounds, that are torn to pieces. There has recently been conducted a campaign against coursing, which honestly bewilders the farmers and sportsmen. Aren't there too many bloody hares chewing up the crops as it is?

Visitors to Ireland are often appalled by the Irish lack of sentimentality about animals. The Society for the Prevention of Cruelty to Animals, holding an international conclave in Dublin, gave the Irish a low rating on their relations with the animal world. A few years ago there was a tremendous outcry in the British press when it was discovered that Irish horses were being sent to the Continent to be butchered for French and Belgian tables.

The horse trade was stopped, though not without bitter reflections from the Irish that English sensibilities had been more aroused by the plight of horses than when hundreds of thousands of Irishmen were starving to death during the Famine. The Irish attitude toward animals is that of most agricultural countries: They are for work or slaughter. A farmer doesn't have time for sentiment; if he keeps a dog, it is because the dog is good at working cattle or sheep. It is also true that animals generally are not cosseted in Catholic countries, though the decent treatment of animals has been the subject of papal encyclicals in the past. The idea of making pets out of them is generally regarded as lunacy in the rural areas of Ireland. The expression on an Irish farmer's face when he watches a car with British plates drive past, with the family dog sitting on the front seat with his fond master and the wife and children crowded into the back, is a study in culture shock. The novelist Leonard Wibberley, an expert on practically everything else, has contended that while the British love animals, animals love the Irish. It is difficult to find supporting evidence for this; there is nothing warier than an Irish dog within range of an Irish boot, and it is my impression that if the channel between Ireland and England were a little narrower, there would be as few dogs in Ireland as there are snakes.

To a considerable extent, however, the Irish attitude toward animals is changing as the country becomes more urbanized. The church has been advocating a more humane attitude, and recently there was a large hubbub raised by television and the press over the plight of two Shetland ponies and six donkeys abandoned on the island of Gola off the Donegal coast when their owners left the island. Such massive public concern would have been unthinkable a decade earlier. It is also notable that city people are keeping more poodles, Yorkshires, and other dogs whose main function is sitting on laps and being spoiled. Ireland may yet see men walking beribboned, rhinestone-collared, pedicured, and pink-jacketed poodles for their nightly airing. They can reflect that the early Irish saints believed that worthy animals went to heaven along with their masters.

When it comes to the horse—the racing or jumping horse, not the poor old plug rapidly being displaced by the tractor—strong emotions are involved. A number of considerations enter into the relationship between the Irish and their horseflesh, many of them practical and fiscal ones, but the most passionate is the fact that nothing delights the Irish eye more than the sight of a horse stretching out into his stride—particularly if he has a few pounds riding on the nose of that horse and the nose is out in front of all the other noses. I know a Dublin businessman whose dedication to his job is all-consuming fifty-one weeks of the year, but who disappears in the direction of Punchestown religiously with a wad of £5 notes in his pocket, and there are many like him. Crazy over horses, or more precisely crazy over betting on horses. It is doubtful whether the fascination would maintain its grip if the element of wagering were suddenly removed from the racing picture.

The economic aspect of the Irish love affair with the running or jumping horse and the status affixing itself to swanking it around the Dublin Horse Show cannot be overlooked. During the past quarter century, Irish-bred horses have made a tremendous impact in international racing, the result of which is a significant boost to the trade balance and the national economy. In 1965, the last year for which statistics are available, Irish-bred horses won a total of £2,000,000 ($4,800,000) throughout the world, and exports of Irish bloodstock were almost twice that amount. The Irish National Stud, at Tully, County Kildare, a thousand-acre breeding farm, is operated by the state for the benefit of Irish breeders. The rolling, grass-covered plains of County Kildare closely resemble the horse country around Lexington, Kentucky. Then, too, there is the Irish Sweepstakes, operated by a private corporation which pays out four-fifths of the take in expenses, prizes, and profit sharing, but which has contributed more than $200,000,000 to Irish hospitals and medical services in the past forty years.

Racing horses has been an Irish tradition since the time of St. Patrick, and the custom of betting on them is probably just as ancient. The punters, as the Irish call bettors, a term that has nothing to do with kicking a football but can entail kicking hell out of a wallet, follow the racing information just as intently as an American horseplayer studying the *Racing Form*. Talk in the pubs centers on horses and politics, usually in that order. Many punters never go near a racetrack, these being the purely fiscal types who have no esthetic interest in the beauty and pageantry of a race. They spend much of their afternoons in the offices of the turf accountants, which are as dingy and run-down—and as profitable—as an American bookie joint. On these licensed premises generally may be found a counter at one side of the room with a brass grille to protect the turf accountant and his money from any forays by a desperate loser. The walls flutter with pages of racing news, always copiously covered in the Irish dailies, torn from the Dublin newspapers. There are two classes of clientele at the turf accountant's, the drop-in trade and the squatters. The former are men with jobs to whom a ten-shilling flutter on the bangtails is a casual avocation. The latter are more dedicated types, many of whom seem to concentrate all their intuitive and intellectual powers on picking the right horses. They settle down in the turf accountant's office to keep a weather eye on the odds, get the results of each race as quickly as possible, and make their calculations accordingly. You will hear little talk from them about the "sport of kings" or the poetic beauty of a closely run race. The Irish bettor, according to one expert, prefers to lay his money on the English races because he is convinced that various forms of knavery are practiced on the Irish tracks; chauvinism ends at the win-place-and-show line. Under the glare of strip lighting, the faces of the punters appear to turn grimmer and greener as the afternoon wears on, and the losers inevitably outnumber those who step up to the counter with winning markers.

The less grimy side of the horseracing fancy may be observed in all its fur, feathers, and tweeds among the crowds which gather for the four most celebrated race meetings at Fairyhouse, County Meath; Punchestown, County Kildare; the Curragh, County Kildare; and Phoenix Park, County Dublin, and for the lesser but possibly more colorful meetings at Tralee, Tramore, and Galway. Here the heroes are such famous Irish trainers as Vincent O'Brien and Paddy Prendergast. The horse and the jockey, who run the race, after all, are less esteemed than the trainers, possibly because brains will always be valued over beauty in Ireland.

Perhaps it is the drama of a race which appeals to the theatrical side of the Irish, for whom any sort of drama is of abiding fascination. The competition on the track, heightened by whatever subsidiary dramas occur in the owners', trainers', jockeys' and bettors' sectors of the racing stage, stands for the eternal human struggle. "The racecourse is a microcosm of life," as Niall Sheridan views it, lending intellectual respectability to what is considered a fairly raffish endeavor in other lands, "a focus for triumph and disaster, glory or defeat, a setting for the endless duel with fate or chance or destiny, call it what you will. As starting-time approaches, there are swift dramatic changes in the betting-market when the 'inspired' money moves in. There is that tense hush just before the start, and the rising fervour of the crowd as the horses rise together to the final fences or the two-year-olds—a wavering spectrum of colour—come thundering down the five-furlong stretch."

The race meeting is the melting pot of Ireland, fusing even such disparate elements as the Anglo-Irish and the Irish-Irish, whose only common denominator is the horse. There is no other place, except haphazardly, at a funeral or a national disaster, where they are likely to meet and meld. At race meetings they are almost indistinguishable, the Anglo-Irish plumage perhaps a little less glossy but worn with greater assurance. Dublin Horse Show Week or an Irish Sweepstakes Derby brings both classes out in a display of elegance that comes close to matching Ascot or Longchamps and easily outshines the Kentucky Derby. It is fascinating to try to single out the representative types of beauty on display, the lean, tailored woman of the old Ascendancy, with a "Hon." attached to her name, posing for a photographer from the *Irish Tatler,* the daughters of the new Ascendancy (composed of the entrepreneurs who have gained affluence in the past ten years), and the miniskirted working girls from Dublin who bear little resemblance to the woebegone heroines of Edna O'Brien's novels. The stylish panorama provided by one of the more elegant race meetings or the bloodstock sales at Ballsbridge, where each transaction is a shot in the arm for the Irish economy, give an impression of the New Ireland as possessing a New Class which would have been incredible to the revolutionaries who died to bring it about.

During one month of 1970, two events connected with the horsy world of the Kildare downs caused more joy and sorrow than anything happening in the embattled North. First Nijinsky, American-owned, but Irish-bred and -trained raced to a victory at Epsom Downs against the ten best colts from England and France. There is nothing like an Irish horse winning an English race to make Irish chests expand. Then tragedy struck: Arkle, "the horse of the century," had to be destroyed. The great steeplechaser had won £146,578 ($351,787.20) in stakes during his racing career and then earned another fortune for his owner when he was retired to stud. Arkle was especially endearing because he liked a drop of Guinness stout with his rations—the sort of parlay an Irishman appreciates—and he was probably mourned more fervently than many a national hero.

None of the amusements, sports, and distractions discussed above can compare with the dismal attraction of a funeral. Funeral-going ranks as a national pastime, for reasons understandable readily to those of Celtic blood. People who ordinarily will travel no farther than the nearest market town for any other reason will journey across half the island to attend the funeral of a second cousin once removed. Outlanders are appalled at the joyful solemnity attending an Irish funeral, are horrified by tales of riotous Irish wakes, and mistake the somewhat festive atmosphere surrounding the event for a callousness unique in the Irish character, an unworthy gloating by the survivors over having outlived the deceased. It isn't that way at all. The Irish from the depths of disbelief in the joys of temporal existence regard birth as a disaster, marriage as an anticlimax, and death as a happy release. A funeral also is a dramatic occasion, people's theater. It is the Celtic way of death, something to be confronted with the same ceremonial intensity as any other fact of life.

3.

Ancient Gods Look Down

It is the land itself that makes the Celt.
—George Moore

The Irish attitude toward death as an occasion for celebration rather than dread and deep mourning was conditioned by centuries of unhappy experience with life as a succession of subjugations. The Irish brood over their history as luckier peoples gloat over past imperial splendors; things seem to have gone wrong ever since the first natives regarded themselves as the "grandsons of Noah" and worshiped a god called Lug, and they can look back on thirty centuries of adversity as a grim cyclorama to one decade of modern prosperity.

History is a brooding, inescapable presence in Ireland, a psychological burden as evident as the Celtic crosses marking the sites of death and martyrdom, ambush and retribution which seem to appear every few miles along the Irish roads. As additional reminders there are the ruined castles, decayed abbeys, tumbling forts, and burned-out great houses of the former Ascendancy. A mile or two from where I live there is the truncated tower of Rossbrin Castle. Cattle graze around the crumbling keep; it is merely a pile of stones in a field being put to good and necessary use. You can reach it only by climbing through hedgerows and crossing the surrounding fields; there are no markers, no efforts to point up a tourist attraction, though elsewhere it would be floodlighted and turned into a national landmark. No one knows who built it—probably the Normans—or the bloody events it must have witnessed as guardian of the approaches to Roaringwater Bay. It is simply there, a worn and weathered testimonial to the times when Dane and Norman and Briton took their turns at ravaging the island. History is so interwoven with the fabric of daily life that its artifacts can be ignored.

The epic of Ireland is the struggle of the many centuries during which the Irish fought and plotted to become masters in their own house, a struggle which shaped the national character, yet, oddly, did not homogenize a race of determined individualists. A subsidiary theme of that effort is the brooding awareness that if the Irish had been willing to surrender some of their individualism, to give up quirkiness to the common cause, it might not have taken so long to get rid of their oppressors. But then they would have been less Irish, and the quality of Irishness is what they hold dearer than anything else. A hint of that quality is visible in Eamon De Valera's statement of long ago that he would rather see Ireland under foreign domination than Ireland not speaking Irish.

The struggle for liberation, but only a liberation on terms which guaranteed the survival of Irish culture, was epitomized in a one-act play by William Butler Yeats which was on the bill at the Abbey Theater, by striking coincidence, on the Easter Bank Holiday weekend in 1916 when modern Ireland was born in a rattle of gunfire. In Yeats' allegory the old Cathleen (symbolizing Ireland) meets two younger persons, Peter and Bridget, as she wanders down a road.

> BRIDGET: What was it put you to wandering?
> OLD WOMAN: Too many strangers in the house.
> BRIDGET: Indeed you look as if you'd had your share of trouble.
> OLD WOMAN: I have had trouble indeed.
> BRIDGET: What was it put the trouble on you?
> OLD WOMAN: My land that was taken from me.
> PETER: Was it much land they took from you?
> OLD WOMAN: My four beautiful green fields.

The four fields, of course, were the provinces of Munster, Leinster, Connaught, and Ulster. Reclaiming them, through incessant political pressure and occasional insurrection, through the loss of its best and bravest men and women, through a thousand chapters of betrayal and self-betrayal, was the story of the past Irish millennium. It gave rise eventually to the figure Sean O'Casey delineated in his play *Shadow of a Gunman,* the young urban or rural freedom fighter, armed with anything he could lay hands on, slipping down back alleys or lurking in the hedgerows. That figure, undeniably romantic but also somewhat sinister, haunts Ireland again and again, a shadow cast not only from the rebellious past but forward into the foreseeable future. The Irish Revolution was one of the few that failed to eat all its young; instead, it spawned new generations of revolutionaries. Finding a cause on which to vent their energies will not be difficult. There is always Ulster, and there is the feeling of the activist young of each generation that the Irish Revolution somehow failed to fulfill itself or accomplish its ideal objectives. And there is no one more adept than an Irishman at conceiving and nursing a grievance to alarming maturity.

The wanderings of the legendary Cathleen from her misty beginnings in Celtic prehistory to the Easter Sunday her sons rose to unshackle her, her long immersion in paganism and her eventual conversion to Christianity form a saga too long and speculative to be handily compressed into a literary time capsule. The main interest, after all, lies in how the Irish became a nation and why they unlike the other Celts (the Scots, the Welsh, the Cornish, the Bretons) could never be entirely amalgamated with another people.

Various racial oddities, tribal fragments of a great westward movement of barbaric peoples after the last Ice Age, made their pre-Celtic appearance on the island. The Fomorians, who devotees of mythical Atlantis believe were migrants from that lost continent, were the first to invade Ireland and subdue the aborigines. According to the *Annals of Clonmacnois,* the Fomorians were "a sept descended from Cham, the son of Noah, and lived by piracy and the spoil of other nations, and were in those days very troublesome to the whole world." They are believed to have arrived in Ireland on a fleet of sixty ships. After about 400 years, they were subdued by invaders, called the Firbolgs, who came from Greece and who divided the island into five provinces. Less than a century later the Firbolgs in turn were conquered by a strange and mystical people called the Tuatha De Danann. The latter were accomplished at various arts and crafts, including metalworking, and had bards, or remembrancers, who preserved their people's deeds and history and recited them on state occasions. The Tuatha De Danann boasted of an artificer named Creidne so talented that when their king had his hand chopped off in subduing a pocket of Firbolgs, Creidne "put a silver hand upon him, the fingers of which were capable of motion." The burial mounds of the Bronze Age people, with about sixty dolmen-type tombs, lay undisturbed and largely unexplored near Carrowmore, County Sligo, with dairy herds grazing among the ceremonial stones.

An Irish-American named Ignatius Donnelly, a protean figure who was also the leader of the Populist Party which polled more than a million votes in 1890, was the chief propagandist of the Atlantis theory. He was convinced that the Bronze Age invaders of Ireland came from Atlantis and buttressed his theory with quotations from the scribes and scholars of antiquity in *Atlantis: The Antediluvian World,* published in 1882. British Prime Minister William Gladstone was so impressed with Donnelly's work that he asked the Cabinet for funds to outfit a ship to trace the supposed outline of sunken Atlantis in the Atlantic Ocean, but his hardheaded ministers rejected the rather romantic proposal. The kernel of Donnelly's argument was that "the population of Ireland *came from the West* . . . that it was one of the many waves of population flowing out from the Island of Atlantis—and herein we find the explanation of that problem which has puzzled the Aryan scholars. . . . In the first place, the civilization of Ireland dates back to a vast antiquity. We have seen their annals laying claim to an immigration from the direction of Atlantis prior to the Deluge, with no record that the people of Ireland were subsequently destroyed by the Deluge. From the Formorians, who came before the Deluge, to the Milesians, who came from Spain in the historical period, the island was continuously inhabited. This demonstrates (1) that these legends did not come from Christian sources, as the Bible record was understood in the old time to imply a destruction of all who lived before the Flood except Noah and his family; (2) it confirms our view that the Deluge was a local catastrophe, and did not drown the whole human family; (3) that the coming of the Formorians having been before the Deluge, that great cataclysm was of comparatively recent date, to wit, since the settlement of Ireland. . . ." In Sanskrit, the strange and persuasive Donnelly points out, there are references to Ireland as Hiranyi, the "island of the sun," meaning of sun worshipers.

If the Irish originally were refugees from Atlantis, it would explain their otherworldliness, their discomfiture in present circumstances, their lack of a funereal attitude toward death, their pessimism about the prospects of improving the human condition. Having a continent sink under you can have a depressing effect on the psyche.

The Tuatha De Danann, or "people of the goddess Dana," disappeared in what was to become a classic Irish tradition: They went underground when the next wave of conquerors washed against the Irish shore. According to the ancient legends, they brought it all on themselves. Prince Ith of the Milesians, a Celtic people who had wandered into Spain from somewhere around the eastern Mediterranean, sailed up the coast of Donegal on a sort of reconnaissance mission and went ashore to find the three sons of King Dagda quarreling over their inheritance, evidence that Irish divisiveness was virulent even in the fifth century B.C. Prince Ith upbraided the three heirs for quarreling in such a beautiful land and became so eloquent in extolling the island's charm that they suspected that he wanted the place for himself, so they slew him. The Milesians then invaded Ireland as an act of vengeance, and the Tuatha De Danann, overpowered by a fleet of thirty Milesian ships, retired into caves far underground to await a better day. Just how the first underground resistance movement turned out is unknown, but it provided a powerful example for the future.

The Gaelic Celts, who came to Ireland sometime in the fourth century B.C., were as much interlopers as any who followed them. Historically, the Celts are a mystery race. No two historians seem to agree on exactly where they came from except, vaguely, somewhere in central Europe. Herodotus casually mentions them as a people living around the source of the Danube in the fifth century B.C. The Greeks were not especially interested in them, though they were accounted the major barbarian race north of the Mediterranean and beyond the Alps. It was known that they were a restless and warlike people, that, as one scholar has written, "the Celts were of tall stature, with blue eyes, white skins, and blond hair; they pass rapidly from courage to despair; they are communicative, impetuous, versatile." Plato described them as susceptible to alcohol, quick to quarrel with other peoples and with each other if no outsiders were available. They were known to have made weapons of iron with which they defeated less advanced enemies armed with bronze swords. During the Roman ascendancy, they manifested themselves all over western Europe, settling down for a time in Gaul, Britain, and Spain and then moving on. For a long time they established themselves in settlements along the Rhine and intermarried with the Teutonic tribesmen roving the forests. Oddly enough, considering the quarrelsome reputation the Celts had made for themselves elsewhere, they seem to have lived peacefully with the Teutons, whom the Roman historian Tacitus described as huge and hairy and ferocious enough to tax the occupying legions of Rome. The Celts stayed just long enough to provide a Celtic leavening in South Germans and then moved westward toward what became their stronghold, Ireland.

The Celts of that period were followers of the sun-worship religion shared by all the ancient races of Europe, Asia, and Africa. Their priests were members of the order of Druids, whose temples may still be found in South German forests. Their chief god was Bel, or Baal, whom the Phoenicians worshiped as the god of the sun. The Druid faith was a conglomeration of borrowings from the Roman pantheon, of a reverence for oak trees they may have picked up from the Teutonic tribes, of sacrifices to placate the elements.

The life-giving divinity of the sun was honored in rites over which the Druids presided. On a certain day all fires on the island were extinguished. At a temple called Tlachta, in what is now County Meath, the divine fire was kindled from the sun. No fires could be started except from this source; for days the countryside was streaked by torchbearers carrying the divine fire throughout the Celtic realm. There were other rites and incantations connected with fire worship. A Druid convocation, at which cattle were driven between two fires to protect them from disease was held at the palace of the King of Connaught on May 1. Long after the Druids went out of business, the first of May was known as Lha-Beul-tinne, the Day of Baal's Fire.

The religion of the ancient Celts came from the Middle East, with additions from Rome and certain embellishments from the order of Druids. They never got around to inventing their own religion, for all their imagination and originality in other fields. On their own they never advanced beyond the animistic stage; something was missing in the Celtic psyche that was found in abundance in the desert peoples of the Middle East, the Greeks, and the Hebrews. "Was it that they had an inadequate ethical sense?" Sean O'Faolain asks. "Was it that they loved life too well, so that one may think, for example, that the concept of the Fall of Man, the greatest contribution made by the Jews to modern religious thought, could never have come from a people so imaginatively in love with Man himself?"

Legends written down in the early Christian period, when Irish history formally began, cast a certain amount of light on the ambience of pagan Ireland. It was a pastoral society without any ambition to build up a commerce even among themselves or to confine themselves to towns or walled settlements, a society as nomadic as the Bedouins, in which it took no great amount of effort to feed and clothe themselves. Occasionally, more for excitement than out of necessity, they bestirred themselves to conduct cattle raids and border wars with other clans. War was a game, an exercise of manliness, a stage on which great dramas could be performed. The island was divided into separate kingdoms ruled by a high king at Tara, whose writ was often challenged by lesser kings. Cattle were the measure of a man's wealth and standing; an important chief or minor king might own as many as 100,000 head.

Except for Tara's hall and a few other rude tributes to authority, there was little permanent building done. Unlike Roman-occupied Britain, Ireland lacked not only towns but roads. There were only a few beaten paths, a few structures of clay and woven branches. For centuries Ireland was a vast pasture covered by herds and their herders, with only an occasional royal settlement at which a local king sequestered himself with his court of poets, musicians, and warriors of the Fianna caste. Since lawyers were also included among the courtiers, it would appear that the Irish love of litigation is deeply rooted.

Aside from the clashes of rival or bordering kingdoms, life in pagan Ireland must have been close to a pastoral idyll. At any rate it produced what more than one authority declares "the finest body of folklore in the world," peopled with tragic lovers, deeds of valor and vengeance, enormous villainies, Deirdre of the Sorrows, and the Knights of the Fianna. The latter, by bardic account, were as pure, noble, and exalted as King Arthur's. They pledged themselves "Never to seek a dowry with a wife, but to choose her for her good manners and virtue. . . . Never to offer violence to any woman. . . . Never to refuse any mortal in need of anything one possesses. . . . Never to flee from less than ten adversaries."

Perhaps partly because of that knightly flavor to pagan Celtic society, the transition from Druidism and sun worship to Latin Christianity in the fifth century was accomplished with amazing swiftness and lack of opposition, considering that the order of Druids had extended their influence over Ireland for a thousand years. It almost seemed to happen overnight, as though the whole Celtic people were struck simultaneously by a common vision. Actually the ordinary folk were converted first; it took almost two centuries to wrench all the kings and chieftains away from their prostrations to Baal, Lug, and the rest of the Druidic pantheon.

St. Patrick has recently been downgraded somewhat by the Vatican, to the shock and dismay of the Irish, but legend credits him with accomplishing the mass conversion. His origins cannot be precisely determined, but it is generally believed by church historians that St. Patrick was a Latin-speaking Christian born in Britain during the last years of the Roman occupation. Rome's power had diminished by then to the point that Niall, the high king reigning at Tara, made frequent raids against Britain. On one of his forays the boy named Patrick was brought back as a captive and sold as a slave. He spent his youth herding sheep on the mountain slopes of County Antrim.

Patrick eventually escaped from bondage and made his way to the Continent, where he studied for the priesthood. A vision came to him, it is said, ordaining that he return to Ireland and convert the people who had enslaved him. Accordingly, he landed back in Ireland A.D. 432 and made a sweeping success of his mission. Oddly enough, the Druids resisted the inroads of his campaign against their religion stubbornly but without calling down a religious war. The only casualty (according to legend) was one of the few kings to subscribe immediately to Christianity, Aengus of Munster, whose foot was accidentally impaled by the spike on the end of St. Patrick's episcopal staff during the ceremony attending his conversion. King Aengus believed it was all part of the Christian ritual and stood silently, in pain he regarded as holy, until the ceremony ended.

For the next 1,500 years Ireland progressed steadily, though not without theological missteps, toward its eventual status as the most faithful daughter of the church. At the beginning of this long history certain Celtic tendencies toward adventurism were detected, along with a leaning toward purgatorial asceticism. For several centuries, in fact, the Irish church was regarded in Rome as a nest of heretics and troublemakers.

One of the early and more venturesome Irish theologians was Pelagius, whose originality in matters of doctrine was deemed excessive. Pelagius was in Rome before it fell to the German barbarians and wrote his *Commentaries on the Epistles of St. Paul,* in which he asserted (in contradiction to church doctrine and the teaching of St. Augustine) the freedom of the human personality, the ability of man to perfect his own soul, his capability of saving himself by good works alone, without the help of the grace of God. It took St. Augustine and a Vatican council to straighten out the church after Pelagius' humanistic views began spreading. St. Jerome referred to him in a letter as "an ignorant calumniator full of Irish porridge." In the eighth century there was an Irish monk named Virgile who was denounced to Pope Zachary for preaching to the innocent Bavarians that the world was round and that there were people living beyond the western ocean, all this in contradiction to contemporary wisdom. Virgile traveled to Rome to plead his case, explaining to the Pope that his people had long believed there was another continent overseas and that his forebears had been "accustomed to communicating with a transatlantic world." Pope Zachary dismissed this as Irish codding, forgave him, and later made him the Bishop of Salzburg. On the other hand, there was Columbanus, the apostle of Christian suffering, who founded a monastic colony in which self-mortification and stern penances were imposed. He served as the founding father of Irish puritanism.

When the so-called Dark Ages enveloped most of Europe west of Byzantium, Ireland became a haven of enlightenment and was indeed the land of saints and scholars. "Whereas," as Terence G. E. Powell, senior lecturer at the University of Liverpool, has written, "in the early Teutonic kingdoms of Post-Roman Europe, the Church found but the most rudimentary machinery for rule and law, in Ireland the missionaries were confronted by a highly organized body of learned men with specialists in customary law, no less than sacred arts, heroic literature and genealogy. Paganism alone was supplanted, and the traditional oral schools continued to flourish. By the seventh century, if not earlier, there existed aristocratic Irish monks who had also been fully educated in the traditional native learning. This led to the first writing-down of the vernacular literature, which thus became the oldest in Europe next after Greek and Latin." Those who transcribed the hyperbolic history of the Celts' thousand years in pre-Christian Ireland did not restrain themselves from embellishing the facts. One fabrication concerned the leader of the Red Branch Knights, who was alleged to have died of rage on being told of Christ's crucifixion. In retelling the pagan legends, the monastic scholars handed down the tradition that Irish heroes become gods through defeat—a reversal of the process elsewhere, and a significant one, which has been repeated in modern history. Such legends, according to the Irish historian Owen Dudley Edwards, have "a chilling relevance for Irish history as a whole." They demonstrate scorn for earthly standards of success, provide a philosophical basis for Irish pessimism, failure, backwardness. "It was as if the Irish realized," Edwards explains, "that defeat gives a psychological (or, as the word is used in Ireland, a spiritual) advantage to those who sustain it. . . ."

Monastic settlements sprang up all over Ireland and became centers of learning, in which illuminated manuscripts such as the Book of Kells were produced, along with the transcription of songs, stories, legends, and epics of pre-Christian Ireland. Europeans came to Ireland to study, and Irish monks went forth to found hermitages and universities in Iceland, England, Scotland, France, Germany, Switzerland, and Italy, one little band even penetrating Russia and establishing a Christian outpost at Kiev.

Eventually Europe regained its stability and forgot its cultural and intellectual debt to Ireland during the dark centuries. But a seventeenth-century English scholar, William Camden, looked back through the medieval gloom to pay the just and proper tribute: "Our Anglo-Saxons of that day used to flock together to Ireland as a market for learning whence it is that we continually find in our writers concerning holy men of old, 'he was sent away to be educated in Ireland.' It would appear that it was from that country our ancestors received the first instructions in forming letters, as it is plain they used the same characters which are still used in Ireland. . . . Ireland, which is now for the most part wild, half savage, and destitute of education, at that time abounded in men of piety, holiness and splendid geniuses, while the cultivation of literature elsewhere in the Christian world lay neglected and half buried." Camden did not find it necessary to add that Europe, as represented by the Danes, Normans, and English, had paid Ireland back by laying it waste in successive conquests.

Through her venturesome and widely traveled monks the Irish can even lay credible claim to the discovery of America. This exploit, attested by eleven Latin manuscripts in the Bibliothèque Imperiale in Paris, all dating well before Columbus' voyage, was undertaken by a Kerryman, Brendan the Navigator, later canonized. In the seventh century St. Brendan presided over an oratory on a mountaintop in County Kerry overlooking not only the lakes of Killarney but Atlantic horizons beyond. Between offering his orisons to God, St. Brendan gazed endlessly over the ocean and caught the glimmering of another land to the west, which was said to be visible to humans every seventh year.

According to the legend, this land beyond the horizon was Hy Brasil, "Isle of the Blessed, Land of the Ever Young." His brothers in Christ had already explored Iceland, so a voyage beyond the horizon did not dismay St. Brendan. A hide-covered coracle, much like that still used by the fishermen of Connemara, was his argosy. With a few companions, St. Brendan sailed across the Atlantic, through a region of icebergs and cold fogs and walruses, down the coast of this new terra incognita to a paradisical land of sunshine and flowers (Florida, if you're a true believer in the legend of St. Brendan). They ventured inland but turned back when an angel appeared to inform St. Brendan that the time wasn't ripe for further exploration and ordered him to return to Ireland. It is possible to doubt the chronicles of St. Brendan's travels to Hy Brasil, just as it is possible to doubt that a glimpse of America could be obtained from an Irish mountaintop every seven years, but supposedly Columbus read the account and was inspired to undertake his own voyage in 1492.

Comparatively few of the newly Christianized Celts took an active part in the enlightenment, which was centered behind the thick gray walls of the monasteries. For the most part their spiritual lives were engaged in a struggle to reconcile their deepest beliefs in unseen powers, in spirits that lived in oak trees, in sprites and demons of all descriptions, with the Christian teachings to which they had surrendered themselves. There was an undeniable longing for the old simplicities, the resort to magic, which demanded less of the believer than Christianity.

A synthesis of Christianity and paganism slowly evolved, with more and more of the Druid magic being exorcised and replaced by the Holy Trinity. Yet there has always been a bit of waffling on the subject, as exemplified by the West Cork woman cited by Sean O'Faolain. When asked if she believed in the fairies, she indignantly replied, "I do not," then reflectively added, "But they're there." The Irish lullaby called "The Castle of Dromore" invokes heavenly protection against the "dread spirit of the Blackwater Clan Eoghain's banshee." As Professor Edwards has remarked, "So powerful a sense of the survival of the pagan does Ireland still invoke, indeed, that we are in some danger of becoming a horror-story writer's paradise."

In a sense these preoccupations laid Ireland open to her conquerors. For almost a millennium the Celts of Ireland had been undisturbed. The centuries were dreamed away. Left to their otherworldly concerns, the Irish made no preparations to receive uninvited visitors from a hostile world to the east. Parochial disputes occupied their kings to the exclusion of any ideas of organizing a common defense of the island, and the high kings at Tara were still attuned to the music of their harps and the voices of their bards and remembrancers.

Then came the fierce Danish raiders in their war galleys, at first, plundering coastal enclaves and exacting tribute, then coming in greater numbers to occupy and settle down. The Danes were not only warriors but city builders. Instead of combining to eject the intruders, the Irish kings sat back and watched the industrious Norsemen build Dublin, Limerick, Cork, Wexford, and Wicklow, among other settlements. Somewhere around A.D. 1000 the Irish decided that two centuries was long enough to put up with the uncouth manners of the men from the north, and in 1014 they were brought together under the banners of Brian Boru, the first native Christian king of kings, to defeat the Danes in the Battle of Clontarf.

Once again the spirit of accommodation prevailed: the Danes were allowed to stay on, intermarry, and be assimilated, incidentally doing a lot of the donkey work the Irish abhorred and building up a foreign commerce which enriched the treasuries of the Irish kings. The end result was a great many more redheads in the Irish population.

Peace was unbroken for another 150 years, until a quarrel among the kings led to the incursion of the Norman barons from England. This divisiveness, among commoners as well as kings, was to be responsible for many of Ireland's sorrows, for its inability to rid itself of foreign domination.

In this new instance, the King of Leinster, Dermot MacMurrough, coveted the consort of Tiernan O'Ruirc, another king, and abducted her without any great amount of protest from the lady. The supreme authority at Tara ordered Dermot to return her to her husband and pay him a hundred ounces of gold for the damage to his self-esteem. Dermot complied, but his wife stealing had caused so much dissension among his peers that Rory O'Conor, the high king at Tara, banished him from Ireland. It was a bad move, because Dermot sailed straight for England determined to have his revenge if it ruined Ireland. Henry II was attentive, agreed that the Irish must be taught a lesson in the dangers of quarreling among themselves, and ordered his restless Norman barons to mount an invasion. Dermot handed over his beautiful daughter to the Earl of Pembroke in return for raising the expeditionary force.

England was still Catholic, and papal approval would have to be obtained before the invasion of Ireland could be launched. The Vatican had long been annoyed with the Irish for their disputatious attitude toward doctrine; furthermore, the throne of St. Peter was occupied by an Englishman, Pope Hadrian IV, who issued a papal bull which not only bestowed his blessings on the venture but in effect rented out Ireland at the equivalent of $10,000 a year. In one of the less Christian documents to be found in the Vatican library, Hadrian IV wrote Henry II:

> Since you have signified to us, dear son in Christ, that you desire to enter into the land of Ireland, in order to subdue the people to the obedience of the laws, and extirpate the vices which have taken root, and that you are also willing to pay an annual pension to St. Peter of one penny for every house therein, and to preserve the rights of the Church in that land inviolate and entire, we are well pleased that you should enter that island. It is likewise that the people of that country should receive you with honor and venerate you as their master; provided always that the ecclesiastical rights therein remain inviolate and entire, and reserving to St. Peter and the most holy Roman Church the annual pension of one penny from every house.

Since he mentioned the matter twice in two sentences, it would appear that the collection of Peter's pence was uppermost in Pope Hadrian IV's mind as far as the Irish were concerned. What was even more surprising, however, was that the Irish never weakened in their fealty to Mother Rome even though it was a Pope who let the English get their foot in the Irish door.

Aside from finding employment for his restless Norman barons, King Henry encouraged the invasion of Ireland out of long-range strategic considerations. Britain would always be in danger if Ireland, a day's sail from continental ports, should fall into French or Spanish hands. Ireland was England's back door and must be barricaded against England's enemies. If only Ireland could be made to understand that it was simply a matter of geography and self-protection . . . but it never would.

Seven and a half centuries of plain and fancy hell began for the Irish the day when the Earl of Pembroke, Raymond the Fat, and a small band of fellow adventurers, soon to be reinforced by King Henry, landed at Bannow Bay in County Wexford. The Normans, greatly assisted by superior military techniques and by Irish disunity, proceeded to conquer the province of Leinster—for themselves, not the spiteful King Dermot, who was forgotten in the joys of plunder and pillage—as well as the Danish-settled towns of Dublin and Waterford. Norman influence spread throughout the island, though the problem of pacifying the province of Connaught had to be turned over to the hardheaded Anglo-Norman De Burgos family. King Henry himself came over to act as referee and parcel out the land to various Norman barons and those regional Irish kings who were willing to pay tribute to him.

The Normans settled down to colonize and build castles and abbeys, whose ruins are still a notable feature of the Irish landscape. In the next century or two, however, the same thing happened to the Normans as the Danes who had preceded them; they were taken in by the gentle-seeming atmosphere, the soft rain, the soporific climate, and the process of absorption—subtly pervasive as the mist—which in Ireland defeats the most determined interlopers. The Normans were a hardheaded and pragmatic people but were easily overcome by the prevailing torpor. The stern and strong-willed De Burgos family soon changed their name to Burke and, it was said, became "more Irish than the Irish," even to the point of defying English authority. "Lord," sighed the poet Edmund Spenser, "how that country doth alter men."

The Irish, however, were under the Norman thumb, they were no longer ruled by a high king at Tara but French-speaking overlords, and there was one law for the Anglo-Normans and another for the native Irish. No Irish were permitted to attend the convocation of the first Irish Parliament in 1297, and subsequent sessions of that body, which was addressed in French or English but never Gaelic, promulgated laws forbidding the Norman colonizers to intermarry with the Irish, dress in the Irish style, or act as godparents to Irish children.

The Celtic civilization, which had been one of the twin beacons from the Bosporus to the Atlantic during the long dark centuries, was systematically destroyed. Why had the Celts failed to surmount their environment, to progress from sainthood and scholarship and form a society capable of protecting itself? For one thing, of course, they had never shown a disposition during their wanderings through Europe to settle down or build anything permanent; as a race they were inclined to let tomorrow take care of itself and concede to duller folk the burdens of permanency; they were always more interested in magical presences than solid things.

Sean O'Faolain believes that there is a palpable inertia in the Irish atmosphere, an element which somehow succeeds in making Irishmen out of foreigners in a remarkably short time, that Ireland is a "very pleasant featherbed." That dreaminess in the atmosphere and in their racial makeup allowed the Irish, before the Danes and Normans appeared, to put off the hard work of unifying themselves and preparing for self-defense.

> The Irish had room and room enough, time and time enough. They made a marvelous start with their romantic literature, and in and after the fifth century they laid their hands greedily on the heritage of Rome and Greece. By the tenth century they had allowed themselves to fossilize, and after it lived like the grasshopper, unready for the storm. They had seven hundred years, from the coming of Christianity to the coming of the Normans, during which they might have organized church and state. They failed to do it. One may imagine the God of History waiting and waiting and waiting, generation after generation, century after century, and finally taking up his pen, writing them off and closing his book with a disgusted snap.

With the Norman conquest and the subsequent English incursion, there came a rigid process of separatism which set apart the native Irish as an inferior and subject people. There were occasional efforts, most of them foreign-inspired, to throw off the yoke. In 1569 the Earl of Munster, defying an edict from England which made conducting the mass against the law, formed an alliance with other Catholic dissidents and obtained assistance from Italy and Spain, both eager to make trouble for the newly Protestant England. That effort was crushed when it made its last stand on the Dingle peninsula. Soon James I initiated the Plantation of Ulster, throwing the native Irish off their lands and settling them with Protestant Englishmen and Scotsmen, not without committing a great number of atrocities. Another rebellion erupted but was crushed by Oliver Cromwell, who, after wiping out the town of Drogheda and 3,000 of its men, women, and children, declared it "a judgment of God on those barbarous wretches." Catholic landowners were cleared out of the provinces of Munster, Leinster, and Ulster and given the choice, in the generous Cromwellian phrase, of going "to Hell or Connaught," that bleak and infertile western province.

The Irish were flung into serfdom, which was hardly alleviated in 1689, when the Catholic James II raised an army in Ireland and was defeated by William of Orange in 1690 at the Battle of the Boyne, in Ulster, on what remains a black-letter day for all Irishmen. Punitive laws were enacted by the British Parliament to teach the native Irish a lesson on the unwisdom of joining forces with England's enemies, one of them an edict forbidding an Irishman to leave all his land to one son but forcing him to divide it equally among all his male heirs, which fragmented the countryside into a patchwork of small holdings incapable of supporting a family except, marginally, on its potato crop.

The bitterly satiric *Parliament of Clan Thomas,* written in Gaelic, provides a glimpse of the new serfdom from the viewpoint of the old native aristocracy: "Clan Thomas spent their time merrily, well-fed and with light minds, as Saint Patrick had ordained for them. They did not use savoury succulent foods nor sweet intoxicating drinks, nor clean well-fitting clothes but crude canvas shirts, slimy coarse swallow-tail coats woven of the foul hair of puck goats and other animals, stinking boots of untanned leather, crooked long-lappeted caps without make or shape, bedunged, bare, rusty, slippery clogs; while, as Patrick had bade them, they watched and waited, served and ploughed and slaved for the nobles and gentry of Christian kind during the reign of every king from time immemorial, and they were craven before the kingly decrees, as was their duty."

Those who did not choose to submit to the privations of the Clan Thomas began that phase of the Irish diaspora known as the "flight of the wild geese." The dishonorable intentions of the English became apparent shortly after the Treaty of Limerick was signed on October 3, 1691, under which the Irish agreed to take the oath of allegiance to William and Mary of Orange. The English promptly broke all their seductive promises. The defeated Irish were left with three choices: give up arms altogether, enlist in their late enemy's army, or migrate to the France of the Sun King. The Irish voted on their alternatives, for the most part, with their feet. Eleven thousand chose to fight under Louis XIV's standards as the Irish Brigade, which became one of the finest fighting forces ever assembled. Only 1,000 decided to throw in with the English, and 2,000 simply turned in their weapons and went home.

The French never made a better bargain than when they imported the dissident Irish. At Fontenoy the Irish Brigade, charging with "Remember Limerick" as their battle cry, won that decisive battle for the French. "Cursed be the laws," groaned George II of England, "that deprive me of such subjects." In the next century thousands of Irish followed the wild geese to France or migrated elsewhere. They fought against the British in India, then in England itself with Bonny Prince Charlie. The general commanding the Irish Brigade requested that it be sent to America during the American Revolution as part of the French expeditionary force because "we have always been in the forefront of any battle against the English."

Not only the most belligerent but the brainiest left Ireland to make careers for themselves and continue the fight against England on more promising fields. Irish families starved themselves to send their brightest children to France for an education. The French aristocracy would include names like that of the Vicomte O'Neill de Tyrone. A marshal of France named Patrice de MacMahon won fame as a division commander in the Crimean War, then surrendered the French army at Sedan during the Franco-Prussian War, and bounded from that debacle to become the second President of the Third Republic. Other Irish names —Dillon, O'Maran, Kilmaine, Lally—appear on the façade of the Arch of Triumph. And the wild geese and their descendants contributed more to civilization than their busy swords. For one thing Marshal MacMahon, irked by the monotony of the cuisine during an Italian campaign, commanded his chef to concoct a new sauce. It became known as mayonnaise, eventually the solace of the American housewife.

The spirit of those refugee Irish was memorialized by Rudyard Kipling:

> . . . The wild geese are flying
> Head to the storm as they faced it before;
> For where there are Irish there's memory undying
> And when we forget, it is Ireland no more.

Irish names, often garlanded with military glory, began cropping up all over the world. Centuries before, Ireland had exported scholars to light a candle in the medieval darkness; now its soldiers appeared in a wild variety of uniforms fighting for widely diverse causes. One Ulysses Brown of County Galway was appointed a field marshal and commanded an army for Maria Theresa of Austria during the War of the Austrian Succession. Marshal Leopoldo O'Donnell threw in with the Spanish, ruled Cuba as governor-general, conquered Morocco, and was ennobled as the Duke of Tetuán. William Brown of County Mayo founded the Argentine navy. John Barry performed a similar service for the American Colonies and commanded at the first naval battle of the American Revolution. The O'Higginses fashioned even more spectacular careers in South America. Don Ambrosio O'Higgins was governor of Chile and later viceroy of Peru under the Spanish. His illegitimate son, Ambrose, returning to Chile after his father's death, led the nationalist uprising against the Spanish. He was proclaimed dictator of Chile after driving out the Spanish but decently retired when his fellow revolutionaries opted for a constitutional government.

For the next several centuries the Irishman abroad was usually a mercenary, adventurer, or scuffler of some kind. The reputation he gained for reckless courage, for impudence in the face of disaster, contributed largely to the self-portrait the Irish cherish and keep well dusted: the brash and frolicsome boyo who outwits or outfights everyone he comes across. The image of that not entirely mythical personage endures despite the collective Irish urge toward a passionate neutralism and a record of nonbelligerence which rivals the Swiss.

4.

The Colonels and the Memsahibs

Ah, Ireland, my dear fellow, that damnable, delightful country, where everything that is right is the opposite of what it ought to be.

—DISRAELI, EARL OF BEACONSFIELD

☘ All over Ireland plentiful evidence still exists of the elegant and enclosed world of the Ascendancy, the Anglo-Irish establishment which held sway over its vast estates and tenants dependent on its amiability for three or four centuries. The physical traces of that vanished world of the lord, the squire, and the bailiff are still visible along the roads. There are the stone pillars, the massive iron gates, the fortresslike gatehouses, the winding driveways through parklands, and the rambling, many-chimneyed, ivy-walled country houses which once were—and in some cases still are—the demesnes of the old landed gentry. Some of the great houses were burned to the ground during the Troubles and never rebuilt, others have been taken over by religious orders, or turned into tourist resorts, or occupied by wealthy fugitives from the roaring European or American industrialism who form a new squirearchy.

There was a considerable literature—the novels of Maria Edgeworth, hundreds of memoirs and dilettante volumes of verse, and all sorts of treatises on the art of fox hunting and other obsessive pursuits—on how that class lived, and bred, and took its pleasures despite the famines which ravaged the island and the periodic threat of a rising which would sweep away all their privileges. It was quite as inbred, ingrown, and exclusive a society as the plantation aristocracy of the antebellum American South, but there has been no such widely popular novel as *Gone with the Wind* to memorialize its passing.

An elegaic sense of how the Ascendancy, too, was blown away almost overnight, with the opening guns of World War I, and the all but inevitable seizure of that opportunity by the latest generation of Irish revolutionaries has been captured by the Anglo-Irish novelist Elizabeth Bowen. She describes a garden party at Michelstown Castle, County Cork, attended by the gentry just after their return from the London season, "an assemblage of Anglo-Irish people from all over northeast County Cork, from the counties of Limerick, Waterford, Tipperary. . . . Ten years hence, it was all to seem like a dream—and the Castle itself would be a few bleached stumps on the plateau."

The great country houses and those who lived in them evidently haunted her imagination; the houses themselves almost become living characters. In *The Last September* she supplies an elegy for a way of life which came to such a violent end as the great houses went up in flame. "A fearful scarlet ate up the hard spring darkness; indeed, it seemed that an extra day, unreckoned, had come to abortive birth that these things might happen. It seemed, looking from east to west at the sky tall with scarlet, that the country itself was burning; while to the north the neck of mountain before Mount Isabel was frightfully outlined." Soon the countryside was desolate. "Next year, the chestnuts and acorns pattered unheard on the avenues, that, filmed over with green already, should have been dull to the footsteps—but there were no footsteps. Leaves, fluttering down the slope with the wind's hesitation, banked formless, frightened against the too clear form of the ruin."

Until a half dozen years ago Elizabeth Bowen retained possession of her family's estate in County Cork, Bowen's Court, which has since been demolished. Her work testifies to the possessive love the Anglo-Irish felt for their lands, their feeling that the Anglo-Irish way of life would endure despite an uneasiness they must have sensed in the countryside, their hope that the Irish peasant someday would come to pray, as his English counterpart once did, "God bless the Squire and all his relations/And keep us in our proper stations." It is only fair to add that along with their sins of vanity and arrogance, the Anglo-Irish in many cases did love Ireland in their own peculiar way and did feel as Irish as anyone else. Actually they were caught in a semantic dilemma: The English considered them Irish, the Irish considered them English, and they considered themselves both. They saw no conflict of loyalties. They were loyal Irish subjects of the British throne.

They turned their faces from and shut their ears to the evidence of their unpopularity and concerned themselves with the pleasures of country life, the fox hunting, the hunt balls, Horse Show Week in Dublin, the race meetings at the Curragh, the exchange of visits with other owners of the great houses, the preservation of manners and mores adapted from the county society of England. They went over to England for the London season, those who hadn't become rentiers and turned their estates over to the management of their stewards. The men often served in the British army and provided some of its greatest generals from the Duke of Wellington to Lord Kitchener to Field Marshal Alexander, then came back to Ireland on retirement, scarlet-faced, choleric, and complaining of hob-nailed livers, old fevers and wounds they brought back from some barbaric frontier of the Empire. Their ladies returned as memsahibs with even firmer ideas on the loftiness of their station and the necessity of preserving the purity of their caste. Colonels and their ladies alike tended to look upon the Catholic Irish as blue-eyed wogs, Caucasian babus, white-skinned Fuzzy-Wuzzies, whom it was necessary to treat with firm condescension.

One of the more damning indictments of the Anglo-Irish was produced by Robert Lynd, the Anglo-Irishman, in a small masterpiece titled *Home Life in Ireland* and published in 1910. It was their shrinking from any sense of duty toward their less fortunate fellow citizens that particularly disgusted Lynd.

> Irish gentlemen as individuals are among the ballad-glorious heroes of the nation: the Ireland gentry as a class are, from Ireland's point of view, one of the most worthless aristocracies in history. The ordinary Irish gentleman who can afford to do so lives largely out of Ireland. . . . When he is at home he lives

as completely aloof from his people as though he were a foreigner treading conquered ground.

His estate is not a thing in which he takes any interest apart from the tribute which he can exact from it. The people do not see him at their churches; they do not find him on their platforms at political meetings. . . . Behind the rent-collecting agent and the rent-defending policeman he stands, a hostile force, believing in no justice save the justice which gives him as much money as he can get for his land, believing in no liberty save the liberty to leave his country a little poorer than he found it, and to subject the interests of an entire people to his own. His relations with his tenants have no sanction of human feeling. . . . They have lived in a little narrow world of bitterness, when they might have been part of a large and joyous struggle towards the making of a civilization. They have experienced all the pleasures of hunting and shooting, of eating and drinking, of comfort and the company of handsome men and women, but they are like people who go through one of the wonderful places of the world in a closed carriage with the blinds drawn.

Dr. Oliver St. John Gogarty, a member of that caste despite the fact he supported the Irish Revolution, would concede that it may have seemed to outsiders like a singularly insular, anti-intellectual class frozen in the attitudes of the seventeenth century. He was also quick to point out the virtues of the landed aristocracy:

Is it any wonder that the "landed gentry" should hold all "ideas" suspect and fight shy of them? . . . It should not be necessary to be clever to retain one's property. They know that frequently they have lost their estates through the machinations of clever people from the steward to pettifogging attorneys. In a world of false notions and false "values" the aristocrat born can trust no man. He has come to place his trust in the horse: the totem of his conquering tribe! . . . To comfort himself he has invented and built up a wonderful form of symbolism, fox-hunting. Here, he who rides may read the meaning of the symbolic ritual—the cleverest animal hunted down by men on horseback. Fox-hunting is the ritual of the aristocrat. In vain does the socially ambitious stockbroker strive to rise socially by falling off his

> hunter. His bandy legs may be more tribal than vocational, but they have not become bandy from horseback. In vain does he emulate the "best people" by affecting concussion of the brain. He may implore the surgeon at the cottage hospital to add to the report of a broken collarbone, "suffering from concussion." The hereditary Masters of Hounds are not to be fooled. They would not accept him were he to have his brain removed.

Obviously the landed aristocracy was not all of a piece; otherwise it could not have supplied so many political leaders of the native opposition (Lord Edward Fitzgerald, Smith O'Brien, Wolfe Tone, Charles Stewart Parnell, and Robert Emmet) or so many literary and intellectual dissidents (Dean Swift, Bishop Berkeley, Oliver Goldsmith, Edmund Burke, Oscar Wilde, George Bernard Shaw, J. M. Synge, Lady Gregory, William Butler Yeats, and many others). The best and brainiest of that class saved it from extinction when the Troubles came.

There were men, such as Captain Stephen Gwynn, a writer and member of Parliament, who were perceptive enough to see that "it is bad for people to be a caste," as he observed in a letter in 1912. "Caste is at the bottom of nine-tenths of our trouble. A Catholic bishop said to me, drink did a lot of harm in Ireland, but not half as much as *gentility*. Everybody wanting to be a clerk. Catholic clerks anxious to be in Protestant tennis clubs, Protestant tennis clubs anxious to keep out Catholic clerks, and so on, and so on. . . . It fills me with distress to see you all standing off there in your own paddock, distrustful and not even curious about the life you don't necessarily touch." As evidence of intelligence and sensibility of the ordinary Irish, he cited a Fenian who had spent many years in Kilmainham Prison and studied *Tristram Shandy* so diligently that "Sterne would have got more than perhaps he deserved in the way of satisfaction" if he could have heard the Fenian discoursing on it.

Among others who sensed that their caste was doomed were two young women, Edith Somerville and Violet Martin (whose joint pen name was Martin Ross), who collaborated on the best-selling *Some Experiences of an Irish R. M.* (Rural Magistrate). Miss Somerville's grandfather was married to a Catholic, who had prayers conducted daily in that otherwise Protestant household for herself and the Catholic servants. She once heard the stableboy groan, as he was summoned by the prayer bell, "Hadn't I the divil's own luck that I didn't tell the misthress I was a Protestant!" Her collaborator, Violet Martin, who lived on her family's estate of Ross in County Galway, pointed out that to many of the landed gentry their estates were anything but profitable. "Life at Ross," Miss Martin recalled in a letter published in *Irish Memories,* "was of the traditional Irish kind, with many retainers at low wages, which works out as a costly establishment with nothing to show for it. A sheep a week and a cow a month were supplied by the farm, and assimilated by the household; it seemed as if with the farm produce, the abundance of dairy cows, the packed turf house, the fallen timber ready to cut up, the fruitful garden, the game and the trout, there should have been affluence. But after all these followed the Saturday night labour bill, and the fact remains, as many Irish landlords can testify, that these free fruits of the earth are heavily paid for, that convenience is mistaken for economy, and that farming is, for the average gentleman, more of an occupation than an income."

Edith Somerville believed that the native Irish, the underdog Catholic Irish, were "immaculately honest and honourable where money is concerned." Her view was not shared by most other Anglo-Irish. On the whole, the Anglo-Irish of high degree looked upon the "natives" as not much more socially or culturally advanced than the heterogenous mixture of races they had observed in other places under the Union Jack. In common they held tenaciously to a number of beliefs about the Catholic Irish that consigned the latter to a permanent, unregenerate underclass: not quite untouchables, often endearing, but distinctly and inescapably inferior. Among those articles of the Anglo-Irish faith were:

The Irish were completely untrustworthy and had to be kept under constant surveillance.

They were too slothful and inefficient to make good farmers, so why shouldn't they have been forced out of the good lands to work the rocky slopes and wade through bog water?

Their ancient language contained no word for gratitude.

They were taught by their priests that it wasn't wrong to lie or steal, especially if they were lying to or stealing from a Protestant.

Many of them lived by poaching from the hunting preserves and salmon streams of their betters.

Those who belonged to the Ancient Order of Hibernians or some such squalid conspiracy took an oath that they would murder Protestants whenever they had a chance.

For all their sinister aspects, as thieves, poachers, and would-be assassins, the natives were, however, comedians and clowns to a man.

And when you got down to it, they were all children who had to be sternly instructed by the people of the great house. They would never be able to govern themselves so there was no point to educating them for the task.

Such attitudes had been hardening into a code for more than a century, since the passage of the Act of Union, which in effect made the Irish nation the prisoner of the British Empire. As Edith Somerville described the process in *Irish Memories,* "Ireland was, in those days [the early 1800's], a forcing bed for individuality. Men and women of the upper classes were what is usually described as 'a law unto themselves,' which is another way of saying they broke those of all other authorities." Only their "native kindliness and good breeding," she believed, kept the Anglo-Irish from becoming absolute autocrats. "They had neither public opinion nor legal restraint to interfere with them. Each estate was a kingdom, and, in the impossibility of locomotion, each neighbouring potentate acquired a relative importance quite out of proportion to his merits. . . ."

The Catholic Irish were not neighbors but subjects. Occasionally the Anglo-Irish would devote some thought and effort to bettering the lot of the natives, of elevating them from hewers of wood and drawers of water, but the programs they conceived often turned out to be impractical at the time. The idealistic George Russell (AE) and Sir Horace Plunkett, for instance, laid elaborate plans for rural cooperatives which would make the small farmers not only more efficient and prosperous but more sophisticated and urbanized. For their pains they would learn that their plan was being satirized by its proposed beneficiaries as being of the "dreamery-creamery school of thought."

The reality of the relations between the underdogs and the top drawer of society, as Arland Ussher pointed out, was that even young boys of the Ascendancy class were addressed as "Your Honor" by the natives. More than a century before, the Ascendancy had given up all interest in integrating themselves with the Catholic population. "Up till the passing of the Act of Union," Ussher wrote of his fellow Anglo-Irishmen, "they were in process of turning into an interesting autochthonous species, but ever since that fatal day they accepted the description of themselves as 'the garrison,' and tended more and more to be an absentee garrison—a class, in the most literal and economically vicious sense, of rentiers rather than landlords." As he looked back on the last days of the Ascendancy, his own boyhood coinciding with the years of its abrupt descent, Ussher regarded it with little nostalgia. "There were in those days a thing called County Society, more usually known as 'the Quality'—families who drove incredible distances in gigs and barouches to drink tea with each other. The males seemed to be every one of them a captain, a major or a colonel; Ireland was a land of colonels as Hungary was a land of counts, and I was secretly a little ashamed that my father and grandfather lacked a military prefix."

The shadowy future was not regarded with foreboding by the hearty, high-living gentry even when the 1903 Land Act was passed by the British Parliament. Land was the basis of their privileged society, their whole reason for being, yet they accepted with equanimity the legislation that provided for government purchase of all lands then leased to tenants, with the former landlord keeping a minimum of his holdings. The tenants could then buy the land on the installment plan.

What interested the feckless gentry was the excellent price they revealed for land that was often close to worthless, which they called the Bonus. Often it was squandered on a gigantic Parisian binge, flung on the gaming tables of the Riviera, or invested in racehorses, mistresses, and madcap ventures in speculative finance. George Wyndham, who introduced the Land Act in Parliament, was walking through a casino in Monte Carlo when an Irish peer plucked at his coattails, pointed to a pile of chips in front of him, and gratefully exclaimed, "George, George, the Bonus!"

Just how large the Bonus was and how extensive were the estates the landed gentry had inherited from some hard-fighting or well-connected ancestor who had participated in the carving out of the demesnes may be grasped in the example of County Cork, the largest of Ireland's counties. The gross inequities of the system are drably cloaked in the *List of Landowners,* a document published in 1871 which is on file at the Cork County Library. One fact leaps out of that compilation. The population of County Cork a hundred years ago was slightly more than 500,000, yet 50 men owned one-third of all its land, and 2,748 owned the balance, a situation comparable only to that of czarist Russia.

The entrenched power of that handful of magnates was indicated by the fact that the Earl of Bantry and his kinsmen owned 86,000 acres; their estates dominated the fingerlike peninsulas from Bantry Bay to Skibbereen. In that one corner of a small island, the Duke of Devonshire (who had larger interests elsewhere) owned 32,500 acres; Lord Bandon, 41,000; the Kingstons of Michelstown, 24,000; Sir George Colthurst, 31,260; the Earl of Cork, 20,165. The Townsends' holdings stretched along the coast, totaled 42,600 acres, and included residences at Clonakilty, Myross, Shepperton, Union Hall, and Whitehall, as well as more of the little whitewashed, twin-chimneyed tenants' cottages than they could count. Other landlords in the western and mid-Cork area included the Earl of Kenmare, 23,000 acres; the Earl of Shannon, 11,200; Wrixon-Becher of Mallow and Skibbereen, 18,933; the Masseys of Macroom, 13,363; the Shuldhams of Dunmanway, 13,000. Many of those landlords also owned extensive estates in England and Scotland. According to *British Landed Gentry in the Nineteenth Century,* such listings as those given above were "exclusive of a large area of, and rental of, perpetually leased lands returned in the name of a middleman."

Over those vast holdings, no matter what was planted there by their tenants, over fences and hedges and kitchen gardens, the local lord and his friends, their horses and dogs, could ride full tilt in pursuit of the fox and exercise of seigneurial rights. And the influence of those vanished sportsmen lingers on. Before me is the deed for a postage stamp of land in West Cork, designated as part of the "barony of Carbery West," one clause of which reads: "The property is subject during the life of the Right Honourable James Francis, Earl of Bandon, K.P., to the sporting rights within the meaning of the Irish Land Act, to which he was entitled previously to the sale under the said Act." The Earl of Bandon is hereby informed that the land has been converted into a fox sanctuary.

Not all the Anglo-Irish were heavy landowners. Some, like the Guinnesses, went into trade and prospered amazingly. There was also a lesser gentry—known to the countryside as squireens, little squires, not an admiring term—who verged on the shabby genteel. Many of them operated flour or linen mills.

There was also a detested breed known as the Castle Catholics, who looked to London rather than Rome for inspiration. They had thrown in with the conquerors a long time ago and owed their prosperity to the patronage of Dublin Castle. Ultraloyal to the British throne, toadying up to the Anglo-Irish, they often sent their sons into service with the British army and navy. If revolutionary storms were in the offing, they comforted themselves with the hope of being sheltered by the British regiments in garrison all over the island.

There was also a Catholic middle class, very small, which sent its sons to the universities and its daughters to the convent schools. This class had its own petty conceits, as Mary Colum (*Life and the Dream*) recalled from her girlhood. "Emigration to America had often a sort of social stigma, and one would occasionally hear an old man or old woman declare haughtily, 'None of my people ever had to go to America, thank God. We always had it,' meaning money or material possessions." Irish-Americans were looked down on; "American vulgarity on top of emigrant vulgarity, my uncle John would say." The attitude toward the Ascendancy, as Mrs. Colum recalled it, was more of contempt than violent hatred. "On the surface they [the landlords] were shown a certain amount of deference by their tenants if they were popular, but locally they were generally referred to as 'Cromwell troopers' or 'William troopers,' for if they sometimes looked down on the natives, the natives had a fine contemptuous vocabulary for them in return. The English rule, though not really accepted, went on smoothly enough as I remember it. It was irresponsible but not really tyrannical in my childhood." It seemed to her that the English sent over to rule Ireland were puzzled and discomfited people who believed that "we were a charming and witty people with an idolatrous Latin religion who could not govern ourselves."

Meanwhile, the Chekhovian self-sufficiency of the Anglo-Irish resisted all efforts from the thinking men and women among them to accept the realities of the nineteenth century. They seemed impregnable so long as the British Empire was the world's greatest power. The great houses, standing on eminences at the end of stately avenues through the surrounding woods, their stableyards full of pink-coated riders, sleek hunters, and clamoring hounds, their tall windows looking out on miles of melancholy beauty, undeniably possessed a quality that haunts the imagination. Yeats described it in two lines about Lissadell, the seat of the Gore-Booths (including the radical Countess Markievicz) overlooking Sligo Bay:

> The light of evening, Lissadell,
> Great windows open to the south.

But all that is romanticism; there is no more need to be nostalgic over that vanished breed than over the Prussian Junkers, the Baltic barons, or the Russian aristocrats. Their smugness alone would have made them insufferable. In his lengthy and now obscure romance *Lavengro,* George Borrow, also the author of *Romany Rye,* expressed their attitude, or posture, in his portrait of what he claimed was a "fair specimen" of the Ascendancy.

The Anglo-Irish were a "most remarkable body of men," he wrote, "who during two centuries have fought a good fight in the cause of civilization and religious truth; they were sent as colonists, few in number, into a barbarous and unhappy country, where ever since, though surrounded with difficulties of every kind, they have maintained their ground; theirs has been no easy life, nor have their lines fallen upon very pleasant places; amidst darkness they have held up a lamp, and it would be well for Ireland were all her children like these adopted sons. 'But they are fierce and sanguinary,' it is said. Ay, ay! they have not infrequently opposed the keen sword to the savage pike. 'But they are bigoted and narrow-minded.' Ay, ay! they do not like idolatry and will not bend the knee before a stone. 'But their language is frequently indecorous.' Go to, my dainty one, did you ever listen to the voice of a Papist cursing? The Irish Protestants have faults, numerous ones: and their virtues are their own, their industry, their energy, and their undaunted resolution are their own. They have been vilified and traduced—but what would Ireland be without them? I repeat it would be well for her were all her sons no worse than these much caluminated children of her adoption."

Not all the gasconade in print would convince the Catholic Irish that the landed gentry were their "adopted children."

They could remember too much deviltry and brutality brought to the island by those alleged benefactors, not to forget such unholy institutions as the Hell Fire Clubs of Dublin and Limerick and a similar group which called itself the Blasters and conducted satanic orgies for about twenty years between 1720 and 1740. They endured in Ireland long after a royal edict was issued in England, in 1721, against "certain scandalous clubs or societies" which "insult the most sacred principles of our sacred religion" and "corrupt the minds and morals of one another." A number of Hell Fire Clubs had been founded in England, one of the more notorious being that of which Sir Francis Dashwood was master of the revels, which took place in a ruined Cistercian monastery at Medmenham. Sir Francis was the "superior" who presided over drunken, mocking reenactments of the Last Supper which ended up in mass fornication.

The ruins of Dublin's Hell Fire Club, organized by Richard Parsons, the first Earl of Rosse, and Colonel Jack St. Leger, still stand on Montpelier Hill near the suburb of Rathfarnham. A demoniac afterglow lingers; the ruins are still avoided by sensible people after nightfall. Montpelier House, the site of the club's anti-Christian social events, was a shooting lodge built from the stones of a prehistoric cairn. It attracted many of the Regency bucks and highborn wastrels within the pale of Dublin; Colonel St. Leger was already notorious for the orgiastic routs he sponsored at Grangemellon, his magnificent country estate near Athy. A painting by James Worsdale in Dublin's National Gallery shows five of the Dublin Hell Fire Club's leading members—Henry Barry, the fourth Lord Santry; Colonel Clements; Colonel Ponsonby; Colonel St. George; and Simon Luttrell, later the first Earl of Carhampton—gathered around a huge punchbowl.

Little is known about the club's more lascivious capers, unfortunately, but the fuel which powered those orgies was scaltheen, a horrendous concoction of whiskey and butter. A black cat, supposedly embodying Satan, was the central figure. To frighten away any people of the neighborhood who might be spying on their revels, one of the club's members would put on a devil's costume, including the tail and horns of a cow, and go howling into the night. Once a crowd of indignant local Irish ventured up Montpelier Hill, but before they could muster up the courage to put an end to the saturnalian carousal, the membership doused a tomcat in scaltheen, set fire to him, and threw him out the door. The fiery apparition quickly dispersed the crowd.

By 1740 most of the membership had either died of their excesses or gone to England. There was enough hellishness left in the residue to commit one last outrage against public decency. At their last outing on Montpelier Hill they soaked a servant in whiskey and set him alight. His death persuaded the authorities, finally, to abolish the clubs in Ireland. A short time later Montpelier House burned to the ground and was never rebuilt.

There were plenty of other villains to be remembered with loathing, not least the lord high chancellor, "Black Jack'" Fitzgibbon, who was one of the chief agents in bribing the Irish Parliament to go out of business in 1801 and who had boasted that he would make the Irish "tame as cats" before he was through with them. Irish barristers hated to appear before him but on occasion managed to let him know what they thought of him. During one proceeding he complained to John P. Curran that he was unable to see any difference between "also" and "likewise." Curran hastened to illustrate his point: "Oh, the distinction is real, my Lord. For many years the great Lord Liffey presided over this court. You also preside over it, but not likewise." He was equally detested by the English when he was rewarded for his Irish endeavors with a seat in the House of Lords. His bad manners so disgusted his peers that the Duke of Bedford informed him, "We would not bear this insult from an equal. How much less shall we endure it from the mouth of an upstart and mushroom nobility." Lord Fitzgibbon was buried in Dublin, where his grave was strewn with dead cats.

And then there was another lordling, Murrough O'Brien, the sixth baron and first Earl of Inchiquin, of whom an Irish historian wrote that "Execrations cling to his memory" two centuries after his death in 1673. Most of all Inchiquin was detested for modeling for that unbecoming style of tailoring known as the turncoat. His uncertain loyalties in politics and religion won him the historic title of "a poor wavering panther." He did waver, and his style was pantherish. Born a Catholic, he went over to the Protestant side after marrying the daughter of Sir William St. Leger, the president of the province of Munster. During the English Civil War of 1641-49, as military governor of the southern province, he expelled all Catholics from Cork City, Youghal, and Kinsale, plundered the towns of Adare and Cashel, and tortured and hanged priests at Castlemartyr, Bandon, and elsewhere.

In 1650 Inchiquin turned his coat again, reverted to Catholicism, opposed the invasion of Cromwell and joined Charles II in exile. His wife, it was said, remained a Protestant and "kept him in a state of continual penance." His reputation as a "murderer of priests and friars" prevented him from receiving command of the Irish troops in their French exile.

Inchiquin returned to Ireland in 1663 but was denied the presidency of Munster because, having turned his coat once too often, he was a Catholic. Charles II did restore his estates in County Clare, a poor reward for a man of his violent ambitions. He was given the dignity of a funeral in St. Mary's Cathedral, Limerick, but it was said that certain persons with long memories took his body from its churchyard grave and threw it into the Shannon.

Viewed from the underside of Irish life, the lords and ladies of the Ascendancy were, at best, representatives of the devil on earth. The native attitude was conveyed in a popular song celebrating the death of a noted sportsman in a hunting accident:

O Lord Waterford is dead,
  Says the Shan Van Vocht,*
O Lord Waterford is dead,
  Says the Shan Van Vocht,
O Lord Waterford is dead
  With the devil at his head
And 'tis hell will be his bed,
  Says the Shan Van Vocht. . . .

The jeering farewell to Lord Waterford may lack something in Christian charity, but he and his peers and those who supported them in a hostile land seemed an unbearable burden to the Catholic Irish around them. In Michael O'Suilleabhain's *Where Mountainy Men Have Sown* he tells of his uncle, when a boy, following the local nabob and his guest, a British army captain, out on a woodcock shoot. The Irish boy was close enough to overhear Sir Augustus Warren and his guest talking as they rested on their shooting sticks and looked out over the terrain with its outcropping of ledge, its thick growth of gorse and other useless vegetation.

"Sir Augustus," the British captain asked, "did I hear you say that you took rents from the people about here?"

"Oh, yes," his host replied, "the land round here is very good."

"Good!" the captain snorted. "Good! Egad, sir, it is good for cock shooting."

As O'Suilleabhain observed, the landlord regarded himself as the absolute master of everything that moved or flew over his domain:

> He "owned" the wild birds of the air and all the ground game. Woe to the man or boy caught chasing a hare or setting a trap or snare. The penalty was meted out according to the humour of the particular landlord, he being also the local dispenser of justice. I can cite an instance, from living witnesses, where the landlord's gamekeeper saw a young man crossing one of the Derrynasaggart Mountains, accompanied by a greyhound. He shot the young man with a rifle and killed him. The gamekeeper was never brought to trial before a court.

* That is, Ireland itself.

Incredibly obtuse were the Anglo-Irish, so insulated from the realities of conditions around them, so satisfied with the righteousness of their position, that they actually believed they had earned the gratitude of the people they had ground down for generations. In the early 1870's the gentry was stunned when their tenants actually began voting in their own interests. A parliamentary seat was up for an election in County Galway, in which a Captain Nolan, a Home Rule candidate, was opposed to a Captain Trench, the Conservative candidate, who naturally was supported by the gentry. The father of Violet Martin (many of whose letters were included in *Irish Memories*) naturally presumed that his tenants would vote as he dictated; instead, he and his fellow landlords were "personally wounded" when the peasantry around Lough Corrib finally declared their political independence.

Violet Martin's father drove to the polling place at Oughterard on election day but was warned by a man he met on the hill outside the town to go back home. "A troop of cavalry glittered in the main street and the crowd seethed about them. My father drove on and saw a company of infantry keeping the way for Mr. Arthur Guinness, afterwards Lord Ardilaun, as he conveyed to the poll a handful of his tenants from Ashford at the other side of Lough Corrib to vote for Captain Trench, he himself walking with the oldest of them on his arm. During that morning my father ranged through the crowd incredulously, asking for this or that tenant, unable to believe that they had deserted him. It was a futile search; with a few valiant exceptions the Ross tenants, following the example of the rest of the constituency, voted according to the orders of their Church, and Captain Nolan was elected by a majority of four to one. It was a priest from another part of the diocese who gave forth the mandate, with an extraordinary fury of hatred against the landlord side; one need not blame the sheep who passed in a frightened huddle from one fold to another."

The reactionary zeal of the Anglo-Irish, their determination to hold their privileged position against all onslaughts were forcefully delineated in Liam O'Flaherty's novel *Land,* which tells of the Land League's efforts in the years following the Great Famine. One of his nastier characters is a Captain Butcher, a nonaristocrat, a land-grabbing, self-made man with a passion for turning Ireland back to feudalism.

Captain Butcher unabashedly recalls how he established himself: "Having a little money on hand, I had married well, I bought Manister. Unlike other Englishmen that were buying Irish land at the time, I had no ambition to become a fox-hunting loafer. As I said before, I come of yeoman stock. I love land. Just to possess it is a passion with me. . . . With industry developing in England at a colossal pace, a man didn't have to be a wizard in order to see that rural Ireland would become England's cattle market. So I decided to clear Manister of peasants and raise cattle. Most of the new English landowners were doing the same thing. I ran into opposition at once. It was really astonishing. The number of Irish people have been reduced by three millions in a few years, through hunger and fever, yet they continued to resist. They fought us tooth and nail. How do you explain it?"

The thick-witted Captain Butcher, who was candid enough about his own greed for Irish land but couldn't understand how the Irish might feel a similar possessiveness about their own country, as though their feelings were subhuman, was representative of the smaller landowners who would fight harder for their holdings than the slack-witted peers who had grown soft in the years of the Ascendancy.

Butcher at least grasped the fact that he was fighting for a privileged position, deserved or not, while his social superiors maundered on about hunt balls and the Dublin Horse Show. "I'm defending the feudal system," as he baldly put it, "and the landowning gentry on whom the power of England is based. If that system and that class are destroyed, then England is doomed within the space of a few generations."

When the Troubles began in 1916, men like O'Flaherty's Captain Butcher naturally demanded the strongest measures to put down the insurrection. The Ascendancy, however, was divided between loyalty to Ireland and to England, between practicality and sentiment. England was their protector, but Ireland was their home. The natives were not inclined to differentiate, to pause and determine just how much the individual Anglo-Irishman might have loved Ireland. When rebellion and later civil war spread through the countryside, many of the Anglo-Irish fled to England to await the outcome of the fighting between the English and the Irish and subsequently between the Irish factions. (The mistress of one country estate in County Waterford received a letter in England from her gardener at home, which reported in part: "Your Ladyship will be glad to hear that both sides admired the dahlias.")

The funeral pyres of the great houses, many of them burned in reprisal for atrocities committed by the British forces, lit up the countryside. It was the end of the Ascendancy as an institution. Most of its membership, however, suffered damage only to their property, rarely to their persons. There was no Night of the Long Knives to avenge centuries of oppression. A retired British admiral was assassinated in County Cork before the Troubles ended, but apparently that was because he persisted in trying to recruit young Irishmen for service in the British navy. It was a miracle, really, that most of the colonels and memsahibs weren't murdered in their beds. The only explanation was the gentleness of the ordinary Irish, their habit of forbearance in personal relations, who showed more nobility in a few years than their escutcheoned, titled, bemedaled "betters" had in four centuries.

The Ascendancy disappeared as a separate, established class, but many of its survivors stayed on in reduced circumstances, preferring the risk of becoming decayed gentlefolk to carving out careers in England. Those country houses which survived the time of arson often lay in near ruin, those which haven't been sold to the tourist industry or newcomers from the Continent, England, and America. Some of the former gentry work hard at farming, at keeping up a semblance of old appearances. They are neither above the Irish around them nor quite a part of them; their fate is to be suspended in social space.

The struggle for survival engages many of them, an unremitting effort to keep ancient roofs from tumbling onto their heads. "Irish estates," says Mark Bence-Jones, who lives on a County Cork estate held by his family for four centuries, "have particular features that are costly to maintain. The lengthy demesne walls can be allowed to fall down, but, sometimes a mile or even two miles, must be kept at least passable. Often there is a bridge; it may be Gothic or even Chinese in style, but its timbers are probably unsound. Even if one can avoid going over it oneself, there is the nightmare that a stranger will fall through it and claim damages."

Some survivors of the former Ascendancy have tried to maintain the old madcap tradition of their lustier ancestors. There was one rakehell known to Arland Ussher who camped out in the ancestral home despite the fact that most of its windows were broken and the roof had lost most of its slates. Most of the furnishings had been stripped by the bailiffs in search of realizable assets, till the only remnant of the old days was a pair of heavy silver candlesticks.

At his frequent drinking parties the master of the ruin and his guests sat on packing cases and slept where they dropped. The drunker guests were invited to duplicate the feat of one of his ancestors and jump out of a certain high window, a leap which his ancestor had survived in frantic flight from his creditors. In various remote rooms of the house the lord kept his several children, all of them known to be imbecilic. One of his pastimes was riding on horseback into a crowded dance hall, scattering the offspring of his family's former tenants, as though renewing the claim to seigneurial rights.

There are fortunately few such lusty survivals of the Ascendancy spirit. Perhaps more than a few resemble the character Lord Patrickstown in Honor Tracy's *The Straight and Narrow Path,* the frightened descendant of a long line of soldiers and viceroys, who was "small and soft and round, where his forebears were straight and hard."

In some places, not many, the influence of the Ascendancy lingered long after its power had evaporated. Less than twenty years ago, but thirty years after the English officially quit Ireland, its stamp was still visible in Doneraile, County Cork, the heart of the fertile Duhallow country. Many of the more prosperous people of the district were retired army officers and their ladies who held themselves aloof from the "locals." On market days, aboard Land Rovers and Bentleys, they swept tweedily and snootily into town. Disdaining to mingle with the common people, they pulled up outside the shops and honked their horns, upon which the shopkeepers rushed out to take their orders.

That sort of curb service is no longer available in the Irish Republic.

5.

The Great Mick, or a Hero for the Irish

The true devotion lies not in melodramatic defiance or self-sacrifice for something falsely said to exist, or for mere words or formulas which are empty, and which might be but the house swept and garnished to which seven worse devils entered in. . . .

—MICHAEL COLLINS, quoted in Oliver St. John Gogarty's *As I Was Going Down Sackville Street*

☘ An interesting sidelight is cast on the Irish people, or any other, by their attitude toward heroes and national leaders. It is a human trait, perhaps not the most attractive one, to delight in hauling great men off their pedestals. The fluctuating fortunes of the Kennedy legend is a case in point, yet a fair number of America's heroic legends remain intact and all but unassailable. Among the Nordic peoples, generally, a national hero is allowed to ride off to Valhalla and stay there with his reputation growing rather than diminishing with time. Latins, with their ingrained skepticism, are less likely to venerate anyone—try to name an Italian or Spanish hero of this century whose luster did not fade the moment he stepped out of the official limelight.

The Celts, however, like their heroes buried safely in the distant hazy realm of the legendary, something for pipers and poets to celebrate without allowing them to impinge on everyday life. Knowing that we all come of common clay, they are not easily swayed by the Führer principle. Anyone who claims the right of leading them is certain to be hemmed in by his countrymen, their bright-blue eyes seizing upon and evaluating every gesture and nuance, questioning every incautious statement. "Mostly," it is said, "your Irishman likes his kings dead."

From their earliest history the Celts regarded a ruler as disposable and expendable. When he grew too old to rule efficiently, he was given a ritualistic sendoff by his grateful subjects. In his study of the Tara kingship stories, Professor T. G. E. Powell has noted: "There can be little doubt that the Celtic king, in fully pagan times at least, met a violent but ritual end, and there are a number of somewhat veiled allusions to deaths by weapon wounds, drowning and burning, in the midst of high magic. . . ." The Irish have always been too individualistic to fling themselves into idolatry of another living human being.

Many of the high kings were killed by their successors without much consternation or protest from the lower orders; *Macbeth* could never realistically have been laid in Ireland because the betrayal and murder of a king simply wouldn't have stirred up all that fuss. The Irishman is quick to suspect anyone who asserts that he is wiser or nobler than his fellows. He can be swayed by a demagogue, but only in the intoxication of the moment.

Anyone aspiring to lead the nation must demonstrate culpability in advance, must recognize the deep-rooted tradition that a leader be capable both of inspiration and self-mockery. He may take his mission seriously, but never himself. When Parnell traveled around the United States to raise funds against a threatened famine and for a campaign to destroy the power of the landlords, he reported that "when Dillon and I had sufficiently depressed the public we went around with our hats." At least one Irish historian (Owen Dudley Edwards) has observed that from antiquity on the Irish patriotic leaders recognized the necessity of playing both the hero and the antihero and "the greatest zealots for a cause can be its most sardonic commentators." Michael Collins, the subject of this close-up, was the chief engineer of the Irish Revolution and was fittingly adored, yet as a student of the ancient folkways he comprehended that it was always necessary to maintain an attitude of self-deprecation. During an internal political crisis he sent a note over to a pub in nearby Duke Street reading: "Send over a bottle of brandy and a syphon to settle the Irish question. Mick, commander in chief." That was the proper style: Mick, commander in chief, with tongue in cheek.

There is reason to believe that John F. Kennedy has achieved the status of near sainthood among the Irish not only because he was of Irish descent but because he was at safe remove from the peeled-eye examination of his idolators.* Their homegrown heroes have fared poorly in modern as well as ancient times. The English may have brought Parnell down, but the Irish finished him off. Nor could Wolfe Tone rally much real support—or Robert Emmet, for that matter—when it counted. During the Troubles an authentic crop of heroes was raised in the forcing bed of revolution, but few survived. The names of Cathal Brugha, Rory O'Connor, Kevin O'Higgins, and Michael Collins all are garlanded with the memory of their deeds—and all were slain by their fellow countrymen. Since then there have been other heroes of the resistance, members of the IRA, but mostly they have remained anonymous, their actions known only to some of their comrades and perhaps to the agents of the Special Branch. Possibly there is a clue to the Irish attitude toward heroes in the career of the one notable survivor of the Irish Revolution. All that his country could bestow upon a man fell to the lot of Eamon De Valera—the most cautious, pedantic, and long-headed of all the revolutionaries, half-Spanish, American-born, rather humorless (in public view) and never given to extravagant gestures. No one would accuse him of being the epitome of the Celtic warrior of the legends; his one moment of recklessness occurred in 1916, when he defended the bridge over the Grand Canal and, significantly enough, was more successful in his exertions than his more flamboyant colleagues elsewhere in the embattled city.

Still, with all their suspicion of that Arabic word "charisma," which has never caught on in Ireland, the Irish like to think of themselves as picturesque and devil-may-care, as living up to the outside world's picture of them as swashbuckling boyos. They have no doubt of the national quotient of courage; the number of Victoria Crosses awarded to Irish soldiers in the British army

* Yet it must be noted that one of Kennedy's more attractive qualities was his self-deprecation; unconsciously he had fallen in with a racial tradition.

alone attests to that. They also like to think of Irish heroism as leavened with a dash of humor. An incident that supposedly occurred in Cork City during the final struggle with the British army of occupation is often cited as an example of this blithe and daring spirit. An IRA detachment based on the city, desperately in need of more transport, entered the Ford assembly plant there. The commandant cornered the factory manager in his office and announced, "We need some lorries."

"Obviously," the American executive retorted, "you have not noticed the flag displayed on this building. This is United States property, and so far as I am aware you are not at war with the U.S. government. You have no right to requisition the property of a neutral nation."

The IRA officer considered the matter for a moment, then took out a pad and scribbled. "As of today's date," he announced, "this detachment is at war with the United States of America. Now hand over them lorries!"

The story may be apocryphal—and in any case the IRA of Cork City was running small risk of facing an American invasion or even much of a reaction from the Ford people, Henry Ford himself being of Irish descent—but it illustrates the way the Irish like to think of themselves in action. To be caught without a ready answer is worse than a defeat.

As proof that such legends have substance, too, there was the career of one man of modern Ireland—the embodiment of what they maintain is the Irish spirit—whom practically all Irishmen would agree was the indispensable hero. Not only was Michael Collins, "The Great Mick," the organizer and propulsive force of the Irish Revolution, but without him, it is safe to say, it could hardly have been accomplished. He was one of those rare men who are thrust to the surface at critical times, who seem to have been born for their crucial role. There was little of the devil-may-care in his makeup, yet he strolled around Dublin with a £10,000 reward on his head and every British agent and soldier looking for him. "The true devotion," he once said, with certain of his countrymen's propensities in mind, "lies not in melodramatic defiance or self-sacrifice for something falsely said to exist, or for mere words and formulas which are empty, and which might be but the house swept and garnished to which seven worse devils entered in. . . ."

He was necessarily a man of action and bloodshed, ruthless with informers and traitors, yet he had Gandhi-like visions of a New/Old Ireland returned to the ancient simplicities—as when he wrote: "One may see processions of young women riding down on the island ponies to collect sand from the seashore, or gathering in the turf, dressed in their shawls and in the brilliantly coloured skirts made of material spun, woven and dyed for over a thousand years. Their cottages are also little changed. They remain simple and picturesque. It is only in such places one gets a glimpse of what Ireland may become again."

During the period that followed the Easter Rising, Ireland was placed under martial law, enforced by a heavy-handed new British commander, General Sir John Maxwell, and the 150,000 troops at his disposal. Twenty-five hundred of the more dangerous rebels had been interned in England, and De Valera was a convict in Dartmoor.

Among the internees was Michael Collins, who, like many others before him in the same circumstances, used his term of imprisonment to consider what went wrong and plan how to make it go right the next time around. "It is so easy to fault the actions of others when their particular actions have resulted in defeat," he wrote a friend from the Frongoch internment camp. "I want to be quite fair about this—the Easter Rising—and say how much I admired the men in the ranks and the womenfolk thus engaged. But at the same time—as it must appear to others also—the actions of the leaders should not pass without comment. They have died nobly at the hands of the firing squads. So much I grant. But I do not think the Rising was an appropriate time for the issue of memoranda couched in poetic phrases, nor of actions worked out in a similar fashion. . . ."

Collins would be a realist, with a continuing profound distrust of idealists, ideal solutions and grandiloquent proclamations. One of the Rising leaders whom he most admired was the crippled Sean MacDermott, of whom he wrote from the Frongoch camp: "Today he is as much alive in this camp as if he were here with us. If I have one quarter of the strength of Sean MacDiarmada I am satisfied. Wherever he walked there went with him the shades of the great Irishmen of the past. He did not seek glory as a personal investment but as a National investment. He was not Sean MacDiarmada, he was Ireland." A fusion of Connolly-like realism and MacDermott-like spirit, he saw, would be necessary to win Irish independence.

Collins was only twenty-six when he was released, along with the others in the Frongoch camp, under political pressure from both Ireland and the United States, but intellectually and spiritually he was prepared for the role he soon assumed. During the months following his release Ireland simmered, waited for another Rising, and was not appeased when the new British Prime Minister, David Lloyd George, proposed Irish self-rule within the British Empire and as a further conciliatory measure released Eamon De Valera from Dartmoor in the spring of 1917. Despite these gestures, the Irish resistance gathered strength on both the military (underground) and political fronts. Its leaders were Arthur Griffith, who had also been released from a British jail; De Valera, who was elected president of the Sinn Fein, and Michael Collins, who was busy reorganizing and reequipping the Irish Volunteers (soon to be designated the Irish Republican Army).

What made Collins, at twenty-six, the leader of a great national movement? Physically he was impressive, fairly tall (five feet ten, but looking taller because of the way he carried himself), strongly built, square-jawed, exuding energy and purpose, possessing a straight firm mouth and penetrating eyes. There is an aura of greatness about him visible even in photographs; his comrades called him "the big fellow," and they were referring to his inner qualities as much as his imposing presence. Robert Briscoe, the Dublin Jewish merchant's son who later became lord mayor of the city, started out his rebel's career as a messenger for the IRA and described Collins as "stocky, but swift moving, with a square, fighting Irish face, and a sort of jaunty swing to him; and that devil in his eyes. Though he was inconspicuously dressed as a bank clerk might be, there was no mistaking the quality of him."

There was a complexity about Michael Collins, as with most great men, that can hardly be defined by a recital of biographical detail or even by the recollections of those who knew him well and worked with him during the six years of his adventurous career. However, details are necessary: he was born in Sam's Cross, a hamlet midway between Clonakilty and Rosscarbery, in 1890. As a boy he acquired a love of books from his aged father, who knew Latin and Greek, and a revolutionary spirit from the writings of various Irish patriots. His schoolmaster noted, among other things, that Collins as a boy "displayed more than a normal interest in things appertaining to the welfare of his country. A youthful, but nevertheless striking, interest in politics. A good sportsman, though often temperamental." For all his bookishness young Collins, like most Corkmen, was more concerned with practical matters than theory or ideology. If he had an ideology, it was simply that Ireland must be free and democratic.

It was a tradition that the brighter West Cork boys entered the British postal service. Michael Collins studied for the civil service examinations, passed them, and was appointed a clerk in the Post Office Savings Bank, West Kensington, London—a colorless beginning for an extraordinary career. In London he was active in the Gaelic League and the Gaelic Athletic Association, and at the age of nineteen he joined the Irish Republican Brotherhood. Several years later he quit the British postal service and took a job in the London branch of the Guaranty Trust Company of New York. Bank clerk by day, aspiring revolutionary by night. He had become one of the IRB leaders among the Irish of southern England. Early in 1916 he returned to Dublin, determined to be on hand when the revolution broke, and thus he was one of the band which held the General Post Office during the post-Easter week.

All this tells us little more than that Collins could change himself within a few months from a staid bank clerk to a flaming revolutionary. A genius for leadership must have been present, because even those who knew him during his clerkship years were impressed by him, and the Irish do not quickly or easily play follow-the-leader. One of his biographers admitted that only the broadest outline of his character was visible, "dynamic, ruthless in pursuit of his objective, domineering, generous qualities allied to those of coolness, calculation, and in lighter moments a gay rumbustious bonhomie."

He was not one of the romantic gunmen, one of those urban guerrillas who fought the underground war against the British occupation, but he was their leader, organizer, and strategist. Desperately hunted as he was, once the British learned of his importance, he never carried a gun; his jaunty self-confidence was better protection than any number of revolvers. He became the strong man of the resistance between 1917 and 1919 through his efforts as the mastermind of an intelligence network which spied upon, and often outwitted, his opposite numbers of the British secret service headquartered at Dublin Castle. At the same time he was building up a guerrilla army which drilled in the mountains and marked time until it would be called into action. In effect, he would become the commander in chief of that army and the chief intelligence officer, as well as assume other duties.

His rise in the underground resistance was propelled by the fact that in 1918 the British again interned many of the Sinn Fein leaders. On April 16 the House of Commons passed a Conscription Act, which would have pressed into service many Irishmen reluctant to volunteer for the British army ever since the Easter Rising. Sinn Fein openly campaigned for resistance to the conscription law. On May 18 the British announced that they had uncovered a conspiracy between the German secret service and the Sinn Fein leaders—it happened to be nonexistent but served the purposes of Dublin Castle—and arrested Arthur Griffith, Eamon De Valera, and many other Sinn Fein leaders, all of whom were shipped back to England and interned.

By then Collins had organized and perfected his own intelligence system, which tipped him off that he was about to be arrested. He escaped the British net and went underground. The British offered a £10,000 reward for information leading to his capture; unfortunately they did not have a photograph of him in their compendious files and, apparently, a very incomplete description. Armed by self-assurance and a bold certainty he would never be caught, Collins went about his business daily in Dublin, on foot or on a bicycle, without a disguise of any kind. The basis of his spy system was the hundreds of pubs; publicans and barkeeps were among his best agents, and he often strolled into a public house jammed with British soldiers, had a pint of stout, made his contact, and casually drifted out.

Collins was one of the several dominant figures at the first Dail Eireann (that is, the rebel Irish Parliament), convened by the Sinn Fein to declare Irish independence and elect De Valera president of a republic recognized only by themselves. The first Dail was called to order on January 21, 1919, several months after the World War had ended. Collins may not have been the number one man at the convocation—that role went to Cathal Brugha, De Valera's chief associate, and a headstrong, hot-tempered young man with whom Collins would often find himself in opposition—but he did succeed in blocking attempts by the socialist-syndicalist wing of the Sinn Fein to introduce the following clauses in the party's declaration: "The Republic will aim at the elimination of the class in society which lives upon the wealth produced by the workers of the nation but gives no useful service in return, and in the process of accomplishment will bring freedom to all who have hitherto been caught in the toils of economic servitude. It shall be the purpose of the Government to encourage the organisation of the people into trade unions and cooperative societies with a view to control and administration of the industries by the workers engaged in the industries." Collins caught a whiff of Bolshevism, and his opposition prevailed; the chief terrorist yielded to the apprentice banker he had once been. The first Dail gave him another post, Minister of Finance, in its shadow government, which he held in addition to adjutant general of the Volunteers and director of intelligence.

Not yet thirty years old but wearing three hats, Collins took on another role on orders from the Sinn Fein executive: jailbreaker. While the Dail was still in session—it was to be declared a "dangerous association" by the British and suppressed six months hence—Collins slipped away to England. He was accompanied by Harry Boland, who kept a tailor shop in Middle Abbey Street but more important was Collins' closest friend and associate, an easygoing man, but able and energetic, whose character complemented Collins' and made him the perfect number two man. Their assignment: to spring De Valera from Lincoln

Prison. A key baked in a cake was their time-honored method. The trouble was, they couldn't find a decent locksmith. Two keys smuggled into Lincoln Prison proved to be the wrong type. A third was rough-cast and smuggled via a cake to be filed down to the proper size inside the prison. On the night of February 3, 1919, Collins, Boland, and a third man, Frank Kelly, went to the prison and opened the outside gate, through which De Valera, Sean Milroy, and Sean McGarry slipped. De Valera was kept out of sight in various safe houses in England until Collins and Boland spirited him and Milroy and McGarry back to Ireland. Several months later Collins smuggled De Valera aboard a liner bound for America, where De Valera was to spend the next year and a half raising money for the Irish resistance—at which he was brilliantly successful—and making propaganda on its behalf. If the streets and hedgerows of Ireland were the fighting front of the struggle against the British, the United States was the indispensable rear area.

Collins, wearing his Minister of Finance hat in the shadow government, was also raising funds totaling $1,250,000 in Ireland for revolutionary purposes. He had several offices around Dublin, each of them fitted by his friend Batt O'Connor, a master builder, with secret cupboards and sleeping quarters and hidden staircases down which Collins more than once escaped a British raiding party. In one Dublin house he kept $75,000 in gold, contained in four boxes and a child's coffin, under the floorboards.

During the winter of 1919-20, the underground war heated up considerably, particularly in Dublin, where British terror was met in full measure by Irish counterterror. England had decided to stamp out the rebellion by whatever means were necessary. The escalation was placed in charge of men who did not flinch at high casualty rates. Field Marshal Sir Henry Wilson, chief of the Imperial General Staff, was an Ulsterman with a born distaste for Irish Catholic rebels. The viceroy was Lord French, who had studied the art of pacification in the Boer War. Neither had been very effective at dealing with the Germans during World War I, but they were confident that a strong show of force would put the damper on the rebellious Irish. The application of terror as a politico-military instrument is a delicate art—too much is as bad as too little—at which neither of the field marshals was adept.

That winter Dublin was a city in a state of siege. A curfew had been imposed, and nothing moved on the streets at night except British patrols, trucks loaded with troops, and armored cars—and the further exception of a few Irish terrorists slipping down the back alleys.

It was the time of Liam O'Flaherty's *The Informer,* with Michael Collins struggling desperately to hold his organization together and build it up for an all-out effort. He had to weed out the Gyppo Nolans who might betray their comrades for money the British handed out lavishly to informers and turncoats and at the same time keep one jump ahead of his British opposite numbers and their Irish allies. Occasionally, for an intelligence executive, he took ridiculous personal risks in his intense curiosity about what the enemy was up to. He even had himself smuggled into one of the enemy citadels, the Dublin Metropolitan Police headquarters. A clerk in the G Division's file room was secretly one of Collins' agents. The clerk smuggled Collins into that document center and stood guard all night while Collins combed through the records and learned just how G Division operated.

At the same time he was supervising the organization and arming of the IRA brigades throughout the island in preparation for a British spring offensive. That winter Collins completed the IRA's order of battle for what he expected would be a long guerrilla war. The operational unit of the IRA was termed a flying column and was composed of up to a hundred men, wearing no uniforms, armed with rifles and pistols, and operating on its home territory. It was designed for the hit-and-run war which Collins knew was the only kind feasible against a vastly superior enemy: ambushes; sudden attacks on convoys and barracks; quick getaways into the bogs and mountains.

Perhaps the most important and effective unit under Collins' command was known with stark simplicity as the Squad, a dozen full-time gunmen who knocked off his opponents in the British intelligence system with deadly effectiveness. Among those assassinated by the Squad, under Collins' direct orders, were various G Division detectives, secret service agents, spies, double agents, and informers. Occasionally it was deemed necessary to eliminate a civilian like Magistrate Alan Bell. Collins' gunmen followed Bell, took him off a streetcar, and shot him on one of the fairways of the Elm Park Golf Club.

The balloon went up that spring, with ambushes, assassinations, raids, and skirmishes all over the country. The British had assembled overwhelming force to crush the Irish Revolution. Their government—all this has a now-familiar ring—refused to admit that it was engaged in waging a war against the Irish. It was designated a police action, and the British regular army was to be held aloof from the dirty work. Quelling the rebellion was turned over to the Royal Irish Constabulary. This force, in turn, was beefed up by two special units of about 15,000 men each. One was the Black and Tans, so called because they wore British army khaki pants and the blackish green tunics of the Royal Irish Constabulary, recruited from unemployed, war-hardened ex-servicemen in Britain who were paid 10 shillings ($2.50) a day and all they could steal for their labors. The other was the Auxiliaries, an "elite corps" of ex-officers who were paid £1 ($5) a day. The Black and Tans became the more notorious of the two commandos, but some historians of the period believe the Auxiliaries were even worse behaved. Both were a scourge to Ireland of almost Cromwellian proportions and an eternal, acknowledged disgrace to Great Britain. The liberal-humanitarian Lloyd George simply turned loose thousands of young men, who had been brutalized in the trenches, on an island which he claimed was part of the British family of nations. Atrocities became commonplace—on both sides. The Black and Tans burned down whole towns in reprisal for IRA attacks. After one of their patrols had been fired upon, the Auxiliaries set fire to the entire business district of Cork City, southern Ireland's second largest city, and held back at gunpoint the firemen who tried to put out the flames.

Backing up the Royal Irish Constabulary, the Black and Tans, and the Auxiliaries was the 50,000-man army of occupation with tanks, armored cars, Crossley tenders (armored troop carriers), plentiful machine guns and artillery. Collins and the IRA executive thus confronted a total force of at least 80,000 men. They could muster only 15,000 men at the time and had weapons for only 3,000 of these. Obviously the man who could surmount odds like those was something of a military genius. Yet Michael Collins' greatest talent in the underground war was not in military action—he was a general who never directed a pitched battle—but as spy master, spy catcher, and innovator of urban guerrilla war. By the autumn of 1920 his network was functioning perfectly. It was a tribute to his efficiency that in the summer of 1920 the British formed what became known as the Cairo Group with the mission of killing off Collins and his principal agents. Sixteen army intelligence officers of long and varied experience in the Middle East, veterans of intrigue and terror during the years when Britain was gobbling up the oil-bearing countries around the Persian Gulf, were recruited in Cairo and sent to Dublin. Posing as salesmen and businessmen, they rented flats and hotel rooms around the city and went to work on Collins' network. Collins decided that this counter-counterintelligence outfit would have to be destroyed.

That decision, along with two unrelated events, resulted in what became known as Bloody Sunday—the second in the Irish Revolution's calendar—November 21, 1920. It was an almost classic study in the workings of terror and counterterror. By then both sides were eager for a bloodletting, some sort of showdown, after months of skirmishing and hit-and-run fighting. Among the Irish the mood was heightened by two occurrences on November 1. That day Lord Mayor Terence MacSwiney of Cork was buried; he had fasted to death in prison after being arrested on charges of conspiring with the rebels. That day, also, an eighteen-year-old IRA man, Kevin Barry, was hanged at Mountjoy Prison; he had participated in an attack on a British convoy in which six soldiers were killed.

The reprisals Collins ordered, however, were in reply to the Cairo Group's dangerous penetration of his intelligence system. He later explained the wholesale killings, which outraged the British people more than any other incident of the time: "My one intention was the destruction of the undesirables who continued to make miserable the lives of ordinary decent citizens. I have proof enough to assure myself of the atrocities which this gang of spies and informers [Cairo Group] have committed. Perjury and torture are words too easily known to them." The statement was apparently typed by Collins himself and was never made public. He was justifying himself to himself, typically, because he was too proud and self-contained to make such justifications to anyone else.

Early on the morning of Sunday, November 21, at his orders, eight groups of men from his special squad and the IRA Dublin Brigade went into action, battering down doors and summarily executing fourteen members of the Cairo Group. Some of the British secret agents were shot in their beds. One tried to jump out of a window, shielded by his screaming wife, but the death squad fired seven bullets into him, and his body was left hanging halfway out the window. Collins' secretary, Anna Fitzsimmons, inadvertently was the witness to one of the killings. One of the British agents was living next door to her, and she saw him led out into the back garden and shot.

The British reaction was swift and merciless. That same afternoon truckloads of Auxiliaries and Black and Tans roared out to Croke Park, where a Gaelic football match was being played. Without warning they opened fire on the playing field and the spectators. They left fourteen dead—the same toll, coincidentally, taken by Collins' death squads—and sixty wounded. And there was more to the British retaliation. Acting on a tip-off, their secret service raided Vaughan's Hotel, an IRA hangout, and took Dick McKee, commandant of the Dublin Brigade; Peadar Clancy, his deputy; and Conor Clune into custody. The three men were questioned under torture at Dublin Castle and then summarily shot. Their friends reclaimed the bodies, which lay in state, dressed in Irish Volunteer uniforms, in the Pro-Cathedral. Despite the evident danger, Collins attended the funeral wearing a trenchcoat, with a slouch hat pulled over his eyes, well aware that G Division detectives were among the mourners and hoping to catch sight of him.

There were many more deaths before both sides began to sicken, to consider another way out. Thus far Irish casualties totaled 752 killed and 866 wounded; the British, about 600 killed and 1,200 wounded. Various peace moves were made, mostly from the British side, particularly after the Orangemen went on a rampage in Ulster and 455 persons were killed in communal rioting.

The British peace feelers were given substance in May, 1921, through Prime Minister Lloyd George's Better Government of Ireland Act, which provided for two Irish Parliaments, one for the six Ulster counties of Antrim, Down, Fermanagh, Armagh, Derry, and Tyrone and another for the twenty-six other counties —partition, in other words. Winston Churchill, as chairman of the British Cabinet Committee on Irish Affairs, proposed that Lloyd George's measure be liberalized and the southern Irish given a greater degree of self-government. If they didn't accept that and agree to a truce, Churchill believed a "tremendous onslaught" against the rebels should be mounted with an additional force of 100,000 troops specially trained for the task.

The Irish were not eager to accept such proposals. De Valera, who had returned from his American mission and resumed the presidency of the underground government, declared: "We cannot admit the right of the British government to mutilate our country." Cathal Brugha, as Minister of Defense, was also opposed to a settling of accounts. Arthur Griffith, the Minister of Home Affairs, was more inclined toward moderation, conscious of the fact that the revolution rested on a rather narrow base of actual fighting men.

Collins, as the driving force of the revolution, provided an answer of sorts on May 25, 1921, when he ordered the IRA Dublin Brigade to destroy the Customs House. Better than anyone else, he knew that the IRA could not keep up the struggle forever, that its resources (depending so much on the financial contributions of the Irish-Americans) were not unlimited. And he saw that if a truce was declared, the Irish revolutionary effort could hardly be maintained if negotiations broke down. A truce meant peace, and there was a question whether the more extreme elements in the Sinn Fein would be satisfied with a partitioned Ireland. As Collins explained, "Once a truce is agreed and we come out into the open, it is extermination for us if the truce should fail. Don't you see that we shall be, in the event of a truce, like rabbits coming out from their holes; and 'potshots' for the farmers should the truce ever fail."

But a truce was declared on July 11, 1921, and De Valera met with Lloyd George the following day to discuss how to make it permanent. The flying columns of the IRA came down out of the mountains all over Ireland, men "on the run" stopped running, and other members of Collins' shadow army surfaced for the first time in several years. But it was an uneasy peace, all that summer, with De Valera declaring that "An Ireland in fragments nobody cares about . . ." and the Dail Eireann was bitterly divided on whether to proceed with the British negotiations. It was also obvious that various factions were moving to gain political control once a measure of self-government was obtained. Collins viewed all this maneuvering with a soldierly distaste, with an unconcealed contempt for the political ambitions coming to the surface, with bitterness stemming from a conviction that all the sacrifices made by men under his orders were merely counters in a struggle for personal power.

He was uneasily aware that his eminence in the revolutionary movement, his very success as a director of guerrilla operations, his prestige with the rank and file, had in a sense endangered him. He had begun to be as wary of his colleagues as of the British enemy. To his old friend Harry Boland, then on an American mission, he wrote: "I think it right that you should be warned of the changes here. There's something about it which I don't like, and I have the impression that the whole thing is pressing on me. I find myself looking at friends as if they were enemies—looking at them twice just to make sure that they are friends after all. I mention no names. After all it may be a wrong impression that's got into me. Frankly, though, I don't care for things as they are now."

He was made even less easy in his mind that autumn when it was decided to send a negotiating committee to London to work out a treaty with Lloyd George and his advisers. He and Arthur Griffith were to head the Irish delegation. The question that probably bothered him, as it did others, was why De Valera didn't take charge of the negotiations. Instead, the President sent the others with a vaguely defined directive to work for acceptance of what he termed an "external association" of Ireland with the rest of the British Empire; it meant, apparently, that Ireland would be independent of the Commonwealth but associated with it and would recognize the Crown as the symbol of authority over that association. Such a foggily pedantic device had little hope of success. De Valèra gave various reasons for not going along with the mission to 10 Downing Street: his place as head of state was in Dublin and his belief that someone with a greater reputation for moderation might be more successful with the British.

A weary, disillusioned, and depressed Michael Collins left with his colleagues for London on October 11 for five weeks of wrangling with the British and even more vexatious disputation with their principals back in Dublin. He knew he was beyond his depth in such intricate matters, that he had been trained to fight a war, not conclude it with the best political brains in the British Empire on the opposite side of the bargaining table. And he was convinced that he was being used as a future scapegoat who would be blamed when the hotheads in the Sinn Fein, like Cathal Brugha, would charge that the best possible terms had not been obtained. As he wrote a friend in Ireland from the house at 15 Cadogan Gardens, where he lived during his weeks in London surrounded by a sizable bodyguard, "You know the way it is. Either way it will be wrong. Wrong because of what has to come to pass. You might say the trap is sprung. This could be a good thing. Enough has been said to put behind as waste the strife of other days. But that's the way it is. Neither I nor anyone else can end or mend it."

Millions of words have been written about the tortuous negotiations which followed. What it amounted to was that Britain demanded a partitioned Ireland, which would be given dominion status, with the British keeping three naval bases and the Irish required to take the oath of allegiance. The alternative, as the British made plain, was an all-out war conducted by 100,000 fresh troops operating from blockhouses over every square mile of the southern provinces of Munster, Leinster, and Connaught. Those who opposed a treaty on largely British terms, the extremist faction led by Cathal Brugha, would have fought on until all of the island was free and united—but how many would have followed them into a protracted struggle, and would they have been enough to defeat a greatly reinforced British army using any means necessary to put down the rebellion?

The position of Collins and Griffith, simply, was that the moment a truce was accepted and their underground warriors surfaced, the continuation of hostilities was impracticable, if not impossible. They did not believe the British were bluffing when they threatened large-scale operations.

His disgust with politicians, English or Irish, had vastly increased. Once during a subcommittee meeting Churchill was reading a long list of truce violations allegedly committed by the Irish. Collins scribbled a note to his aide asking whether any answer could be made to the charges, and the aide shook his head. "For Christ's sake," Collins roared, slamming the table with his fist, "come to the point!" Then he laughed uproariously, and Churchill, in spite of himself, joined in.

The upshot was that, under conflicting pressures from Lloyd George (a threat of "war within three days . . . immediate and terrible war") and from the Dail Eireann in Dublin, the Irish delegation signed the treaty on December 5, 1921. The agreement to sign came after hours of nerve-racking debate and recrimination. The mistake that Griffith and Collins made, as leaders of the delegation, was in not informing Dublin of the failure to win last-minute concessions. By hindsight it is possible to see that, though the delegation was given plenipotentiary powers, they should have made De Valera and the others signify agreement; a midnight phone call might have done the trick. For their own good, and for the political unity of the Irish Republic, Griffith and Collins should have shifted the responsibility to the Cabinet and the Dail Eireann. Apparently they felt they could not prolong the negotiations without risking the renewed war which Lloyd George threatened and which Collins, as head of the disbanded resistance, did not believe the Irish capable of fighting. Instead of another war with the British they got a civil war among the Irish.

Even the most magisterial historian cannot say today whether it was best for Ireland that the treaty was signed. Had it not been, taking the diehards' viewpoint, Ireland might now be unified, without the constant spiritual and political drain of the Ulster problem. Or Britain might have carried out its threat of a bitter-end war, and Ireland today would be the conquered province it had been for 700 years. Or if it had won the ultimate struggle with Britain, it might have been engaged in suppressing another kind of rising, that of the Protestants in Ulster, who would not have accepted union with Catholic Ireland without resistance of the bitterest kind.

Collins felt no triumph over the treaty. He roamed the streets for hours after the signing, then went back to Cadogan Square and wrote an Irish friend living in London: "When you have sweated, toiled, had mad dreams, hopeless nightmares, you find yourself in London's streets, cold and dank in the night air. Think—what have I got for Ireland? Something which she has wanted these past seven hundred years. Will anyone be satisfied at the bargain? I tell you this—*early this morning I signed my death warrant.* I thought at the time how odd, how ridiculous—a bullet may just as well have done the job five years ago. . . ."

De Valera was outraged, not only by the terms of the treaty but by the fact that the negotiators hadn't consulted him before the final agreement. De Valera's anger was more than matched by that of Cathal Brugha and the extremist wing of the IRA, the leaders of which demanded that Griffith, Collins, and the others be arrested for treason the moment they returned from London.

On their side, as soon became evident, Griffith and Collins had the war-weariness of the Irish people. It was reflected in a Cabinet vote on whether to present the treaty to the Dail for ratification, which went four to three in favor of presentation.

On January 7, 1922, the Dail finally voted on the treaty question, ratifying it by a narrow margin, 64 to 57, which was an indication on how sharply divided the country was. Within a few months there were four factions claiming the right to rule Ireland: the Provisional Government, headed by Collins and Griffith and supported by most of the Irish Republican Brotherhood; De Valera's Republican Party; the Dail Eireann, which became a mere formality; and a splinter group, headed by the small, fiery Rory O'Connor, which seceded from the IRB and called itself the Irish Republican Army.

The strong man of the legitimate Provisional Government was chairman Michael Collins, with Griffith acting as president of the Dail. On January 16, accompanied by a number of his ministers, he took over Dublin Castle, the stronghold of British imperialism in Ireland. Down came the Union Jack, and out marched the last British troops. The handover was not entirely a triumphant occasion, according to one departing Britisher, who described the Irish group as sullen and depressed. By then Collins knew he had a fight on his hands. Rory O'Connor and his followers, the most radical of the antitreaty forces, occupied the Four Courts, a massive edifice on the bank of the Liffey, the high seat of Irish justice, as a rather curious means of "saving the country from Civil War now threatened by those who have abandoned the Republic." Actually the Four Courts seizure started the civil war. From April 13, 1922, when O'Connor and his followers, including Liam Mellows as his deputy, Robert Briscoe, Sean MacBride (Maud Gonne's son), and Sean Lemass, a future prime minister, barricaded themselves in the green-domed building, to the end of June, they constituted a visible and unbearable thorn in the side of the Provisional Government. How could it claim credibility, seek recognition from other sovereign powers when one of the more important seats of government was occupied by an armed force?

During the weeks of O'Connor's occupation of the Four Courts, a number of attempts were made to mediate, to persuade the dissidents to leave the building, but all failed. Meanwhile, antitreaty members of the IRA were digging out their guns and taking to the hills again. In County Cork late in April there was an outbreak of ambushes and shootings, in which ten Protestants were killed after a Catholic IRA man was shot to death by a Protestant.

Collins was trying to administer the affairs of his besieged government, keep the British calmed down, talk the antitreaty forces out of doing anything rash, and rally the country to his support. He dashed around the country making speeches. In highly volatile Cork City, his appearance was described by one of his listeners: "He was at one and the same time the youthful dashing leader we had learned to love and admire; and yet a figure on which strain, worry, and overwork had taken its toll."

Several times he appeared to be on the verge of a nervous breakdown. The strain on him was more severe than during the underground war against the British because the issues then were clear-cut; now he was faced by his ex-comrades instead of the ancient enemy. The threat of British interference became more critical on June 22, when Field Marshal Henry Wilson was assassinated outside his house in London. Now the British were demanding that O'Connor and his "garrison" be removed from the Four Courts by whatever force was necessary, with the explicit threat from Winston Churchill that if this was not done, "we shall regard the Treaty as having been formally violated." Collins' anguish must have closely resembled that of Abraham Lincoln when he ordered the bombardment of Fort Sumter. Six days after Wilson's assassination he moved decisively against O'Connor and his 150 followers barricaded in the Four Courts and two nearby hotels in O'Connell Street which they had also occupied. By then De Valera had indicated his support for the extremist faction, and Cathal Brugha, armed with a Thompson submachine gun, was among those occupying the Hammam Hotel.

To root out O'Connor and his followers, the Provisional Government, having no artillery of its own, borrowed two eighteen-pounder field guns from the British army. It also had no gunners except for General Emmet Dalton, who had once served in the British army. The guns were set up across the Liffey, on Bridgefoot Street, under Dalton's direction, and a scratch crew of apprentice gunners was recruited. Shortly before dawn on July 28, the bombardment of the Four Courts began. It took them a day to get the range, another day before their concentrated fire began cracking the massive walls of the building. The Hammam and Gresham hotels nearby were also brought under siege. Masonry crashed; machine guns rattled; Irishmen were killing Irishmen, sadly enough, with all the zeal they had directed against the British.

On the third day, with the Four Courts tumbling down around their ears, and fires raging all along the east side of O'Connell Street, Rory O'Connor decided there was no alternative to surrender. The white flag went up at the shattered Four Courts, and its survivors were taken into custody. (Six months later, in reprisal for the assassination of a Free State member of the Dail, O'Connor and three others were executed by a firing squad.) Elsewhere the fighting went on for several more days, until finally the Gresham Hotel was stormed and taken. The Hammam Hotel was on fire, and its occupants came out with their hands up—all except Cathal Brugha. The latter not only refused to surrender, with a hundred rifles zeroed in on him, but came out with his tommy gun firing full automatic and was cut down.

Of all the death and agony caused by the events from June 28 to July 5, the most painful to Michael Collins personally was the desperado's ending to Cathal Brugha's life. They were the bitterest of political enemies, but Collins had always admired Brugha's honesty, integrity, and courage. Quelling the insurrection would be the hollowest of victories, Collins saw, if it only further divided the country. On July 1, when the street fighting was reaching its climax, he wrote himself a memo: "Must make a record of this. . . . We don't want any humiliating surrender. We want order restored. That only. Maintained for the future." Vain hope. The flying columns were out again, this time pursued not by the British army but Michael Collins' Free State troops. Guerrilla warfare had broken out, and from September, 1922, to the end of July, 1923, the only period for which casualty figures are available, there were 665 killed and 3,000 wounded on both sides. Thirty million pounds sterling in property was destroyed, including many of the great houses which had been spared during the war against the British. Among them was the country house of Oliver St. John Gogarty, the Dublin poet and physician, whose crime was to be a protreaty member of the Senate. "Damn the vampire dead," raged Dr. Gogarty, "who have left us nothing but a heritage of hatred which operates equally against the 'Foreigner' and against ourselves."

Gogarty provided an affecting portrait of Michael Collins that troubled summer, in the last days of Collins' brief life. Collins occasionally took refuge in Gogarty's Dublin house—he rarely slept two nights in the same bed, as much a man on the run as any IRA irregular in the hills, knowing that gunmen on the other side had been ordered to shoot any member of the Dail who had voted for the treaty and anyone wearing the uniform of the Free State army above the rank of lieutenant. During the earlier Troubles, with hundreds of British police and secret service agents hunting for him, Collins had gone around unarmed. Now, the head of the legitimate government, he carried a revolver in his pocket and lived like a fugitive. Only thirty-two years old, his drawn and haggard face, his haunted eyes, made him look ten years older.

By then Collins had assumed supreme responsibility for putting down the insurrection. The Dail was prorogued on July 13, without any regard for constitutional niceties, by a committee of fifteen, including Collins, W. T. Cosgrave, Arthur Griffith, and Kevin O'Higgins. Until hostilities were ended, the governing powers would reside in a war council consisting of Collins, as commander in chief; Richard Mulcahy, chief of staff; Eoin O'Duffy, commander of the southwestern division; and Diarmuid O'Hegarty, commandant general.

Early in August Collins was roving the countryside in an armored car, supervising operations against the antitreaty forces which had seized control of a number of towns and key points in the west, the three counties of Limerick, Kerry, and Cork. Haggard and careworn, "tragically dejected" as one companion described him, he inspected units of the national army, many of them what he called "sunshine soldiers" who had joined up after the British were withdrawn, others Irishmen who had been honorably discharged from the British army and had come home to help restore order.

On the road to Limerick his party halted to inspect the prison at Maryborough, where on August 12 he received the news that Arthur Griffith, the supreme personal totem of his career, was dead. Barely fifty years old, the man whose writings had inspired the Easter Rising suffered a stroke and died instantly. Gogarty believed that Griffith's epitaph might be King Arthur's: "I perish by this people which I made."

The funeral procession for Arthur Griffith, which Collins headed with General Mulcahy at his side, both crisply outfitted as generals of the national army, was the last glimpse Dublin would have of the young man who had come to the capital in 1916 as a recruit in the Irish Volunteers and six years later was effectively the chief of state.

Collins' own health was failing, though a couple of months out of the bog of Irish troubles would undoubtedly have restored it, when he set out with an armored convoy on the road to Cork City several days after Griffith's funeral. His friends tried to dissuade him, not only because of the bands of irregulars swarming throughout the southwest but because he looked so ill.

The illness undoubtedly was more psychological than physical: He was literally sick of death, sick of war, sick of unending dissension, and he felt doomed. Before his departure for Cork, he remarked to Cosgrave, who would soon assume the burden of reuniting the nation, "Do you think I shall live through this? Not likely!"

His forebodings were not alleviated on the journey from Dublin to Cork by jeering slogans chalked on the walls and buildings of the towns through which he passed. "Collins marches through Cork," they read, indicating his enemies knew more about his movements than was healthy for him. "Why not Belfast?" On August 20, Collins and his party arrived in Mallow, on the road from Limerick to Cork, and halted to inspect the local garrison. Before moving on, the group picked up Private John O'Connell to act as guide, many of the roads in the southwest having been mined or blocked and many of the bridges wrecked. To avoid such obstacles, they had to travel over a mountain road through Whitechurch to reach Cork City that evening.

Collins and his fellow officers were billeted at the Imperial Hotel, which also served as headquarters for General Dalton, who had taken charge of operations in County Cork against the guerrillas. The city was pacified, more or less, but there were still many bands swooping down from mountain hideouts, and County Cork as a whole was strongly antitreaty, antigovernment, and therefore anti-Collins.

The next day, August 21, Collins and his aides spent in inspecting the garrisons in and around Cork City and conferring with groups of citizens. On August 22 the group set out early in the morning for a trip up the West Cork coast, Collins' home territory, where he believed he would be welcomed personally, even though many of his old neighbors were politically opposed to him. The convoy consisted of a motorcyclist, Lieutenant Jack Smith, followed by a Crossley tender (with two officers, eight riflemen, and two machine gunners aboard), a Leyland Thomas touring car in which Collins, Dalton, and two drivers rode, and a Rolls-Royce Whippet armored car bringing up the rear.

They proceeded to Bandon and Clonakilty, where they had to make a detour over a rough road which took them through Sam's Cross, the hamlet near which Collins was born. He stopped to look at the ruins of the house where he was born, which had been leveled by the Black and Tans, and then stopped at the pub kept by Collins' cousin, where they had a round of Clonakilty Wrestler, the locally brewed stout. At Rosscarbery and Skibbereen they halted to inspect the garrisons. So far no one had even raised a fist at them. On the way back they were again forced to take a circuitous route because of the blocked roads. It was early evening, with the light fading fast and a haze covering the glens and hollows, when they came to the bleak and narrow valley of Beal na mBlath. The road was bordered by a stream on one side, heavy brush and alders on the other—a good place for an ambush. Collins, his sense of danger alerted, picked up a rifle from the floor of the touring car and placed it across his knees. His car was now traveling ahead of the Crossley tender and its machine guns, for some unexplained but fatal reason.

The motorcyclist, Smith, riding fifty yards ahead, suddenly applied the brakes when he almost ran into an overturned brewer's dray, in front of which was a mass of bottles and broken glass. Machine-gun and rifle fire began from a concealed position in the brush, concentrating at first on the Crossley tender.

"Drive like hell," General Dalton ordered the driver of the touring car.

Collins, however, countermanded the order and leaped out of the car with the rifle in his hand, determined to fight it out with his ambushers. It was a foolish and reckless gesture for the head of the Provisional Government. His first duty was to preserve himself for something more important than a fire fight on a backcountry road.

Collins and Dalton joined the riflemen behind the Crossley tender, all of them banging away furiously, but so far without casualties on either side. Suddenly the fire from the ambushers stopped. Collins moved away from the shelter of the Crossley tender and stood in the middle of the road inserting a new clip in his rifle. He was standing there when firing suddenly broke out again. A hitherto-charmed life ended when a bullet crashed into his head. He was killed instantly. The firing continued for several more minutes until the ambushers fled.

Collins' body was placed in the rear of the touring car, and the convoy proceeded to Cork City, from which the news spread throughout Ireland that night. It was placed aboard the steamer *Inisfallen* for the journey to Dublin, where a huge and silent crowd awaited its arrival at North Wall.

The funeral was massively solemn, utterly unlike the personality of the man it celebrated. His coffin was borne from the Pro-Cathedral to Glasnevin Cemetery on one of the gun carriages borrowed from the British for the bombardment of the Four Courts—an irony Collins would not have appreciated. He might, however, have been amused by a message the IRA irregulars chalked on his gravestone: "Move over, Mick. Make room for Dick." Dick was his chief of staff, General Richard Mulcahy, who thus far has escaped the malediction.

Without undue hero worship, it can be said that in his brief life Collins reflected the most shining qualities of the Irish character. There is nothing false about the legend he inspired. Without his commanding presence the Irish resistance could never have been so quickly successful. Without his restraint and example, the civil war would not have guttered out the spring following his death, which epitomized for both sides, in a strikingly tragic fashion, how much the country was losing through internal strife. How much Michael Collins, with his enormous energy and varied talents, would have accomplished for Ireland had he been allowed another thirty-two years of life is a matter of sorrowful conjecture.

6.

"More Catholic Than the Pope"

O Ireland my first and only love
Where Christ and Caesar are hand in glove.
—James Joyce, *Gas from a Burner*

Religion is the most pervasive element in Irish life. In other nations God may be proclaimed dead with impunity, but in Ireland His stern presence is inescapable. The air reverberates with church bells; the Angelus informs the people when day is done. There are more new and modernistic churches going up everywhere; more nuns, priests, and members of religious orders visible in the streets than anywhere outside Rome.

It's not quite true that everyone in the Republic is Catholic—only 95 percent of the 99.5 percent professing some form of Christianity. Nor is it true that the Catholic Church constitutes a spiritual dictatorship, with the hierarchy dictating to the government and every parish priest a local tyrant. Irish prime ministers have gently put cardinals in their places. The Irish Catholics are obedient, yet a large proportion are using the contraceptive pill against clerical sanctions, and back when Parnell died in 1891, and the clergy instructed their followers not to pay their last respects because he was a Protestant and had married a divorced woman, more than 160,000 turned out for his funeral.

If you want to understand why the Irish are called "more Catholic than the Pope," if you have the stamina to witness what seems to less fervent Catholics of other lands as a medieval act of mortifying the flesh, you can make the pilgrimage to Lough Derg, a remote lake in County Donegal hard by the border of County Tyrone (Ulster). There is no reason to doubt that this has been nominated the hardest Christian pilgrimage in the modern world, though it does not quite come up to the hardships of the Mohammedans' pilgrimage to Mecca.

This is the Mecca of Irish Catholicism: a mist-covered island where St. Patrick is said to have experienced a vision of purgatory. In the past fifteen centuries millions of the faithful from all over the world have sought that premonitory vision through prayer and fasting, a shriving of the spirit still undertaken by 30,000 persons a year . . . and no matter that some doubt of St. Patrick's validity has recently been expressed by the Vatican.

All through the summer months the pilgrims make their way to Lough Derg; for some it is an annual event. Often drenched by storms sweeping over the Blue Stack Mountains, they spend three days at their rugged devotions, sustained mainly by "Lough Derg soup," which is hot water with a dash of pepper and salt. Many give up part of their vacations to make the pilgrimage to that most remote part of the Republic.

A long hard road, whether taken by sea to Donegal Bay or overland. Yet here in the northwest corner of Ireland more than at Armagh, the seat of the hierarchy, or the Pro-Cathedral in Dublin, you can sound the uncritical, unquestioning depths of the Irish faith.

On the road from Pettigo, through the bleak hills of Donegal, you round a bend and come to the boat landing on the shore of Lough Derg. Across the water on Station Island stand the buildings of St. Patrick's Purgatory: the copper dome of the basilica surrounded by the large square buildings of the men's hospice and the women's hospice and the church where the prior hears confessions. It is a rocky outcropping of an island which you will be expected to traverse on bare feet, in penitential fashion, just as the saints and sinners of the fifth century did.

You may be sustained by reflections on the greater difficulties in reaching the place experienced by pilgrims of a long time ago. A document found in the state papers of Richard II attests that St. Patrick's Purgatory was more famous in Europe in his time than it is now. On September 6, 1397, he issued a safe-conduct pass to Raymond, Viscount of Perilleux, Knight of Rhodes, which was addressed to all constables, marshals, admirals, seneschals, governors, bailiffs, prefects, captains, castellans, majors, magistrates, counselors of cities and towns, guardians of camps, ports, bridges and passways—a revealing glimpse of the medieval bureaucracy. The king's pass declared that Raymond "intends and purposes to come into our Kingdom of England and to cross over and travel through the said Kingdom to our land of Ireland, there to see and visit the Purgatory of St. Patrick, with twenty men and thirty horses of his company." Richard II shrewdly appended the directive that the French knight be unmolested only so long as he paid for his company's food and fodder at any town, camp, or castle where they presented themselves. Presumably the diet of "lake water and bread" then offered by the Purgatory was on the house.

At the pier today's pilgrim hands over a £1 ($2.40) note in return for a disk which is to be surrendered to the boatman. You wait for the motorized whaleboat to fill up with fellow pilgrims and wonder how many such traditions, anywhere else, could have survived for 1,500 years.

If you are doing things properly, you will have been fasting since the previous midnight, though you face a physical and (possibly) spiritual ordeal which will last three days. The old saints held that fasting made prayer significant, that lack of sleep, endless repetition of a long prayer aloud, and the physical suffering caused by walking over sharp stones on bare feet forced the soul to the surface of one's consciousness. Only through suffering, privation, and penance could the human being come to a glimmering of understanding God's purpose.

The boat slowly fills up with about sixty pilgrims: a number of farmers with their wives, a Dublin solicitor, a number of priests, three tinker women from County Westmeath, and a mixed bag of shopgirls, students, spinsters, elderly bachelors off the family farm.

The boat lands you at the island's pier in midafternoon. Off come your shoes forthwith. And on comes the realization that a barefoot boyhood in Indiana, scuffling on soft dusty roads, was nothing like this. The sharp-edged stones of Station Island seem to have been specially cut to make penance truly penitential, and you can only envy the gray old farmer from County Fermanagh with the horny feet who claims to have made the pilgrimage forty times.

From then until evening you walk and pray among the penitential beds in the middle of the island. Underfoot are the splintered foundation stones which centuries ago formed the cells of the Celtic monks who kept the vigil on the site of St. Patrick's vision. Mist swirls up from the lake as twilight falls, and you are allowed to break your fast with black tea and bread or oatmeal cakes.

In the men's hospice, as in the women's, there is a brief respite of foot nursing and bruise counting. Dinner is "Lough Derg soup" ladled out of a copper urn—you can have all you want.

The pilgrims who arrived one or two days earlier are permitted to go to their hard beds at ten o'clock, but the night, the Ordeal of the First Day, is just beginning for the newcomers. You scratch the midge bites on your ankles, wait for the bell which signals the start of the vigil. You troop over to the basilica to make more stations, seven of them, with prayers at each lasting about forty-five minutes. No sleep, only the click of rosary beads, the murmur of prayers. There is something zombielike in the pilgrims' treads, a sleepwalker's glaze in the pilgrims' eyes. Between fasting and not sleeping, the pilgrim's mind occasionally reaches a plateau of giddiness, possibly in some cases godliness. You think back to the afternoon when you raised your arms between the statues of St. Patrick and St. Brigid, huge metal crosses down in the penitential beds, and renounced the world, the flesh and the devil. Now your flesh seems to be renouncing you.

You rest for an hour or so in the men's hospice, footsore, legweary, eyes with leaden lids, bug-bitten, chilled to the bone after a walk through the mists curling around the lake's edge and over the dewy grass. You rest, head nodding and eyelids fluttering, but you do not sleep. There is a mass to be attended shortly, with a prior thundering from the pulpit. You wonder whether the reverberations of his voice are not calculated to prevent anyone from dozing off. There is no easy way to make the pilgrimage to Lough Derg, not even if you have endowed a cathedral.

There is another twelve waking hours of the Second Day of the Ordeal ahead of you.

In midmorning you go to confession, kneeling on lacerated knees, in the small church at the edge of the lake. Then you make another, more gingerly circuit of the penitential beds, paying your respects to St. Brigid, St. Catherine, St. Brendan, St. Columba, St. Davog, St. Molaise, and St. Patrick.

At noon you receive communion at mass in the basilica. Another prayerful tour of the penitential beds. By six o'clock you may be thinking of the pubs in Dublin, the thick foam on a pint of Guinness, the fog of cigarette smoke, the easy laughter—or even more compelling of a plate of steak and chips. Here there is only mist, groaning pilgrims, nodding heads, the commanding bells, the sharp stones lying in wait for penitential feet. If you lack some of the makings of a true pilgrim, you may hate the people in Dublin sluicing their throats and stuffing their bellies. Your own repast will consist of black tea, bread, and oatmeal cakes.

A bell summons you to evening prayer and benediction in the basilica. The prior in the pulpit is still in good voice. You make the stations of the cross before returning to the men's hospice around 10 P.M., still capable of faint surprise at the long summer twilight coming through the narrow windows before you fall on the hard monastic bed. Outside, it is some satisfaction to know, the pilgrims just arrived that day are shuffling off to the basilica for their night-long vigil.

Somewhat refreshed after a night's sleep, you are awakened by bells summoning you to mass, communion, and another round of the penitential beds and of the stations in the basilica. The Ordeal of the Third Day is over; your pilgrimage has come to an end. The motorboat takes you across the water to the pier and the outside world. As you look back, Purgatory Island seems to be sinking under the weight of the basilica, the hospices, the churches, the penitential beds, the great crosses, and the centuries of pilgrims who have subjected themselves to St. Patrick's vision.

A really durable Christian would probably also make the pilgrimage, as 20,000 annually do, to Croaghpatrick. On that mountain overlooking Clew Bay, County Mayo, St. Patrick fasted for forty days and forty nights, during which the legendary snakes fled from him. On the last Sunday of July thousands make a predawn climb of the 2,500-foot mountain, its face surfaced with loose rock, to attend mass at a chapel on the summit. This, too, for the more pious, is an ordeal by bare feet.

Why has Catholicism so vigorously survived in Ireland when in other countries it seems to be losing its hold in a clamor of ecumenicism, of modernizing the ritual, of rebelling priests and nuns leaping the walls? As Sean O'Faolain sees it, the Irish priest has the advantage of "a powerfully strategic relationship to the public. One can see this over and over in the puzzlement, sometimes the exasperation, of the layman at a loss to know where the human element and the professional element begins and ends. The priest, like the soldier, will always explain his acts in professional terms, never in merely human terms." But there is more to it than professionalism, or the mystique of spiritual leadership, or even the psychology of domination: centuries of history when the church appeared to be the shield of the people, comforting them in subjugation, even while instructing its followers that they must be loyal to the government of the conquerors. Yet in Mexico, where the church also sided with the foreign interlopers, the church suffered accordingly when revolutionary governments took over. Obviously there is a differing quality in the faith of the Irish, partly accounted for by their long isolation from the mainstream of Catholicism.

Among the strongest influences that made Irish Catholicism unique was the negative factor that the Romans never appeared in Ireland and thus Christianity came to the island later and in a different form. And the Irish took to the new faith with all the hectic enthusiasm of converts; its purgatorial tradition, which even today brings thousands of pilgrims to Lough Derg and Croaghpatrick, goes back to the ancient monastic settlements. The faith was tested when the College of Propaganda at Rome consistently ordered that the Irish church must display unswerving loyalty to the British Crown "at all times and places." It was also tested by, and easily survived the Reformation, largely because most of the people spoke Irish and the bishops of the reformed (English) church made no great effort to convert them to the Protestant faith because of the language barrier. After the Catholic defeat at the Battle of the Boyne in 1690, the English concentrated on trying to extinguish Catholicism (no priests could be ordained, the Catholic bishops were banished, and the religious orders were banned); naturally this only made the Irish more fervently Catholic.

Nor did the Irish determination to remain Catholic wilt when the English adopted more conciliatory tactics with the passage of the Act of Union, upon which the English allowed the establishment of the great seminary at Maynooth in 1795. The fact that the first faculty of Maynooth was staffed largely by monarchist and Jansenist refugees from revolutionary France also contributed to the special quality of Irish Catholicism by instilling holier-than-thou attitudes and a rigidly puritanical doctrine that was denounced as pseudo-Calvinistic by the Jesuits. The word from Maynooth, propagated by the priests it graduated and ordained, was that the love of God must be demonstrated by sacrifices, by fleshly privations greater than going to mass and making confession.

The church began acquiring temporal power early in the nineteenth century, when Daniel O'Connell, who was determined to weld the Irish into a nation, won equal civil rights for the Catholic subjects of the Crown in Ireland. From then on, the Catholic hierarchy opposed all nationalistic/revolutionary movements directed at evicting the British and establishing an independent republic.

Its conservatism was epitomized by Paul Cardinal Cullen who returned from Rome in 1849 thoroughly alarmed by the Mazzini brand of republicanism in Italy. He equated Fenianism and other rebellious elements with a godless radicalism, placed Catholic control of education ahead of breaking up the estates of the landed gentry and dividing them among his own followers. His conservatism was also evidenced when he persuaded Dr. John Henry Newman (later Cardinal Newman) to come over and establish a Catholic university to counteract the "godless colleges" already in existence. Soon enough Newman and his sponsor found themselves in bitter opposition over the issue of lay control of the new university. If the cardinal's views prevailed, as Newman wrote, the university would "simply be priest-ridden.

. . . I mean men who do not know literature and science will have the direction of teaching. . . . The deep difficulty is the jealousy and fear which is entertained in high quarters of the laity. . . . Nothing great or living can be done except when men are self-governed and independent. . . ." Cardinal Cullen finally dispensed with the great Newman, unable to banish memories of Mazzini taking possession of Vatican property and of the cardinal himself saving the College of Propaganda only by persuading the U.S. minister in Rome to fly the American flag over it. Thus in 1865 the sacraments were forbidden to any Irishman taking part in a revolutionary movement.

Some of the bishops were strongly opposed, as has been noted, to the Easter Rising and subsequent events, and they sided with the Treaty State government after independence to the extent that antitreaty irregulars were excommunicated. Again the church maintained its hold on the people, partly because its conservatism was a reflection of its followers and perhaps even more so because the parish priests had always kept the closest possible ties with their parishioners, and to the latter the local priest represented the church more than the distant and aloof hierarchy, whose edicts he sometimes pretended not to hear.

Reckless deviation, particularly if it came from intellectuals rather than political dissidents, has never gained much sympathy. Both the Catholic press and the public were affronted in 1924 when a new journal appeared in Dublin, for which the manifesto was supposedly composed by William Butler Yeats (who included it in his volume *Tomorrow*) and signed by a number of contributors. "We are Catholics," it declared, "but of the school of Pope Julius II and of the Medicean Popes, who ordered Michelangelo and Raphael to paint upon the walls of the Vatican, and upon the ceiling of the Sistine Chapel. . . . We proclaim that we can forgive the sinner, but abhor the atheist, and that we count among atheists bad writers and bishops of all denominations. 'The Holy Spirit is an intellectual fountain.' . . . What devout man can read the pastorals of our Hierarchy without horror at a style rancid, coarse and vague, like the daily papers? We condemn the art and literature of modern Europe. No man can create, as did Shakespeare, Homer and Sophocles, who does not believe with all his blood and nerve that man's soul is immortal, for all the evidence lies plain to all men that where belief has declined men have turned from creation to photography. . . . We dismiss all demogagues and call back the soul to its ancient sovereignty, and declare that it can do whatever it please, being made, as antiquity affirmed, from the imperishable stuff of the stars." The manifesto created a furor; the concept that "bad" bishops could be considered atheistic was wrathfully rejected. In other countries, even Roman Catholics would not have been affronted by that idea. It created such an atmosphere of hostility in Dublin, however, that the journal was laid to rest after its second issue.

Priest baiting, for all its perverse attractions to the more cross-grained intellectual, has never become a popular pastime. There have been occasional displays of literary candor, however, such as Edward McNulty's novel *Misther O'Ryan,* published in 1894, in which the priest is a whiskey-swilling bully adept at political intrigue. A priest in Paul Vincent Carroll's play *Shadow and Substance* is depicted in violent opposition to the building of a local public library, which he charged with "teaching the latest ideas of blackguardism." The novelist Honor Tracy, who has lived in Ireland for considerable periods and was associated with a literary review edited by Sean O'Faolain, will find few of her books on rectory tables. Some years ago she wrote an article for a London newspaper relating how the people of an impoverished parish were being bullied into donating more than they could afford for the building of an expensive new house for the priest. The latter sued the newspaper for libel, but the case was settled out of court, and the newspaper published an apology. The doughty Miss Tracy then sued the newspaper on the grounds that *she* was libeled by the apology; she won the case and several thousand dollars in damages. Not content with having profitably proven her point, she then wrote the novel *The Straight and Narrow Path* (1956) which was a best seller in Britain and the United States but *not* in Ireland. One of its leading characters was Canon Peart, whom she portrayed with an affectionate malice as a man who loved his comforts and did the Lord's work with a Jansenistic enthusiasm:

> Under the kindly influence of the sun a dangerous spirit was stirring among his flock. It was not by accident that he made so mean a score during his nightly forays through the lanes. The young people were nesting further afield, in haystacks, beds of rushes, behind scented gorse bushes up on the hills, beyond his reach; and, as the Canon ruefully told himself, he could not be everywhere at once. And now the inevitable had happened, and little Bridget MacCarthy was with child. It was a terrible shame on himself and the parish. . . . The routine the Canon followed in cases of this sort was admirably simple. He would seek out the young man responsible, threaten him with hell fire, everlasting torment and the loss of his earthly job and then, having reduced him to a jelly, go on briskly to discuss the details of the wedding. . . .

The position of the church is as secure in Ireland as any institution could be, far more than it is in other lands. Under the Constitution of 1937 people of all faiths are guaranteed their religious liberty. But it adds: "The State recognizes the special position of the Holy Catholic Apostolic and Roman Church as the guardian of the Faith professed by the great majority of the citizens." A constitutional lawyer might consider there was a slight ambiguity here: Does it mean all faiths are equal but the Catholic is first among equals? The Constitution does not elaborate; it's one of those "understood" things the Irish are adept at grasping ("I'll say no more"). In practice, there is complete tolerance; even the Jehovah's Witnesses are free to proselytize in their aggressive fashion and distribute pamphlets on the steps of churches and chapels of the other faiths. Just how much direct influence the church has on the affairs of the state is a matter of opinion; undoubtedly it is less than Ulster suspects, and there have been no striking examples of overt clerical interference since the quashing of Dr. Noel Browne's Mother and Child Welfare program in the early fifties. All this, of course, refers to national politics. On the local level the parish priest exerts more control and influence over daily life than anyone else. He is not only the guardian of morals but the tribal chief; he settles family disputes, quarrels over land boundaries or livestock ownership, controversies over the selection of the local football team. No occasion can be called official or formal without his presence. At his frown, proposals to build a drive-in movie or open a nightclub quickly expire. He may no longer scour the hedgerows nightly to scatter the courting couples, but his writ is absolute throughout the parish.

His image has changed perceptibly, if not drastically, in the years since Honor Tracy depicted him as the local tyrant, because the church is gently modernizing itself, trying to accommodate itself to the changing temper of Ireland and the freer thinking encouraged by television and other "outside" influences.

Maynooth College, as the premier seminary, the one which has supplied two-thirds of the present hierarchy, is adapting to change and anticipating more. The young priests it is sending out to the parishes are being educated along more progressive lines. *The Furrow,* a review published at Maynooth, discusses such matters as married priests and film censorship with a more liberal attitude than most of the newspapers. In its columns there are echoes, however discreet, of the tumult raised by progressive Dutch, German, French, and Belgian theologians.

In other Catholic periodicals it is apparent that a sort of debate is going on among the clergy—not the layman, for he is distracted by other things and is willing to leave such matters to the professionals while confining himself to the routine of attending mass—over how much adjustment the Irish church must make, how permissive it should become, how much it must yield to the Vatican councils.

Some commentators believe the priest should be more "involved" in social controversies, such as the settlement of the itinerant population, and that he can no longer count on enjoying an unchallenged and unquestioned role in modern Irish society. Father Patrick Brophy, writing in the widely circulated *Catholic Standard,* asserts: "The privileged position of the priest—and of course more so the bishop—which shielded us from comment and from analysis of our viewpoint must give way to a new kind of leadership. It was too often assumed that we priests spoke for the church when in fact we were expressing opinions of a personal character shaped by our own background. The office of being a priest was invested with an authority in matters that were not closely related to the gospel." Father Brophy believes the clergy might interest itself in such matters as the plight of "the young, house-deprived, postponing marriage year after year while good money goes down the drain in fancy schemes and futile inquiries. . . . Priests are now being looked to for moral leadership. The time for preaching by word is never as opportune as the witness of example. The gap between the ideal of Christian living and its external expression in Ireland widens."

At almost the same time a Father Crane was lashing out in the *Irish Messenger* on "bogus ecumenism, which frowns on any action taken by Catholics on their own" and against "humanist pressure groups," particularly in England, "which sneer at any Catholic group that dares to make a stand on its own in defence of faith and morals." To Father Crane, a Jesuit, there could be nothing worse than "involvement" in dubious causes, in "defence of the new-found liberalism" to which he believes many Irish Catholics have succumbed. To his mind the "new theology" is inextricably linked to left-wing agitation. Father Crane further warns: "The last thing to do is to ask a pop theologian, or left-wing, liberal, Catholic layman for any solution of the concrete problems which face the Church in her relations with the world of men. Few have anything intelligent to offer in this very practical field. Yet their opinions are constantly sought and as readily given in terms of magic words like 'involvement' and 'commitment,' which add up to nothing so far as effective policy is concerned. This, of course, is exactly what one would expect, for both these words are more concerned with thought than with action. What each calls for from Catholics is not Catholic action but merely passive association with already existing causes. Such Catholics no longer think of the Church as having a specific contribution of its own to make to society. Instead they bid the faithful take their cue from the crowd about them, which is thought of as having some peculiar dynamism of its own."

Another writer in the same periodical alerts its readers to the prevalence of priests who are said to be "seeking a self-identity, priests who are questioning their place in modern society." Such troubled priests, tossed by the winds of change, can be "helped immensely" by their parishioners, "whose/deep faith convinces them of their dependence on their priest at the altar." The flock, in other words, must rescue the straying shepherd.

Several years ago another Catholic writer, David Thornley, warned in the Jesuit quarterly *Studies* against a clergy too "self-congratulatory" about its hold on Irish Catholics. The faithfulness of the Irish in attending to their religious obligations might be attributed, he speculated, to the conformity engendered in a largely rural country rather than any superior devotion to Christianity. He feared that "the consequences of the unsophisticated and dogmatic anti-intellectualism of Irish religious upbringing are all too often shown when the product is suddenly exposed to the English environment." Undoubtedly he had in mind the high crime rate among the Irish who migrate to England—higher in many areas than that of the Pakistanis or West Indians. It has also been a matter of concern for many years that Irish emigrants tend to lose their faith in considerable numbers. "For any subsequent disasters," Thornley continued, "we invariably blame the English for their lewdness and materialism. Are they really the ones to blame? Irish Catholicism, lay and clerical, has no mandate from God and no guarantee from the inevitability of history which will allow it to opt out of the soul-searching which is the unique task of the Universal Church in the second half of the twentieth century."

The Irish church may not be ready for vigorous soul-searching on all levels, from parish priest to hierarchy, but it is beginning to move decisively in other directions, particularly social welfare. The younger clergy feel the necessity of initiating Catholic action beyond the salvation and protection of souls. They realize that the church could lose its primacy if it remains a purely religious institution, that it must care for minds and bodies as well as souls and become more significant in daily lives and more responsive to mundane problems.

One vigorous step in this direction is a seamen's club called Anchor House near the quays of Cork City. Recently there was a public scandal over an increase in prostitution around the city's port facilities, much consternation over Irish girls selling themselves to foreign seamen. The church, not the police, provides the vice squad in Ireland. (The old brothel quarter of Dublin, largely but not solely patronized by troops of the British garrison, which Joyce called "Nighttown," was located on the north side of the Liffey west of the Amiens Station. The Legion of Mary, supported by a series of missions preached at the Pro-Cathedral by the Jesuits, cleaned up the red-light district shortly after the British were evacuated. The streetwalkers and the inmates of brothels were persuaded to enter the hostel of Sancta Maria. It would be interesting to know how they made out later, but no information on the subject is available.)

Anchor House was established by the port chaplain, Father Lennon, who shares the supervisory duties with the Reverend Mr. Kennedy of the Church of Ireland—a grass-roots form of ecumenism that seems to be spreading. The place provides a bar, a dance floor (with local girls volunteering to provide partners), and a room in which a Maltese seaman may be glimpsed watching *The Virginian* on Irish television. There are other recreational facilities scraped together by Father Lennon and his Protestant associate.

The novelty of Anchor House isn't only Catholic and Protestant clergy working together, rare as that has been in the past, but Father Lennon's attitude. The old Catholic obsession with proselytizing is entirely absent. "The majority of the seamen who come here will not go to church," as Father Lennon explains. "They're not interested in organized religion. The whole idea puts 'em off. So we never talk religion. But they know this is a Christian club. . . . I believe that Christianity goes over by way of decency, by way of concern and hospitality."

The success of the venture is proved by the 16,000 names of almost every nationality and race in the world which have been signed on the Anchor House's visitors' book. It is open from six o'clock to midnight every night, and the atmosphere of the place does provide a spirit of anchorage. Father Lennon and the Reverend Mr. Kennedy have simply come up with a reasonable and inviting alternative to the company of prostitutes for the lonely men off the ships.

At the same time Father Lennon, as port chaplain, is trying to have the Cork quays closed to the public so the prostitutes won't be able to board the ships in search of customers. As for the girls who formerly walked the quays, he is trying to persuade them to find another way of making a living and to set up a shelter or rehabilitation service to ease their passage to respectability.

A signal that this new concern for social welfare was penetrating the Irish hierarchy was observed recently with the appointment of Dr. Eamonn Casey as Bishop of Kerry, at which dismay was registered among the more conservative element of his peers. Supposedly the decision to bring Dr. Casey from his immensely successful endeavors in Britain among the Catholic emigrants there was taken by Cardinal Conway himself. Brisk, practical, and energetic, the youthful Bishop Casey is nothing like the stereotype of the senior churchman, nor does he display the crustily dogmatic character of some of his peers in the church.

Aside from having a cultivated taste for brandy, Churchill-sized cigars, and driving a fast car, he sprinkles his talk with such unclerical expletives as "bloody," "blooming" and "damn," possibly from long association with the British. He now resides in the large granite mansion adjacent to the cathedral at Killarney, which is filled with antiques and ornately framed paintings.

Bishop Casey made his reputation in the social welfare field after being assigned in 1960 to Slough, Buckinghamshire, with special responsibility for the Irish emigrants. Homesickness and disorientation, which can cause alcoholic and sexual misadventures, was the first problem he confronted. To keep the newcomers away from the temptations of the English industrial towns, he founded a number of social clubs. Next he took up the difficulty Irish workers had in finding suitable lodgings and housing. Since the situation was the most critical around London, he moved his headquarters there and established the Catholic Housing Society in 1963 and several years later an organization called SHELTER, which now finds homes for 1,200 Irish families annually.

Presumably it was his practical approach to the daily problems of Irish Catholics that resulted in his summons to the diocese of Kerry, one of the less developed sections of Ireland with tourism and hardscrabble agriculture as its economic mainstays. He admits that it was difficult to make the transition from housing expert to the administrative and spiritual responsibilities of a bishop. "When I was in the housing business," he says with a deprecatory smile, "I knew exactly where I wanted to go. Now I'm suddenly put in a role which one has no real feel for and no real understanding of. As a priest you have very little idea of what is involved in being a bishop. The first thing I have to do is to identify myself with my priests. It doesn't matter a damn what views I have, or what aims I have, unless my priests are doing it with me. I have to release the energies, the commitment, and the experience that exists within my diocese."

From his conversation it is evident that Bishop Casey intends to direct much of his priests' energy toward solving his diocese's social problems. One of them is the effects of tourism. Kerry is dependent on that trade, yet many Kerrymen are disturbed by its effect on the character of the people, on the change they have noted from traditional hospitality to dollar and pound chasing. As everywhere else in the world, tourism brings its corruption of values, its destruction of the old simplicities.

Bishop Casey sees it more or less as a necessary evil whose effects can be ameliorated. "I'm not denying there are problems involved; we're going to have a meeting on this soon. Take the very obvious problem of children being taken in to work at hotels at the age of thirteen and fourteen. One must be conscious that you are creating a situation in which these children are being asked to make decisions which you or I would have had to make at twenty-one or twenty-two. These kids are at their most impressionable age, and I want them to see only the best and nicest things—there are enough awful ones later in life."

His experience in England with Irish emigrants thrust into an urban environment, most of them from impoverished rural homes, arouses his concern over the implications of the Buchanan Plan. The Dublin planners envision a largely urbanized Ireland; the people of the Kerry mountains would be transplanted to Killarney, Tralee, and Limerick. Such a program, he believes, should take into account a "basic sociological factor that creates all kinds of other problems.

"Should we let Killarney grow like Dublin or London?" he asks. "Over my bloody dead body! I want to ask the question—if Buchanan's terms of reference were simply total employment by 1980—is that all we know at this stage of civilization? I remember all too well that in London jobs were five a penny, but, my

God, could people *live* as human beings crushed into rooms with no proper facilities for the kids? Surely there are other things which go to making the good life besides a job."

The most celebrated of the progressive clergymen in Ireland is the outspoken (for Ireland) Dr. Peter Birch, the Bishop of Ossory, which includes the city of Kilkenny. A tall, stooped, well-read man with tired eyes, Bishop Birch has been vigorously active in setting up in Kilkenny a social service center, a program under which young girls are sent to Holland to learn housekeeping and other skills, and a network of voluntary workers who help the aged, the ill, and women with large families.

Bishop Birch is not a patient man and occasionally blazes out at public and governmental indifference to human suffering. "It's a pity in some ways we haven't got a Communist Party here," he has been quoted as saying, "so that we would sit up and do something about the gaps in our social legislation. We must stop looking on help for others as a handout. . . . People say of a woman, 'Why should she be helped? She gets eight pounds fifteen shillings from social welfare.' But she will also very likely have eight children. Some standards of charity are just middle-class notions that are out of date."

Bishops Casey and Birch, as can be sensed from their private and public discourses, are hardly flaming radicals to any but the most crustily conservative of their fellow churchmen. What sets them apart is their demonstrated feeling that a social conscience is not incompatible with their responsibilities as religious leaders. Their hopes of reforming Irish society to a limited degree would be regarded as modest indeed elsewhere. What must be taken into account is the moral courage required for any Irishman—a churchman particularly—to speak out on any subject, to deviate from the norm. Rocking any kind of boat is not something to be undertaken without sober forethought.

William Cardinal Conway, Primate of All Ireland, Archbishop of Armagh (one of the four ecclesiastical provinces), is a moderate, statesmanlike figure who presides over the 4 archbishops, 24 bishops, more than 6,000 priests and 13,000 nuns, and is the arbiter between those who think the church is challenged by a necessity to modernize itself and those who regard it as immutable, an institution which cannot radically change without destroying itself. By his appointment of Dr. Casey as Bishop of Kerry and many other actions—not least a cool and broad-minded attitude maintained during the recent troubles in Ulster—Cardinal Conway has demonstrated that he believes the Irish church must be adaptable. Not long after his consecration in 1965, he announced that "The directives of the [Vatican] Council are being steadily and methodically implemented in Ireland; every meeting of the bishops is predominantly concerned with this great task. . . . The *aggiornamento* is a much deeper thing than putting the Mass into the vernacular or the re-designing of churches. It involves above all a deep spiritual renewal, a readjustment of attitudes, a developed capacity to relate the unchanging Gospel to the circumstances of the modern world."

Among those in the hierarchy who are charged with being more resistant to change are the Most Reverend John Charles McQuaid, Archbishop of Dublin; Dr. Michael Browne, Bishop of Galway; and Dr. Cornelius Lucey, Bishop of Cork.

Archbishop McQuaid is remembered as the leader of the clerical opposition to the Mother and Child Welfare scheme; on the other hand, during his thirty years as head of the Dublin archdiocese, he has built up the largest system of charitable institutions in the country, everything from boys' centers to rehabilitation homes for unwed mothers. He has indicated a certain disinterest in schemes for revitalizing the church such as agitate many of the younger priests and some laymen. On returning from the Vatican Council session in 1965 he remarked, "You may have been worried by much talk of changes to come. Allow me to reassure you. No change will worry the tranquillity of your Christian lives." Such pronouncements have prompted the *Irish Times,* Protestant and modishly liberal, to label him "the very incarnation of all that it was believed Pope John with his loving heart was trying to rid his Church of—obscurantism, self-righteousness, arrogance and spiritual apartheid."

Dr. Lucey, Bishop of Cork, also seemed to consider the recent Vatican councils as having no great direct importance to the spiritual life of Ireland. After the Second Vatican Council, he was quoted as saying, "The Council is all right for a week or so, but it doesn't seem so interesting when you are watching it. A lot of the problems they discuss are of no interest to us. The Jews, religious liberty . . . we already have it here. The only time there's any trouble, the Jehovah's Witnesses cause it. Our people don't want them."

He became involved in a particularly acrid controversy growing out of the papal encyclical *Humanae Vitae,* which in effect forbade the use of contraceptive pills and which the Irish hierarchy was quicker than most to praise and support. There is much underground enthusiasm *for* the pill and use of it (through plain-wrapper shipments received from Belfast or London), but there was no public protest from the Catholic laymen most affected by the ban. The lone voice of dissent was raised by an unusually brave cleric-educator, the Reverend Dr. James Good, professor of theology at University College, Cork, who stated (to a brandishing of croziers): "Assuming that the accounts so far received are substantially correct, I think that Pope Paul's statement on birth control is a major tragedy in the Church."

Naturally the statement made big waves and front-page stories. Dr. Good's ecclesiastical superior, Bishop Lucey, was away on vacation when he loosed that bombshell. On his return a week later Bishop Lucey suspended Dr. Good's rights to preach and hear confessions. At a subsequent meeting of the Irish hierarchy at Maynooth, its full support was given the Pope's edict against the contraceptive pill. Cardinal Conway's statement on the subject was considerably more mollifying than Bishop Lucey's. "I really don't live on the moon and have, in fact, a fairly good monitoring service," he said. "I think that the great bulk of the ordinary people simply accept what the Pope has said. Among some classes there has undoubtedly been much disappointment and some criticism, although not as much as is sometimes thought." Rather surprisingly, considering the tradition of the primate's aloofness from the laity and its opinions, Cardinal Conway ordered what he called a "limited spot-check" among people of the professional classes. This informal poll indicated, he said, that "six out of seven of the men felt that the Pope could not have come to any other decision, although with the women it was different. I'm not suggesting this was the general pattern, but it is interesting to note that a National Opinion Poll survey among young people of the fifteen to twenty-four age group, where you would naturally expect to find revolt, indicated that a substantial majority approved of the encyclical."

Bishop Browne of Galway, a tall and distinguished man in his mid-seventies, was Bishop Lucey's collaborator in defeating the proposal for free medical care for mothers and children. His principal objection to that scheme, he recalls, was the possibility that a non-Catholic doctor might be charged with giving prenatal care to Catholic mothers, which could have resulted in an infringement on Catholic teaching. Regarding the Second Vatican Council, Bishop Browne thought it extraordinary that it should have been convened when there was no threat to the church such as Luther's Reformation. He agreed with the council's pronouncement that all mankind, not the Jews alone, was responsible for the death of Christ. At the same time he felt that the church should likewise be relieved of total culpability for the Reformation. "If not the Jews for Christ," he demanded, "why Catholics exclusively for the Reformation?"

The views of the conservative bishops, however, are coming under heavier and more frequent attack. Bishop baiting, of course, is as old as heresy and almost as old as the church. In Ireland a distinction is drawn between bishop baiting, which is legitimate if kept within bounds, and denying acknowledgment that the bishop is the baiter's "father in God." A bishop may be mistaken in his beliefs and criticized for them, but his religious authority is not challenged. Thus, Sean MacReamoinn, a former diplomat who comments on religious affairs over Irish television, writes that "very few" of the Irish "dioceses are 'ruled' by men whose virtues of heart and head make them seem to be what their office supposes them to be—fathers, and at the same time, servants of their people. The rest, however devoted and honest—and I believe they are all that—or however learned—and some of them can make claims to a scholarship superior to that of most of their critics—the rest are, it must be admitted, sadly but truly, men whose relevance to the hard facts of Christian life in Ireland today is scarcely visible to the naked and, at times, the cold eye of their flocks."

To liberals and progressives such as MacReamoinn, it is distressing that Irish morality covers such a narrow field of vision. By immoral, they point out, the Irish invariably mean sexually wayward. Immorality would not be charged to a corrupt politician, for instance, or tax cheaters or dishonest merchants or slum landlords. A society which tolerated free love would be regarded as irremediably evil, but not one which neglected the poor, the sick, and the aged.

Clerics and seminarians determined to renovate the Irish church, he points out, can cite the documents of the Vatican councils as "warrant for their questioning of, and reluctance to conform to, hitherto sacrosanct attitudes." Under the impact of the councils and with the appointment of younger bishops, it appears that the church will be much less autocratic and paternalistic in the near future, that increasingly the hierarchy will be more aware of and sensitive to the needs and feelings of its followers.

To the Catholic Irishman the worst thing a man can be is not a Protestant—he is generally, if a trifle reluctantly, respected for that—but a pagan, a word heard oftener in Ireland than anywhere else. There are few pagans in Ireland, where Protestant piety is as fervent as the Catholic, though the number of Protestants has been steadily dwindling. Only half of 1 percent of the Republic's citizenry professes no religious faith. About 5 percent is Protestant: roughly 125,000 members of the Church of Ireland (Episcopalian in American terms, Low Church in English), fewer than 25,000 Presbyterians, about 8,000 Methodists, fewer than 4,000 Jews, and about 7,500 in other denominations, including a scattering of Quakers (President Nixon's Irish connection stems from his mother's side, German Quakers who fled persecution in their homeland and settled for a while in Ireland before going on to the United States).

Between all these faiths there is a general amiability that might surprise anyone who, reading the dispatches from Belfast and Derry, has the idea that the whole of Ireland is a religious battlefield. The Catholics in the South, however, are such an overwhelming majority that they can afford an easy tolerance of the one in twenty Irishmen who is not a Catholic. It is true enough that any Irishman is a trifle uneasy until he establishes, by indirect questions and with the utmost tact, just what faith you are. Once that matter is settled, he is willing to accept you no matter how exotic or outlandish your beliefs. On a West Cork road I know well, there are several Protestant farm families among the preponderance of Catholic ones; on both the working and social levels they get along fine; the only division comes on Sunday when they go their separate ways to church. In the village of Ballydehob there are three churches, Catholic, Church of Ireland, and Methodist. The Church of Ireland has a small but devoted congregation. The Methodists have dwindled to three families, and their church is served by a circuit-riding pastor. But the Protestants rarely abandon a church, even though it is falling in ruins and only a few of its parishioners survive. There is said to have been one Protestant church in County Cork where services were held so infrequently that a goose hatched her eggs in the pulpit.

Although dwindling in numbers, the Protestant Irish maintain a surviving ascendancy in business, industry, and the professions. Out of every 1,000 Catholics, only 9 occupy top managerial or executive positions and only 43 are members of a profession. Among Protestants, 65 in 1,000 are executives, and 83 are professional men. There is an apparent cachet attached to being a Protestant even in Catholic-owned firms; possibly it has some connection with the fact that so much Irish commerce is transacted with Britain and other largely Protestant countries, as well as the tradition that a Protestant is likely to be better educated, less of a country boy.

The assured place of the Protestants in the Irish community undoubtedly owes much to the fact that during the last two centuries so many of them were involved in the movements for political independence. As a whole, of course, they were devoted to the union with Great Britain; many of them still display pictures of the British royal family on their walls. But there was a considerable number, whom they could only regard as renegades, who worked mightily for independence from the British Crown. Wolfe Tone, Robert Emmet, and Charles Stewart Parnell all were Protestants; so were such later figures in the rebellion as Yeats, O'Casey, Countess Markievicz, Erskine Childers, Robert Barton, and Dr. Douglas Hyde.

The Church of Ireland, as their chief bulwark on a Catholic island, was disestablished in 1869, by which time the Protestant middle class had been steadily declining. This was the class which kept the shops and catered to both the landed gentry and the British garrisons. After independence, with the garrisons withdrawn and the gentry losing much of its wealth and purchasing power, the shopkeepers either emigrated to England or moved to Dublin, within the old "Pale," where the Protestant population has increased in step with the city's growth and where they maintain two of the finest cathedrals. It gives visitors quite a turn to learn that St. Patrick's Cathedral of Dublin is a Protestant church.

The seats of both the Catholic hierarchy and the Church of Ireland—this is another Irish anomaly—are located at Armagh, in County Armagh, Northern Ireland. They stare at each other from respective hilltops as though determined to keep an eye on each other. The Church of Ireland's primate, Archbishop George Simms, unlike his opposite number, Cardinal Conway, is headquartered in Dublin. With the Catholic primate staying in Northern Ireland and the Protestant leader in the South, it is almost like an exchange of hostages.

Dr. Simms is a classical scholar and a leading expert on Celtic literature. His first visitor when he and his family moved into their suburban Dublin house was the man whom liberal Dubliners regard as a bigoted mossback, the Catholic Archbishop McQuaid. Dr. Simms is a member of the Anglican-Catholic world commission, which meets in Rome to discuss the furtherance of the ecumenical movement. The most difficult problem, he says, is intermarriage, which is complicated by Catholic insistence that the children of such marriages be reared as Catholics. It is unwise to proceed with haste, he adds, because "True ecumenism is in understanding each other. People on both sides have to be educated." There is greater friendliness between the Catholic and Protestant clergies, he indicated, than among their followers, who would rather nurse old grievances.

The bitter truth of that statement was apparent when the film *Cromwell* opened in Dublin. It was a healthy sign, of course, that Ireland's number one Protestant devil could be sympathetically portrayed in a Dublin theater; a few decades ago the theater would have been bombed or burned down. Less healthy symptoms could be detected inside the theater, which was packed, mostly by men with their young sons in tow. It soon became apparent that the audience constituted a Protestant cheering section. There were cheers when Cromwell, played by the Limerick-born Richard Harris with a nonpartisan zeal, invaded a Catholic church and knocked the crucifix to the floor by way of desecrating a papist symbol. The cheers were thunderous when King Charles' head was lopped off, and shouts of "Well done!" There was precious little of Dr. Simms' ecumenical spirit present in those members of his flock who had come to cheer on their long-dead hero.

In addition to its tolerance of the 5 percent Protestant minority, the Irish Republic can boast of a generally amiable attitude toward its small Jewish colony. Most of the Irish Jews found sanctuary there after fleeing from pogroms in Russia and Poland, many of them settling in Dublin, which has a grand rabbi. Less fortunate were those who settled in Limerick, where they met with considerable prejudice at one time. On the whole they are as well integrated as the Protestants, it is said, though there are reports that they encounter difficulty in obtaining membership in some of the golf clubs. The most famous of the Irish Jews was the late Robert Briscoe, lord mayor of Dublin, whose appearance on American television, lauding the spirit of tolerance in Ireland, put a brighter polish on the country's image than a boatload of shamrocks. Briscoe attained high rank in the native establishment through his services in the rebellion, his record as an IRA diehard (one of those besieged with Rory O'Connor in the Four Courts), and a lifelong follower of Eamon De Valera. His son has been a Fianna Fail member of the Dail. Very few Irish Jews have migrated. In Ireland they found one of the few relatively comfortable resting places in their Diaspora.

Religious separatism no doubt will be a long time disappearing from Ireland. Presently there are signs of a tentative drawing together, more and more "mixed" marriages, Catholic priests, and Protestant ministers sharing the same platform, Catholic priests addressing Protestant meetings, both sects attending funerals together, above all, a greater feeling of ease between them. It's a form of grass-roots ecumenicism; the flocks moving ahead of their shepherds.

A microcosmic example of the new togetherness is offered by the seaside village of Fethard in the Hook district of County Wexford. Fethard has its own niche in history: Eight hundred years ago an English valiant named Raymond the Fat landed with his knightly spearhead to establish a foothold for Henry II's invasion of Ireland. Somewhat later Fethard was notorious as the base for Wexford smugglers who outran the British customs' vessels and engaged in illegal trade with the Lowlands countries.

About fifteen years ago the fishing village was shaken by religious feuding. Today nobody wants to talk about it, understandably enough, but it grew out of an interfaith marriage which gave rise to some highly divisive and ugly rumors. It was also a study in the human effects of the ancient *Ne Temere* decree issued by the Council of Trent in 1564. This decree is interpreted, particularly in Ireland, as providing that the children of a "mixed" marriage shall always be baptized and brought up as Catholics. In Fethard, its practical results included a Catholic boycott of Protestant shops for a time and a complete breakdown in relations between the Catholic majority and the small Protestant minority.

The breach was partly closed when both sides realized they had to get together and do something about Fethard's economy. There was a high rate of unemployment and emigration in and around the town, which was unable to maintain itself on the fishing and small farming. To counteract this, a cooperative effort to find new markets was made through various rural organizations; tourism was promoted, with the local catch of lobsters, crabs, mussels, cockles, and clams as one of the attractions. It also helped when women of both faiths were drawn into the local branch of the Irish Countrywomen's Association.

What really speeded the process was the assignment of two young clergymen to Fethard several years ago. Taking over the Church of Ireland, next to Fethard Castle, and its tributary churches of Saltmills and Tintern, was an energetic young man, the Reverend James Grant, formerly of Grand Falls, Canada, and the Seamen's Mission in Dublin. The new priest was Father Richard Hayes, a wiry ex-football player and a Wexford man.

The Reverend Mr. Grant and Father Hayes formed an immediate alliance, realizing the community would slowly die if the cooperative movement weren't pushed for all it was worth. One of their more valuable allies was Maurice Butler, who had retired from the Indian tea business and settled in Fethard. In the old Ascendancy days Butler would have lived in a big house behind iron gates and held himself aloof from local problems. Butler, however, is chairman of the Fethard Development Association.

Most of all, the two young clergymen set an example for the rest of the parish by constantly being seen in public together. Soon people who hadn't spoken to one another for a dozen years thawed out, and the communal spirit was restored. One scheme concocted by the two clergymen was the Sea Food Festival of 1970, which commemorated the landing of Raymond the Fat in 1170. People opened guest houses, the noted actor Cyril Cusack was lured down to preside over the festivities, and Fethard-on-Sea was established as a tourist attraction, convenient for the English coming over on the Rosslare car ferries.

Other efforts were launched to keep the economy turning over the year around, Mrs. Sheila Auld reviving the local handcrafts and producing seashell souvenirs and embroidered linen, new markets searched out for the mackerel fishing as well as shellfish. In the long wet winters, townspeople and those from farms in the Hook are participating in nonsectarian amateur drama societies, which throughout Ireland are almost as popular as bridge parties. To encourage that movement, the Reverend Mr. Grant and Father Hayes collaborated in getting the Abbey Theater Company to make an appearance in the parochial hall and to give acting lessons in the Church of Ireland school. They believe that all of these efforts have resulted in halting emigration and making Fethard-on-Sea a place where people can make a living again.

Probably the most hopeful sign of all is the remark frequently made by the town's Catholics: "You know, we'd like to see more Protestants in Fethard."

7.

The Bachelor Boys

The thing that has taken and torn me in twain,
Has pricked me with pangs, plagued with me pain,
Is the number of women, old and young,
For whom no wedding bells have rung. . . .
—BRYAN MERRYMAN, *The Midnight Court*

In the display cases of commercial photographers in the Irish market towns there is mute but graphic evidence of the terrors which marriage holds for the Irish male. Testimony to the foreboding the Irishman feels about matrimony is written unsparingly in the displays of wedding-party photographs. The centerpiece is always the bridegroom, trussed up for once in his life in formal attire. He stands there stiff with fright and stares wildly into the camera's eye. Ranked beside him is the best man, who looks almost as miserable as his doomed friend. The other males in the wedding party try to conceal an expression of pity or contempt, if unmarried themselves, or a sort of gloating commiseration, if married. On the face of the bride there is often a look of bewildered triumph, as though she were still unable to believe the trembling specimen beside her has knelt with her before the parish priest. She may also be conscious of the fact the bridegroom's mother, even though he may be a boy of forty-eight, is looking daggers because a scheming female has snatched her son away in the prime of his youth.

The wariness, the foxy elusiveness of the Irishman when it comes to marriage have long been celebrated in literature. Until recently few married before the age of thirty-five. Many feel they are being deprived of their youth if the banns are read before they are fifty. They are encouraged in their broken-field running by those who have lost the game. "A young man in this country who is engaged to be married," wrote Seamus Heaney, "is regarded with sympathetic puzzlement by his elder married friends. They convey to him a sense not so much of climax as finale. 'It's a blister you'll sit upon for the rest of your days.' Images of strangulation and fettering recur—you know, the noose, hitched, tied up—and euphemisms such as 'having the job done.' When he returns from the honeymoon, they admit him to their company with a new intimacy—he finds himself part of a secret order of broken spirits."

There are many reasons for the Irishman's unique resistance, some of them valid. The strongest, perhaps, is his conviction that he lives in a man's world—a delusion propagated by his womenfolk, who know better but are clever enough to conceal the knowledge. At least until recently he has been inculcated from birth with the theory that he is superior to all women (except his mother), that the female has never advanced much beyond the Adam's-rib stage. Other factors can be gleaned from observation and the writings of sociologists and clerics concerned with the problem. The oversexed Irishman is a rarity; he has either to migrate to London or Stockholm or to live in grinding frustration. Irish Catholicism is the most puritanical of all the daughters of the church; a man living a hundred yards from the Vatican's walls can now get a divorce, but not a Dubliner. The Irishman's energies go into work and sport; his money is spent on downing pints and gambling or is saved with a fervor that only a French peasant could appreciate. "Ninety-five percent of Ireland's eligible women," Edmund J. Murray, the Catholic scholar, has observed, "would marry tomorrow were the eligible men of the nation to transfer their affections from horses and dogs and football matches to the nobler activities of courtship and marriage."

And he is a skeptical fellow who refuses to be codded about the joys of matrimony. For many years he has been designated a sociological free-fire zone, urged to marry and propagate, to comprehend that he may be committing "race suicide," and all the propaganda only makes him more suspicious of the proposition, particularly when the coals are heaped on his head by writers in the newly emboldened women's magazines.

He is not persuaded by women writers who picture him as a boozy, smug, irresponsible, heartless fellow who is driving Irishwomen abroad to find husbands, who claim that an Irish girl would rather marry a hot-blooded Englishman than endure a five- or ten-year engagement with a perpetual adolescent who has to be frog-marched to the altar. Nor by remarks such as that of the young French teacher living in Ireland that "When *The History of Great Irish Lovers* is written, it will be the thinnest book in the library." (No thinner, he will retort, than an equally ephemeral volume which might be titled *The History of Irish Nymphomania.* Even the Irish-born dancer-courtesan who called herself Lola Montez could not legitimately be included in such a volume because she was the daughter of a British officer.)

History, tradition, and economics, the Irishman will point out, all operate negatively on romantic love in Ireland. History made marriage a practical matter, tradition ordained that the male's whims are more important than the female's deepest urges, and economic necessity, at least until the last decade, has made it a step to be considered with a long searching intensity.

Under English rule for centuries, under a political and economic system that showed the ugliest facets of colonialism, the Irish had to be practical about adding to the burdens of making a living off a few acres of bog and rocky hillside. Even after the English were sent packing, the bachelor, working only a few more unproductive acres, could not plunge into matrimony because he usually had aged parents and unmarried sisters to be considered, and family loyalty, forged through centuries of famine, oppression, and other historic adversities, still comes first. Nor can the Irishman be faulted, he maintains, if his religious education has been interpreted, rightly or wrongly, as defining marriage as "permission to sin." Nor that Mother Machree is not only a sweet old lady dozing by a turf fire but in her subtle way the most ironhanded of the world's matriarchs.

Only with the wryest of grins can he read Paul Jones' playlet, which recites the bachelor's dilemma in capsule form.* The

* Published in its entirety in the symposium *The Vanishing Irish,* edited by John A. O'Brien (New York, 1953).

characters are Malachy, a ninety-three-year-old farmer, his son, Seamus, who is sixty-nine, and their dog, Tray. The last half of the mini-drama goes:

MALACHY: I've been thinking, and I sitting here, that it's time you settled down and got married and made a home for yourself. What happened to that nice girl of the Dalys you used to have an eye for? Annie Daly, wasn't that her name? The dark-haired one that used to wear a red ribbon in her hair.

SEAMUS: She went to England ten years to be a nurse.

MALACHY: And the little Sweeney girl, that won the prize for dancing at the Feis at Gortnatubber?

SEAMUS: She went to Swansea and married a Welsh miner.

MALACHY: Did she, did she? They do say there's a lot of them gone. Right enough, I haven't seen many young girls in this part of the world in the last few years or so.

(*The dog stirs uneasily in his sleep*)

MALACHY: (*patting the dog's head gently*) Poor Tray, he's thirteen years old now. He's dreaming of the times he used to be out after rabbits. . . . Do you know, Seamus, I'm beginning to think I'm getting past my work. I think you ought to be out looking for a good wife for yourself and settling down. I've only at most another three or four years to go, and then the farm will be yours.

(*Seamus bites the dog.*) CURTAIN.

Way back, though, qualified observers have been less inclined to place the blame on the bachelor tied down by family exigencies than on the footloose fellow determined to be one of the boys forever. More than 200 years ago Bryan Merryman demanded in verse of the ubiquitous bachelor:

And what have you done to restore the nation?
Shame on you there without chick or child
With women in thousand running wild.
What matter to you if their beauty founder,
If belly and breast will never be rounder,
If ready and glad to be wife and mother,
They drop unplucked from the bough of life?

The concern over the population decline in Ireland, owing to both the elusiveness of the Irish bachelor and emigration, became especially acute in 1953, when a symposium titled *The Vanishing Irish* was published. It even spread to North America, where it was quickly garnished with statistics showing that the Irish who had migrated to the United States and Canada were also afflicted by a falling birthrate and a high incidence of aging bachelors and spinsters. The alert was also sounded by Sean O'Faolain in a lively and scornful magazine article titled "Love Among the Irish." Soon every qualified expert and a number of the unqualified were rushing into print with their theories on why the Irishman resisted marriage and how that condition could be made more attractive for him, the tone of these jeremiads ranging from the admonitory (the clergy) to the furious (women journalists) to the sardonically sympathetic (male journalists).

O'Faolain, as the groundbreaker in the movement to persuade the Irish to marry in greater numbers and be quick about it, avoided any suggestions of male chauvinism. The trouble with his sex, he declared, was that the Irish bachelor wanted only one thing from a prospective wife: the assurance that she would be a good housekeeper and mother. He was balking at marriage, O'Faolain added, because he didn't believe the modern young Irishwoman wanted it either; she was too interested in film stars, clothes, household gadgets, and other frivolities. He quoted as fairly typical one bachelor's pragmatic attitude toward finding a suitable wife:

> I am a bachelor, aged 38. I am in no hurry to get married. Next September, or the September after, I will take a holiday with an object at Lisdoonvarna, County Clare. I will inform some of the priests on holiday that I am on the lookout, and that I am a bachelor of some substance who requires wife with a dowry and of a certain minimum figure. In due course a girl will be selected and the wooing will proceed on a sane plane. At Christmas my people will visit her people and her people will investigate my background, credentials and relatives. I will meet the young lady again on some such occasion as the Rugby International in Dublin during the following Easter. In due course the nuptials will take

> place. If I marry at 40 on the lines I have indicated I will guarantee that at 60 my wife and myself will be fonder of one than any couple of the same age who married in their youth for what Hollywood miscalls love, but which is in fact lustful infatuation. . . .

That "sane" approach was not greatly esteemed by the young women to whom O'Faolain spoke. Perhaps most of them had been converted to the obsession with romantic love displayed in films and other forms of fiction. One of them characterized modern Irishmen as a "race of male cuckoos and beer sharks" who get all the affection they really want from their mothers. She affirmed:

> The men of today are mammy's darlings. They have everything at home so why should they leave it? Their mothers slave for them and they expect that their wives will slave for them in the same way.
>
> It is no wonder they used to marry early long ago when they even expected their wives to polish their boots for them. But we women now want marriage on a 50–50 basis, so the darlings have slowed up. Look at the way a man can drink Lough Erne dry and it is not called a binge, but if a poor woman gets a cold she is told to cure it with buttermilk boiled with onions. There is little doubt either that parents do influence their sons to wait a little longer, and you know what that means—10 or 15 years maybe. The odd thing is that these mothers are more than anxious to find other mothers' sons to marry their own daughters. . . .

O'Faolain heard all sorts of explanations for the marriage shyness of the Irishman, the four most plausible of which were that "sexual desire is sublimated by religion, exhausted by sport, drugged by drink, or reflected by either an innate or an inculcated puritanism." Poverty should be ruled out on the basis of statistics showing that a century before, when social and economic conditions were much harder, 57 percent of the Irish married between the ages of twenty-three and thirty-four, against only 25 percent in the early 1950's. He was inclined to lay the blame to the peasant caginess of the Irishman, with his yearning for a dowry, his calculations about which girl in the neighborhood could add the most to his own small holdings.

The Irishman, he believed, was "much more calculating in love than a foreigner might think if he based his notions on the reckless and dashing figures of Anglo-Irish fiction. Those gallant rakes were bred in the big houses of a minority landlord class. The mass of the people were hard-pressed peasants for whom love had to take a second place before the essential tie of blood and economy. Today this basic, rural class is dominant in Ireland, and they have brought into the towns the traditions and techniques of the country."

Arland Ussher was even less sympathetic to the antimatrimonial tendencies of his fellow Irishmen and once bluntly stated that they had too little interest in sex to "perpetuate their own cantankerous species." He considered them the most graceless of suitors, bemused by the certainty that there is nothing less dignified than the spectacle of a man in love. "Whatever one is told about Irish 'blarney,' I have almost never heard an Irishman pay a *compliment* to a woman. So unused indeed are women to such graceful forms of address that they would probably in most cases reply by a rebuff, fancying an intended assault upon their virtue. . . . The Irishman in love feels ridiculous; and to drive home the feeling, an enamored couple in any country parish are exposed to derision." He could fault Irishwomen only for developing a defensive posture of "ungraciousness and tartness."

A couple of women writers had a go at the bachelor boys during the race-suicide alarms of the early fifties and exhibited a good measure of that "tartness" to which Ussher referred. The playwright and novelist Maura Laverty, though happily married to an Irishman, asserted: "No woman in her senses would trade even one moth-eaten Spaniard for a whole team of All-Ireland Hurling Finalists, referee included," because Latins even at their worst "have a happy knack of making a woman feel that in merely being a woman she enriches the world." Bottom pinching in Rome, she asserted, was greatly preferable to the "cold indifference she encounters at home." She was outraged by the Irishman's preference for masculine company, by his stinginess ("The improvident Irishman will, of course, be with us always, but it is not in such nonsense as presents for women that his money will be spent, but on liquor and gambling"), and by his inveterate caution about taking the plunge, which "forces his fiancée to waste her best years waiting for him to make her his wife."

Maura Laverty, like most urban observers, nominated the Irish mother as the largest clinker in the domestic grate. It was and is true, however, that caring for the older people, seeing to it that they always have the "closest chair to the fire," is part of Irish tradition. Age, as in prerevolutionary China, is venerated to a greater extent than elsewhere. Not only the aged mother but the work-worn father, in rural areas especially, is guaranteed a place in the home they have always occupied. Sending them away is regarded as cruel and venal. Unmarried sisters are usually assured of similar protection. Often, still, on the Irish farms you will find a family composed of the older son—his younger brothers usually have emigrated because the land will not support them all—either or both parents, and one or two unmarried sisters. The aging bachelor boy may have wanted a wife for years, but he knows he is trapped by conscience, as well as by the strongest bonds of affection.

Nevertheless, Mrs. Laverty considered the Irishman the "world's prime example of the Oedipus complex. He is anchored to his mother for as long as she lives. . . . Mothers prize their sons far above their daughters—and they have no compunction in showing this favoritism while their sons are young. (Query: Do Irishwomen lavish this inordinate love on their sons in an effort to compensate themselves for inadequate husbands?) Sisters are taught at an early age that their duty is to dance attendance on their brothers. I myself remember that my nightly duty was to clean my brother's boots. The inevitable result is that the Irish boy grows up with an exaggerated affection for and dependence on his mother and with a contempt for all other females."

Mary Jane Keating, the Dublin journalist, believed that the Irish male not only hates marriage but "doesn't really like the company of women except inasmuch as they confer some luster on him. He doesn't mind taking a lovely creature out for an evening; he likes to chat with a witty conversationalist and bask in the adoration of a girl who subscribes to the theory of the super-Celtic male." Materialism and puritanism, aside from the Irishman's refusal to consider marriage seriously until he is middle-aged, were nominated by Miss Keating as the worst blights on romantic love. "Why do they let a cold and materialistic outlook govern their actions and their dealings with one another until malice and frustration come to triumph over love and the fulfillment of a normal life? . . . As a matter of strict fact, normally sound people would not be so bitterly sex-conscious as we are now in Ireland. It is bad and humiliating to be undersexed as to be oversexed. Surely sex is inherent in every human being living in a natural and unaffected way, and it is utterly wrong to seek to impose an education which tends to outlaw sex as an indecent and unworthy thing. Yet that is the general tendency of education both in the home and in the school."

The decline of the unromantic but practical matchmaking system, a tradition going back to pagan times, was decried by Bryan MacMahon, the playwright and short-story writer from County Kerry, where the old ways are slower to fade away. He recalled that the professional matchmaker held an honorable and useful position in the Irish villages. He explained:

> The matchmaking system, which has had coals of fire heaped upon its head, resembled a complicated game of patience with young nubile people as cards in the matchmaker's hand. The appearance of a key card could ensure a series of swift moves. ("Mary's waitin' to get her money; the fortune comin' in with her brother's wife will carry her into Connor's of Castleacre. That'll let the Connor girl into the Glebe farm at Mallymehan." And so on.) It is possible to follow a fortune the round of a parish and find it unbroken at the end of the mating season of Shrove. But, cumbersome and exhausting as this system was, with its incursions into "clear title," it *did* provide a solution of sorts. The most regrettable feature of its decay is that there is no other system left to take its place.*

* The mechanics of matchmaking early in this century were described by Stephen Gwynn in his *Holiday in Connemara.* The old "bartered bride" system lasted longer in the Irish-speaking districts than anywhere else, indicating it was rooted deep in the old tribal way of life. A bargaining session was a serious occasion, its grimness alleviated only by lashings of porter and whiskey. The prospective bridegroom and eight or ten of his supporters and advisers marched to a house which served as neutral ground. "They were shown into a room with

The matchmaking tradition with all its down-to-earth aspects was destroyed, MacMahon believed, through the importation of "foreign" ideas that love, not a sensible touch of self-interest, should lead to marriage. "Magazines, popular songs, plays of outmoded English vintage, the talk of returning emigrants—all these poured scorn upon the old ways of finding a life partner. Thus, semi-ashamed of matchmaking, and complete neophytes in this new art of love, the Irish sit glowering in their chimney corners."

Bryan MacMahon apparently was on to something. Within a decade, the ancient and honorable role of matchmaker was taken up, but without the commercial aspect of it, by a number of the Catholic clergy, who are operating with considerable success in the rural areas where such efforts are needed the most.

Another factor, perhaps the overriding one, enters into the calculations of the Irish when confronted with the possibility of marriage. The bachelor boy is taking on a more considerable burden, with little or no chance of unshouldering it, than his counterparts in other countries. There is no divorce in the Irish Republic, and whether a marriage is happy or wretched, it is for keeps. If wretched, his only recourse is to the pub and the sympathy of his fellow males. And whether he has prospered or not, the teachings of his church encourage him to reproduce himself manifold. A large family combined with an unhappy marriage means that he will not even be able to seek the consolation of pints at the pub or place an occasional ten-shilling piece on the dogs or horses.

---

three long tables furnished with uncut loaves and butter, a glass and tumbler to every place, bottles of whiskey on the board, and a barrel of porter somewhere handy. The bride's friends were there in equal numbers, and the parties ranged themselves at opposite sides of the table. . . . The boy's spokesman, backed by the others, began praising the suitor: how he had a well-stocked farm; was sober as well as rich; had no brothers to divide his income. To this the bride's party answered by praising the girl as industrious and skilled in needlework." A dowry of one hundred pounds was finally settled upon. Neither the bride nor any other females were present at the bargaining session because it was regarded as "unlucky." It is also possible that the men excluded them because the women were fierce bargainers and would have kept the men from their drinking. The women were summoned when the bargain was struck, the room was cleared for dancing, and the older men gathered around a table in the corner for some serious drinking which lasted until near daybreak.

As for the sophisticated European alternative of consoling himself with another woman—all but unthinkable. Even in the largest cities of Dublin, Limerick, and Cork, the chances of successful cheating are so slender as to be a fairy light in the gloaming. Irish eyes may be smiling, on occasion, but they are always watchful. The man who steps out of line is sure to be observed no matter where he may whisk himself and his extramarital romance, and he will be reported on and roundly condemned. The hard eye of the parish priest will be on him forevermore.

Ireland thus far has insulated herself against the permissive atmosphere of other Western European nations, with gray and Georgian Dublin as far removed in spirit from swinging Elizabethan London as though they were separated by the Indian Ocean instead of the Irish Sea. Marital infidelity in Ireland is not only a heinous moral offense, but a frightful inconvenience, calling for the talents of a Scaramouche and a Scarlet Pimpernel if one hopes to avoid surveillance.

There is something debilitating in the Irish climate that militates against exertions of that kind. Tony Gray, the Dublin-born journalist and novelist now based in London, believes that husbands and wives are more faithful in Ireland "partly because the men can't be bothered, and partly because the opportunities crop up less often than in countries with larger populations. There isn't the same choice of potential material; and the chances of being spotted are far higher. Cozy, extramarital liaisons develop in golf clubs, yacht clubs and so on, it is true, and they seem to be tolerated by complaisant partners because the absence of any provision for divorce in Ireland ensures that they will not escalate into crises likely to endanger the family unit." Only a tiny fraction of the population, it should be noted, can afford to join clubs, let alone the expense of skulking around with another man's wife. "The fact that you cannot get a divorce in Ireland also helps to limit the amount of extramarital activity between married men and young girls. If an English secretary finds herself drifting into an affair with the boss, she can always persuade herself that he intends to talk his wife into giving him a divorce. Even if she doesn't really believe this at least it offers her a formula by which she can always rationalize her behaviour. An Irish secretary, on the other hand, knows very well that this can never happen, and is forced, right from the outset, to face up to the reality of the situation."

The rarity of domestic scandal in Ireland was measurable in the spring of 1970, when the Irish newspapers played up stories, three and four columns in length, about an extramarital affair involving a senator from County Donegal and the wife of a road mender, even though space was scarce at the moment because the Dublin government was being rocked by the gun-running conspiracy charged to several of its members. The proceedings before the High Court in Dublin also demonstrated how much energy had to be expended in conducting such an affair and the physical and financial hazards it entailed. The middle-aged senator, who was also a hotel owner, was charged with "enticement" and "criminal conversation" with the plaintiff's wife, Victorian phraseology not at all out of place in Ireland. The plaintiff testified that his wife was lured away from his home by gifts of jewelry and a fur coat. Testimony showed that the defendant suffered in various ways from his alleged adventure: He not only lost the case and several thousand pounds, but had the hoardings advertising his hotel defaced with the word "brothel" inscribed over them and was assaulted by the plaintiff with an iron bar during a County Council meeting. During the plaintiff's testimony, this exchange took place:

Defendant's counsel: "Did you injure him?"

Plaintiff: "Yes, I did."

Plaintiff's counsel: "Unfortunately, not fatally."

The plaintiff's counsel was not rebuked for his bellicose remark, even though it was uttered before the High Court. Adultery in Ireland still calls forth feelings of Biblical intensity. And those who venture into adultery, according to Alan Bestic, another Dublin journalist who fled to Fleet Street, suffer mightily for their sins. "Men certainly stray much more frequently than women," Bestic observed, "though immediately after they have made love, they are whipped with guilt. To get out from under the lash, they turn a fierce resentment on the unfortunate women, who have taken them illicitly to bed. 'It was all her fault . . . the dirty disgust.' This attitude is not surprising, when it is remembered that husbands have this subconscious guilt even about their wives."

* * *

In the past ten years, neatly coinciding with the economic upturn, Ireland has been taking a more modern, if not at all permissive, attitude toward sex, love, and marital relations. The quick spread of television viewing has helped promote this change, along with burgeoning women's magazines, what is left of foreign-made films after the local censors have finished snipping, and the effects of prosperity in thawing out the reluctance of the Irish bachelor.

Marital relations are now discussed with a frankness that would have been incredible ten years ago. The contraceptive pill has made its shy appearance, though the channels of distribution are largely underground. Furthermore, fewer young people are migrating. Within a year or two, the Central Statistics Office forecasts, the number of married men under the age of thirty will rise to 60,000, compared to half that number in 1961.

The sexual inhibitions of the Irish are now being assaulted by a variety of publicists, sociologists, marriage counselors, women's magazine writers, and intellectuals. The bachelor boy may soon be a lonely and isolated figure, unable to count on the moral support of the boys in the pub around the corner.

The anecdote of two middle-aged persons who had been engaged for twenty years, presenting them as comic instead of pathetic figures, indicates the trend toward marriage-mindedness. Whipping up her courage, Mary one evening suggests to her long-term fiancé: "Paddy, don't you think it was time we were thinking of getting married?" "What? Married?" the startled Paddy replies. "Sure and who would have us?"

The Paddys and Marys are under intense scrutiny now, and efforts are being directed against what has been called the "Sean O'Oedipus Complex," which places so much emphasis on maternal and sisterly love and so little on the sexual kind. The main thrust of the sociologists' campaign, it appears, is to loosen what they regard as the overly restrictive bonds between parents and children.

Parental possessiveness was the subject of a recent pamphlet, *The Dilemma of the Human Family,* specifically the Irish family, by Drs. Ivor Browne and T. J. Kiernan. The domestic crunch, they observed, comes when the children attempt to break away and lead their own lives, especially in homes where the mother or father have coddled the children to compensate for hostility between the parents.

> It is only when the children attempt to move out and progress towards independence that trouble becomes manifest. It is not, therefore, enough to speak of such a home as being good or bad —the further question must be asked: is it good or bad for the stage of the cycle which it has reached? What may be reasonably appropriate behaviour in a mother toward a six-month-old infant may be a highly pathological behaviour if directed towards a twenty-six-year-old man! Yet this is characteristically the sort of thing found in many families with an adult schizophrenic—the mother or both parents behave towards him as if he were a small dependent infant.

The Irish are being told, in effect, that they are "lousy lovers" and had better learn that there are pleasures, as well as duties, connected with the marital bed. Most of the blame for that joylessness is chalked up against the male of the species, just possibly because most of those who write on the subject are women. One of the blunter counselors is Dorine Rohan, whose frankness in *Marriage Irish Style,* a widely circulated paperback, shocked many of her readers.

In assaulting the traditional inhibitions of her countrymen, using terms that would have raised an indignant outcry ten years ago, she pondered the sexual mores of the Irish and found it depressing that "many Irish people do regard what should be making love as an animal desire to be ashamed of if not carried out with the express (!) intention of having children. It is indicative that so many Irish people feel only inclined to make love when they are alcoholically inebriated; as if the fact of being anaesthetized took away from the awareness of their distasteful behaviour. . . .

"More than any other factor in a marital relationship the sexual problem is probably the one most likely to drift (where it is a problem), and if allowed to develop as a problem, it is likely in the vast majority of cases that neither party will do anything towards solving the problem. This is the case in many marriages where sex is not a definite physical problem, but rather where love and tenderness and sensitivity play no part in the 'love-making.' One of the most frequent complaints I have heard from Irish wives was that their husbands were completely insensitive to them as lovers, and many husbands complained that Irish girls are frigid or not interested in the sexual side of marriage."

The concept of sex as sin, with the production of children as only a slightly mitigating factor, is being examined with scant sympathy. That the roots of this theological determination are deeply rooted in the history of the Catholic Church in Ireland only urges on the critics. "The Irish are lousy lovers," Desmond Leslie wrote in the English magazine *Scene,* "and if they are, it's not their fault. They have been castrated by their catechisms since the impressionable age. They have received such horrific drubbings on the sinfulness of sex, it's a wonder they can function at all."

The Irish will straighten themselves out sexually, he believes, only when they find the happy medium between the traditional repression of their instincts and the more permissive tendencies of Western Europe. He makes it clear, however, that he does not advocate turning Ireland into an island outpost of Venusberg. Instead, the Irish must turn back to the mystics of all religions who understood the "life force" and looked kindly upon a fusion of flesh and spirit.

"Permissive promiscuity will not find the way," he wrote, "for like repression it is death to love's poetry and majesty. Frightening us will not do it, for the taint may last throughout adult life, making couples afraid of the joyous abandonment love demands. Where then lies the answer? In wartime England when food was strictly rationed we all became obsessed with greed, and thought only of food. Came a return to plenty, no one worried much about eating and mealtimes returned to normal. The present hippy permissiveness reminds one of the days when food rationing ended and everyone ate themselves sick. But it was shortlived and we soon ceased to slobber at the sight of a juicy steak. Just as complete freedom from censorship in Scandinavia has practically put the pornographers out of business (except for tourists) if love could be shorn of its abuses, finding its proper level, half the crimes and neuroses would disappear." Leslie foresaw a more joyful, less sexually neurotic Ireland, not least of all because "a growing generation of young priests is alive to this need and less bookbound than their elders."

A more relaxed attitude toward sexual morality is already visible, particularly in the larger cities, according to Rosita Sweetman, who specializes in the subject of domestic relations. She wrote in the Irish newsmagazine *This Week*:

> Up to a decade ago there was a conspiracy of silence about sex in Ireland. Parents and educators pretended it didn't exist; children "found out" about it from friends or stolen books, and marriage on the whole was embarked on with the scantiest knowledge of the "facts of life." Through television, radio and communications, through tourism and travel, Ireland is now wide open to the cultures of America and Britain. The society we seem hell-bent on developing is one in which human communications become more difficult. Sexual mores, and sexual expression, are a basic form of human communication. How do we stand in this area? In contrast to the old idea of children marrying in accordance with their parents' wishes couples now marry whom they wish—as one wife said, "Marriage was the real pointer in my life which made my parents realize that I was not just their child but a person as well."

In the course of her researches, Miss Sweetman discovered that urban attitudes had relaxed sufficiently to make interracial marriage, largely between Irish girls and African students attending the universities in Dublin, not only possible but fairly accepted. She cited a couple named Roger, a Nigerian attending Trinity, and Valerie, an upper-middle-class girl from Belfast, who met when they joined a Maoist group. A few years ago that would have been an unthinkable conjunction, African student, respectable Irish girl, and Chinese Communism.

"We didn't start off by sleeping together," Roger casually remarked. "It was quite a long time before we got to this stage; we started living together after we'd known each other about a year." As Valerie continued the story, "A kind of crisis developed—I found out I was pregnant. We were in London at the time. When I told Roger I was pregnant he said he didn't want to get married. . . . Then my parents found out of course about the baby—they first of all didn't want me to marry Roger, that was a racial thing, then they felt I should get the baby adopted, but I decided that was out. I came back to Dublin determined to have the baby and thinking it was all over between Roger and me. While I was away he had been doing some thinking and decided he did want to get married." Her chief anxiety, she indicated, was that other girls were "after" Roger. "They feel there will be no complications attached and it's a kind of game to sleep with married men." Presumably she was speaking of girls in the radical semibohemian circles of Dublin, mostly students or camp followers at Trinity who plaster the hoardings with Maoist posters and station themselves behind tables stacked with pamphlets on College Green.

Probably a more typical couple were Jenny, a country girl, not unlike one of Edna O'Brien's much-beset heroines, and Bob, a middle-class Dubliner, who had married five years before over the violent objections of both their families. "I got married to Bob when I was twenty," Jenny recalled, "and this caused frightful rows at home." (Country people have a strong prejudice against what they call the jackeens of Dublin, viewing them as tricksters and guttersnipes, no matter what their background.) "During our engagement Bob's mother also caused tensions. She had bitter rows with him and was trying to maintain her control over him. This all eased after we got married, as I was surer of my position and could invite her out to *my* house, and so forth. . . . We never slept together before we were married. We eventually got our facts straight during our engagement, when we went up for a couple of talks with a Jesuit priest." Bob explained that in his circle premarital sex was taboo because "we all had hangovers from the age of moral restraint."

That age lasted for centuries. The credit for placing a chastity belt on the whole Irish nation, aside from pagans and Protestants, is generally bestowed on the heresy known as Jansenism, which has been defined in Scottish Catholic novelist Bruce Marshall's epigram as "the impression that God made an artistic mistake when He planned the mechanics of procreation."

There were earlier influences than Jansenism, however, to encourage the Irish Catholic view that intimate relations with a female were degrading, that in sexual congress the male was lowering himself to being coupled, literally, with a subhuman. St. Thomas Aquinas preached that a woman was only a "maimed male." St. Augustine of Hippo, who exerted so indelible an influence over theology for 1,500 years, handed down the dictum that even sex in marriage was barely tolerable in a Christian. To St. Augustine marriage was preferable only to fornication outside the law. Those who abjured matrimony, in fact, would reach his envisioned City of God much sooner than those who married. And there were other Fathers of the Church who preached that women, even as wives, were a constant threat to a Christian's rationality and virtue. The Celtic mind, in the darker recesses of its mysticism, welcomed such flagellation of the fleshlier urges.

Jansenism, the heretical infection of Dutch origin but carried to Ireland by French theologians, found a home among the Irish hierarchy. Under the pretext of returning the church to a purer and more primitive Catholicism, its followers insisted on the necessity of an almost inhuman rigidity in all moral and spiritual concerns, on denial of the orthodox Catholic doctrine of freedom of the will.

All this stemmed from the Lowlands theologian Cornelis Jansen, who was the Bishop of Ypres at his death in 1638. His most influential work, *Augustinus,* was published two years after he died and became a rallying point for all sorts of yearners after an illusion of a past purity. Jansen died in a state of grace, so far as the Vatican was concerned, but his teachings—or more particularly the way fanatics interpreted them—were proscribed by the Inquisition in 1641. The Jansen doctrine was stamped out in most of Europe, but ideas often arrive a little late in Ireland. It was implanted at Maynooth College, the premier seminary of the Irish church, shortly after it was founded in 1795, by French Jansenite theologians who had fled their country during the Revolution. Its absolutism, reflected most glaringly in the imprisonment of any and all sexual urges, greatly appealed to the Irish clergy and has never entirely lost favor. It was transmitted from Maynooth to the clergy at large and finally to the totality of laymen, a continuing challenge to that part of the Celtic spirit which demands more of itself than seems humanly possible or plausible. And a touch of that ancient fervor lingers on.

New Catechism, Question 256: "What are the chief dangers to chastity?"

Answer: "The chief dangers to chastity are idleness, intemperance, bad companions, improper dances, immodest dress, company keeping and indecent conversation, books, plays and pictures." (Company keeping in American terms means, roughly, going steady.)

To the mind of a child memorizing his catechism, it might seem that association with the opposite sex, all books and plays and films, by being bracketed with the other threats to chastity, would lead to a loss of virtue. Oliver St. John Gogarty, perhaps because he was a Protestant, once remarked that there must be some way to persuade his countrymen to love God without teaching them to hate women.

In the past decade, with Jansenism's influence diminishing amid the more liberal attitudes of the Irish hierarchy and the much greater liberalism of the younger clergy, many priests have come to realize that some practical way must be found to marry off their parishioners. Father Patrick B. Noonan, born on a County Limerick farm, in participating in the forum on the "vanishing Irish" admitted that changing the attitude of the Irish toward marriage was an educational problem. "They should be taught, not merely in the schools, but from the pulpit and through all the modern channels of information, that the normal age for marriage is before, not after, thirty."

The Catholic Standard now runs a sort of lonely-hearts column, in which such appeals as the following appear: "Bachelor, late forties, Government position, large capital and private business interests, good appearance, wishes to meet refined affectionate business, professional lady or farmer's daughter. . . . Lady with good capital seeks introduction to bachelor 45-50, business gentleman with capital or business of own. . . . Would educated, cheerful, devout Catholic man (Northern Ireland or Donegal) correspond with lady Civil Servant, 43? . . . I am 29, nondrinker and genuine person, would like to hear from nice Pioneer girl 25-30 in Kerry or Cork. . . ." Obviously the sexual, even the romantic element is missing from most of these appeals. They remind one of the story of a County Meath bridegroom who woke up the morning after the wedding, stared in bewilderment at the face on the adjoining pillow, and demanded, "Miss Ryan, whatever are *you* doing here?"

A number of rural priests have taken up the challenge of thawing out the reluctance of the Irish to march up the aisle together. In Knock, County Mayo, Father Michael Keane operates what he calls an Introduction Bureau to which 3,000 men and women have applied in the last three years for the opportunity to meet prospective wives or husbands. Of that number 150 marriages have resulted, statistical confirmation of the wariness of both sexes. According to Father Keane, "the girls are reluctant to marry a farmer earning less than fifteen hundred pounds a year when they can go to Dublin and make almost twice that. The men aren't looking for romance or glamor, but for someone to provide them with children."

Another priest who labors in the marriage-promotion field is Father Reynolds, who enrolls bachelors and spinsters from all over Ireland who have signified their wish to find a husband or wife. He believes that simple lack of opportunity has prevented many Irishmen from marrying and deplores the cartoon figure of the marriage-dodging bachelor drawn with a certain fond malice by academic or journalistic observers, as well as the tendency to blame the clergy for freezing the sexual impulse.

"Many small farmers," he says, "simply never get to meet a woman aside from those on the neighboring farms. They are tied to their bits of land, since most of them raise cows that have to be milked morning and night. They go to the creamery with their milk later in the morning, perhaps once a week they travel to the nearest village or town to buy their supplies, and to church on Sunday, and that's all they see of the outside world." Father Reynolds sorts through the applications he receives from all over the island, arranges introductions between his applicants, and then steps aside to let nature take its course. During the past several years, as a new-style matchmaker, he has brought about hundreds of marriages which, without his practical approach to the mating game, would probably never have taken place.

In the cities, Dublin especially now, but with the rest of the country predictably following her lead, love and marriage, Irish style, are undergoing rapid changes. With increasing vehemence the Irishwoman is insisting on her rights with the encouragement of television, women's magazines, and the other forms of propaganda which reach her. A few years ago she was informed by *Nova,* the English woman's magazine, that Irishwomen could be considered the "last victim of slavery in Western Europe."

Women's magazines are available in every supermarket and other shops throughout Ireland, and their rapid growth in readership testifies to the expanding influence of the ideas they propagate—not merely recipes and household hints, but the necessity of standing up for their rights as human beings. As much as anything else, they are changing the pattern of Irish courtship and marriage. A prominent feature of most such magazines is the column devoted to marriage counseling, which is offered with a frankness that dismays older women.

"I knew I had to submit myself often," a thirty-seven-year-old woman named Nellie, who had recently married a fifty-two-year-old farmer, wrote, "but I did not think it would be so often. . . . I think often of doing away with myself."

The blunt comment of the magazine's marriage counselor was:

> The trouble is that Nellie has been trained from childhood, more by implication than actual word, to regard anything concerning the difference between men and women and the mystery of procreation as something sinful and obscene. . . . The intimate side of Nellie's marriage (and there have been quite a few Nellies in my postbag) is a crude, unsavoury and bewildering failure. Her husband is one of the thousands of inexperienced, middle-aged, lonely countrymen, who have only a rudimentary knowledge of the facts of life and with their natural capacity for love and tenderness totally underdeveloped. . . . When Nellie has learned to live in marital harmony, she will be able to train her husband to gentleness. The only danger is that many ignorant men regard any response in a woman as evidence that she is promiscuous and he will be watching her for signs that she is being unfaithful.

The priggishness of Irish husbands, from the viewpoint of emancipated women, is a continuing burden on their wives. Recently Monica McEnroy, the wife of a County Wicklow doctor and a frequent contributor to Irish periodicals, reported in *Women's Way* that she knew a girl who was expecting her first child. "The neighbors," her husband nervously remarked, "will be guessing when they see you going to early Mass." "Why should we be going to early Mass?" the young wife asked. "We always go to the twelve o'clock." "Surely," he retorted, "you're not going to the twelve o'clock Mass, pregnant!" Mrs. McEnroy added that from that moment the girl "knew her marriage was finished. He never knew, of course, never realized the damage he had done, and she never told him. A permanent adolescent—that's what he was."

Perhaps the day of the bachelor boy is done, and that of the bachelor-husband who drops in on his wife and children in the manner of an honored guest is going fast. Yet it is too soon to dismiss the marriage-shy Irish male as being outmoded as the Druids. In his own way he has been an amazingly effective practitioner of birth control, and if the overcrowding of this planet continues at its present rate he is likely to be looked upon as a visionary and a demographic hero.

One can easily get the impression from sociological treatises and some of the women's magazines that Ireland is dominated by a cult of masculinity, that the Irishwoman is a poor spiritless downtrodden creature who has to be content with following her husband at a discreet three paces to the rear. It is true that Irishwomen do not ordinarily raise their voices to command, nor do they exercise their influence publicly. One can see them cringing inwardly when they hear an American tourist ordering her husband around like an unpaid lackey. And one can also see them smile indulgently when an Englishwoman in a West Cork pub asks the proprietor whether he thinks the women's liberation movement will ever gain momentum in Ireland and he replies with a roaring "Never!"

Although they speak gently and are the only demure women left in the Western world, their strength of purpose is the underpinning of Irish society. Their femininity is the most ineffable this side of Suez, and in youth or age they have more than their share of charm, beauty, and fascination. They may have their undeserved troubles in snaring and domesticating the elusive Irish male, but they are not addled by faddish concerns over the "search for identity" or the "quest for a role." Their time-tested role is to keep "himself" on a loose rein and conserve their energies for the molding and guidance of their sons.

Ireland itself is symbolized by a woman, Cathleen ni Houlihan, and its history is filled with earthy, passionate, and dominant females like Queen Maeve of Connaught, the Galway pirate queen Grace O'Malley, and the numerous heroines of the Irish Revolution. In Celtic mythology their vibrant passions might be compared with the curious conduct of the ancient hero Cuchullain, whose wild fury in combat could be stilled immediately if the enemy sent forward a naked woman, upon which Cuchullain would cover his stricken eyes. As one commentator on the ancient legends has remarked, "The male is a characterless, wailing and complaining figure, acting not from the heat of the blood but in conformity with a destiny laid upon him by spells and oracles." The women, however, were figures of splendid wrath and active dispositions.

Nor is it any dramatic fallacy that Synge's *Playboy of the Western World* is dominated by the earthy magnificence of Pegeen Mike or that Juno of O'Casey's *Juno and the Paycock* dwarfs such male characters as the bellicose but nimbly prudent Fluther. O'Casey's mother, as he characterizes her in *Drums Under the Window* and other volumes of his serial autobiography, was one of those fighting Irishwomen who hold the domestic fabric together by force of character. Arland Ussher believes that a "sort of polarization" between the sexes occurred and made Ireland "a country of Junos but not, certainly, of Jupiters." Possibly it was the psychological consequence of having been conquered so many times; conquest breaks men but only strengthens women.

If Irishwomen needed an outside figure to rally around, there was the swashbuckling O'Malley, uncrowned queen of the Galway coast, whose spectacular career is largely recounted in the state papers of Queen Elizabeth I, who was first her enemy and then her ally. "A most famous feminine sea-captain," one of Elizabeth's viceroys called her; "a nurse of all rebellions in Connaught," reported a less admiring English administrator.

Grace O'Malley was described as a tall, swarthy, black-haired, dark-eyed woman born in County Mayo around 1530. She was married first to Donal O'Flaherty, who was killed in a sea battle, and then to Richard Burke, formerly De Burgos, a member of the powerful Anglo-Norman family. Her career as an outlaw began modestly enough when as the fourteen-year-old bride of O'Flaherty she assisted in his smuggling operations. Subsequently she turned to piracy and captained her own raiding vessels—galleys with thirty men at the oars and another fifty or more warriors for the boarding party—to prey on Spanish and English shipping. She made her headquarters in Clare Island, in Clew Bay, just off the English garrison town of Westport. Later as the profits from her forays accumulated, she established a sort of country retreat in an island castle in Lough Corrib, the ruins of which are visible on the road between Cong and Headford in County Galway.

She was feminine enough to fly a burgee with a white sea horse rather than the customary skull and crossbones, but she displayed a masculine expertise in handling a cutlass or blunderbuss when her boarding parties stormed over the side of a Spanish galleon or an English merchant vessel. Once she was confined to her cabin awaiting childbirth on a far-ranging cruise interrupted by the appearance of Turkish corsairs. Grace clambered out of bed, came out on deck with a blunderbuss in each hand and dispatched two of the Turkish intruders, supervised mopping-up operations, and then went back to bed to give birth to the future Viscount Mayo.

The O'Malley tamed down a bit after her second marriage, for which the more vehement Irish patriots and any contemporary feminists might have faulted her. Richard Burke evidently exerted considerable influence over her and persuaded her that her countrymen would be better off cooperating with rather than rebelling against their English overlords. In 1576, it is recorded, she offered her three galleys and her armed followers to the service of Queen Elizabeth.

Thereafter the Galway pirate queen and the heiress to the power of the Tudors were allies. It wasn't until 1593, however, that Grace accepted one of Elizabeth's invitations to visit the court in London. The interview took place in Hampton Court Palace. When she made her appearance in the throne room, she was announced as Grace O'Malley, not Madame Burke, a contemporary historian noting that "it is customary among the Irish women to retain their maiden name after marriage." Furthermore, Grace treated Elizabeth with a rough camaraderie, which first surprised, then amused the English queen.

There is no surviving transcript of the confrontation between the dark lady of piracy and the red-haired Saxon queen, but the Reverend Caesar Ottway reconstructed that moment of high comedy from documents in the Dublin archives. First Elizabeth, noting Grace's enthusiastic use of snuff and the tremendous sneezes it caused, presented her Irish ally with a richly embroidered handkerchief which Grace took "indifferently, used loudly and cast away carelessly, and when asked by Sir Walter Raleigh why she had treated the gift of Her Majesty in such a way, the answer was of that coarseness which ought not to be heard by ears polite."

Trying to please her difficult guest, Elizabeth ordered that one of her lapdogs be presented to Grace, who ungraciously handed it back, saying, "It's little the likes of me would be doing with such a thing. It is fit only for idlers such as you." Elizabeth protested that she was kept busy indeed ruling her kingdom. "Maybe so," Grace retorted, "but as far as I can see of your ways, there's many a poor creature in Mayo, who has only the care of a barley field, as has more industry about them than you seem to have."

With equal asperity Grace refused the offer of a title. "Aren't we both equals?" she demanded. "If there be any good in the thing I may as well make you a countess as you me." She agreed that her son might be ennobled as Viscount Mayo, first of the Earls of Mayo, but wanted nothing for herself, whether a lapdog or a coronet. On her way back to Galway she demonstrated that presentation at the English court had not gentled her disposition. When her ship landed at Howth outside Dublin, she requested food and lodging at Howth Castle but was turned away at the gate. Before continuing her journey to Galway, she kidnapped the son of the master of Howth and would not return him until the father promised that Howth Castle would always be open to wayfarers, in the Irish tradition. She lived out her remaining seven years as a snappish old lady who crusaded for liberalization of the laws affecting women's property rights.

There were enough similar examples, outside the annals of piracy, to bolster and sustain the quiet self-assurance of Irish womanhood. If you asked most Irishwomen outside the Dublin intellectual orbit whether they yearned for liberation, they would probably reply—it being an Irish habit to answer a question with a question—"Liberated from what?"

No doubt Tanis O'Callaghan, writing in the Dublin *Evening Press,* was speaking for the majority when she commented on current demonstrations of the American women's liberation movement, declaring that she and her countrywomen wanted no part of sexual separatism:

> Surely the true liberation of all females would be the removal by society of all obstacles which hinder any woman from attaining her full role of womanhood. What the Women's Liberation women seem to want is the removal of all obstacles which hinder a woman from fulfilling the role of a man. . . . Perhaps Irish women, far from having their heads in the sand and failing to recognize the new freedom their American sisters would like them to wrestle for, have decided wisely to dismiss the whole Movement as the grumblings of a bunch of cranks. And perhaps this is because the majority of Irish women are in fact truly liberated and far too busy enjoying their freedom in being real women—utilizing in the full sense their feminine abilities as wives and moulders of the new generation.

Women's rights in Ireland, in fact, were much more expansive under the old Celtic laws before the English legal system drastically reduced the female status, an indication that intrinsic sexual equality is deeply embedded in the Irish ethos. Foreign invaders may have slaughtered the menfolk and placed the survivors in captivity, but they also ended what must have been one of the historic heydays of feminine independence. Under the Brehon laws of the eighth and ninth centuries, the Irish female possessed rights which even a modern feminist might hesitate to demand.

The Brehon laws provided that a woman could get a divorce if she considered her husband sexually unsatisfactory, if he did not promptly make her pregnant, if he embarrassed her in front of visitors, if he struck or abused her physically or verbally, or if he was unfaithful.

Further, she was enabled to divorce her husband if he did not provide sufficient food and drink, especially when her relatives came calling, if he got too fat or contracted some disfiguring disease, if he went away to war and came back with disabling wounds (an echo here of "Johnny, I Hardly Knew Ye"), or if he became ill and took too long to recover.

In many cases the woman could opt for what amounted to a conditional divorce, allowing her the privilege of changing her mind. She could leave her husband, for instance, during lean times when there weren't enough ox joints and mead to keep his in-laws well stuffed and then return to his bed and board when times were better. Alimony, too, was provided the disaffected wife under the Brehon laws. When she was divorced, she was entitled not only to repayment of her dowry but to compensation for her services and punitory damages as well.

All this signifies not merely that Celtic womanhood was willful but that the menfolk, before they were demoralized by successive conquests, were self-confident enough to allow women such a privileged position.

The concept that Irishwomen may be the real rulers has been circulating for at least 300 years, long before the first English and American suffragettes chained themselves to lampposts and kicked constabulary shins. It was rather playfully suggested by a poetic parish priest, Father Domhnall O Colmain, of Glounthaune, who apparently decided that any of his countrywomen over the age of thirty were more honorable, intelligent, and capable than those of the opposite sex. In his poem "The Parliament of Women," written about 1670, he envisioned a women's rights convocation atop Carragain Mor, near Glanmire. Equally playfully, it must be presumed, he dedicated the work to the youngest son of Sir James Cotter, the local landlord, who would be hanged (as Father O Colmain foresaw), in Broad Lane, Cork City, when he could no longer hold back the swift-running tide of feminism.

The all-female Parliament would legislate against lust, envy, backbiting, drunkenness, and laziness, which were regarded as the chief masculine failings. From its opening session, as Father O Colmain imagined it, the ladies would formulate plans for obtaining control of the national life, confident they would be more competent at the task than men. Among the laws they would pass would be a reversal of the prevalent practice whereby sons would be raised by their fathers while the daughters would be raised by their mothers. Girls were to be admitted to higher education and encouraged to enter medicine, the law, and the clergy. Men were to be permitted to administer local affairs for another ten years until women had been sufficiently educated to take over.

"The Parliament of Women" did not become a historic fact, but it was widely read and evidently made some sort of impact. The Limerick-born Lola Montez helped rearrange the affairs of Bavaria in collaboration with its addled monarch, but Ireland itself wasn't ready for the Montez touch. Not much later, however, the Countess Markievicz ("a spluttering Catherine-wheel of irresponsibility," as Sean O'Casey called her) and Maud Gonne MacBride were in the forefront of the Irish revolutionaries. During the civil war the Cumann na mBan, the women's auxiliary of the Sinn Fein, came down solidly on the side of De Valera, Brugha, and others who favored a continuation of the struggle. Women members of the first Dail—including Countess Markievicz; Maud Gonne MacBride; Mary MacSwiney, the sister of the late Lord Mayor Terence MacSwiney of Cork, who had fasted to death in a British prison; Mrs. Kathleen Clarke, the widow of Tom Clarke; and the widow of Lord Mayor Michael O'Callaghan of Limerick, who was murdered by the Black and Tans—were among the stanchest of antitreaty partisans.

During the fight against the British, Irishwomen had served as active auxiliaries either as members of the Cumann na mBan or on their own hook. They participated in protest marches, tended the wounded, sheltered the fugitives, distributed literature from the underground presses, and made life hell in the way women know best for the British forces. Perhaps the most stirring tribute to their unsung heroines was paid by Michael Collins in a speech in Cork City shortly before his death:

> No one knows better than I what the women have done during the past two or three years, and it was not only the Cumann na mBan but the ordinary unorganized women of Ireland. Everywhere we went throughout Ireland we were treated well by the women. The women endured more during those years than some people who talk big words today.
>
> I know old women who lay awake at night in houses where I and others slept during the conflict. . . . The women who sheltered the real fighting men know what the fighting men think of them. I don't go in for displaying my feelings in a cheap way, but any one of us who went through the conflict knows that the women had to face things which we had not to face. We were armed and had that advantage when the enemy came. But the women were subjected to all sorts of indignities, and they had not the protection we had. Few appreciate what Ireland owes to the women who stood their ground during the past few years, and no thanks that anyone can bestow upon them will be too great.

Two of the selfless women Collins had in mind when he delivered that tribute were Nora and Sheila Wallace, who opened a small shop in Cork City around 1910 which sold newspapers, books, and magazines, especially those dealing with Irish nationalism. The shop kept by the spinster sisters subsequently became a message center for the Irish Volunteers and later the IRA. Both sisters, during the struggle against the British occupation from 1916 to 1922, not only used their place as a drop for rebel communications but served as IRA intelligence officers. The strain on their health and nerves was so severe that Sheila Wallace died soon after the struggle ended, and Nora had to spend a long time in Switzerland recuperating. The IRA displayed its esteem for their services when its members carried Sheila Wallace's coffin all the way from SS. Peter and Paul's Church to St. Finbarr's Cemetery on their shoulders.

The torch of dissidence, the tradition of female activism have passed to Bernadette Devlin, the five-foot fury of the barricades in Northern Ireland, member of the British House of Commons at twenty-two, imprisoned a year later, and more famous than any member of Prime Minister Lynch's Cabinet. With a paving block in one small hand, Bernadette has summoned up memories of Queen Maeve and Grace O'Malley and put all the bachelor boys to shame.

8.

The Shadow Army

My name is Brendan Behan. I came over here to fight for the Irish Workers and Small Farmers Republic, for a full and free life, for my countrymen, North and South, and for the removal of the baneful influence of British Imperialism from Irish affairs. God save Ireland.

—His statement on being arrested in England as an IRA operative

☘ The Irish Republican Army, not to be confused with the Army of the Irish Republic, is the world's oldest paramilitary organization. Its history is tightly interwoven with the nation's, yet for long periods it is belled as a moral and political leper; its leaders proclaim themselves progressives and visionaries, yet their cause is linked to a day in the distant past when Irish representatives decided not to continue the fight against Britain and hold out for the inclusion of Ulster's six counties in the Irish Republic. For more than half a century, it has endured as Ireland's secret army. It has survived denunciation by the Irish government, excommunication of its members by the Irish Catholic Church, periodic manhunts by Irish police and British constabularies, one bitter civil war, and a thousand skirmishes, raids, and ambushes. It has spent most of its harried existence underground, avoiding pitched battles, surfacing and striking only when its principal objective comes in sight: the liberation of Ulster and the establishment of a workers' republic over all the island.

The IRA was the graduate school of President De Valera,

former Prime Minister Sean Lemass, and many of the nation's leaders, now the established and antirevolutionary, who condemn it as subversive, outmoded, unneeded, and a menace to internal security. Under the Offenses Against the State Act, passed during the emergency of 1939, it is technically illegal even to mention the IRA in print, on the radio, or on television.* Illegal, kept under constant surveillance, publicized and possibly overpublicized as the most daring and expert of the world's underground armies, headlined recently as the motive force behind the civil rights movement in Belfast, the IRA is anything but senile for all its venerable age.

Although it may have been a prototype, it resembles only slightly the underground armies elsewhere. It claims sufficient knowledge of gun smuggling, plastic explosives, organized sniping, sabotage and infiltration, and all the other techniques of violence. Some of its men are "on the run," as in the old days. Its operatives still move down alleyways on missions of terror and death, supposedly, and many also attend mass regularly and keep in touch with their families. The IRA obviously has its own traditions, going back to the Easter Rising and before that to the Fenians and Wolfe Tone's United Irishmen, and no need to adapt to the modern revolutionary life-style. Outwardly at least the IRA is as homespun, and sturdily Irish, as a bolt of Donegal tweed.

In the Irish style, it is both visible and invisible; secret, yet unsecret enough for its chief of staff to pose in his office for an English newspaper photographer (*The Observer,* April 12, 1970). It is not at all difficult to get in touch with the IRA; all you need are a few coppers and a phone book. The Dublin telephone number is 4-10-45, which is the listing for the *United Irishman,* its monthly mouthpiece.

If you want to reach Cathal Goulding, the present chief of staff of the IRA, you only have to look him up in the Dublin section of the phone book, in which he is listed, along with his daylight occupation: house painter.

Homely Irish, unmilitary, and drab as some missionary society struggling for a half-forgotten cause are the headquarters of

* And yet the title of the latest book by Tim Pat Coogan, the editor of the *Irish Press,* operated by the De Valera family, is of all things *The IRA.*

the IRA, which would disillusion anyone expecting it to be crammed with radio transmitters and crawling with mysterious characters. IRA headquarters is in a run-down four-story brick building at 30 Gardiner Place. On the ground floor are the offices of the *United Irishman* and its editor Seamus O Tuathail. On the second floor are the headquarters of the Sinn Fein, the political arm of the republican movement. Above that are two floors marked off as "private" and supposedly containing the nerve center of the IRA directorate.

At ten o'clock one morning I found the building deserted, but unlocked and unguarded. Anyone with a screwdriver could have entered any of the offices. There was a mop standing in an open sink on the staircase, but no more lethal weapons in evidence. There was a wanted poster tacked to the bulletin board which sparked momentary interest but it turned out to be an example of Irish codding:

WANTED
Peter Berry, Secretary,
Department of Justice,
for collaboration—
the Beria of our time.*

Waiting for a few revolutionaries to show up, I took shelter in a pub down the street, where a Dubliner told me, "Out of Ireland's three million we have five hundred thousand clergymen, several hundred thousand IRA men, and the rest are all politi-

* Peter Berry is the permanent civil servant in charge of operating the department, and therefore director, of the Special Branch, which has responsibility for internal security. A somewhat shadowy figure, he is described as a dedicated and dogmatic opponent of any institution which attempts to set itself up against the state.

The American writer Jimmy Breslin, who recently went over to Ireland with his family to do research for a novel, departed from Ireland in a flurry of headlines after a run-in with the Special Branch. He came under suspicion, as he tells it, for associating publicly with Eamonn McCann, the Catholic civil rights leader in the North, who happened to be in Dublin. "He is considered dangerous by the secret police in Northern Ireland," Breslin explained. "Therefore, the secret police in Dublin feel the same way about him." Breslin quit Ireland in well-publicized disgust after a man from the Special Branch visited his house at 11 P.M., while Breslin and his wife were out, and demanded to know whether the Breslins were harboring a suspect in the shooting of two U.S. servicemen on the Dublin docks.

cians." This was a pardonable exaggeration, at least in respect to the IRA.

The current issue of the *United Irishman* contained little that could be considered inflammatory; the situation in Belfast had quieted down in recent months. Late in 1969, however, the readers of the *United Irishman* were invited to contribute to "a dynamite fund to help Irishmen fighting behind the barricaded areas in the North" and were reminded of the statement of the Fenian leader O'Donovan Rossa that he would use dynamite or hellfire to drive the English out of Ireland.

At the moment the *United Irishman* was campaigning vigorously against the take-over of Irish companies by foreign conglomerates, largely British, and warning that "the Irish people would lose control of the economy and so of their destinies. . . . The headlong rush of Irish business interests into the ruin of the Common Market shows the bankruptcy of their position as stooges of foreign capitalists." The *United Irishman* also played up its "fish-in" campaign against the owners of fishing rights on Irish lakes and rivers. There had just been a successful operation mounted on Inver Bay, one of the richest salmon estuaries. Anyone who wanted to fish in Inver Bay, as in most cases where such privileges are controlled by the owner of the land bordering the water, had to obtain the permission of Lord Adair, an absentee landlord. Obviously the *United Irishman* had a point in claiming that the Ascendancy and its privileges had not been entirely eliminated a half century before, with Irish industry being taken over by the English (in the boardroom rather than on the battlefield) and Irish salmon being under English bounty.

Closer acquaintance with the premises at 30 Gardiner Place demonstrated that the joint headquarters of the *United Irishman*, Sinn Fein, and IRA are often lively and well populated enough. Hatless, tieless, with rumpled hair and an easygoing manner, Cathal Goulding strolls into the building unattended by a bodyguard or the staff of which he is chief. He must be the world's least pretentious and unassuming revolutionary. Late in the morning the offices fill up, mostly with young people, but others not so young, including Tomas MacGiolla, the bespectacled president of the Sinn Fein, one of whose predecessors was

Eamon De Valera, President of the Irish Republic, who looks and acts in the same schoolmasterly manner.

Not on the scene at the moment was a young woman named Mairin de Burca, who is secretary of the Sinn Fein. It was later revealed, when she failed to make a court appearance to answer police charges against her in connection with a demonstration in defense of squatters on Pembroke Road that turned violent, that Miss de Burca was conferring in Jordan with leaders of Al Fatah and other Palestine guerrilla leaders. When she finally made her court appearance, it was disclosed also that the Sinn Fein-IRA are reaching out into the Third World and becoming less parochial. They are demonstrating their sympathy for the Arab cause and for Marxist revolutionaries elsewhere, though some older members insist on recalling that Sinn Fein means "Ourselves Alone" and object to foreign ideological ties of any kind. A number of younger members, however, are reportedly associated with the Irish-Arab Friendship Society founded by Sean Ryan, a prosperous Dublin businessman who once was interned for IRA activities. The society was formed just after the Six-Day War to counter the organization of the Irish-Israel Friendship League. Many of its members are wealthy businessmen and Arab professional men who were educated in Ireland and chose to stay there. What has an Irish revolutionary movement to do with the Arab-Israeli struggle? According to John Feeney (*This Week*, September 24, 1970), "The left wingers of Sinn Fein have developed an ideology which claims Ireland is similar in most respects to a Third World country. They believe that it must be liberated from imperialist control before it can be made socialist under the dictatorship of the proletariat. Sinn Fein blends in Irish xenophobia and prejudice with anti-imperialism by agitating on selective issues. Ground rent, fishing rights, housing and anti-large estates agitation appeal, at one and the same time, to justified dislike of economic exploitation and to national ('anti-imperialist') xenophobia."

For all its unexceptional surface, its atmosphere of student protest rather than revolutionary professionalism, the narrow brick building at 30 Gardiner Place is kept under constant surveillance by officers of the Special Branch, which assumes many of the functions of the FBI in the United States, Scotland Yard in Britain, and the Sûreté in France. The present headquarters, however, has never been raided by the Special Branch. Once it was burglarized; the loot was recovered and promptly returned by the police when they arrested the culprits.

Generally, a few doors down from the building, a black sedan occupied by two detectives of the Special Branch is stationed to keep an eye on who goes in and out of 30 Gardiner Place. The watchful paternal eye of the government does not greatly discomfit the people who work in the offices. Sometimes they make a sport out of throwing the watchdogs off balance. One day the game of "shooing the Branchmen" took this form: Half a dozen men from the *United Irishmen* and Sinn Fein offices, along with a girl secretary, picked up placards and sauntered out as though heading on a picketing mission. One of the signs read: BRITISH IMPERIALISTS GET OUT. They walked down the block to where a Volkswagen was parked at the curb. By then the two Special Branch men had got out of their car and were following. Instead of getting into the Volkswagen, their quarry marched down the street to the end of the block, then up the other side, with the Branchmen in dogged pursuit. The detectives suddenly realized that they'd been had, climbed back into their car, and drove off to some farewell jeering by the young revolutionaries. A short time later, apparently in reference to this contrived incident, the Sinn Fein picketed Dublin Castle, the Special Branch headquarters, with signs protesting "harassment," though if anybody had been harassed, it was the Special Branch men.

Dublin Castle . . . an ironic echo from the time of the rising against the British. History seems to travel a circular course in Ireland. Once it had been the citadel of British authority; its lower courtyard had rumbled under the treads of Whippet tanks and armored cars. From its stone walls, also, had been directed the counterterror campaign against the IRA when Michael Collins was running it. Still later it had served as headquarters of the Treaty State forces during the civil war in which the IRA was again hunted down. IRA men have been tortured and killed there, and the wonder of it is that those who regard Dublin Castle as an eternal symbol of repression, with their talent for dynamiting whatever they find detestable, haven't blown it up.

* * *

The long struggle for Irish independence, of which the IRA was the most spectacular offshoot, was marked by psychological factors of which the Irish eventually took full advantage. They had gotten to know the English very well, and with the native genius for sorting out human strengths and frailties they divined that British power could be turned against itself. They had early realized that there were two sides to the British character, mirror images of each other, that of the hard-nosed conqueror and that of the tender-minded libertarian, the apostle of fair play, whose sensibilities could be outraged and manipulated. The Irish turned their national defeat into a moral victory. Eventually the British found the moral superiority of the Irish so intolerable that they gradually relaxed their hold on Ireland, and British liberal-humanitarianism became the fulcrum on which British power was overturned.

There was of course plenty for the British to feel guilty about. By the Statutes of Kilkenny they had reduced the Irish to pariahs in their own land, designed as they were to keep the Anglo-Normans from amalgamating with the natives; later the Penal Laws, by ensuring and strengthening the hold of the Protestant proprietors over their stolen land, virtually cast the Irish into serfdom.

The Irishman was no longer a farmer or a freeman, nor was he a member of what the English called the yeomanry, a sturdy and independent spirit capable of establishing English-style democracy and fighting for popular liberty. He was turned into a peasant, a forelock-tugging dependent of the squireen and landlord, with many of the passive but few of the active virtues. The tenant state of mind does not encourage any sort of forward looking. It was a wonder that even a small minority of the Irish could be roused from their apathy to join in the sporadic revolts. Sparks flew across the water from the French and American revolutions and touched off a young Dublin barrister, Wolfe Tone, who organized the United Irishmen in the 1790's to detach Ireland from the British Empire. He obtained the support of the French in two abortive risings, one in 1795, when the French admirals refused to land their troops during a storm in Bantry Bay, the second three years later, when the French succeeded in landing about a thousand troops in Mayo. Tone, a Protestant, was captured and sentenced to the gallows. Gallantly witty to the end, he had joked about the British practice of hanging and disemboweling traitors, quipping, "A fig for the disemboweling if they hang me first," but cheated the hangman by committing suicide.

Little more than five years later Robert Emmet and a small band recklessly tried to take over Dublin Castle. He was hanged in the street after addressing future generations of the Irish from the gallows: "When my country takes her place among the nations of the earth, then and not till then, let my epitaph be written."

By then the Act of Union, eliminating the Irish Parliament, providing for the 100 Irish MP's in the British House of Commons, had been passed. It reduced Dublin from its status of a capital city to the provincial rank of a Leeds or Edinburgh, and it made Ireland a part of the English homeland, the British Isles henceforth. She was now "John Bull's other island," part of the United Kingdom of Great Britain and Ireland.

Daniel O'Connell, a County Kerry lawyer elected to Parliament in 1828, tried to rouse his countrymen from their apathy. He fought against the Act of Union and for Catholic emancipation, but in the bitterness of his struggle for Home Rule he groaned that "nobody would ever believe the species of *animals* with whom I had to carry on my warfare against the common enemy." Such outcries would often be echoed by Irish militants. The sullen passivity of the Irish mass could be as distressing to its leaders as to the British.

Political and religious freedom became minor issues during the several years before O'Connell's death in 1847. The potato famine had struck Ireland just at the time its potato-fed population was expanding on a geometric scale. In the early 1840's the Irish population had risen to more than 8,000,000, or almost twice the present one, a large proportion of them living on tiny patches of land.

The definitive horror of the famine has been recounted in Cecil Woodham-Smith's unsparing *The Great Hunger*. Statistics can provide only a vague outline: more than 1,000,000 dead of starvation and disease from 1846 to 1851, another 1,000,000 migrated (mostly to America) after ghastly hardships on the corpse-littered roads to the sea and on the hell ships which transported them. What happened after the potato blight appeared in 1845-46, leaving the fields a reeking mass of garbage, has been called genocide. It was the result, if not the aim, of British government policy, which prevented the Irish from developing a healthy and diversified agriculture and also industrialized the Protestant counties of Ulster while preventing the industrialization of southern Catholic Ireland.

Many of the famine victims would not have escaped if the Irish already in America had not sent money for their passage. Others were kept alive by remittances from their American relatives, thus bringing to folklore the "American letter" as a synonym for "manna from heaven." The pitifully inadequate efforts of the British government, then the richest and most powerful on earth, to alleviate the suffering in Ireland did little more to endear Crown and Parliament to the Irish than the fact that British shipping interests, using what one New York newspaper called "damned plague ships and swimming coffins" in the North Atlantic crossing, made a handsome profit off transporting the luckier famine victims.

Perhaps the saddest and bitterest commentary on the Irish famine was not that the English democracy allowed it to happen, for all the robust humanity resident in the individual Englishman, but that the Irish expected nothing more from their alleged protectors in Whitehall and Westminster.

Instead of crushing all hope and resistance out of the Irish, the famine quickened realization that their situation was intolerable, and equally important, it made the Irish who had fled their homeland all the more determined to bring about Home Rule. The Irish in America soon became a crucial factor, as a British Home Secretary noted. Formerly the British had had to contend with rebellions in Ireland, he explained, but "Now there is an Irish nation in the United States, equally hostile, with plenty of money, absolutely beyond our reach."

There was also a half-American Protestant Irishman sworn to destroy the "rack rent" system and the power of the Anglo-Irish landlords. Charles Stewart Parnell, a wealthy landowner himself, was the new Jeremiah, the son of Sir John Parnell and of an American mother, whose grandfather commanded the *Constitu-*

tion during the War of 1812. He saw that land was the key to the Irish dilemma and with John Devoy and Michael Davitt organized the Land League. The idea was to apply the nutcracker to the Anglo-Irish overlords, through a combination of financial and political pressure. Irish-Americans sent more than $1,000,000 to finance the Land League's activities and got good value for their money. Landlords and their agents—many of the former being absentees—were given the Captain Boycott treatment if they refused to reduce rents or if they evicted tenants for nonpayment of rent. Open resistance followed, with armed bands called Moonlighters roving the countryside and striking at the more oppressive landlords. All this was combined with a parliamentary campaign by Parnell which resulted in the passage of the Land Acts, a form of rent control, with the courts empowered to fix rents and the tenants guaranteed tenure as long as they paid the lawful rents.

Now hope revived among the Irish that they might eventually reclaim their land, be freed of their bondage to those tiny fields, and be able to obtain enough land to support their families. The intensity of the Irish feeling about those rocky slopes from which they wrenched a subsistence of sorts was conveyed by Michael O'Suilleabhain in his memoir of a violent life in the mountains of County Cork, *Where Mountainy Men Have Sown*. "What of the people who made the little fields?" he wrote. "Driven long ago from the fertile inland by successive plantations, they took root among the rocks. It is significant they all bear old Irish names. You will rarely find a [British] Planter's name among them. If you do you will find that it is located on a spot worth occupying. It is hard to visualize how any human being, no matter how strong and courageous, survived the winters before the first little field was made. One could build a house of some sort in a short time, but to make a field in the wilderness takes time and energy."

With Parnell leading the Irish contingent in the House of Commons, all that seemed to be changing. Home Rule for Ireland, in the 1880's, became the paramount political issue in Great Britain. William E. Gladstone, as intermittent Prime Minister and leader of the Liberal Party, supported Parnell's Home Rule plan in return for the backing of the Irish members of the

House of Commons. In 1892 he succeeded in pushing a Home Rule bill through the Commons, but it was defeated in the House of Lords.

Two years before that, however, the cause had lost its most brilliant and forceful leader. Parnell was named corespondent in a divorce suit brought by one of his followers, Captain William O'Shea. Parnell not only refused to deny the charges but married Kitty O'Shea after the divorce. Victorian England was outraged, and Gladstone demanded Parnell's resignation. To their shame, but understandably enough in the light of the Irish moral code, the Irish also abandoned Parnell, and his career lay in ruins. Home Rule was to wait a long time for its revival.

Meanwhile, there were increasing numbers of Irish who became convinced that Ireland would detach itself from the United Kingdom only through violent action, not political procedure. Various forces were working, though not combining, toward that objective. When Irish passions are engaged, they tend through their volatility to fragment the common effort instead of welding it for greater strength of purpose, the opposite of the Teutonic-type of thrust for power; this makes the Irish more endearing and picturesque but somewhat less effective.

Between 1890 and the Easter Rising of 1916 at least fifteen different revolutionary organizations were formed. Sinn Fein ("Ourselves Alone") was an extremist faction founded by Arthur Griffith, a highly talented journalist who edited the *United Irishman*—an ironical logotype indeed—and who believed there should be a dual monarchy for England and Ireland with separate parliaments. There was the Irish Republican Brotherhood, which grew out of the old violent Fenian tradition (which included an invasion of Canada by the American branch in 1867) and was headed by Tom Clarke, a mild-looking tobacconist who had spent fifteen years in British jails for revolutionary activity. The IRB demanded the establishment of an independent Irish republic. An activist, armed offshoot of the IRB was the Irish Volunteers, which a young mathematics teacher named Eamon De Valera, born in New York City to a Spanish father and an Irish mother, hastened to join.

Also prominent among the revolutionary factions was the Irish Labour Party, headed by James Larkin and James Connolly, with a young Dublin workman named Sean O'Casey, his playwriting career still in the future, as its secretary. The Labour Party was Marxist, and Connolly was known later as the Lenin of the Irish Radicals. Larkin was also the leader of the Irish Transport and General Workers Union, which was locked out in 1913 during disturbances leading to "Bloody Sunday," August 30, when more than 600 persons were injured in Dublin rioting. He subsequently left for America to organize Irish-Americans against participation in World War I. After Bloody Sunday and Larkin's departure, Connolly organized the Irish Citizen Army, which with the Irish Volunteers was the military foundation stone of what became the IRA, with the ultimate objective of establishing a workers' Socialist republic. Lenin called it the first Communist army in Europe. Some of its recruits testified to the curious attraction of proletarian revolutionary movements for those whose privileges they would destroy. One of the first commandants of the Irish Citizen Army was Jack White, the son of a British field marshal. Its soup kitchens were supervised by Countess Markievicz, the wife of a Polish count, herself Anglo-Irish, a highly combative feminist born in one of those "great houses" soon to be gutted by her comrades in arms.

And there was the Gaelic League, which promoted the teaching of the Irish language and history and the playing of Irish sports (hurley and Gaelic football) rather than cricket and rugby. It was part of a cultural revolution which preceded the political. The literary revival in which Lady Gregory, J. M. Synge, William Butler Yeats, and others less renowned were providing the Irish with a new pride in their heritage was an important element in the revolutionary process. Put another way, the writers, particularly those whose works were produced at the Abbey Theater, were teaching the Irish to be Irish, not mock-Englishmen.

In addition to all those factions, there was the Nationalist Party, led by John Redmond, which represented Ireland in the House of Commons. Probably a majority of the Irish supported this legal (from the viewpoint of British officialdom) political movement dedicated to gradualism. It succeeded in persuading the ruling Liberals to present a Home Rule bill in 1913, whereupon the Ulster Unionists reared back in alarm, organized the

Ulster Volunteers, and imported 35,000 rifles from Germany just before the outbreak of war. The war ended the last best hope of Home Rule, thus placing the moderate Nationalists in the position of trying to catch up with the revolutionary process. The gun-running efforts of the Ulstermen were matched by those of their opponents in the South. Again it was a number of Anglo-Irish, turning against their own kind, who provided the muscle and ingenuity with which to armor the often merely verbal efforts of the Irish revolutionaries. One big consignment, 1,500 secondhand Mausers and 50,000 rounds of ammunition, was landed at Howth, near Dublin, by a yacht whose crew included the English-born Erskine Childers and Mary Spring-Rice, the cousin of the British ambassador to Washington. Later another Anglo-Irishman, Sir Roger Casement, once of the British Foreign Office, plotted with the Germans to land 20,000 captured Russian rifles at Tralee but found no one waiting to take delivery of the arms. The German freighter was scuttled by its crew, and Sir Roger, sent ashore from a U-boat, was captured and hanged for high treason.

Meanwhile, a quarter of a million Irishmen were volunteering for the British army to fight in Flanders and the Middle East. Before the Rising and the excessive response by the British military, the Irish Revolution was making a less than impressive case for itself. To the ordinary people, the whole spectrum of revolutionary factions was composed of malcontents, dangerous labor agitators, bohemians, pretentious intellectuals, deracinated jackeens from the big city. The Irish mass is always resentful and suspicious of change, slow to take any action against law and order. Probably, and naturally enough, they were leery of a movement in which so many of their ancient enemies, the Anglo-Irish, were so prominent. Arland Ussher, the author of that penetrating study *The Face and Mind of Ireland,* lived through those times and was sympathetic to the aspirations for independence, but as he recalled, the republican movement, in its various guises, did not have widespread support before Easter, 1916. The word "republic" was suspect; it suggested to most Irishmen the atheism and bloody-mindedness of the French Revolution. Ussher also believed that "Irishmen, in the mass, make bad revolutionaries." Others have remarked on the crucial difference between a rebel and a revolutionary; the Irish are born rebels but resist the process by which a rebel becomes a revolutionary. Certainly the planning that preceded the Easter Rising —the division of opinion and authority among its leaders, the lack of coordination and foresight—was almost farcically inept. In place of an agreed strategy there was a muddle of provisional committees, grandly titled paramilitary officers, supreme councils of this and that.

Revolutions are nourished by concessions, and the slackening of British rule in Ireland, the relative prosperity of the past several years, worked in favor of the revolutionaries. Another thing that favored the uprising, apparently, was the bumbling of the British, all of whose police spies and counterespionage agents based in Dublin Castle seemed to have been sleepwalking just before and during the fateful Easter bank holiday. The British refused to take alarm even when the Irish Volunteers drilled openly, when Connolly's Citizen Army was being trained in house-to-house fighting and taking part in maneuvers designated "Attack on Dublin Castle" and "Capture of the Magazine Fort." For all the tension to be felt in the Dublin streets that holiday weekend, British officers of the Dublin garrison flocked out to the Fairyhouse race meeting and toddled around the paddock with their field glasses trained on Irish horseflesh instead of the armed columns marching along the Liffey quays.

The men who planned the uprising did not count on a few patriotic deaths to rally the whole Irish nation. They gambled on victory over the British army of occupation and the establishment of a provisional Irish republic. One trouble was that the leaders couldn't agree on how the gamble was to be undertaken. Connolly was threatening to take action with his Citizen Army, with or without the support of the Irish Volunteers. And the Volunteers were divided among themselves. Their commandant, Eoin MacNeill, professor of early Irish history at University College, Dublin, was opposed to starting the rebellion while England was still at war, while other members of the military council favored the Easter Rising.

Those in favor of immediate action—including Padraic Pearse, a gentle and introspective schoolteacher; Sean MacDermott, former barkeep and full-time organizer of the Volunteers; Thomas MacDonagh, another teacher; and Joseph Plunkett, a mystic poet and amateur military strategist whose father was a papal count—held secret meetings without the presence of the nominal leader, MacNeill, and decided on the Easter Monday D day. MacNeill got wind of the plot somehow—even military secrets aren't sacred in Ireland—and three days before Easter Monday, April 21, sent out orders to Irish Volunteer units throughout the country *not* to attack. Thus, part of the forces of the rebellion were alerted to go into action Easter Monday while the bulk of the Irish Volunteers, elsewhere in the country, had been ordered to stand down.

The result was that, instead of mustering the full strength of the Irish Volunteers, about 18,000 men throughout the country, only 1,200 (including about 200 of Connolly's Citizen Army) reported on Easter Monday morning when the balloon went up. The operation proceeded briskly enough. Six of Connolly's men captured the guardroom at Dublin Castle, the nerve center of the British regime, and ate the guards' breakfast before fleeing. Commandant Eamon De Valera and the Third Battalion, Irish Volunteers, occupied various key points on the southern approaches to Dublin.

Meanwhile, the main body, headed by Padraic Pearse as commander in chief of the Army of the Irish Republic and James Connolly as commandant general of the Dublin Division, and armed with rifles, sledgehammers, pikes, and homemade grenades, marched down O'Connell Street toward the General Post Office. Little attention was paid them by the holiday crowds, who believed it was just another training exercise or gesture of defiance. As they marched along, Connolly was heard to mutter, "We're all going to be slaughtered."

They ran the green, white, and orange flag up the mast at the General Post Office, seized the building, and in that moment inaugurated the history of modern Ireland.

While the main body occupied the General Post Office, knocked out the windows and sandbagged them, other contingents took over Jacob's Biscuit Factory, the South Dublin Union, the Four Courts area, and a group of hospital and poorhouse buildings on the Liffey quays. Another force of 104 men and 14 women (with Michael Mallin as commandant and the Countess Markievicz as second-in-command) was digging trenches in St. Stephen's Green in the heart of the city. Monday night mobs looted the stores on O'Connell Street. Late Tuesday the British had set up machine guns at such vantage points as Trinity College, the Fire Brigade Tower, the Customs House, and the Shelbourne Hotel overlooking St. Stephen's Green, from which the entrenched rebels were soon driven out.

The British viceroy warned the people of Dublin that "the sternest measures were being taken . . . for the prompt suppression of the disturbances." He would not deign to call it a rebellion. It was Wednesday before a sizable artillery force was assembled to blast the various rebel strongholds, and the gunboat *Helga* steamed up the Liffey to bombard the General Post Office. That day, too, a large British force was reported to have landed at the port of Dun Laoghaire and was marching toward the city. This provided Commandant De Valera with his moment of glory. He gave the soon-to-be-aborted uprising its one hour of military success. His battalion was stationed in the houses covering the approaches to the Mount Street bridge over the Grand Canal. Though the British column outnumbered the Irish by more than 10 to 1, the latter held out for three more days and inflicted heavy casualties, 18 British officers killed or wounded, 216 other ranks killed or wounded.

By Thursday fires were raging throughout the city, most of them set by British artillery fire or incendiary bombs. The next day fires in various parts of the General Post Office forced Pearse and Connolly to evacuate the building and occupy a row of shops in Moore Street. Connolly by then had been twice wounded and had to be carried to the new headquarters on a stretcher.

The Easter Rising was guttering out. Its sparks had not struck fire elsewhere in Ireland. Many of those who had put their lives on the line were openly disgusted by the way it had been mishandled. That weekend the rebel strongpoints, one by one, blossomed with white flags. The Pearse-Connolly contingent was the first to surrender on Saturday morning, De Valera's the last on Sunday noon. The defeated revolutionaries were marched off to Richmond Barracks. Many in the crowds that watched the processions, particularly those with relatives fighting with the British on the western front, were raucously hostile and shouted, "Bayonet the bastards!" The Catholic hierarchy was opposed to the insurrection. Only in later years would so many Dubliners claim they had fought with the Volunteers or the Citizen Army that week, and obtain jobs on the strength of the claim, that it was said the General Post Office couldn't have had room for them all.

That week, as William Butler Yeats declared in his celebrated poem on the Easter Rising, "a terrible beauty was born." Most of the country, a week after Easter Monday, would have agreed that it had been terrible but would have denied the beauty part. Fifty-six republicans had been killed, along with 216 Dublin noncombatants, as well as 130 British officers and men. The damage to public and private property was estimated at more than $7,500,000. On May 10, with some of the leaders of the rebellion still awaiting sentence, the *Irish Independent,* which was owned by the man who had broken Connolly's streetcar strike in 1913, published an editorial expressing the hope that Connolly and some of the others would not escape the British firing squad. "When, however, we come to some of the ringleaders, instigators and fomenters not yet dealt with, we must make an exception. If these men are treated with too great leniency, they will take it as an indication of weakness on the part of the government. Let the worst of the rebels be singled out and dealt with as they deserve."

The *Irish Catholic* several days earlier had suggested the attitude of most of the higher-ranking Catholic clergy: "The movement which has culminated in deeds of unparalleled bloodshed and destruction of property in the capital of Ireland was as criminal as it was insane. Only idiots or lunatics can have supposed it could prove successful. Traitorous and treacherous as it undoubtedly was, it was most traitorous and treacherous to our native land."

What turned public opinion in favor of the unsuccessful revolutionaries? The stupidity of the British military courts in condemning and making martyrs out of the ringleaders. Ninety-seven of the prisoners initially were given the death sentence, but only fifteen of those actually faced the firing squad. De Valera was among those condemned, but because of a question of citizenship (he was American-born), the sentence was commuted to imprisonment at Dartmoor. Hundreds of other Irishmen, either participants in the Rising or suspected of plotting against the regime, were also hauled away to British prisons.

But it was the executions, shots heard around the island and eventually around the world, which brought the Irish mass to the realization that it was engaged, like it or not, in a death struggle with the British. Tom Clarke, Padraic Pearse, and Tom MacDonagh were shot to death on May 3, and a few more each day thereafter, until a week later the crippled Sean MacDermott and James Connolly, who had to be carried to the stake on a stretcher and propped up to face his executioners, who was half-dead already, and whose wounds stank of gangrene, were the last of those to be executed at Kilmainham Jail.

Suddenly pictures of the Kilmainham "martyrs" began appearing on the mantelpieces of Irish cottages. The slain rebels' effect on the popular imagination, as Arland Ussher recalled, "was due not merely to the list of their virtues, but to the fact they represented a new type of Irish leader, who was not ashamed—as men like Redmond were—of the language and folk-culture of Ireland. These men differed, not only from the old type of parliamentarian, but also from the old type of rebel." The new breed of revolutionary was inspired by the discovery broadcast by the literary revival that the Celtic mythology was as glorious as the Greek, that a considerable civilization had existed in Ireland long before much of Europe was civilized. To such men and women, rebels in both the cultural and political sense, the rising against the Saxon was more important than the struggle between the Allies and the Central Powers; the fact that Irish was spoken only in the bogs and mountains of the west was more alarming than the possibility the Germans might march into Paris again. Quixotic, yes, but to an Irishman his island is not merely the center of the universe, but the universe itself.

To the more peace-loving Irish who believe that Irish problems can be settled without violence, apparently a majority, the IRA is a throwback, an unwelcome reminder of the tragic past, an irritant in the forward-looking eye. The IRA has also suffered from the Irish syndrome of factionalism, which even now splits

its ranks when unity would seem to be required for survival against a growing hostility from the central government.

Ever since 1916 there has been a constant process of fragmentation over both personalities and the means of achieving IRA objectives. Just before the 1916 uprising it was epitomized by Padraic Pearse romantically declaring that Ireland needed a "blood sacrifice" and James Connolly, disdainful of such Anglo-Irish fancies, replying in his down-to-earth manner, "No, I do not think the old heart of the earth needs to be warmed with blood. I think anyone who does is a blithering idiot."

To the Irish majority, in untroubled times, the IRA seems an anachronism that should have disintegrated in a modern society. And yet something atavistic stirs when the Orange drums reverberate louder in the North, when the tread of British boots is heard from Belfast, when Catholic lives and property are endangered in Derry or the Bogside. The Irish pulse tends to beat faster when the IRA, in a voice combining the Fenian and the Marxist, announces that once again it is prepared to take up the fight against the oppressors of the Irish people.

Love it or fear it, the IRA is woven into every strand of modern Irish history. Through the years since the civil war and its virtual disbandment, it has always found something to oppose, something to inflame the imagination of youth and keep boys dreaming of the day when they would be sworn in as IRA men and given an automatic pistol to slip into their belts.

The mystique is what fascinates. By what process is a young Irishman turned into a gunman, a saboteur, risking his liberty and often his life? Not for fame or glory, because his deeds will be performed anonymously, and he will never be a "Red Rudi" or a Bernadette Devlin or make Strawberry Statements for fun and profit. His career will call for more austere dedication, and less promise of reward, than any of the other revolutionaries in the world.

Undoubtedly a large proportion of the IRA's recruits through the years have come from the Dublin slums, for much the same reasons that the Black Panthers in America are drawn from the black ghettos. They are moved by despair at their own future, by the belief that anything will be better than what they have, and very often—like Brendan Behan—they come from "IRA families" with a long and well-remembered tradition of keeping up the fight from generation to generation. Behan, when he was imprisoned in England, would remember how his father had taken him for walks on Sunday and how they often passed Kilmainham Prison. "It was where he had first seen me, from his cell window, during the Civil War. I was born after he was captured, and when I was six weeks old my mother brought me up to the jail and held me up, on the road outside, for him to see from the cell window." In such families the IRA tradition was often stronger than their Catholicism. As Behan succinctly put it (in *Borstal Boy*), "the Church was always for the rich against the poor."

When Behan was arrested on his first and last terrorist mission to England, caught in a Liverpool lodging house with a suitcase full of gelignite, chemicals, and detonators ("my Sinn Fein conjuror's outfit," as he called it), he refused to answer any questions at police headquarters but made the defiant statement: "My name is Brendan Behan. I came over here to fight for the Irish Workers' and Small Farmers' Republic, for a full and free life, for my countrymen, North and South, and for the removal of the baneful influence of British imperialism. God save Ireland."

Behan was only sixteen when he was arrested by the British police and was sent to a Borstal institution (reformatory), too young and homesick not to wish "I could wake up at home, and say, well, that's how it would be if you were pinched in England, and not attend any more parades, and drop out of the IRA and attend more to my trade, and go out dancing or something, and get married. . . ."

In the Borstal he would remember throwing rocks at the upper-class boys from the Belvedere Jesuit School and the Mountjoy Protestant School as they went to play rugby at Croke Park, "toffs and toffs' sons . . . it was a holy and a wholesome thought to give them as bad a time as we could." College for the rich kids, the IRA for the slum boys. One lot learns how to pass the port beneath the high table at Trinity, the other studies bomb making and guerrilla tactics. Someday there may be a collision between the toffs' sons and the slum boys of a sort not envisioned by the founders of the Irish Republic.

* * *

The IRA has been the subject of more wordage in every medium, more footage in films, more romanticizing (before revolutionary movements lost their appeal, as they loomed closer home, for mass audiences) than any similar organization. Yet its inner life has never been publicly analyzed, its psychology never explored, perhaps because it could be done only by someone who had served in the ranks. It would also require a sense of detachment which IRA veterans never seem to achieve.

Frank O'Connor relived his experiences as an IRA man in his various writings, but that was the old IRA of the Revolution and civil war. When he joined up during the Revolution as a teen-ager, "it was a brief escape from tedium and frustration to go out on the country roads on summer evenings, slouching along in knee breeches and gaiters, hands in the pockets of one's trench coat and hat pulled over one's right eye." Disillusionment came later when he served as a courier during the civil war. Once he brought dispatches to the headquarters of General Liam Deasy and learned that rations take precedence over ideals in even the most highly motivated fighting forces. He was awakened by a disturbance in the barrack square and went down to investigate. "There was a column of men lined up there—the angriest-looking men I've ever seen." The officer in charge of the column roared at O'Connor, "We're after fighting our way down from Patrickswell, and when we got here the Corkmen had meat for breakfast and we had none. Tell General Deasy if the Limerick men don't get meat there'll be a mutiny!" O'Connor was captured by the Treaty State forces on one of his missions and later admitted (*An Only Child*) that imprisonment came as a relief, that "each morning the nightmare of the Civil War grew fainter in my mind, the sleepless nights, the aimless skirmishes, and the futile, sickening executions."

The paucity of insiders' accounts of life in the shadow army may be attributed to the fact that most men of action aren't given to introspection or literary activity. Another reason for reticence has been candidly, if briefly, put forth by Owen Dudley Edwards, an Irish historian now teaching at the University of Edinburgh: "IRA men of the present and recent past have reason to fear any deep analysis. . . . Their blunderings and bickerings can only ask of the world the charity of its silence, as Robert

Emmet put it, and some of them have gone to considerable lengths to insure that such charity will cover their sins."

What it means to take the IRA oath has been explored with more intrepidity in fictional forms than in any factual memoirs. The implications of committing violence on order, impersonally but ruthlessly, of submitting to a relentless revolutionary discipline, of surrendering oneself to a cause not always perfectly understood have been examined in some detail and with considerable insight in such novels as F. L. Green's *Odd Man Out,* Liam O'Flaherty's *The Informer,* and Arthur J. Roth's *A Terrible Beauty.*

None of these could be mistaken as the product of an IRA propaganda bureau, nor would they serve as IRA recruiting aids. Informers, turncoats, and doubting Thomases figure largely. What sensible Irish youth would want to risk emulating Gyppo Nolan in *The Informer* and being executed by his comrades? What loving Irish parents would wish upon their son the transformation noted by the heroine of *Odd Man Out* in her IRA friend: "He was pledged already. His whole nature was submitted to his ideals, submerged beneath the purpose of the Organisation. Looking at his hard, fair features, and touching his hard flesh, she felt only the coldness of him. . . . He had been a member of the Organisation since his seventeenth year. Since then his life had been a fantastic record of illegal exploits, arrest, trial, imprisonment, escape, flight and pursuit, murderous forays against the Police, and successful enterprises. . . ."

Green and O'Flaherty were primarily interested in telling a story, but Arthur J. Roth in *A Terrible Beauty* served up a cautionary tale which warned against the dangers of a casual, romantic involvement in a dead serious and ruthlessly prosecuted cause. Roth was born in Ireland and served in the Irish army for three years before migrating to the United States.

The hero of *A Terrible Beauty* is a twenty-year-old farmer's son named Dermot O'Neill. Lightheartedly, his head stuffed with colorful legends of the IRA's war against the British, lent a sharper focus by the murder of his own uncle, Dermot joins a local unit of the IRA during the pre-World War II phase of its activities in Northern Ireland. Soon he finds himself more deeply involved in violence than he had bargained for. He takes part in a raid on an ordnance depot, and on another mission his best friend is captured and sentenced to ten years in prison.

Sick of it all, threatened by excommunication from the church, Dermot finally tells off the fanatical local commandant of the IRA: "Your head is full of plans of being a great hero—another Dan Breen. . . . The only thing you want is to be a genuine rebel on the run. You can't wait until you're dragging yourself all over the mountains with your trenchcoat and a revolver in your pocket." *A Terrible Beauty* ends tragically with Dermot O'Neill himself on the run and his young sister shot to death by the IRA fanatic when he mistakes her for Dermot.

The reality of the IRA's continuing struggle for its objectives —the liberation of the six counties of Ulster, the setting up of a Socialist regime in Dublin—may be glimpsed in the newspaper reports, police summaries, court proceedings, and government documents which recapture events but drain them of the terror, blood, and anguish which must have accompanied them. The Irish are a kindly people, especially to strangers, but they can be terribly hard on one another.

Little mercy was shown by the IRA or its enemies during the campaign it launched just before World War II in England and Ireland. Just before the outbreak of war, England was plagued by 127 separate bombing incidents, with the explosives usually placed in pillar (mail) boxes and public lavatories, in which one person was killed and fifty-five were injured. Later in 1939 one man was killed and five maimed by an explosion set off in Victoria Station, London, and in Coventry, soon to be heavily bombed by the Luftwaffe, five persons were killed and seventy injured by a bomb left on a bicycle in a crowded street.

A considerable number of Irishmen suspected of membership in the IRA were deported from England, just in time to make trouble for Prime Minister De Valera's government when it was concentrating all its efforts on keeping out of the war, which meant that, above all, it had to avoid giving offense to the British government or providing Churchill with a pretext for seizing Irish bases. De Valera had already rushed emergency legislation through the Dail, the Offenses Against the State Act, which allowed the government to deal with the IRA under powers amounting to martial law.

Official concern over what the IRA was plotting mounted steadily when it increased its terrorist activities in the North and banks and post offices in the South were robbed to support that campaign, when it became known that Nazi agents were arriving by U-boat, parachute, and more conventional means to provide a link between the Irish underground and the German government.

Fearing that the IRA was planning a large-scale operation in the North, which might result in a British invasion of the South, the government began rounding up IRA men in wholesale batches by swooping down on their mountain camps and making house-to-house searches in the cities. The condign punishment meted out, the haste with which the IRA men were tried before military courts and consigned to an internment camp at the Curragh, if not summarily executed, indicated how strongly the government feared that the IRA might drag Ireland into the war.

It was a ruinous time for the IRA. Its chief of staff, Sean Russell, had taken off early in 1939 on a fund-raising mission to the United States. Early in 1940, when his visa expired, he faced deportation and internment at the Curragh. German agents smuggled him to Genoa, then to Germany, where he was trained in sabotage and subsequently boarded a U-boat which was to land him secretly on the Irish coast. Russell, ill-fated as Sir Roger Casement on a similar mission during the previous world war, died of a perforated stomach ulcer a hundred miles off the coast of Galway. Meanwhile, a Wexford man named Stephen Hayes had been serving as chief of staff of the IRA. With much of its membership in the Curragh prison camp, some of the IRA directorate decided the only reason for the disaster must have been treachery committed by someone high up in the organization.

Somehow Hayes' comrades decided that Hayes was the traitor and decided to place him on trial for his life. A group of IRA men from Northern Ireland kidnapped Hayes on June 30, 1941. With his legs chained, Hayes was taken to a house in the Wicklow mountains, then to another in the Dublin suburb of Terenure. For the next three weeks he was kept shackled, questioned endlessly by his comrades, and barely kept alive on a diet of bread and water. Finally, he was hauled before a court-martial reminiscent of a similar scene in O'Flaherty's *The Informer* on charges that he had betrayed the organization by "having deliberately forwarded information of a secret and confidential nature concerning the activities of the Irish Republican Army to a hostile body, to wit, the 'Irish Free State Government.' "

Hayes was sentenced to death, but on the morning of September 8, after more than two months of captivity, Hayes escaped by jumping out of the window and shuffling along on shackled legs until he reached the Rathmines police station.

The shock of that affair, Hayes' account of being maltreated and sentenced to death by his own comrades, the spectacle of an IRA chief of staff seeking protection from the government he had so recently been operating against, shattered what was left of the organization outside the internment camp.

Yet in the decade following the war it slowly came back to life, as it presumably always will so long as its reason for being, the complete liberation of Ireland, exists as a rallying point for adventurous youth.

In 1953 the IRA decided to launch a campaign against Northern Ireland and revived the old flying column tactics of Michael Collins' day. Several hundred men, often sleeping in the open, sometimes in dugouts, participated in well-planned attacks on the barracks of the Royal Ulster Constabulary, oil refineries, British Broadcasting Company transmitters, bridges, railroads, and arsenals. The hit-and-run attacks by a comparative handful of dedicated young men cost seven lives and £700,000 ($3,500,000) in property damage and greatly embarrassed the government in Dublin in its efforts to get along with the British.

There were seriocomic moments in the tightrope act performed by the Costello coalition government, which did not want to enrage the IRA and at the same time had to mollify the British, who were demanding that the Republic do something to curb its extremists. A minister in the Costello government got word to the IRA Army Council, which then met over a bookmaker's establishment in Fleet Street, Dublin, that it would be considered a great favor if the IRA would omit the Dublin dateline from its communiqués. The IRA directorate agreed, and the government was then able to inform London that the Army Council had moved its headquarters to Northern Ireland.

The new generation of activists included a young man named Cathal Goulding, whose father had fought against the British. Goulding attracted the attention of the IRA directorate by leading a raid in England to build up the organization's armory. He and several other men raided the Felstead Officers' Training School in Essex and made a haul which included ninety-nine rifles, eight machine guns, ten submachine guns, an antitank gun, and a mortar. They were picked up the following day, however, and were subsequently sentenced to eight years in prison. "We believe," Goulding told the court, "that the only way to drive the British army from our country is by force of arms. For that purpose we think it is no crime to capture arms from our enemies." Goulding is now the IRA's chief of staff, a man whose determination to "drive out the British" is undiminished from his fiery youth.

Despite the presence of such firebrands in its ranks, the IRA went into another of its periods of hibernation in 1962 after a decade of sporadic campaigning across the border. There were a number of reasons—the "era of good feeling" which temporarily emanated from the unprecedented meetings between Prime Minister Lemass of the Irish Republic and his opposite number in the North, Pope John's amelioration of Protestant and Catholic differences, increasing prosperity in the South, a certain amount of distaste in the Republic and among Irish-American supporters of the IRA over incidents in which lives were taken—but probably the main one was a growing conviction in the South that the partition of Ireland could not be ended by force. There had also occurred a splintering in the ranks. Perhaps the luckless Stephen Hayes had put his finger on the problem after he escaped to police protection from his former comrades when he remarked that the Irish are "rebels but not revolutionaries." They have courage, dedication and daring to spare, but find it difficult to yield up individualism to any cause. Scratch an Irishman—politely—and you will find a Celt.

It turned out to be a shorter hibernation than usual, more of a breathing spell than a sound sleep. The IRA made itself visible in various actions between 1962 and 1969, blowing Nelson's statue off its pillar, firing on British warships (with rifles) when they made courtesy calls in Irish ports, and taking an increasingly forceful role in various demonstrations and sit-ins over housing. It has also been campaigning against the inroads of foreign capital and foreigners, especially Germans, buying up large farms in Ireland. American-owned enterprises have not been spared. In 1968 the IRA claimed credit for burning £60,000 ($144,000) worth of buses which transported workers to the American-owned E. I. Company in the Shannon industrial complex.

The outbreak of rioting in the North in the summer of 1969 brought the IRA into the spotlight again, particularly after Catholic working-class neighborhoods in Belfast were attacked by Protestant mobs and many homes were destroyed. According to the best available information, the IRA was caught off guard by the fighting in the North, and reportedly only six of its members were active among those trying to defend the Catholic areas of Belfast and Derry. In any case, the IRA had to compete with the presence of charismatic Bernadette Devlin; it boasted that it was sending carloads of street fighters to Belfast while the image of little Miss Devlin clawing up a chunk of paving stone was being televised and wirephotoed around the world. Then too, the IRA was outflanked in a sense when Prime Minister Jack Lynch announced that he was sending regular army units to the border along with field hospitals to care for those injured or made homeless during the Bogside battles—a risky gesture, perhaps, since the Irish army is outnumbered by the Royal Irish Constabulary plus British regiments, while the Irish air arm consists of four obsolete Vampire jet fighters to confront a Royal Air Force equipped with atomic bombs.

The IRA necessarily became more active in the North, sending up men and arms to reinforce the Catholic civil rights movement, while in the South it seems to be concentrating on political and social action. Much of its energy is also absorbed by internal politics—the old tendency toward factionalism—with one wing emphasizing its Socialist orientation and the other a more traditional nationalism. The leftward drift was accentuated by the appointment of a young Marxist intellectual, Roy

Johnson, to the Army Council and by a Sinn Fein report, titled "Ireland Today," which speculated on the possibility of joining forces with the minuscule Communist Party in the Republic, and a familiar-sounding proposal for the formation of a "National Liberation Front."

At the annual Sinn Fein convocation in early 1970 the ideological split was widened when about two-thirds of the delegates voted to enter parliamentary politics, from which it has generally abstained on the grounds that a republic which does not include the six Ulster counties is still under British domination. The so-called Socialist Republicans who voted to end abstention take the position of the European Communist parties that nothing can be accomplished without working from within the government and taking what political power they can. The other third of the delegates, largely the older Sinn Feiners who resent radical influence subverting the nationalist impulse, walked out. That left the Republic, in effect, with two secret armies—the Marxist "provisional" IRA and the old "official" IRA with its roots in the conservative countryside. But it's all rather minor league by international revolutionary standards, a matter of a few thousand (at most) underequipped and largely untrained young men quarreling among themselves. Lenin would have given them up as a lost cause.

The leftist Sinn Fein and IRA faction is meanwhile seeking to broaden its base of support by taking up causes which would enlist the sympathy of the thousands of small farmers who have always supported the regular political parties. It has formed land leagues aimed at breaking up the larger farms and surviving estates and redistributing the land into small holdings. In a recent issue of the *United Irishman,* Roy Johnson, as the resident dialectician, proposed a $168,000,000 farm subsidy program, which would amount to $714 annually for each of 200,000 farmers. Johnson is a computer scientist, but what runs smoothly through his computation machine would find a stormier passage in budget sessions of the Dail.

Sinn Fein president Tomas MacGiolla meanwhile talks of reaching out to enlist the Protestant working class of the North and combining it with that of the South to bring about an upheaval that would topple democratic capitalism in both parts of the island. Could there be a reddish bar in the making for the green, white, and orange flag of the Irish Republic? "Because of its social actions and attitudes," Proinsias MacAonghusa wrote recently in *Hibernia,* "the IRA is now a people's liberation army in a classical revolutionary sense, is conscious of its role and is now possibly more dangerous to the British government at Belfast and the Whitehall-controlled Government at Dublin than at any time in the past."

Perhaps MacAonghusa's prognosis was correct. The government seemed to agree with it several months later, when Prime Minister Lynch suddenly assumed emergency powers under the Offenses Against the State Act against what he called an "armed conspiracy." This gave him the right to intern any citizen without trial, and several were immediately placed in internment. The Dublin newspapers reported that the conspirators had planned a series of bank robberies and the kidnapping of influential persons, including a British diplomat. At the same time the U.S. embassy was being harassed with daily threats of violence and the kidnapping of its personnel. The American military attaché in Dublin recently was summoned to the door by a mortician, who announced that he had come to "collect the corpse" as requested in a telephone call.

The Irish think of themselves as law-abiding, civilly obedient, and it is true enough that you can walk down most Irish streets, your pockets stuffed with ten-pound notes, with little risk of being robbed. The gun, however, is still a potent political symbol. The man who carries it in Ireland, you may be sure, is a romantic idealist as fervent as Wolfe Tone or the men who died in the General Post Office the morning after Easter.

9.

The Wild Irish West

Ireland, like Israel, has a sense of some special destiny, which enables her to bear her discomfitures with fatalism and secret pride.

—Arland Ussher

☘ If you could find one of the occasional Irish romantics, he would probably tell you that the real, the traditional, the genuine Irish-speaking Ireland still lives only along the bleak, gale-torn western coasts, with its old, sad, and overburdened heart still beating somewhere in Connemara, that part of County Galway lying west of the Lough Corrib. You can believe it on a misty autumn afternoon, looking down on that sleevelike lake at the island, with its ruined castle, where the pirate queen Grace O'Malley held forth four centuries ago.

On the other hand you could take the word of the late Oliver St. John Gogarty, whose country house in Connemara was burned to the ground during the Troubles, that there is an irremediable blight on the wild and lonely coast with its storm-racked islands. He was haunted by the memory of the hunched figures in a Connemara pub, the dark-faced and silent men bent over their pints of stout. "They chew on melancholy as a cow on a cud. Shane Leslie attributes it to 'hushed hate.' It is more than that. It is independent of external circumstances. They take pleasure in darkening with melancholia God's sweet air. They sin against the light. Accidia! Of course, the obsolete deadly sin."

Dr. Gogarty's recommendation was that the western province be cleared of people and planted entirely with trees.

Ireland's wild west, which includes the Gaeltacht, or Irish-speaking sections, can claim some of the most bleakly beautiful scenery in the world. Gaunt and desolate one moment and, when the sun breaks through and makes lustrous the lakes and purple and gold hillsides, achingly lovely the next. It begins in the north with the coast of Donegal, making a left turn around the shoulder of County Mayo, continuing south along the Connemara section of County Galway, Galway Bay with its Aran Islands mournful in the mists, on down the bays and fingerlike peninsulas of County Kerry and West Cork. Along that often foggy perimeter facing the Atlantic, with fjords like those of Norway, with offshore islands like those of northern Scotland, with primeval silences and rock-strewn fields and the few trees bent into fantastic shapes by the eternal wind, the Ireland of the past, picturesque and forlorn, struggles for its existence. Here were driven thousands of the Irish who had been dispossessed by English settlers from their more fertile lands elsewhere, too poor to emigrate, and here they literally carved out homesteads from the rocky hillsides in the old province of Connaught ("To Hell or Connaught," as the English gracelessly put it).

For hundreds of years the western scene was unchanging: the whitewashed rectangular cottages with thatch on the roof; the smoke from a turf fire torn by the wind from the chimneys at either end; the tiny fields enclosed by walls made of the rock cleared from them (the irregular checkerboard of a Connemara slope has only to be glimpsed to induce a sympathetic backache); the thin topsoil nourished by dung and seaweed; the black water of the bogs where strips of turf have been cut and laid out to dry; the roaring sea below and the granitic mountains looming above; the small flocks of sheep and the sturdy little Connemara ponies; the villages and towns from which the young, bright, and able-bodied have fled in search of something better than living on the verge of destitution.

A queer isolated existence for those who cling to it, whole settlements where the majority are the very old and very young. It represents a concentration of the Irish tragedy, that of its youth who can only say, "There's nothing for us here," and of their elders who watch the young go away and often never return. There is more than one steep hill in the west called the Hill of Weeping in Gaelic because from its summit those leaving it would pause to look back for the last time over the fragmented fields, the little white houses, the narrow, twisting roads, and the rough gray sea.

You can study the tragic dilemma—stay and starve, or go and be half-miserable the rest of your life—on the tiny West Cork island of Cleire, nine miles out in the sea, where 197 persons struggle for a living. Two-thirds of the island community are over sixty years old. They stayed on Cleire, they will tell you, because they had to look after their elders, until finally they were trapped by time and too old to migrate themselves. In a sense Cleire is to Ireland what Ireland is to Europe, an outpost isolated by the sea and the mists rising from the Gulf Stream as it meets the winds from the Arctic. Yet the people of Cleire cling like the survivors of a shipwreck to their barren refuge and want nothing changed. More than anything else they fear outside influences and the corruption of an outer world they consider has gone mad with permissiveness. They want no part of the tourist trade or the summer hotels; they would ward off any unlikely incursion of industry unless it were based on their "natural" way of life and left it undisturbed. They will not compromise with the modern world, yet they must send their more promising children away to confront what they most fear themselves. In that, perhaps, they are like the majority of the Irish people, only more so; they are caught in the pincers of the new economics and the old tranquillity, the choice between tourist hordes and impoverished isolation.

The people of the west are tough enough, however, to cope with the latter. Their character partakes of the granite ledges which break the soil everywhere. Undoubtedly it also owes something of its grim strength to the Normans who settled there. One exemplar of that quality was James Lynch Fitz-Stephens, the head of a great Galway mercantile family, originally Norman, for whose actions the term "lynch law" somewhat mistakenly came into usage. The mansion of the Lynches still stands on Shop Street, Galway City, with the carving of an ape on its façade. The ape, brought over from Spain, rescued one of the children when the house caught fire.

James Lynch Fitz-Stephens was elected mayor of Galway in 1493, shortly after Columbus stopped by to attend mass at the Galway Cathedral and (according to some accounts) pick up a Galwayman to serve as his navigator. Soon after the election the new Mayor went to Cádiz to visit Spanish merchants with whom he had long been associated. One family which entertained him was the Gómezes, who had a son about the age of the mayor's son Walter. He insisted that young Gómez return with him to Galway as his guest. Young Gómez and young Walter hit it off from the start, but the friendship was blighted when Walter's girl began flirting with Gómez. Walter kept a watch on the girl's house and one night caught Gómez slipping away from a rendezvous with the girl, stabbed Gómez with a poniard, and threw his body into the sea. An incoming tide washed the body back on the shore, and Walter fled from the city.

The youth was the pride and hope of the House of Lynch, but to James Lynch Fitz-Stephens, who was chief magistrate, as well as mayor of Galway, justice was an absolute. He led the posse which captured his son, then presided over his trial and condemned the youth to the gallows. At first the people of Galway were appalled at the verdict and held riotous demonstrations for clemency. The mayor refused all entreaties. At a final meeting with his son, he gave the boy his last blessings and prayed with him. No hangman could be found to conduct the execution, so James Lynch Fitz-Stephens placed the noose around his son's neck, fastened the rope to an iron bar projecting from the wall of the jail, and (in the graphic phrase of a contemporary) "launched him into eternity." Galwaymen came to understand the nobility of the mayor's action, the reason for his insistence that justice must be evenhanded at all costs; their Celtic ancestors had always believed in equality of justice with a Biblical intensity. It is one of the ironies of histories that the name of Judge Lynch should be associated with lawless mob action, when his condemnation of his son actually was justice of the most painfully lawful sort.

* * *

The west is Ireland's Appalachia, where the farms are too small and infertile to support a reasonable life, where even the sea is yielding smaller harvests every year while foreign trawlers outstrip the efforts of the Irish fishermen. One of the principal cottage industries is the knitting of the heavy "Aran" sweaters which most tourists take home with them. The women of the Connemara countryside knit sections of the sweaters at 2 shillings (24 cents) an hour, $12 for a fifty-hour week. Later the sections are stitched together in a central workshop. There is melancholy overlaying the whole western scene, yet it does not have the quality of despair to be found in West Virginia or the Cumberland Mountains; the Irish are seasoned veterans of the poverty war, and in Connemara they have not known even the hope of relative affluence for centuries.

Here you can walk up a country lane overlooking Galway Bay, up to an abandoned cottage surrounded by wind-warped trees, and look westward over the gunmetal sea as you stand in the ruined doorway. Years ago those who lived in the house departed for the factory slums of Detroit or Manchester, leaving little but the rusty nail from which an oleograph of the Sacred Heart had hung.

Whole towns and villages have been abandoned, such as the County Mayo settlement described by the great German novelist Heinrich Böll in his nostalgic *Irish Journal*:

> If anyone tried to paint it, this skeleton of a human habitation where a hundred years ago five hundred people may have lived: all those gray triangles and squares on the gray-green slope of the hill; if he were to include the girl with the red pullover who is just passing along the main street with a load of peat on her back, a spot of red for her pullover and a dark brown one for the peat, a lighter brown one for the girl's face, and then the white sheep huddling like lice among the ruins—he would be considered an unusually crazy painter: that's how abstract reality is. Everything not made of stone eaten away by wind, sun, rain, and time, neatly laid out along the somber slope as if for an anatomy lesson, the skeleton of a village. . . . Here no one razed anything to the ground, and the softer parts of abandoned dwellings are left to feed the wind, the rain, the sun, and time, and after sixty, seventy,

> or a hundred years all that is left is half-finished buildings from which no carpenter will ever again hang his wreath to celebrate the completion of a house; this, then, is what has been left in peace after death.

The rest of Ireland, it is said, has a bad conscience about the desolate west—to the same extent, perhaps, that other Americans feel an occasional twinge about Appalachia. Actually the plight of the Gaeltacht is part of the agricultural problem, which may or may not be eased by the prospective entry of Ireland into the Common Market system. The key to a majority in the Dail lies with the heavily populated areas around Dublin, Cork, and Limerick; therefore, the politicians favor the industrialized areas over the agricultural. The farmers are required to supply cheap milk, meat, grain, and vegetables to the cities, at half the price English farmers receive, and to be content with a barely marginal existence. When the land was redistributed, it was parceled out in acreages too small to make farming a viable proposition. A land of small peasant proprietors was envisioned, with emphasis on the "small." Unforeseen or ignored was the struggle of even the hardest-working farmers to wring a living out of small plots of thin topsoil. A West Cork farmer I know has worked from early youth to his mid-forties to expand his family's ten or twelve acres to slightly more than forty acres, to reclaim each bit of land he acquired by covering its rocky outcroppings with kelp and manure, to build up his dairy herd to sixteen cows.

The Gaeltacht, as an enclave where the Irish language is preserved in all possible purity, though it probably bears little resemblance to that spoken by the ancient Celts, is also part of the nation's cultural heritage. It is the preserve of the old stories and songs and poems, the place where history came to a full stop and where the past is pickled in memory from generation to generation. That, too, is why the rest of the country feels an occasional pang of remorse, an attitude which Donald S. Connery has defined as "much like that of a young couple in a city apartment who know they should be doing something for the old folks withering away on the broken-down family farm, but who are too busy to do much more than send off a little money now and then."

To the outside world the preservation of the Irish branch of Gaelic might seem little more than an endearing foible, one of those little obsessions to which every nation is entitled. To many of the Irish, including President De Valera and left-leaning intellectuals alike, it is rooted deep in history and destiny. All too well it is remembered that successive conquerors did their best to destroy, in turn, the language, the culture, and the Catholic Church. Under Oliver Cromwell's "final solution," which introduced the English and Scottish plantations everywhere but Connaught, the Irish language was declared illegal, and speaking it was harshly punished. That meant Irish was spoken only in the remoter and poorer sections of the west where the English writ did not bother to run, and English was the tongue of those who lived with the overlords in the rest of the country.

What survived of the native tongue, culture, and religion was in the keeping of hedge school masters, wandering minstrels, and fugitive priests. Meanwhile, the uninstructed masses were allowed to sink to the educational level of the Hottentots and the Russian serfs. As late as 1831 the British were still so determined to stamp out the vestiges of Irish-speaking that they organized the national schools, the first principle of which was to wipe out any hand-me-down remnants of the Celtic language and culture and in which Irish children were made to learn by rote such gems of misinformation as "On the East of Ireland is England where the Queen lives; many people who live in Ireland were born in England, and we speak the same language, and are called One Nation." From 1851 to 1901, accordingly, the number of those speaking only Irish steadily declined. The statistics show that in 1851, 319,602 persons spoke only Irish and by 1901, only 20,953.

All this was turned around, to some extent, when the language-revival movement and the recovery of the Celtic legends by Yeats, Synge, and others preceded the political revolution which overturned the British. If conquests had been completed and solidified through destruction of the Irish language and culture, the reasoning ran, they must be restored to make Ireland whole again, independent and unique. Irish must be made the first language again, English would be learned only as a matter of necessary communication with the outsiders. The Gaelic League was founded in 1893 by Dr. Douglas Hyde, Father Eugene O'Growney, and Eoin MacNeill to extend the Irish language "as a spoken tongue," with the republication of Gaelic literature and the formation of a new literature written in Irish as further objectives. Such leaders of the coming political revolution as De Valera, Pearse, and Collins were enrolled by the Gaelic League. Thanks to the diplomatic efforts of Dr. Hyde, a Protestant, as were many members of the movement, the British finally permitted Irish to be placed on the curriculum of primary schools in the Gaeltacht and eventually that of the National University, at which Dr. Hyde and MacNeill were appointed to the faculty. Apparently the British failed to realize that Irish-speaking was more than yet another eccentricity of the natives, whose wayward impulses provided them with so much amusement.

Once the English departed, the Treaty State immediately ordained that Irish was to be the "official language," and in the Constitution of 1937 it was defined as the "first official language." It still is. Road markers give directions in both English and Irish, government documents and announcements are published bilingually, there is a nightly news broadcast on Telefis Eireann in Irish and several weekly programs on which only Irish is spoken (during which thousands of viewers repair to the fridge, the bathroom, or the backyard), and the Dublin newspapers carry editorials and report certain events in the ancient language.

The case for preserving the language has been vigorously defended. Father Martin Brennan has pointed out that Irish literature was "the first articulate literature in Europe outside classical Greece and Rome." Maire Cruise O'Brien, language scholar, former diplomat and wife of Conor Cruise O'Brien, not only volunteered to teach in a Gaeltacht school threatened by closure but defended the survival of the ancient tongue in an essay titled "The Two Languages," in which she explained:

> The education that will fit an Irishman to take his place as a fully-equipped human being either within or outside his own

> country must begin by giving him a pride in himself, not as he might be, but as he is, and a knowledge and love of Irish seems to me an essential part of this education. The Irishman must realize his English speech not as a regrettable sub-standard variety but as a rich and beautiful hybrid before he can, first, make the necessary concessions to Standard English to be understood without humiliation and psychological damage, and, second, acquire a genuine competence in that tongue.

To those less concerned with linguistic integrity, the controversy is regarded as the vaporings of the overeducated, the American equivalent of forming a Society for the Preservation of Choctaw. They are quick to point out that debates on the subject of preserving Irish necessarily are held in English, that people in the Gaeltacht complain of Dublin intellectuals speaking "broken Irish," not the real thing. It is also a matter for scornful comment that government bureaus begin their communications with the salutation *A Chara* and end with *Mise, le meas,* but everything in between is written in English. An Irish scholar enraged by this tepid concession to the "first official language" replied to a government writ by beginning his letter "Dear Sir" and ending "Yours Faithfully," but the rest of it in Irish, for which, no doubt, a translator had to be summoned.

The ordinary Irishman wonders how the Italians would like being forced to learn Latin, whether they had any use for it or not. Hardly anyone outside the more fashionable intellectual circles or in one of the more remote pockets of the island where Irish really is the first tongue will admit that he has any practical use for the smattering of Irish he remembers from his school years. (One exception, it is said, occurred in the Congo when the Irish contingent of the United Nations forces spoke Irish over their radio network as a security measure.)

Yet Irish-speaking is still a matter of governmental concern, and every child must pass in that subject to obtain his school-leaving certificate. Anyone joining the police, the army, or the civil service is required to have a certified knowledge of Irish, and in the national universities fluency is necessary for matriculation. A large part of the educational program is thus devoted to learning a language spoken only in enclaves of the twenty-six counties of the Irish Republic and by a few scholarly specialists abroad.

There is a public assumption that Irish-speaking is a matter of national urgency, a private and bitter resentment of its impracticality. Most Irish will tell you they would prefer having their children learn French, German, or Spanish if a second language is to be required. The letter columns of the newspapers are frequently enlivened by complaints on the subject, the theme of most being that Irish-speaking is an anachronism benefiting nobody but the paid professionals of the language-revival movement, and replies from the other side alleging that such objectors are un-Irish or possibly anti-Irish.

Even those residents of the Gaeltacht, to whom Irish is the mother tongue, often regard it as a quaint encumbrance. An Aran islander will remark, "What use is it once we leave the Kilronan pier?" where the ferry for the mainland calls. "They laugh at us in the Galway City shops if we ask for something in Irish." And there are protests from the same people over the propaganda issued by Dublin intellectuals and bureaucrats, such as a letter in the Connacht *Tribune*: "If there was only half as much meetings about jobs for people, the people might be better off. I don't expect any of these Gaelic League people, or whatever they are, care a straw for my three sons, but I care for them and I would rather hear them speak English as they worked in a Galway factory or a Galway shop than know they could talk Irish to themselves as they worked on an English railway station."

Then too, there are certain academic difficulties arising from the question of just how sound is the structure of the language as it is spoken and written today. The scholars say there were four different periods in the language's development; Old Irish (A.D. 700 to 950), Middle Irish (A.D. 950 to 1200), Early Modern (1200 to 1650), and Late Modern (1650 to the present), The Old Irish exists only in the few surviving ancient manuscripts, while that taught today, so far as a nonlinguist can follow the commentary of experts in the field, is a verbal melting pot of the three later periods with an admixture of Chaucerian and later Anglo-Saxon traces. Spelling in the Gaelic script can quickly bring on a headache to any but the dedicated mind; for example, there is no *v, w, x,* or *z,* except in the schoolbooks which attempt to simplify the learning process.

In 1970 the government indicated it was aware of the rumbles of discontent over the presence of Irish as an indispensable hurdle in the educational system. One way in which that awareness was fostered was through the activities of the Language Freedom Movement, which campaigns against compulsory teaching of Irish on the grounds that it entails "unlimited financial expenditure, many educational handicaps on Irish children, and even denial of basic human rights to those who want their children taught through English, the home language."

The government's answer to such protest movements and to the common knowledge that the majority of the Irish people regard Irish-speaking as something of an unfunny farce was to appoint a commission to study the matter under the guidance of the Minister for the Gaeltacht, George Colley (who is also the Minister of Finance). Undoubtedly the fruit of such deliberations will be a solemn temporizing, in which the Irish bureaucracy is inordinately skilled.

Certainly the gesture appeased few, but amused many. The spokesman for the Language Freedom Movement was quick to point out that most members of the commission are "by and large well-known Gaelic establishment figures. They include some of the staunchest defenders of the unproven assumptions on which the Fianna Fail language policy is firmly based. What kind of objectivity can these people display?" The spokesman, Mrs. John O'Brien, president of the LFM, added the advice that "If the Government really wants objectivity, it can easily engage a professional body of public opinion analysts. It did something like this two years ago; the resultant Dichter report—which cost the Irish taxpayer £7,242 ($17,380)—was hushed up and has never been published."

Equally outraged by the decision of the government to "investigate the attitude of the public to the Irish language" was the stoutly conservative *Irish Independent,* which maintained any such commission should find out why, not if, the people resented compulsory teaching of Irish:

> If the Irish people, or a big majority of them, do not love their language, do not treasure it, do not care two hoots if it is allowed to die, there must be good reasons for their attitude. . . . Mr. Colley once spoke of low standards in high places. He was not referring to the Irish language, but we have no hesitation in saying that so far as Irish is concerned, the standard is very low in high places. In spite of all the *blather,* Irish is rarely spoken in the Irish Parliament. . . . Boys and girls exclaim: "I hate having to waste time doing the old Irish language." We hold that those boys and girls, usually aided and abetted by their parents, are basically wrong in their outlook towards their native language. But they have heard so much about the base uses to which the language has been put that they have lost respect for it; even worse, they often despise it.

Possibly it is the compulsory aspect that causes much of the resentment. Obliquely recognizing that possibility, the Language Commission report of 1963 recommended that the phrase "compulsory Irish" should not be used in discussions of the curriculum, that the proper designation was "essential Irish." What is resented above everything else is the fact that a child cannot be certified as having graduated from primary school if he fails in Irish, even if his marks in every other subject are superlative. The Irish, above everything, hate compulsion. They might be cajoled into accepting Irish-speaking as a matter of national pride, but they will not be dictated to.

There are many who believe that the teaching of Irish will not be placed on a realistic—that is, voluntary—basis until the old guard of the language-revival movement dies out. These veterans of the Irish-speaking campaign tend to romanticize the Ireland of pastoral days, to see the language as a means of resurrecting a golden age which never existed except in myth and legend. "The concept of the Gael as propagated by the extreme wing of the movement," Tim Pat Coogan has observed, "is of a man approximately six feet and five inches in height, noble-browed and with the faraway look in his eye which comes through perusing Erin's past glories. His wife is serene, beautiful and the mother of eleven children."

Meanwhile, the government of the Republic expends millions of pounds annually in preserving and propagating the ancient tongue. Ever since independence the Gaeltacht has been provided with special grants and subsidies, and special schools were established in the region at which teachers could learn Irish in its purest possible form. The Ministry for the Gaeltacht gives each Irish-speaking family an annual bonus of £5 ($12) for each child, obtaining social welfare has been made easier for them, and they receive grants toward the building of new homes. For the past forty years a government-financed organization called the Gaeltarra Eireann has operated small factories to provide employment in the region.

A sort of "dole mentality" has been unwittingly fostered through subsidization, and many families in the Gaeltacht piece together a living out of social welfare, child bonuses, and boarding students who come out from the cities to learn Irish among people who speak it as a matter of course.

Yet even in Connemara, the heart of the Gaeltacht, the children say they want to study English so they will be equipped to obtain employment, if not in Galway City, then in England or America. They may have heard complaints from the outside world of the difficulties encountered in attempting to be bilingual—the Irish army cadets, for instance, who tried to study Rommel's African campaigns from commentaries translated into Irish from German or the public accountants who occasionally grapple with the problem of converting Business English into Business Irish, with "final dividend" translated into *dibhinn chriochnaitheach* and "uncertified bankrupt" into *feimheach neamhdheimnithe.*

Although the Gaeltacht has been treated as a special case by the government and a long and earnest bureaucratic effort has been made to revive the area, it remains as forlorn as its stretches of uninhabited land, its gorse-yellowed hillsides, and its black mirrors of bogwater. It contains the essence of the modern Irish tragedy—the slow death of the rural areas, the forced emigration, the failure of all schemes to maintain the people in decent circumstances on their native soil. Maurya, the mother in Synge's

Riders to the Sea, said it all in one sentence: "They're all gone now, and there isn't any more the sea can do to me."

"The west is dying," they say, despite the £2,500,000 spent annually on the Gaeltacht. Five to six hundred farmers a year are reported to be leaving the land in County Mayo alone. The farm families move to the cities; small government-subsidized factories start up and close down when they prove uneconomic; whole villages are abandoned to the wind and rain. The people of the Gaeltacht say they feel like second-class citizens because they can't keep pace with the material progress in the more prosperous parts of the country. "The West today is a version of the 'Irish towns' outside the walls of garrison towns in the darkest days of the conquest," an Irish radical wrote. "Squalor is lacking, for the disowned people today are free to fly the country and they know where to go."

All over Connemara the population hemorrhage is visible both in statistics and in the countryside. In the Cois Fharraige district the population was 24,584 in 1956; ten years later it was 21,716—cold figures which can be translated in more human terms by the scene at a bus stop where an aging mother sees her sons and daughters off on a bus for Dublin or the night mailboat across the Irish Sea to Holyhead. In the Cor na Ron section of that Gaeltacht district there are 240 people making a chancy living. Year after year, more of the young ones go to the cities. The youth choosing to stay fall into a pattern of dependency. They leave school at about fourteen, go to work in a small factory (toys, seaweed processing, tomato packing) until they are eighteen, when they are eligible for the dole and can receive £7 ($16.80) a week if single, £10 ($24) if married. Only the more ambitious stay in school after they are fourteen and go on to secondary or vocational schools.

Farming, mostly raising oats, is the main occupation of the people of Cor na Ron. The land would defy even a Japanese farmer, however, because there is only a little topsoil covering the ledges which run down to the sea. Tractors can't be used because the laboriously cleared fields are too small. Donkeys pull the plows and reapers. It is a heartbreaking sight to look down from a ridge over the checkerboard of tiny fields, few of them larger than a Long Island swimming pool, each of which had to be cleared of boulders and rocks; the whole landscape appears to have been the playpen of some giant infant who pelted it with every rock he could lay his hands on. So picturesque, the tourists coo, all those lovely quaint walls snaking up and down the hillsides.

In the Ally district, halfway between Spiddal and Inverin along the south Connemara coast, looking out over Galway Bay toward the Aran Islands, there are a few hundred people clinging to their native rocks. They could enjoy some of the most spectacular scenery in the world, with the Twelve Pins looming to the north, if they had not grown indifferent to it. Those harvesting the sea put out in the frail curraghs, made of tarred canvas, as their ancestors did. Those living off the land raise potatoes, oats, and barley and collect sea rods from the shore for the manufacture of animal feeds. The land is so resistant to cultivation that it must be cultivated with a long-bladed spade, such as is used to cut turf. The farmers eke out a living by cutting turf from May to September, an occupation which nets them about £200 ($480) if they have enough grown children to help out in the bog.

The young people either go to work in the Lurgan marble factory and make ornaments and jewelry out of the sea-green Connemara marble for the tourist trade, or they migrate to the cities as soon as they acquire their school-leaving certificates, or they go on to the secondary school in Spiddal. The governmental obsession with Irish-speaking has resulted in a curious transformation. At the beginning of the century English was the first language of the school, Irish of the home. Since Ireland became independent, Irish is the language of the school, English of the home, and most children are bilingual. In the Ally district discontent with this situation and with the fact that the national school is considered antiquated resulted recently in a strike during which parents kept their children home.

In the district which includes Leitir Mor and the islands of Galway Bay, the population has decreased from 2,845 in 1961 to 2,557, from 548 families to 530, and life remains almost as hard, as risky and full of privation as when Robert O'Flaherty made his famous film many years ago. Almost everyone is on some form of the government dole except for a few professional people. For connoisseurs of old folkways, day-tripping over on the ferry from Galway City, the Aran islands of Inishmore, Inishmaan, and Inisheer are as fascinating as they sound, with the islanders clad in their homespun bawneens and wearing pampooties (a rough hide shoe without a heel) even when the folklorists disappear into the mists back to their hotels in Galway.

On Gorumma Island to the north of the Arans about the only occupation for the men is cutting turf which is sold for $48 a boatload to be burned in the stoves and fireplaces on the Arans. They also go out in curraghs to gather seaweed, which they sell for $14.40 a ton, and it takes a lot of kelp to make a ton. The teen-agers attend a comprehensive school at Carraroe, on the mainland, but most of them eventually leave for the cities. The only amusements they can find are the family television set, the pubs of Carraroe, or the "western" dance hall at Beal a Daingean.

Connemara, in its bleak and lonely and almost Gothic magnificence of mountains tumbling toward the wild gray sea, is something other than the paradise it appears to the sport fisherman or the antiquarian prowling its Druid altars, its ruined abbeys and friaries, its ancient stone ringforts and Celtic burial grounds. The people of Connemara regard it as a wide-open ghetto, imprisoning them with the roaring sea to the south and the bogs and mountains to the north. What have they to do, except the slavey's work, with such establishments as Ashford Castle on the Lough Corrib, which has been turned into an elegant tourist hotel providing salmon fishing and snipe shooting once enjoyed by Lord Ardilaun and before him by the powerful Norman family of De Burgos (later Burke)? Their concerns are finding work for their children in the new plastic-toy factory on the coastal road to Spiddal, growing sugar beets for the nearby refinery, or lining up for jobs in the industrial estate outside Galway.

Elsewhere in the Gaeltacht, it is much the same, the desperate pursuit of subsistence in a land where human life, unaided from the outside, is all but insupportable. A case history of disintegration is the half-empty town of Charlestown, in County Mayo near the Sligo border. It is a relatively modern town, having been built shortly after the Great Famine. Twenty-five miles away, around Castlebar, was the demesne of Lord Lucan, one of the notorious dunderheads involved in the Charge of the Light Brigade, who became even more infamous in County Mayo for devising a battering ram to level the cottages of his starving tenants. That part of East Mayo was owned by Lord Dillon, who got in a row with his agent, Charles Strickland, over a social snub administered at a hunt ball. To avenge himself for having been treated as a lackey, Strickland decided to build Charlestown as a commercial rival to Lord Dillon's own village of Bellaghy. He laid it out with the three streets converging on the town's square, one of them leading to the border of County Sligo, the second to the port of Ballina, and the third to Dublin.

Eventually Charlestown thrived while Bellaghy declined. It was famous for having more pubs per capita than any other town in Ireland, a sure sign of prosperity. But it fell into a decline during the long years of the economic war with England.

Like so many other Irish towns which paid in human suffering for the proud De Valera's refusal to truckle to the British, for the Dublin politicians' boasting that Ireland would go it alone and be damned to the English marketplace, Charlestown lost its market for cattle and other farm products. It had nothing to export but its sons and daughters, consigned to the English labor market, and emigration reached floodtide during the World War II years. Nationalistic politics, in effect, dictated that the Charlestowns of Ireland must export their children and keep their cattle at home. Those left behind survived on the money orders sent back from Britain. Thus Charlestown lived on borrowed time, and in the succeeding decades it turned into a shell, emptied of its youth, with only the old and the very young staying on.

For a time the money sent home from England provided a flush of false prosperity. A few people tried to protest, but they were drowned out by the rustle of those lovely English money orders. John Healy, the Dublin journalist who was born in Charlestown, recalled in an *Irish Times* series and a subsequent book that "we never had it so good" during and just after the World War II years when the Irish were at a premium in the war industries. In the forties the unaccustomed security of bank balances erased memories of the thirties and "a town and countryside of living, marrying, breeding, working people."

Learned explanations of how the Charlestowns came to exchange their human potential for money earned in England will not satisfy Healy or the few people who still live in his native town. "The economists and sociologists," Healy wrote, "will now say that the Charlestowns of the West of Ireland were overpopulated and the economic infra-structure, based on agriculture, and the economy of the small farm, could not support the population we had: they had to go. They will summon up statistics from France and Belgium and Germany and the Unites States to demonstrate the correctness of their findings." But to Healy the forces which swept the Irish west of people who had lived there, through wars and famines, for generations were not measurable in statistics but originated in "our failure to recognize the vacuum in rural Ireland." The political and moral leadership failed to supply the values, the examples, even the heroes the west needs to be persuaded that life there is worth living. Talk of infrastructures somehow does not inspire people to fight for their way of life.

Much too late to save Charlestown and its surrounding farms, the £6,000,000 ($14,400,000) Moy Valley Drainage Scheme was launched several years ago with an invasion of earth-moving machines. If agriculture is revived, however, it will be industrial farming. Large plantations will replace the small holdings; another goal of the revolution will have been discarded.

For Charlestown's tragedy John Healy is more inclined to blame the politicians and their failure to keep their promises that local post-primary-school education would be upgraded than the dependency of the townspeople on the money orders from abroad:

> Politicians, good, rank bad, and totally indifferent, have come to spurious power and survived for years on the promise to end [emigration]. Others refused to recognise it: social economists, recognising the word's bad odour and fatalistic connotation of political defeat, have abandoned the word and substituted the euphemism of "outward social mobility" for emigration. To the

people of our town, it doesn't matter any more what they call it. The game is lost: it was over and finished with before they knew it had started. Today a few leave Charlestown every year but it is merely the muscular spasms of a corpse. . . .

The answer of the political and economic planners to such jeremiads as that of John Healy is "regional development" to provide jobs and slow down or halt emigration. Growth centers have been designated for industrial development to take place gradually between now and 1986—a long time to expect of impatient youth. The urban district councils of two of the principal towns in County Mayo, Castlebar and Westport, recently sponsored a study which provides for the establishment of regional complexes as "counter-attractions to the present inordinate rate of growth within the Dublin region."

Spurred by the continuous fall in Mayo's population figures, in spite of a rising birthrate, the plan would promote the growth of Castlebar and Westport as "towns which have already shown dynamism, which contain the necessary basic infrastructure, and which have a good supply of labour and are most likely to give the quickest return on invested capital." Six thousand new jobs would be created in the Westport-Castlebar growth centers, along with the lesser satellite towns of Ballinrobe and Claremorris. Aside from the growth of tourism, no suggestion is made of how new industry will be attracted to the regional-development centers. Under the country-wide Buchanan Plan, too, Galway City is designated as growth center of the west, into which government funds presumably would be channeled. Whether regional planners like the Urban District Councils of Westport and Castlebar could prevail over the Buchanan Plan is problematical, and it will be Dublin which decides where the subsidized industry goes, where the money for new housing, schools, roads, water, and sewage systems will be committed. Politics will be another X factor as rival towns demand that their own growth be subsidized by the central government.

The lovely old seagirt city on Galway Bay is not only the unofficial capital of the Gaeltacht and the center of western tradition with a civic sword that dates back to James I and a great mace that was fabricated in 1710, but the key to the west's hope of survival. If Galway City, its present 28,000 population growing by 1,000 each year, can provide jobs and education for the youth of the Irish-speaking enclaves, all will go well. Its industrial estate recently has acquired garment, china-making, printing, fertilizer, crystal glass and marble-ornament-making plants, not to mention a government-subsidized French firm to manufacture oil heaters which went bankrupt before production started. Tourism has been heavily promoted, especially in the suburb of Salthill, a seaside resort with a splendid mile-long beach and a promenade as impressive, if not as overcrowded, as one of the English beach towns. Even more hopes are invested in the expansion of University College, Galway, with its English Gothic buildings dating back to 1845. The brightest young people in the Gaeltacht are recruited with scholarships provided by the various county councils.

Some years ago Kate O'Brien saw Galway City as one of the brighter hopes of keeping Irish youth, if not in their native villages or townlands, at least within a half day's bus journey from their homes. In Galway, she wrote, "potentially, in our now so wonderfully mechanized and minimized world, is everything that the 1960's and 1970's are going to have to show." Aside from University College, it has a number of technical schools. "To be a student in Galway is a true felicity nowadays. The city is small, and conditioned to the leisure that students like; also it is a city where talk, youth, and extravagance, of idea as of purse, are taken for granted."

Anyone taking a weekend train from Galway to Dublin, crammed as it is likely to be with students still bending over their books and papers, can see that those amenities and opportunities are appreciated to the fullest extent. Their hairstyles may be exuberant as that of university youth anywhere else, but there is not a whiff of cannabis in the air, and their political concerns are more likely to be centered on Northern Ireland than Maoist revolutionary fantasies.

Relatively prosperous, lively, and forward-looking as Galway City is, it also reflects the troubles of its south Connemara hinterland. Ironically, it is the city's growth along the twenty-mile stretch of gray and rugged coast from Galway to Tully that causes much bitterness and controversy. Building construction is permitted only along the north side of the road so as not to block the spectacular views of the thundering sea to the south. Here hundreds of new houses have been built, most of them far more luxurious and costly than more than a few Irishmen could afford. They symptomize a new form of colonization. Most of them are being built by Englishmen, and a few Americans and other nationals, who have fled from their own smog-covered and crime-ridden homelands. Looking at the homes of the newcomers, an Irishman will groan, "We kicked the English out fifty years ago, and now they're all coming back. An Irishman wanting to buy or build a new house is priced out of the market." Along certain streets on the outskirts of Salthill or on nearby Gentian Hill there are rows of houses occupied by retired British army and navy officers; Ireland as a whole, in fact, is the new Valhalla of pensioned British warriors.

A newspaper report on this invasion by leasehold characterizes it as "a new type of heartache and frustration spreading through the area like a cancerous growth and building up into such dangerous proportions that some sort of showdown between local people and the Galway County Council seems inevitable." Gallwegians feel that rich outsiders are being courted while natives, somehow, are neglected. "Basically the Irish-speaking population of Galway feels that the County Council has laced them up in a straitjacket over housing affairs . . . that the Gaeltacht is being steadily anglicized by the new inhabitants. . . . South Connemara, because it is on Galway's doorstep, is fast becoming the place for moneyed people to live and even speculate in property. Sites for houses are now fetching £2,500 [$6,000] from Spiddal backwards while completed houses can fetch from £6,000 [$14,400] upwards."

The natives are caught in a bind of the sort which can be observed elsewhere as people opt out of the world's cities in search of remoteness, serenity, and natural beauty. The newcomers may represent a form of colonization, but they pump fresh money into the local economy and indirectly provide more employment. Meanwhile, the local people are finding it difficult to build their own homes along the coastal road, which will soon constitute a striplike suburb of Galway City, because of the zoning restrictions which prevent building on the south side of the road. "The tourists," says Peadar Mac an Iomaire of the Gaeltacht Civil Rights Movement, "are more important to the planning authorities than the livelihoods of the people of the area. The local people aren't all that interested in beauty and while we agree that certain restrictions are necessary, we would be against them if the ordinary man is suffering as a result of them."

Various outrages of the county bureaucracy are reported: A Galwayman was refused planning permission to build a caravan site on a piece of property he had bought, while across the road from him a foreign business firm had no difficulty in obtaining permission to build thirty chalets, a restaurant, and a swimming pool. A man from the Cor na Ron district was refused permission to build on the sea side of the coastal road, then bought another site on the north side and this time was turned down on the grounds his proposed house would "interfere with the beauty of the locality."

All this, of course, is symptomatic of a region which is struggling to develop itself, to provide work and housing, commensurate to a rising level of expectation, for its long-deprived people. The money of the outsiders is needed to build up and sustain the economy, but their presence, their foreignness, their ability to pay for what they want are nevertheless envied and resented. The conflict of interests, naturally, is all the more emotional among a people which has so long suffered a physical as well as financial domination. What the local people want from the outside is new industry rather than real estate development favoring retired people from abroad; the good of that is felt immediately in larger paychecks. The Steinbock fork-lift truck factory was established in Galway in 1960 by a German company. It employed local people on the production lines, with German foremen supervising them until the Irish became sufficiently knowledgeable. Batches of thirty boys from the technical school were sent to Germany for basic training until a work force was built up. Three years ago the factory was bought by Americans. Welders there make from £20 to £30 ($48 to $72) a week, good enough to lure a number of Galwaymen back from England.

In the southwest corner of County Donegal, a bootstrap-type operation was also launched as a foreunner and possible pilot model of the "Save the West" campaign. Sometimes known as the Miracle of Glencolumbkille, the effort to revive a remote corner of Donegal is watched with considerable interest by all the depressed areas of the Gaeltacht and by small farmers elsewhere who are confronted by the same problems of isolation and finding a profitable market for their produce.

The motive force around Glencolumbkille, as so often in Holy Ireland, is supplied by a rugged, rawboned, hard-driving priest in his mid-fifties. Father James McDyer, the son of a small farmer who spent his formative years in England, looked around his parish, and decided it was dying of inanition, of the youth drain, of hopelessness. The farmers were relying on the old way of doing things, weren't bothering to get the most out of their hillsides. Youth was fleeing the countryside, its bleak glens wedged between the gray sea on one side and mountains on the other, because of a total lack of social life and an absence of opportunity.

From his first days as curate of the Glencolumbkille parish, Father McDyer observed that the whole west of Ireland was afflicted by what he calls a "creeping paralysis." As he warned at public meetings on the subject, "Now we have only the old people and the children still with us. Soon it will be only the very old. After they die comes the wilderness."

A start had to be made on reversing the process, and Father McDyer picked his own parish—typical as it was of so many others—as the starting point. He pledged himself to get the local economy turning over again through cooperative efforts, to keep the young people home by providing at least a minimum of social amenities and improved education.

About all that the priest had going for him was enormous physical and moral energy and an overpowering personality, which showed up, with his dark flashing eyes and beetling brows, on Irish television when his work at Glencolumbkille had made him a national celebrity.

Bulldozing his way through the apathy and inertia of his parishioners, persuading them to organize a cooperative to find markets for their produce, encouraging them to build a hall at which the young people might find recreation, he infused new life and hope into the community. At first this was accomplished by force of personality. He urged the people to get off the dole and opt instead for subsidies for the small holdings. Vegetables were grown and cooperatively marketed for processing, and such traditional crafts as weaving Donegal tweed, so tough it is almost impervious to wind and rain, were revived.

All this needed help from the outside, not only from the government but from individuals with a philanthropic bent. Father McDyer took off in a whoosh of black skirts to raise financial support totaling $93,000 from other sections of Donegal, from Donegal emigrants who had prospered in other countries, from the Guinness brewery, and from a whirlwind trip to the United States. Within a few years he had established a vegetable canning factory, which keeps local girls from migrating, brought in electricity and piped-in water, and built a tweed-weaving factory. He has also inspired farmers to till their land more productively. But not without a certain amount of scurrility from less fortunate communities and some suspicion from his clerical superiors, largely based on the calumny that a cooperative movement resembled the Communist collectives. Once he straightened out the semantic confusion over cooperative and collective, he became something of a national hero, with Prime Minister Sean Lemass opening one of the Glencolumbkille factories, the fashion designer Sybil Connolly trekking over to preside at the agricultural show, and the government handing out an additional subsidy of $70,000. Whether other deprived areas could be brought back to life in similar fashion depends on how many Father McDyers there are in Ireland. Probably not enough.

In Ireland as a whole, as in the Gaeltacht regions where Irish problems attain a ghettolike intensity, the main hope of the people lies in education. A people trying to "catch up" sees the schoolhouse door as the entry into everything that is good, modern, and uplifting. "Education is our only hope," John Healy wrote in *The Death of an Irish Town,* "an education that will aid us to look back upon our past to discover our mistakes as well as our accomplishments; an education that will help us appreciate the realities of the present and the potential of the future." He convicts the successive governments of failing to equip the postrevolutionary generations with the knowledge they needed to cope with the changing world, with being too little concerned with those young people who had to leave their homes to compete with better-educated youth in England and America. For five decades the politicians have been promising higher standards of teaching, more and better schools, a secondary education available to more students in state-supported schools. Education is now the "in-thing in Government circles and among the high priests of economic politics," as Mr. Healy sees it, but he is obsessed by memories of the promises made by other politicians twenty-five years ago when his native town was going down the drain.

Educational reform is the "in" topic of discussion from the rural villages to the solemn panels assembled for the Telefis Eireann cameras, to the smart cocktail parties around Merrion Square, Dublin, to the front pages of the national dailies. Suddenly the Irish public has awakened to the fact that it has been shortchanged. Primary school education, compulsory for all children up to the age of fourteen or fifteen, is still what Padraic Pearse, the schoolmaster and poet martyred in the Easter Rising, called "the murder machine."

If minds are not murdered, the reformers say, they are being put to sleep, closed against even the possibilities of self-education that come with maturity. The trouble is, some add in lowered voices and with nervous glances over their shoulders, that direct supervision of the schools is done by the Catholic and Protestant clergy.

Others have organized to stop the corporal punishment of schoolchildren, claiming their children are brutalized into learning by rote instead of gently introduced to the joys of learning. An organization calling itself Reform, with Martin Reynolds as chief organizer, has dedicated itself to halting the practice of teachers using canes, whips, rubber hoses, and other implements as teaching aids. It charges that parents have been "cowed" by the clergy into accepting harsh treatment of their children. A shock wave went through the country when Irish television picked up an American documentary on child beating in the Irish schools and showed it to a panel of experts, most of whom defended the unsparing rod. The church offers no apologies for its unofficial doctrine, anathema to progressive education elsewhere, that an occasional "walloping" is likely to make the child a better pupil.

Educational reformers, in essence, claim that the state has virtually abdicated its responsibilities for education to the church, that recent studies have unanimously shown that the system is antiquated and undemocratic, that the philosophy guiding it dates back to the British, who were not greatly interested in having to deal with an educated subject people. These allegations would have come as no surprise to the few Irish who may have read Paul Blanshard's polemical and anticlerical *The Irish and Catholic Power* (1954), which declared that the school buildings are "often wretchedly dirty, overcrowded and cold. . . . The oversupply of teachers is so great that only the highest-ranking students in lower schools are admitted to professional training." On the other hand, Blanshard conceded that Ireland was scrupulous in obeying both the letter and spirit of the 1937 Constitution and its clauses protecting the rights of the Protestant minority. "On the whole, Southern Irish Protestantism is satisfied with the present system of school control. In its financial operations, the scheme is administered with scrupulous impartiality. . . . No child is compelled to receive religious instruction to which his parents object; and if a school cannot be found which fits the theological outlook of his parents, the child cannot be compelled to attend any school."

In the West Cork village of Ballydehob, there are two national schools, one managed by the parish priest and the other by the Church of Ireland minister, though one school could comfortably accommodate all of the district's children. Yet there is a separate school for the children of less than a score of Protestant families in the vicinity. Such scrupulousness is admirable from the viewpoint of religious liberty, as an aspect of the tolerance which is certainly one of the finest achievements of the Irish Republic as conceived and shaped by De Valera, but from the educator's position it would appear that one good school would be better than two dividing the available resources.

The historic oddity is that the Irish have been much more obsessed with preserving the Irish language than concerned with modernizing their educational system, though both were proscribed by the English conquerors and survived only through clandestine effort and though equipping the young to cope with the modern world ought to be as important as mastering the ancient tongue. The memory of the hedge schools ought to be sufficient as a goad to giving education a top priority.

Irish education, in fact, had been suffering successive setbacks ever since the Danish invasions late in the eighth century. Until then the monastic schools had kept the lamp lighted in the general European darkness, as the earliest records show. A.D. 550, for instance, fifty students from the Loire district of France arrived at Cork to be educated in the monastic schools, even to be fed and furnished books, at no expense to themselves. Meanwhile, Irish scholars were spreading knowledge all over Europe, as well as preaching the Gospel in places where Wotan and other gods were supreme. "That fierce and restless quality which had made the pagan Irish the terror of Western Europe," Helen Waddell (*The Wandering Scholars*) noted, "seems to have emptied itself into the love of learning and the love of God; and it is the peculiar distinction of Irish medieval scholarship and the salvation of literature in Europe that the one in no way conflicted with the other." Columbanus established more than a hundred monastic schools in France, Germany, Switzerland, and Italy, and such great scholars as Sedalius of Liège, Virgilius the Geometer, and John Scotus Erigena all were Irish-educated.

With the Danish invasion, however, the monasteries were pillaged and burned, the monks put to flight, and their manuscripts seized or destroyed to the point where only ten pre-1000 manuscripts are still preserved in Ireland. The English, too, were determined to keep the Irish masses in a state of servile ignorance. Two years after Henry VIII made himself head of the Church of Ireland, he ordered the monks expelled from the monasteries, which were either torn down or allowed to fall into ruin. Equally stern measures were taken against the Irish schoolmasters.

A royal commission appointed by James I reported on ferreting out those who persisted in trying to keep the learning process alive among the Irish:

> We found in Galway a publique schoolesmaster named Lynch, placed there by the Citizens, who had great numbers of Schollers,

> not only out of that province but also out of the Pale [Dublin], and other partes resorting to him. We had daily proofe, during our continuance in that citty, how well his Schollers profited under him. . . . We sent for that schoolesmaster and seriously advised him to conform to the Religion established, and not prevailing with our advices, we enjoyned him to forbear teaching.

The English monarchs continued their program of stamping out Irish education to "prevent the corruption of the youth of this nation with Popish principles," and schoolmasters who defied their edicts were transported to the Barbados. During the reign of Charles II, despite the most repressive measures, one of his representatives in Ireland admitted that "the people retain an ardent desire for learning." During the seventeenth and eighteenth centuries education in Ireland was driven underground, except for that conducted under Protestant auspices. Anyone setting up a school had to take the oath of allegiance to the British Crown.

From the beginning of the seventeenth century, however, Irish children were being secretly educated in what were called hedge schools. That is what they literally were. The fugitive schoolmaster gathered his pupils in the concealment of a hedgerow and taught in the open air during the warmer months. In the winter he assembled the children in a byre, or barn. A Frenchman named Latocayne who walked from one end of Ireland to the other, carrying an umbrella and a pair of dancing pumps, finding much use for the former and little for the latter, wrote: "It appears to me quite as good to give or receive a lesson in the open air as in a stuffy school." One schoolmaster in County Tyrone had a sod house built by the roadside for him, the tuition for each pupil being two chunks of turf to be burned in a rude fireplace in the center of the classroom when the weather turned cold. The thirst for education, against all the barriers erected by the English, constantly amazed the overlords. Lord Palmerston wrote of his despised tenants on his County Sligo estate in 1808 that there were three or four hedge schools operating on his demesne. "The people join in engaging some itinerant master; they run him up a miserable mud hut on the roadside, and the boys pay him half-a-crown, or some five shillings a quarter. They are taught reading, writing, arithmetic, and what, from the appearance of the establishment, no one would imagine, Latin and even Greek."

Among many of the fugitive schoolmasters there was an enlightened attitude toward both their tasks and their pupils that even today would be accounted progressive. A teacher named Carleton wrote a sort of manual for hedge school colleagues in which he admonished: "We should never forget that they are children, nor should we bind them by a system whose standard is taken from the maturity of human intellect. We may bend our reason to theirs, but we cannot elevate their capacity to our own. We may produce an external appearance, sufficiently satisfactory to ourselves but, in the meantime, it is probable that the child may be growing in hypocrisy, and settling down into the practice of a fictitious character." Children, he believed, should be allowed to behave with as much freedom in school as they did outside it. Learning by rote, he declared, was like forcing a milk-fed infant to "gorge on ox beef."

One of the great difficulties of the hedge schools was obtaining a variety of reading matter, books being expensive and hard to find. What were known as cottage classics were used in County Clare to teach reading, and they included some rare specimens which would have been banned by the keepers of the Index in the Vatican: *Irish Rogues and Rapparees; Fair Rosamund and Jane Shore,* the story of two prostitutes; *Jack the Bachelor,* the biography of a noted smuggler; *Donna Rosina,* the story of a Spanish courtesan; Ovid's *Art of Love;* Defoe's *Moll Flanders;* and the somewhat more edifying *History of the Seven Champions of Christendom.* The above-mentioned Carleton was especially critical of the reading material placed in the hands of schoolchildren, "most inflammatory and pernicious in nature . . . as far as religion and morality were concerned, nothing could be more gross and superstitious than the books which circulated among them." Later they were replaced by sixpenny reprints, published in Dublin, Cork, and Limerick, which were of a more elevated, if less interesting, sort.

Among the Irish the underground schoolmaster enjoyed the highest honor and prestige. Like the parish priest today, he was prominently on display at weddings, christenings, harvest homes, and other social functions. His advice was sought on all sorts of matters, he drew up wills and petitions, and often he served on the side as parish clerk. The English, however, saw him as a rogue of the worst sort. "He is the centre of the mystery of rustic iniquity," wrote one Englishmen in 1820, "the cheap attorney of the neighborhood, the fabricator of false leases and surreptitious deeds and conveyances. Possessed of important secrets and of useful acquirements, he is courted and caressed; a cordial reception and the usual allowance of whiskey greets his approach, and he completes his character by adding inebriety to his other accomplishments." Another English traveler, Sir John Carr, described the schoolmaster as "a miserable breadless being . . . generally a man who was intended for the priesthood, but whose morals had been too bad, or his habitual idleness so deeply rooted, as to prevent his improving himself for that office."

What particularly outraged the English was the belief that the schoolmasters were propagating treason against the Crown. One Thomas Crofton Croker wrote that in the southern province of Munster, especially, the schoolmaster was regarded as an oracle, that in the "evening assembly of village statesmen" he could be heard agitating for a free Ireland; "he talks downright treason; he reasons on legitimate liberty; he is an enemy to royalty and English domination; he is the frequent promoter of insurrectional tumults; he plans the nocturnal operations of the disaffected. . . ."

The establishment by the British of a national school system in 1831 eliminated the hedge school teacher. Padraic Colum wrote an elegy for "A Poor Scholar" who realizes that his day is done and his teaching of Latin and Greek regarded as useless in the nineteenth century. It ends:

> I teach these by the dim rush-light
> In smoky cabins night and week.
> But what avail my teaching slight:
> Years hence, in rustic speech a phrase,
> As in wild earth a Grecian vase.

The hedge schools were one of the glories of the Irish past; the "thirst for education" among the ordinary people surprised the

English, who preferred to think of them as mindless bumpkins, but for many decades Irish education was allowed to decay. People were satisfied that the major responsibility for overseeing education was placed in the hands of the religious denominations, that the illiteracy rate was reduced to 1.6 percent, that education was made compulsory between the ages of six and fifteen.

Admittedly the children of middle- or upper-class homes are given a considerable advantage over the majority of their fellows. A caste system almost as rigid as that of the old Ascendancy is the result, just as in most countries officially dedicated to democratic principles. The boy or girl graduating from primary school has the choice of going to work, which most of the poorer ones do; or attending a secondary school (roughly equal to an American high school), which charges fees; or going to a state-run vocational school, where the fees are nominal, and learning one of the trades for boys, secretarial work or home economics for the girls.

The major advancement of Irish education will be the provision of free and possibly compulsory secondary schooling. The last two ministers in charge of the schools have indicated they realize the necessity of the state's assuming a major responsibility if progress is to be made. In 1964 Dr. Michael Hillery, then Minister of Education, remarked in a magazine interview that "I have to take the initiative all the time. More and more the state is coming out as the only body that is geared to take the initiative, and the Minister now has to be somebody planning and pointing the way, instead of just going around with an oilcan and keeping the machinery in order." His successor, George Colley, who recently stepped up to the Treasury, agreed: "We must improve our system if we are going to progress. I'm talking to priests and educationalists every day telling them what our plans are and what the need is. But in the last analysis, it's my job. I have the power to enforce the rules. The fact that they haven't been enforced doesn't mean they won't be in the future."

Dr. Hillery's metaphorical oilcan, however, is still being employed more frequently than the monkey wrench. The Ministry of Education is combining smaller schools, especially those with only one or two teachers (modeled after the "little red schoolhouse" of American legend), and replacing them with larger centralized schools, which often requires busing. In the rural districts a typical school will remind the middle-aged American with a small-town or rural background of his own childhood. It is attended by about fifty pupils, twenty of the younger taught in one classroom, the thirty older in a slightly larger one. The toilets are dry closets, close enough to the old American outhouse in design and purpose to summon up a wave of nostalgia or revulsion, which are cleaned out several times a year. The school was built shortly after the turn of the century. The only teaching aids are a blackboard and chalk. Water is conveyed from the wellhead in a bucket. There is no electricity, so school hours are adjusted in the winter months to the available daylight. The rooms are drafty and hard to heat, but Irish children mostly are not spoiled by central heating or unaccustomed to chilblains. American devotees of the 3-R principle would be delighted by the curriculum: reading, writing, arithmetic, a smattering of Irish history and geography, religious instruction (Catholic in this case), and the Irish language.

Most of the secondary education is controlled by the teaching orders of the church, particularly the Christian Brothers, for the boys, while the girls are taught by nuns. A separation by class, by religion, and by sex occurs when children are educated beyond the fifteenth year. As one expert says, the Irish educational system is "clearly and uncompromisingly based on money and class. The child of the better-off parents will get the best education available, no matter how unintelligent he may be. The working-class child will leave school at fourteen or fifteen, no matter how promising or talented he may be." Thus the rich and poor are separated from mid-teens, the first going to a private secondary school, the second to the state's vocational school (unless the child has obtained a scholarship) or onto the job market. The number of children attending secondary schools has doubled in recent years, thanks chiefly to increased grants to cover the tuition of those with parents unable to afford the fees. "Comprehensive" secondary schools operated by the state in areas where there are few such facilities are also being introduced. However, those with the best chance of succeeding in life, as with Americans who attend prep schools versus those who graduate from high schools, will continue to matriculate from such posh academies as Belvedere, Clangowes, Blackrock, and Castleknock or the even more fashionable Catholic boarding schools in England.

This inequality of educational opportunity has been officially stigmatized as a "dark stain on the national conscience," but about 40 percent of all Irish children still end their schooling with only the primary leaving certificate in hand. There is also considerable controversy, now including parents as well as teachers and members of the educational establishment, over the effectiveness of teaching methods, the emphasis on examination, the rigid orthodoxy of the religious teaching orders.

"Teachers in Ireland are on the whole conservative," wrote Rosita Sweetman in a recent survey published by *This Week*. "They come in the main from a rural background, have been through a training college or a university where their attitudes to formal instructional teaching were ramified. . . . One of the urgent requirements is a proper re-training scheme for teachers at all levels; this should include the clergy, in day to day control of hundreds of schools, who are notoriously conservative in their outlook."

Miss Sweetman calls the examinations the "bogeyman of education" because they overemphasize the ability to memorize and stifle the student endowed with an imagination or with talents in other directions than mere brain stuffing. Assistant Secretary Sean O'Connor of the Ministry of Education agrees: "The syllabus tends to be dominated by the examination—that is a tragedy. . . . I see no reason why children shouldn't bring in their dictionaries and reference books to examinations. We have gone to absurd lengths in memory testing; it would be a good thing now to give priority to comprehension and the intelligent use of information. . . . The leaving-certificate doesn't give enough scope for conceptual thinking. It is too much a regurgitation of information. I think we should be past that." O'Connor hopes for the establishment of a separate university for the training of teachers.

Higher education is also being expanded. The bastion of the Protestant ruling class has always been Trinity College since its establishment by Queen Elizabeth I; it is Ireland's Harvard/Oxford, but until recently no Catholic could attend Trinity without a special dispensation. Its Catholic rival is the National University, with colleges at Dublin, Cork, and Galway. The effects of the ecumenical spirit fostered by the Vatican councils were slow in being felt in Ireland, and it wasn't until 1965 that the Archbishop of Dublin, Dr. John McQuaid, omitted the usual warning from his Lenten Pastoral that any Catholic who attended Trinity without receiving a dispensation was "guilty of a mortal sin and while he persists in disobedience is unworthy to receive the sacraments." When the ecumenical glow reached Dublin, it was announced that Trinity College and University College of Dublin would be amalgamated as the University of Dublin—the greatest "mixed marriage" ever permitted in Ireland, as the wits noted.

That marriage has not yet been consummated. Meanwhile, the lordliest social and cultural cachet is affixed to a Trinity graduate, un-Irish as any sort of caste system may seem. I once met a man in the bar section of the Cork-Dublin train who displayed all the Irish swiftness and subtlety in establishing his credentials. Within the space of a quick drink, he managed to inform me that he was suffering from a hangover induced by too much port—not porter or Paddy, mind you—which had been imbibed at a reunion with several of his Trinity classmates. To cap it all, before tottering away, he offered me a pinch of snuff from a chased silver snuffbox.

10.

Dev: Odd Man In

> *For a joke, some seraph must have touched the lips of De Valera with a chilled coal from God's altar, to laugh henceforth at the sturdy mouth's efforts to blow it into flame, to turn it into a song of derring-do for everyone to whistle o'er the lave of it.*
>
> —SEAN O'CASEY, *Drums Under the Windows*

The heading of this chapter would be regarded as highly disrespectful around the presidential quarters in Dublin's Phoenix Park. Nobody calls President Eamon De Valera Dev to his face, and very few did when he was young and lowly enough for ordinary familiarity. But then, how many people were really permitted to call Eisenhower Ike? If President De Valera is consciously Olympian, if he demands the utmost respect for his person, if he flouts the ancient Gaelic urge toward the equalitarian, perhaps he has earned the privilege. He is the only surviving member of the World War I generation still occupying a seat of power. Almost ninety years old, almost blind, he towers over modern Irish history not only physically, with his tall unbending figure, but in every manner of political and moral presence. The most remarkable thing about the man and his career is that he accomplished it all with a manner as forbidding as that of the Dalai Lama, the antithesis of all that the Irish in politics usually signifies.

The Irish worship the heroic—Mick Collins was the man for glorification, particularly after he was safely dead—but when it comes to the ultimate political leadership they seek the hard man, the practical man, and to hell with charisma.

The creation of modern Ireland was almost an act of De Valera's will. His paternal feeling toward his country was epitomized in the statement "Whenever I wanted to know what the Irish people wanted, I had only to examine my own heart, and it told me straight off." It also expressed a breathtaking arrogance, for the Irish themselves seldom know what they want, and very often it does not coincide with what De Valera's heart tells him they want.

In or out of power, but seldom out of it, De Valera has dominated the Irish political arena for more than fifty years, largely by holding himself sternly aloof from the mob, by maintaining an air of absolute authority, to the point where it seems indubitable that Charles de Gaulle used De Valera as a model in raising himself above an equally volatile electorate. He is the old-fashioned Irish father, down to the last ironfisted gesture, the last unbrookable pronouncement. He is not to be argued with; he is the master of the national household.

In the old viceregal lodge, which he did so much to detach from the British proconsuls, he maintains himself as the national totem whom, to be frank, few Irishmen love or like but whom most of them fear and respect. The nation's more distinguished visitors are brought to him for a courtly audience. Occasionally he may be glimpsed standing stiffly at attention, imperious profile indifferent to the wind and rain, at yet another unveiling of a martyr's plaque or a funeral of a sufficiently eminent veteran of the "Old IRA"—De Valera's IRA, before it was outlawed and became less than respectable. His vision is so clouded he can see little of his surroundings, the rambling official residence in Phoenix Park, the gardens and immaculate lawns, which are a legacy of the dispossessed British. A military aide is always at his side to guide him through the ceremonial functions which take up most of his official life.

His wife, a woman of gentle beauty who keeps out of the limelight, writes fairy tales for children. The late Oliver St. John Gogarty would probably say that De Valera has written fairy tales for the adults, believing as he did that "fairy tales are our politics," that Ireland sustained herself on illusions which De Valera did little to destroy. "Woe betide the reputation of anyone who wakens us up from our dreams," Dr. Gogarty told an American friend. "The reaction of this on Ireland, whose politics are supported by the American Irish, can be imagined. It leads to a perpetuation of the politics of the Famine. It keeps alive resentment and encourages the demagogues here to hawk hate."

De Valera's constituency is not swayed by such considerations. There is a large "nest of simple folk" out back of the beyond, in the whitewashed cabins of the countryside where the majority lives, which intuitively understands and supports De Valera's vision of what Ireland should be. It is conservative in every sense and undismayed by the fact that De Valera was, as a liberal commentator bitterly complained, "the genius who took socialism out of Irish Republicanism." It would be fairer, perhaps, to say that De Valera is a determined centrist. During more than twenty years as Prime Minister, he displayed a remarkable command of the ability to meet challenges from both right and left, from the IRA and an Irish offshoot of Fascism known during the uproarious thirties as the Blueshirts.

Certainly it was his ability to strike a balance, to remain above the clash of street politics and the clamor of contending personalities, to maintain an Olympian reserve, that accounts for his survival when other strong men, such as Michael Collins, Kevin O'Higgins, General O'Duffy, and others have been snuffed out either by an assassin's bullet or by losing their hold on their followers. Certainly it is not because, like certain Irish-American politicians, he was able to make himself a lovable figure (Al Smith, for instance), the epitome of grace and intelligence (John F. Kennedy), or the symbol of raffish benevolence (like Curley, Murphy, and other political bosses). The chilly self-containment of his personality was etched in acid by Sean O'Casey in *Drums Under the Window:* "For a joke, some seraph must have touched the lips of De Valera with a chilled coal from God's altar, to laugh henceforth at the sturdy mouth's efforts to blow it into flame, to turn it into a song of derring-do for everyone to whistle o'er the lave of it. Though Sean knew not even of De Valera's existence, there he was walking beneath the gentle clouds caressing Dublin's streets: a young man full of the seven deadly virtues, punctual, zealous, studious, pious, and patriotic . . ."

If De Valera did not quite succeed in making Ireland into his own austere, schoolmasterly image, it is still true that up to 1970, at least, it is the most old-fashioned, pious, and tradition-bound of Western democracies. There are many who claim it is Sicily West. But the question is whether this is due mainly to De Valera's influence or more likely because De Valera is a reflection of the determined conservatism of the Irish majority.

His career, as an act of will, as a monument to the "seven deadly virtues" for which O'Casey and many of his countrymen indict him, prevailed against bone-deep prejudices of the Irish against all politicians. They are the most political of peoples, as their history there and abroad demonstrates, but they are also the most cynical and skeptical about their politicians. Practically all Irishmen, with an easy fatalistic laugh, are convinced that all politicians are entirely governed by self-interest—not least those who based their careers on deeds allegedly performed in the rebellion or the civil war.

This attitude is hilariously conveyed in John B. Keane's *Letters of a Successful T. D.* (that is, a member of the Dail), which has been reprinted a number of times in paperback and is regarded as almost a guidebook to the political psyche. Its antihero is Tull MacAdoo, member of the Dail from a backcountry parish, who believes that he and his colleagues are "the men who freed the country and we are entitled to certain considerations." In one of his letters home Tull ingenuously reveals his own venality: "As you know the new housing scheme for Kilnavarna is long overdue and it looks as if the County won't be able to afford it for many a year. McFillen knows how I can get 25 prefabricated houses at £250 a house. That's £6,250. A pal of his will be importing fifty of them from Europe and I can have twenty-five. I'll probably get a friend of mine here in Dublin to buy them and I see nothing to prevent me from flogging them to the county for four or maybe five hundred apiece. In the name of the sainted mother of God, destroy this letter! Because, if wind of this move got out, I was finished. It would be a front page scandal. It's a clever move, you'll have to agree. The houses are being imported as an experiment, and, if they are a success, they will be manufactured here. McFillen will be a sleeping director of whatever company gets the concession." Tull forebodingly adds, "If this country knew one-tenth of the things I know, there would be a revolution tomorrow morning."

To which millions of Irishmen would add a fervent amen. To a constituent who threatens to expose Tull MacAdoo, T. D., for the fraud and corruptible he is, however, Tull gives the lie to that amen: "Listen, Flannery, why don't you go for the Dail? You have a following who think you're God Almighty. You would definitely get in. No bloody fear, Flannery: you leave the dirty work to me and my equals and criticize us with safety from a distance."

For a subtler view of the political hack in his natural surroundings, there is the James Joyce story, "Ivy Day in the Committee Room," from *The Dubliners.* It ironically exposes the gap between idealism and practice, and the custom of venerating the safely dead hero. " 'This is Parnell's anniversary,' said Mr. O'Connor, 'and don't let us stir up any bad blood. We all respect him now that he's dead and gone—even the Conservatives,' he added, turning to Mr. Crofton."

One difficulty in dealing with the Irish electorate is its amazingly long memory. The events of the early twenties are still spoken of as though they happened the day before yesterday. Thus any political figure in Ireland is dogged relentlessly by his missteps. And thus there were questions about De Valera, not to mention rumors and suspicions, which bedevil him occasionally in his present Olympian isolation. There are many who still criticize him for not having taken a more active combat role in the Revolution; for having insisted that Michael Collins and others negotiate the treaty with the British when he possessed iron-bottomed negotiating powers equaled in modern times only by Comrade Molotov; for not having participated in the actual fighting against the Treaty State forces during the civil war. All through his career, too, he has had to reply to charges that he isn't "really Irish." Half-Spanish and born in Manhattan, he was reared and educated in Ireland.

The failure of the insurrection against the Treaty State left De Valera, politically and personally, in desperate circumstances. He had ordered the stand-down in 1923, when the badly outnumbered IRA had been broken into small fugitive bands, when

12,000 members of the antitreaty forces and their sympathizers had been jailed by Collins' successor as chief of state, William T. Cosgrave.

De Valera himself was still at large in August, 1923, when he made a speaking appearance in Ennis, County Clare, his old constituency. Wearing a black suit, black tie, and black hat and a funereal manner appropriate to his circumstances, he stood up to address his supporters. "I have come to tell you," he told the hundreds in the crowd, "I have never stood for brother's hand being raised against brother—"

Before he could elaborate on that rather curious preamble, a column of Free State soldiers marched into the square and arrested him on orders from Prime Minister Cosgrave.

De Valera thereupon spent a year as a prisoner of the state at Arbour Hill Barracks.

Shortly after his release he returned to Ennis, the scene of his arrest, and uttered one of his few known witticisms: "People of Ireland," he began, "as I was saying before we were interrupted. . . ."

From then until 1932, when he finally obtained the power he had sought so long, De Valera occupied an equivocal and cautiously employed position as leader of the opposition in and out of the Dail. Ireland, though the civil war was officially over, stayed in a state of turmoil for several years, marked by an army mutiny and an underground resurgence of the IRA. De Valera had renounced the tactics of force in overturning a government he considered to be a betrayal of the Irish Revolution but on at least one occasion reluctantly took part in abortive negotiations aimed at obtaining arms from Soviet Russia.

During that time in the political wilderness he moved steadily toward a centrist position. Then and for years to come, Ireland would be obsessed with issues growing out of the civil war, a situation that continued for three decades while the country stagnated socially, economically, and politically. The old feud between the pro- and antitreaty forces would reverberate for almost two generations. Cosgrave was the standard-bearer for the urban bourgeoisie, the slowly rising middle class, and to the right of him was Kevin O'Higgins, the Vice-President and Home Minister in charge of tracking down dissidents. To the left was the

Sinn Fein and its violent twin, the IRA, with their leftmost faction composed of those who believed in the establishment of an Irish workers' republic. So there was room for a man who raised himself, cautiously and gradually, above the factionalism, who could promise to vindicate the Revolution without stirring up more violence.

Toward that end, early in 1926, he and his followers organized the Fianna Fail (Soldiers of Destiny) Party. Most of the Sinn Fein followed him into the new party, constituted along more politically practical lines, and left the diehards to plot and swear vengeance in the decades to come.

Months before the election, the "hard man" of the Cosgrave government, Kevin O'Higgins, was assassinated. He had been in charge of the repressive measures directed against the IRA and to a lesser extent De Valera and his followers, both of whom he detested individually and collectively. His heroes were Arthur Griffith and Michael Collins, whom he considered to have been the victims of De Valera's intransigence. O'Higgins' enemies—a number greater than those of any man in Ireland, with the possible exception of De Valera—accused him of trying to emulate Benito Mussolini, with the ultimate ambition of becoming dictator of Ireland.

Actually O'Higgins was an intensely ambitious man, young, ruthless, and energetic, but there is no evidence that he intended to work outside the democratic system. Like Griffith and Collins, he believed that Ireland needed civil peace and time to recover from the troubles that had been pulling down the country for a decade. Further, he believed that Ireland could be unified without drastic action in the northern six counties and that he was the man to do it. The year before his death, in 1926, he ably represented Ireland at the League of Nations in Geneva. Privately, with his active disposition, he got fed up with the proceedings, one of the reasons for his disgust being the fact that the Americans "buzzed" around Geneva as unofficial meddlers. He was one of the few Irishmen of that period who felt little gratitude toward the United States.

There was no doubt at all of Kevin O'Higgins' willingness to act sternly against those whom he considered enemies of the state, to wield his executive powers ruthlessly. Although he had been best man at the wedding of Rory O'Connor, he did not hesitate to order O'Connor's execution for his leading role in the Four Courts siege, which inaugurated the civil war. A heavy drinker in his early youth, he nevertheless decided that drink, next to revolutionary intrigue, was the worst problem facing the Irish. The sale of alcohol was prohibited on St. Patrick's Day at his command, and pubs were (and still are) required to shut from 2:30 to 3:30 P.M. (the Holy Hour) to break the habit of extended and boozy lunch hours.

Undoubtedly O'Higgins would have become Cosgrave's successor as Prime Minister, though he himself, feeling that he was "walled in by hate," did not expect to live that long. On Sunday, July 10, 1927, he was walking to church in Booterstown, County Dublin, alone and unarmed. A car with three gunmen and a driver was waiting at the top of Cross Avenue. The moment O'Higgins came within pistol range the gunmen jumped out of the car and emptied their guns. O'Higgins fell with one bullet in the head and six in his body. For five hours his will to live struggled against the inevitable. To friends gathered at his bedside he remarked that he looked forward to sitting on an Irish cloud with Mick Collins, both of them playing harps and talking politics. Among his last words were a warning against the ambitions of Eamon De Valera: "Tell my colleagues that they must beware of him in public life; he will play down to the weaknesses of the people."

The IRA, to wide disbelief, denied responsibility for O'Higgins' assassination. In any case, that event brought the proposal from Prime Minister Cosgrave for much sterner laws, including the death sentence for possession of firearms, which would be presented to the next sitting of the Dail. O'Higgins' death also removed De Valera's most dangerous and determined opponent. De Valera saw that it would be necessary for Fianna Fail to take its seats in the Dail to combat Cosgrave's sterner measures and to build up the party's base through parliamentary action. In the general election of 1927, Fianna Fail won 44 seats to Cosgrave's government party's 47, with others scattered among the Farmers', Nationalist, Independent, and Sinn Fein parties.

Now arose a situation which called up all of De Valera's talents for sideslipping. He and his fellow members of Fianna Fail could not legally take the seats they had won without taking the oath of allegiance to the British Crown, nor could they remain politically effective by sulking on the sidelines. De Valera's appearance on the floor of the Free State Dail on August 10, 1927, was a masterpiece of quibble and evasion. Gloomy as an undertaker in his frock coat, he stepped up to the clerk of the Dail and announced: "I am not prepared to take an oath. I am prepared to put my name down in this book in order to get permission to go into the Dail, but it has no other significance." There was a Bible in front of him for the oath taking, but he carefully shoved it aside, adding, "You must remember I am taking no oath." The government did not object to this saraband of legalisms, and De Valera and his followers were allowed to take their seats. Sardonically watching, Cosgrave commented that "they all seemed to have been blown in here from an outer world like little winged angels."

Thus began De Valera's cautious advance toward the governing power. It would take time to explain away his yielding on the point of the oath taking. Though he did not swear on the Bible, there was undoubtedly an oath of allegiance prefacing the register he signed, which he later explained as nothing more significant than an "autograph."

There was a touch of sanctimony about De Valera's performance as leader of the legal opposition which greatly annoyed many of his colleagues. Puritanical in his personal life, a nonsmoker and nondrinker, he wanted the bar in Leinster House, next to the members' dining room, closed down; he campaigned against the evils of jazz, gambling on the horses, and reading indecent literature, which he believed should be proscribed by a rigorous censorship of books, films and the Sunday papers from Britain.

His gravity, his self-righteous air particularly irritated Oliver St. John Gogarty, who was then a senator. Anyone who led Fianna Fail, meaning De Valera, had to "dress like the manager of the Cats' Home," Gogarty declared. "He had to look grave; he had to be filled with the milk of human kindness but touched withal by a gentle melancholy on account of the dope he must administer in the end."

All of De Valera's plans came to fruition in 1932, when Fianna

Fail won 72 seats in the Dail to Cosgrove's party's 57 and De Valera was named president of the executive council (in effect, Prime Minister, although that office was not formalized under the Gaelic title *An Taoiseach* until the Constitution of 1937). From then until 1948 he held that office and molded the nation according to his own visions and principles, his view of an ideal Ireland (not much different from Michael Collins'), his fervent hope of reviving the Gaelic culture and language.

A radio broadcast in 1943 encapsulated his dream of what Ireland should be: "The Ireland which we have dreamed of would be the home of a people who valued material wealth only as a basis of right living, of a people who were satisfied with frugal comfort and devoted their leisure to the things of the spirit; a land whose countryside would be bright with cosy homesteads, whose fields and villages would be joyous with the sounds of industry, with the romping of sturdy children, the contests of athletic youths, the laughter of comely maidens; whose firesides would be the forums for the wisdom of old age. It would, in a word, be the home of a people living the life that God desires men should live."

And what leader, good or bad, would not aspire to a country so satisfied with "frugal comfort," a people docile, unambitious, and with their minds fixed on the rewards of an afterlife? It was a thoroughly paternalist dream; father figure knows best; let somebody else mind the store up in Dublin.

Single-minded, he proceeded to abolish the oath of allegiance and end the payment of land annuities as required by the treaty with Britain, upon which the British imposed duties on imports from Ireland. This hit the Irish farmer hard. In retaliation De Valera placed a heavy tariff on imports from Britain. That was the beginning of the "economic war" with Britain, which could not have come at a worse time, the beginning of the worldwide Depression.

His measures to alleviate the effects of the economic crisis met with little legislative favor, in either the Dail, where he ruled through a small margin, or the Senate, which was composed of sixty members, thirty elected by the Dail, thirty nominated by the executive. The upper house, including William Butler Yeats and Dr. Gogarty, often tried to block his legislation. De Valera's program of self-sufficiency was mocked with particular acerbity by Senator Gogarty, who charged that De Valera was a "sixpenny Savonarola in a Woolworth world," that his was "a voice from a mathematical madhouse, from some algebraical world of minus values where everything is upside down and all the quantities are negatives." Gogarty demanded whether, under self-sufficiency, the potato should be extradited because it had been introduced into Ireland by Sir Walter Raleigh. In the first six years of De Valera's administration, it was estimated, the economic war cost Ireland £48,000,000 ($240 million).

His prestige, significantly, was higher abroad than at home. Only months after taking office, he went to Geneva to preside over the thirteenth session of the Council of the League of Nations. There he was praised for statesmanlike vision in pleading that the League's sanctions be obeyed, that each of the member nations live up to their obligations. Best speech ever made by a Council president, said the Manchester *Guardian*. But it was one thing to play the frock-coated messiah on the rostrum at Geneva and another to work out Ireland's problems. The country probably had never been poorer since the Famine. Irish children, until about ten years ago, were rarely seen wearing shoes except to school and to attend mass. The depression that ended for most of the world around 1940 hung on for another twenty years in Ireland. Meanwhile, De Valera's world reputation rivaled that of Gandhi, and his people, basking in that reflected glow, came to agree that "Dev" must be some kind of genius.

While De Valera labored to solve Ireland's economic problems, he was caught in a nutcracker situation peculiar to the thirties and common to other Western democracies: the power plays from right and left, near-Fascist and near-Communist, that in different forms afflicted Britain, France and the United States, that in more naked forms overwhelmed Germany, Italy, and Japan. It must be said that De Valera, in his confrontation with extremism, came off as well as anyone, if not better.

The challenge from the right was presented by an organization calling itself the Blueshirts, which was so indigenous that the ordinary people saw no connection between them and the Brownshirts then taking over Germany or the Blackshirts which had assumed power in Italy. The Blueshirts were an outgrowth of the Army Comrades Association formed in 1932 by Thomas O'Higgins, a brother of the late Kevin O'Higgins, with the ostensible purpose of protecting the meetings and rallies of the Fine Gael (Cosgrave's) Party from violent intrusions by the IRA. Unarmed and undermanned police were unable to keep order on such occasions, and there was little reason to suspect that O'Higgins' musclemen were the nucleus of a praetorian guard. Fine Gael supporters also had a point in their favor when they claimed that De Valera could have acted more forcefully in protecting the rights of free speech and assembly when it came to his opposition. At any rate, the Army Comrades Association evolved into something more alarming when the leadership was taken over by General Eoin O'Duffy, a bluff and hearty military type, and when such intellectuals as William Butler Yeats (who wrote their marching song) gave it their support for a time.

The IRA, meanwhile, had set itself up as the Blueshirts' front-line enemy, as well as De Valera's political opposition. IRA activities, after all, had given rise to O'Duffy's organization. A corporate state, to the IRA, meant an Ireland modeled after Nazi Germany and Fascist Italy; the country needed stronger protection against such a menace than the schoolmasterly, overly patient De Valera could provide.

De Valera had little hope of appealing to the nobler instincts of General O'Duffy, whom he had recently fired, so he turned to the IRA with an appeal for reason. He knew that there had been considerable Communist infiltration of the IRA, that his old comrades now regarded him as a "defector," but he apparently felt he had more influence in that quarter than with the Blueshirts. So he called in Sean Russell, then operating head of the IRA, for a sort of peace conference. The IRA, he admitted to Russell, was his toughest problem; time would deal with the Blueshirts, the economic malaise, and the others. It was an inconclusive meeting, but De Valera knew that sooner or later he would have to drive the IRA underground.

A more sinister possibility than IRA intransigence had presented itself: that of a rightist rising on Memorial Sunday, August 13, 1934, when the triple anniversary of the deaths of Michael Collins, Arthur Griffith, and Kevin O'Higgins was to be commemorated. General O'Duffy announced that he and his

Blueshirt legions would march to the bronze and stone cenotaph standing near the government buildings on Leinster Lawn. De Valera and his advisers suspected that once they laid their wreaths, the Blueshirts might keep on going and take over the seat of government, much as Mussolini and the Blackshirts had in Rome. De Valera accordingly cracked down hard. The Public Safety Act of 1931, which had been largely responsible for Cosgrave's overthrow and De Valera's accession, was revived along with the military tribunals which would try anyone caught defying it. Furthermore, De Valera forbade any Blueshirt to march to the cenotaph or elsewhere on Memorial Sunday. On that occasion most of the Irish Army was deployed on the approaches to the Leinster Lawn. Had De Valera not taken such forthright action, there might well have been a massacre of Blueshirts, who were poorly armed for all their strutting and stiff-arm salutes, by the IRA, which was well equipped with machine guns and other weapons.

It was all rather un-Irish, a reflection of European political violence as much as a reignition of civil-war issues. Soon enough the Blueshirts fell apart as a national organization, and in 1936 De Valera made his move against the IRA. Its chief of staff was arrested, and the IRA was declared an illegal organization.

Once the extremism of right and left had died down, De Valera proceeded on what he regarded as the most important business of his government, the new Constitution of 1937, which effectively converted the Irish Free State into the Irish Republic, all but completely severed from Britain (the exception being the three treaty ports the British retained). In drafting that document, he consulted the works of those who had written the American Constitution as well as Abbé Sieyès and the third Earl Grey and other authorities. He told the Fianna Fail convention of 1936 that he was writing a new constitution "as though Britain were a million miles away."

It was published in the spring of 1937. Henceforth Ireland would officially be known as Eire. The link with the British Commonwealth was preserved through "external association" with Britain, a pet phrase of De Valera's, which hardly anyone but De Valera entirely understood. At any rate it preserved Ireland's imperial preference while furthering political independence. The Senate was abolished, as was the ceremonial office of governor-general. Censorship of the newspapers, books, and films was formalized. (Foreign authors like Hemingway, Faulkner, Huxley, and Sinclair Lewis and native writers like Sean O'Faolain, Sean O'Casey, and Liam O'Flaherty had been banned for years.) One of the finest legacies of De Valera's long years in power, however, was the clause guaranteeing religious freedom to all faiths, while recognizing the Catholic Church as the religion of the majority. He was determined that religious strife would never reappear in the Irish Republic, and it never has. It is a paradox that Ireland, for all the religious persecution she had experienced, for all the fervent Catholicism of its majority, is a model of tolerance—and for that much is owed Eamon De Valera.

The new constitution was approved by a plebiscite, and the following year De Valera made solid progress toward bettering relations with Great Britain. Such amity was and probably always will be necessary to achieving and maintaining prosperity in Ireland. De Valera went to London and negotiated an agreement to end the economic war. A reciprocal trade treaty was signed, by which certain British and Irish goods were allowed duty-free into the respective markets. Persuading the British to give up the treaty ports at a time when German invasions of the Rhineland, Austria, and Czechoslovakia raised the prospect of another continental war was much more difficult—especially since Churchill warned that "In a war against an enemy possessing a numerous and powerful fleet of submarines, these are essential bases." The British, however, agreed to evacuate their bases, to accept £10,000,000 in settlement of the £98,000,000 due as payment on the lands reclaimed from British proprietors.

De Valera came home in triumph, sensibly called a general election to claim the political spoils of his diplomatic triumphs, and his party was returned to the Dail with a sizable majority. "Now," he said, "it is possible to pursue a steady path." Under the new constitution De Valera had become the Prime Minister in name as well as fact, and Dr. Douglas Hyde, a Protestant long preeminent in the revival of the Irish language, was installed as President at the viceregal lodge.

When war came to Europe again, all of De Valera's talents as the head of a nation determined to preserve its neutrality under any possible combination of events were severely tested. Every bit of Irish self-interest was involved in keeping out of the conflict. De Valera stood firm even when the United States became involved, though the Irish Republic could hardly have been established without American aid and sympathy.

The Irish supported their leader in maintaining a stance of "aggressive neutrality," in warning any nation which threatened to invade the Irish Republic and use it as the base for military or naval operations that the Irish would resist to the full extent of their powers, in rejecting Roosevelt's demand that German and Japanese diplomatic representatives in Dublin be sent packing, in turning down appeals for British and American occupation of the former treaty ports to guard the sea lanes against German submarines. De Valera was so fastidious in walking the knife-edge which kept his country out of war that he paid the diplomatically correct call on the German legation to express his condolences on the death of Adolf Hitler. In his victory speech Churchill could not resist jibing at De Valera—with whom he had less in common, personally and politically, than any other man alive—that despite all temptations his government had left Ireland to its isolation and De Valera to "frolic with the German and later with the Japanese representatives. . . ." De Valera stiffly replied that Churchill should have been generous enough to "acknowledge that there is a small nation that stood alone, not for one year or two, but for several hundred years, against aggression," by which he meant British aggression.

During the postwar years, De Valera's party was swamped in the Dail by an alliance of its opponents, and a coalition took over the government for three years. De Valera was replaced as Prime Minister by John A. Costello, who moved swiftly to end "external association" with Britain and the British Commonwealth and to proclaim Ireland an entirely independent republic. He lost the executive power from 1948 to 1951, when Fianna Fail, forming a coalition of its own with the Independents, was again ascendant. During the fifties Ireland's industrial and social progress was slow; it was afflicted by an adverse balance of payments, high unemployment, the emigration of 30,000 of its young people annually. De Valera was still Prime Minister and the father of his country, but there were newer and younger men pressing for recognition, for social reform and industrial progress that would bring Ireland closer to the standards of other Western nations.

It also seemed that he hoped to turn the clock back rather than provide the material things for which the Irish were experiencing much stronger urges. Thus he was touching, perhaps, but out of step, when he would remark, "Sometimes I think it would be a fine thing for us in this country if we could shut ourselves off from the rest of the world and get back to the simple life I knew as a boy in Bruree."

In 1959 he surrendered the prime ministership and was elected President. In that eminence he remains Ireland's first citizen and the world's senior statesman. By masterly maneuvers, by patiently educating the electorate, he brought his nation out of the delirium of the civil war, detached her from the British Empire, kept her safe during World War II, and nurtured a career longer than Stalin's or Franco's or Salazar's as head of state. If he failed in any major effort, it was to keep his promise of 1932 that he would engineer the radical programs required to "provide the fundamental needs of our citizens." It has not escaped notice that Ireland did not begin to share in the general prosperity of Western nations until very late in the day, until in fact a year or two after De Valera was tucked away in the presidential mansion in Phoenix Park.

His successor as Prime Minister was a member of the old guard—Sean Lemass, who had been a sixteen-year-old rifleman during the Easter Rising, an IRA guerrilla, a member of De Valera's staff during the civil war, Minister of Industry and Commerce during Fianna Fail's long ascendancy . . . his credentials were impeccable. If De Valera was the supreme practical politician, Lemass proved himself the master of practical economics. He turned Ireland around, promoted economic growth, restored good trade relations with Britain without sacrificing sovereignty, made himself the "general manager of Ireland."

The prosperity that peeped over the horizon almost from the day Lemass took over the government brought a transformation visible from Donegal to Cork, though it may have skipped a few areas. It is characterized by the outcropping of television aerials, the displacement of the donkey cart by the automobile, the better clothing and plumper faces of the Irish people, the spreading industrialization of the Shannon estuary and around Dublin, Cork, Limerick, Galway, and other cities, by the flood of consumer goods, the fleet of Aer Lingus jets flying to Europe and America, and the booming tourist industry.

The blueprint for Lemass' program of modernizing and bringing prosperity to Ireland, of switching the emphasis from agriculture to industry, was contained in the Whitaker Plan. This was the work of Dr. Kenneth Whitaker, secretary of the Department of Finance, who proposed that much of the budget be devoted to encouraging productive investment, establishing new industries to build up exports, attracting foreign capital through grants and tax holidays. German, Japanese, American, British, and French industrialists soon appeared on the scene, not always to the heartiest of welcomes from the rural Irish, who feel that the government is willing to "lash out the money to any foreigner" with a scheme for building a factory at the Irish taxpayer's expense, but reluctant to back a native entrepreneur.

During Lemass' seven years as Prime Minister Ireland began looking outward, too, as an enthusiastic member of the United Nations and an ardent sympathizer with the aspirations of the underdeveloped Third World. Thus Irish contingents joined the UN peace-keeping forces at various times in Lebanon, Kashmir, Cyprus, the Congo. The Congo operation, in particular, left a tragic mark on Ireland. Dr. Conor Cruise O'Brien, the educator, writer, and occasional politician, had been sent to Katanga as UN representative and played a controversial role in the suppression of the Katangese revolt. The cost of international idealism was borne home when ten Irish soldiers were killed by Baluba tribesmen in an ambush; the whole country went into mourning on November 22, 1960, when their coffins were carried down O'Connell Street in Dublin. But Ireland's interest in the Third World was unabated, particularly in Africa, more recently in the Nigerian civil war, largely perhaps because for generations Irish missionaries by the hundreds have been active in Africa. As a result, many African students are choosing to attend Irish universities.

Lemass' successor, after he retired from politics in favor of a highly successful business career, was a tall, reticent, relatively youthful man—born in Cork a year after the Easter Rising, the first Irish leader to break what seemed an unbreakable link with the Troubles—Jack Lynch. Like the pedantic De Valera, like the brusque Lemass, he seems an odd type for an Irish politician, with melancholy blue eyes and the sensitive features of a minor poet. Yet Jack Lynch, who had served as Minister of Finance in Lemass' Cabinet, had risen to political eminence partly because of a striking athletic record; in his youth he was the hurling star of Cork City, six times an All-Ireland medalist, whose feats with the hurley stick are still a glowing memory in a nation which regards the hurler as a man among men.

It soon appeared that the euphoria of Lemass' years, the surging industrialism, the burgeoning tourism, even the possibility of amiable relations with Ulster, might not carry over into Lynch's administration. Prime Minister Lynch has been beset by bank strikes, Maoism among the university-educated youth, the outbreaks of rioting in the North (bringing appeals for the South to help in some militant fashion it is not prepared to undertake), the problems connected with entering the Common Market, a slightly overheated economy which has resulted in a spiraling cost of living, and challenges of his leadership within his own party.

The old wounds keep reopening. Just when things were going smoothly, Ulster exploded in the summer of 1969 and reminded the Irish, if they needed reminding, that Ireland was still not unified, that British troops could be summoned to keep the peace on Irish soil. When Ulster quieted down again in the spring of 1970, thanks largely to British pacification efforts, the Republic was shaken by a gun-running scandal which indicated there was a faction within Fianna Fail, and worse yet within Lynch's own government, which strongly favored more assistance to the beleaguered Catholics of Ulster than the government was prepared to supply.

The Prime Minister apparently was speaking for the majority

when, shortly after the rioting in Belfast and Derry which followed the arrest of Bernadette Devlin in late June, 1970, he adopted a moderate tone and pleaded for restraint. Five persons had been killed in that outbreak, and Lynch expressed his regret over their deaths, but added: "Apart from the personal tragedies involved, violent protests and provocation parades can only retard the attainment of social justice, the promotion of peace and brotherhood between Catholics and Protestants and the implementation of reform." A poll taken by *This Week* magazine indicated the people favored the same attitude of restraint. There is no doubt they want the border erased, but 83 percent of the persons polled disapproved of arms being smuggled from the South into the North. As for armed intervention—the invasion of Ulster by the army of the Irish Republic, which reportedly is ill equipped for any such aggressive purposes, especially if it were to be confronted by British forces—77 percent disapproved of such an action, and only 17 percent approved.

Even the perpetual critic of those in political power, Dr. Noel Browne, spoke out in favor of Jack Lynch's determination to keep the situation damped down and the hotheads under control. "I have been a life-long bitter critic of Mr. Lynch," he said, "but he has now been transformed into a strong determined man of action. He is the first influential Irish leader who is not merely mouthing the platitude that peace is the answer to partition. He has proved in the fire of his tough decisions that he really means it."

Even more surprising, and a lot more shocking than Dr. Browne's approval of a Fianna Fail first minister, was the announcement that two of Lynch's ministers had been fired and a third had resigned for alleged implication in a plot to smuggle arms and ammunition from Europe, via Dublin, to Northern Ireland. Minister of Finance Charles J. Haughey, the son-in-law of Sean Lemass and therefore a top-drawer member of the Irish Establishment, and Minister of Agriculture Neil T. Blaney were those fired by Lynch. Minister for Local Government and Social Welfare Kevin Boland then promptly tendered his resignation. The Irish public is relatively shockproof when it comes to the antics of their politicians, but this was the sort of crisis that would have toppled a government anywhere else, and hours after Lynch made his dramatic announcement at three o'clock in the morning a large crowd milled around the gates to Leinster House.

Subsequently Haughey and Blaney, along with three other men, were arrested on charges of conspiring to smuggle arms and ammunition (500 pistols and 180,000 rounds of ammunition, consigned from an export firm in Vienna to Antwerp for forwarding to Dublin, as it later developed) into the Republic for use in Northern Ireland. The charges against Blaney were later dismissed for lack of evidence. Early in September, 1970, however, Haughey was brought to trial in the heavily guarded High Court of Ireland in the old Four Courts building which had once been the scene of an even more violent schism between factions disputing the course of the island's history. Standing trial with him were Albert Lukyx, a Belgian-born businessman who had become an Irish citizen; Captain James Kelly, a former army intelligence officer; and John Kelly, the chairman of the Belfast Citizens' Defense Committee.

It became apparent that a serious split had developed within the Fianna Fail Party over how far the government should go in reclaiming the six counties of Ulster. That Kevin Boland, though he had not been charged in the arms-smuggling conspiracy, was the leader of a faction urging more forceful intervention in Ulster was indicated when Prime Minister Lynch summoned a meeting of Fianna Fail members of the Dail—in which he held a majority of seven over the combined opposition—and demanded successfully that Boland be expelled from Fianna Fail's parliamentary party. Ten other members voted with Boland against his expulsion, and those eleven votes could threaten Lynch's majority if turned against the government.

Lynch withstood a clamor for a general election, but it was obvious that his troubles with the activist wing of his party had not ended.

In American terms, an analogous situation, roughly, would be for President Nixon to claim discovery of a plot within the highest echelons of his administration to send more forces to Vietnam, after he had begun his troop-withdrawal program, followed by his peremptory removal of the Secretary of the Treasury and the Secretary of Agriculture and the resignation of his Secretary of Health, Education, and Welfare.

Until the arms-smuggling crisis, Lynch had been known as "gentle Jack," but his determined moves against the opposition within his own party, including the orders to arrest two of his ministers which could have come only from him, showed he possessed sterner qualities than affability. "Something has happened to easygoing Jack," a newspaper columnist wrote. "I told on another occasion how he once got a skelp on the head at the beginning of a [hurling] match and only smiled, but went on to get the winning goals later."

Lynch undoubtedly will need all the courage first tested in the organized mayhem of the hurling field. In almost half a century, there have been only five prime ministers, but the *Taoiseach* is as beset by powerful and contentious personalities as any tribal chief of ancient times.

He must answer to the constant questioning and probing of rivals within his own party and those of Fine Gael, Labour, the Independents, and all the way down to the noisy young Maoists. Fine Gael, headed by William Cosgrave's son Liam, is still the major parliamentary opposition party, the lineal descendant of the old pro-Treaty State forces once led by Collins and Griffith. It has been trying to fabricate a more modern approach, along the lines suggested in the statement of a youthful Fine Gael senator, Garet FitzGerald (the Senate was abolished but then in characteristic Irish fashion reconstituted as the Senead, a mostly honorary body). "Politicians today," he said, "have to choose between the length of old memories and the impatience of young minds." As he summed up the ideological position of the two parties, "Fianna Fail tends to concern itself with getting things done, to achieve quick results. Fine Gael is more concerned with the liberty of the subject. Fianna Fail was a party of the Left and we were to the Right. Now it has moved Right and we have moved Left."

Essentially, however, Fine Gael attracts the support of the various strata of the middle class, as Michael Viney and Owen Dudley Edwards observed in their essay "Parties and Power." *

* Published in *Conor Cruise O'Brien Introduces Ireland,* edited by Mr. Edwards.

These include "recent entrants to the urban lower middle class," a growing multitude, and "a swelling generation of urbanized Irish whose regard for technology and the modern devices of capitalism has led to their rejection of what they see as at best an irrelevant, at worst a handicapping, adherence to the outmoded Gaelic culture. This culture is seen as entrenched in the countryside and the small towns, for whose economic ills they may hold it responsible."

Labour, with its power centered mostly in Dublin and a few of the larger cities, operates along the lines of similar Socialist parties in Britain, West Germany, and the Scandinavian countries, but with considerable more panache, having the polemical services of such brilliant and articulate people as Dr. Conor Cruise O'Brien and Dr. Noel Browne. Brendan Halligan, the Labour Party's secretary and a member of the Dail, believes it is the only one with a clearly defined program, which with modifications is that of James Connolly and his vision of a workers' republic. "Fianna Fail and Fine Gael don't really relate to anything but historical differences," Halligan declared, pointing out that the two major parties are the result of civil war issues. "Fianna Fail is a conservative-type government. Fine Gael are caught in a cleft stick, seeking a philosophy, having an identity crisis."

Yet it is plain that all three major parties suffer somewhat as Democrats and Republicans in the United States from a sort of schizophrenia. Many of the left-wing members of Fianna Fail and Fine Gael are more Socialist-minded then the right wing of the Labour Party.

Among the gadflies who swarm over the political scene none is more stingingly iconoclastic than Dr. Noel Browne, who criticizes his own Labour Party, as well as the conservative tendencies of the Irish workingman, with a sometimes startling lack of inhibition; it was perfectly characteristic of him to lavish praise on Jack Lynch when he stood up against the militant faction of Fianna Fail. Browne came of a poor family up North, in Derry, where his parents did piecework in the shirt mills. Later the family moved to England, where his mother was buried in a pauper's grave and one of his brothers died in the workhouse. Through the patronage of a wealthy Dublin family, he was educated at Trinity College and graduated with a medical degree. After practicing for a time in England, he returned to Ireland and was appointed to the staff of a County Wicklow sanatorium. Shortly after World War II he conceived a plan for fighting tuberculosis —from which his mother died and he has intermittently suffered —which required a fund of £250,000 ($600,000). Fund-raising speeches somehow led him down the political path and into the office of Minister of Health during the Costello interregnum of 1948-51.

As Minister of Health, Dr. Browne made himself highly controversial through his Mother and Child Welfare scheme, which raised the specter of Socialized medicine and eventually led to the breakup of the Costello coalition. Essentially the program provided for free maternity treatment and free medical attention for all children up to the age of sixteen. Not only the medical profession but the Catholic hierarchy assailed it, the latter because Browne's plan did away with the means test (by which recipients must prove they need medical attention and are unable to pay for it). The church declared that the state would usurp the "rights of the family and of the individual" and the program would be "liable to very great abuse." There was also a sexual education clause which the hierarchy claimed would "give local medical officers the right to give instruction to Catholic girls and women in regard to this sphere of conduct." Browne also ran into clerical difficulties when he refused to appoint a nun as matron of a hospital.

A brandishing of episcopal croziers was then—and to some extent still is—sufficient to put the quietus to any scheme. Dr. Browne lingered long enough in office, however, to build facilities for the treatment of tuberculosis and bring down the death rate from that disease from 3,103 in 1948 to 432 in 1961.

A member of the Labour Party since 1964 and a member of the Dail from a southeast Dublin constituency, Dr. Browne, certainly one of the most fascinating men in public life, continues his career of smashing idols and breaking political china, including that of his own party. Recently he made a speech guaranteed to offend practically everyone, except those numerous Irish who delight in the spectacle of someone else verbally cracking heads.

Expressing what he called the "hard truth" about the Irish working class, Dr. Browne called it "the end product of a deeply conservative socio-economic educational and cultural environment. . . . He [the workingman] is as conservative as the most august elder of the Carlton Club. Virtually all our politicians have been afraid to come into conflict with this truth and instead have simply come to terms with it as a reality of their political strategy. Those who in private protest their left-wing convictions supinely continue to preach the kind of right-wing conservative pap that gets them elected to a pleasant job in the Kildare Street Club known as Leinster House."

All that most politicians of any strike yearned for, he said, was the "back seat of a ministerial Mercedes." Labour had to shake the clinkers out of its own grate, make its leaders declare themselves for or against a continuance of the capitalistic system. The old catchwords of republicanism were "ideologically meaningless and emotive words" brandished during a "half-century of political make-believe." The Irish have to choose between the social reformism of the British Labour Party or the Marxist revolutionary Socialism of James Connolly. "I am a socialist in the Connolly tradition. Each of us who now proclaims his socialism must make clear what kind of socialism he believes will achieve our ends." There could be no mere "tinkering" with a capitalism and trying to make it work along Socialist lines; there could be no more patience with Fianna Fail, "born in a period of romantic idealism and idealists, corrupted over the years from the top." His hard question: "Must we not destroy capitalism as we know it, in all its vicious inhumanity in Ireland, and on its remains create a truly socialist society? If the avowed capitalist cannot make it work, how could we?" What he proposes is "a workers' socialist republic in a united Ireland in the Seventies."

To the outsider who believes Ireland is a political paradise from which the radicals, as well as the snakes, have been driven, it would come as a shock to realize that Dr. Noel Browne's call for the overthrow of capitalism is one of the milder voices raised in the cities. Slow and careful Erin is not about to be converted into an island outpost of Russian or Chinese Communism, but there is a rising militancy from the left and the encouraging turmoil in Ulster which sends shock waves through all Irish society, to raise hopes far from the Liffey. Russia has become so interested in the Irish situation that for the first time it has dispatched a resident correspondent of Tass, the Soviet news agency, usually the forerunner of more than merely journalistic interest, to be posted in Dublin. And Ireland has evolved quite as much as the United States from the automatic anti-Communist reflexes of the McCarthy period. Which is to say that even a Communist—if not always one of the Maoist variety—is tolerated.

Mick O'Riordan, who used to be a conductor on the Dublin buses but is now the proprietor of a left-wing bookshop in Pearse Street, is the resident commissar, the leader of the Irish Workers' Party. He has never been subjected to any violence because of opinions generally unpopular—his fellow workers on the bus line gave him a chiming clock when he retired as a conductor—and is optimistic about a more receptive spirit among the Irish, a willingness to look beyond the old orthodoxies. As leader of the Irish Communists the most he can claim, at the moment, is a reported Communist infiltration of the IRA, whose pronouncements grow more leftist every year.

Not only prosperity but a willingness to open their minds came to the Irish in the sixties, O'Riordan claims. "Pope John and the first sputnik set a lot of people thinking, and that is always a healthy exercise. The Vatican revolution opened their eyes to a new world."

It is true enough that urban, educated Irish are searching for a new direction, but whether university-educated youth will choose to sip at the philosophical fountain in O'Riordan's bookstore is another question. As with radicalized youth elsewhere, they find the standard Russian-brand Communism just another tawdry orthodoxy and seek the madder music broadcast by Peking and formalized in the homilies of Chairman Mao. The Little Red Book and the wild slogans (more Celtic than Chinese in their style) scrawled or painted on the hoardings in Dublin and other university cities bear frequent testimony to the intense flirtation with Maoism. Undoubtedly many of its followers are foreign students enrolled at Trinity, but there are plenty of the native breed. They demonstrate vociferously against the American presence in Indochina, but they tend to ignore Irish political questions, which they regard as part of the mess their parents made. Their parents are more than content that their children should concern themselves with events half the world away and leave the serious business to their elders.

Generally their antic behavior is tolerated in Dublin, so long as it does not turn to violence, but there is a growingly repressive attitude in other cities with smaller and quieter contingents of Maoists. They are likely to turn up on any occasion at which notoriety can be garnered from their actions. A Maoist squad moved in when Dr. Benjamin Spock appeared at Mansion House in Dublin, some of them carrying pictures of Chairman Mao and others with signs reading "Spock, U.S. Fascist Imperialist Agent"—something which even American Maoists have not accused Dr. Spock of being. The Garda had to be called when some of the female Maoists stormed the platform and tried to take over the proceedings.

A few years ago there was head cracking when the Maoists staged a sit-down on O'Connell Bridge and blocked traffic on Dublin's busiest street. The large force of Garda did not interfere until a youth on a motorcycle came roaring out of Westmoreland Street and began weaving in and out of the squatting demonstrators; later the Maoists charged he was an agent provocateur employed by the Special Branch, which infiltrates and keeps a close watch on radical student movements. Several of the demonstrators tried to haul the motorcyclist off his machine, the Garda promptly deployed in a baton charge, and many of the demonstrators were left inert with head injuries.

In Cork and Limerick, recently, the city authorities warned that they would not tolerate any more nonsense from the Maoists. The sentiment in Limerick City, which the leftish commentator Proinsias MacAonghusa labels "Ireland's most intolerant city," possibly a reference to the fact that something like a pogrom was once carried out against the small Jewish population there, is hotly anti-Maoist. The mayor, Stephen Coughlan, a Labour Party member, loudly praised those constituents of his who attacked a Maoist bookstore, while James Kemmy, former chairman of the Labour Party in Limerick, has defended the Maoists on civil-rights grounds.

Predictably the church has frowned on Maoism, with the Most Reverend Dr. Michael Browne, Bishop of Galway, observing that "We are going through a period of unrest when press, radio, and television give exaggerated publicity to the statements and actions of very small groups and even individuals. . . . Our young Maoists never refer to the fact that even in the highest ranks of their own Chinese party, life has no value or security. In the recent so-called cultural revolution, 100 of the 135 top-level Communist leaders were put to death."

Occasionally a cause or pseudocause pops up to enlist a fairly wide political coloration from liberal to far left, such as when the Dublin police moved in massively to evict a number of persons squatting in the old Georgian houses in Hume Street, which were to be demolished to make room for modern office buildings. Here was an event which enlisted the sympathies of the liberal Jesuit Father Michael Sweetman, Dr. Noel Browne, and many others who spring into the arena with alacrity. From across the Irish Sea such expatriates as Edna O'Brien, Spike Milligan, and Sean Kenny added their verbal weight to the protest.

Their support from across the Irish Sea was not enough to satisfy Dr. Browne, who wrote in a letter to the *Irish Times*: "As one who protested at Hume Street but who—of greater importance has consistently expressed this abhorrence of Leinster House [that is, the headquarters of the ruling party], their ineptitude, petty-mindedness and poltroonery over the past fifty years here in Dublin, I am reminded of the incident where a harassed and beleaguered Mick Collins received a telegram from the ultra-militant arm-chaired Yanks, 'Fight on, Mick,' it taunted, 'we're all behind ya,' and Collins' comment, 'Yes three thousand miles behind me.' " The trouble with O'Brien, Kenny, Milligan & Co., Browne wrote, was that "so many of talent such as the above-named wouldn't stay here and fight, and so the yahoos won."

One of his heroes, James Connolly, would have approved of those sentiments. Writing of earlier times, Connolly, as though sensing that his hopes for a revolution aaginst the Irish bourgeoisie as well as the British imperialists would be betrayed, observed shortly before his execution: "The Irish Gael sank out of sight, and in his place the middle-class politicians, capitalists and ecclesiastics laboured to produce a hybrid Irishman, assimilating a foreign social system, a foreign speech and a foreign character." It is still the "hybrid Irishman" who serves as the left wing's devil figure, along with the materialism and conformity, the yearning for respectability which characterizes the middle classes everywhere.

The Irish Babbitt is under increasing attack from the left, but President De Valera and his other defenders need not be unduly disturbed. Intellectual ferment isn't likely to boil over into revolution; the country is still safe for yahoos and anti-yahoos alike, and the De Valera legacy of a tranquil nation, of toiling and pious masses, certainly is not threatened seriously from within. More than by revolutionary threats Ireland is still bemused by the sad and bitter truth that afflicts so many other former British colonies: the fact that all its worldly troubles were not stamped "made in England."

11.

The Celtic Difference

I am not making a plea for the existence of ghosts and extra-human influences. I would be more inclined to argue that in the context of Ireland the traveller would be well advised to suspend both belief and disbelief in this connection.

—OWEN DUDLEY EDWARDS

With their lives circumscribed by the Irish Sea, St. George's Channel, and the open Atlantic, and their history until recently encouraging a belief that they were surrounded by hostile forces, the Irish long preserved an attitude toward their ancestral superstitions, the mythic and legendary that delighted and amazed the European scholars studying their folkways as palimpsests of humanity's earliest speculations on the nature of its world. The Irish have retained their hold on that attitude; their racial memory is no fuzzy-minded cliché. After all, they can boast that it served as the foundation of possibly the most remarkable edifice in modern literature, which has found houseroom for Yeats, Moore, Joyce, O'Casey, O'Faolain, and even that rambunctious lodger Brendan Behan. It also resulted in that blend of the romantic and mystic with the realistic which became the bench mark of Irish drama, prose, and poetry.

If you would dismiss the prevalence of witches, the profusion of fairies, the plenitude of things that go bump in the night, as the result of peasant superstition or the products of a cottage industry fabricating quaintness for tourists, you would probably not be expelled from the country. The Irish would probably agree with you that it's all a lot of nonsense—including the housewife who avoids throwing dishwater out the door after dark for fear of drenching a passing fairy or the farmer who plows around a hawthorn tree in an otherwise cleared field because it might be bearing a fairy thorn and there's no sense taking chances.

The Irish fairies, by repute, are no Tinker Bells; they can react malevolently to trespasses on their domain. There was the case of the thorn tree near Downpatrick which had to be uprooted and hauled away in the process of clearing the site for a new building. The workmen sensibly refused to have anything to do with that phase of the project, so the superintendent had to haul it away himself. A horse shied; the superintendent was kicked in the leg and had to have it amputated.

There is so much supernatural lore to be extracted from the Irish countryside that a few samples will have to suffice. Pookas, which are sometimes said to take the form of horses or large black dogs, have been rampant in the not very distant past, particularly in the vicinity of drinking men. The Doneraile family in County Cork has been plagued by an assortment of apparitions, including the resident banshee (which wails advance notice of a death in the family), various pookas, several lively and diligent ghosts, a coach drawn by four headless horses, and other spectral heirlooms. It is notable that the richer a family has been, the more such visitations it receives from the other world; the affinity of ghosts for castles is notorious, and the possibility of snobbishness in that realm is worthy of speculation.

In the Curragh the Earl of Kildare is said to rise from his grave every eleven years and ride to his castle on an enchanted horse. The Anglo-Irish were anything but immune to talk of banshees and little men, much as they scorned the mentality of the "ignorant Irish peasant." One of the more intelligent specimens of that caste, the writer Edith Somerville, recalled a banshee encounter in her own family, and she wasn't writing with her tongue in cheek. One night her younger sister ran into Miss Somerville's room wailing that she had been awakened by the figure of a woman—the form often taken by a banshee—keening and moaning in the garden under her window. In the morning they learned that six children of the district, on an outing celebrating the eve of St. John, had been drowned that night when their boat capsized in Rosscarbery harbor. The tragedy occurred just about the time the woman made her appearance in the Somerville garden. Miss Somerville also wrote of a shoe two and a half inches long which had been found in a pass through the Bantry Mountains; a leprechaun, it was locally believed, had made it for a fairy.

Other curiosa whose manifestations have been more or less solemnly recorded are the Nine Green Cats of Ballydineen, the Flying Yellow Dog sometimes observed in the Oldchurch graveyard, the Death Coach drawn by phantom horses, and the Radiant Boy of the Mallow Road, a friendly ghost who sits on a gatepost in a nimbus of stars which he playfully hurls at passersby.

Regarding all this, the historian Owen Dudley Edwards comments that, while "not making a plea for the existence of ghosts and extra-human influences," he would advise the foreigner in Ireland to "suspend both belief and disbelief in this connection. . . . We find ourselves perpetually surrounded by imponderables which mock at our investigation, from the early monks who knew too much to reject coexistence with pagan survivals, to Yeats, who in poetry strove with success to catch a glimpse of these intangibles. . . ."

Pagan beliefs, especially those relating to the supernatural, endured in Ireland long after the church moved to stamp them out as heretical and un-Christian. Centuries after St. Patrick and other missionaries began their campaign against the old Celtic gods, their Druid spokesmen, and their attendant demons, the old superstitions were still lustily coexisting with Christianity. Witchcraft, often of a rather benign sort, was regarded with respect as late as the last century, especially in rural Ireland, where even the rational mind can be persuaded of the possibility, at least, of unseen powers moving out there in the moonlit boreens and the shadows of the marching hedgerows.

The most celebrated of the latter-day wonder-workers was a woman born an O'Connor but better known as Biddy Early. Much of her legendary powers of healing and occasionally of working mischief may be questioned, but not the sway of her remarkable personality and the hold she exercised on the imagination of her contemporaries.

Her extraordinary fascination, even as a bent and toothless

crone in her eighties, may be glimpsed in a brief item published in the Limerick *Chronicle* of July 29, 1869:

> We understand that a marriage of an extraordinary kind was celebrated this week in Limerick by one of the parish priests, that of an old woman known as "Biddy Early," who resides near Tulla, and who, among the peasantry, has the reputation of a witch or sorceress, who could cure all kinds of diseases. Such was her power over a fine young man named Pat O'Brien, from Glonnagruss, that she succeeded in inducing him to become her fourth husband, although she is said to be over eighty years of age.

Lady Gregory, the playwright, gleaned much of Biddy Early's story for *Visions and Beliefs in the West of Ireland,** and her close associate William Butler Yeats mentioned her in one of his poems:

> Dim Inchy Wood that hides the badger and fox
> And marten cat, and borders that old wood
> Wise Biddy Early called the wicked wood.

Biddy acquired and demonstrated her powers at a time when the church was vigorously campaigning against such survivals of the pagan tradition, having expressly forbidden "all dealings and communications with the devil; and inquiring by improper means after things which are lost, hidden or to come." Things lost, hidden, or about to happen were exactly what interested her.

She was born some time late in the eighteenth century in the townland of Feakle, at the head of the Lough Graney, about twenty miles north of Limerick City, a district still rather remote, as though hiding from modern influences, even with the flight patterns of Shannon Airport overhead. During Biddy's lifetime the village of Feakle also served as headquarters for the Irish Rabelais, Bryan Merryman, whose *Midnight Court* was regarded as giving off satanic emanations. Perhaps there *was* something a trifle unhallowed in the misty air, the feathery glens, the little lost woods of the Feakle townlands.

* Recently reissued as part of her collected works.

As a girl Biddy O'Connor went into service as a maid in the nearby village of Tulla. One of her responsibilities, according to the tales still told in the district by such local historians as ninety-six-year-old Jim Fitzgerald and eighty-seven-year-old Jack Horan, was caring for an unearthly and delicate infant of the household which employed her. Legend has it that the child was a changeling—one the fairies had left in the cradle to replace an earthly child they had spirited away—who would soon return to the netherworld. A transference of powers, it was said, took place when the changeling decided that Biddy O'Connor was wise and gentle enough to use them for the general good. One day the infant suddenly told Biddy: "I won't live long. Take down that bottle from the shelf. It will give you power. Be sure to do good with it."

Biddy's miraculous bottle began acquiring fame in the neighborhood about the time she married her first husband, a man named Early, the first of three she was to bury. She was described as a tiny redheaded woman with strange blue-green eyes, who always wore a white bonnet when she traveled around the district with her magic bottle and practiced her sorcery.

Biddy was denounced by the parish priest, and his parishioners were forbidden to consult her, but she soon acquired a sizable clientele around County Clare. Pilgrims came to Tulla with their physical or spiritual problems, which Biddy Early referred to her magic bottle for solution by peering into its interior and finding the answer. Money never crossed her palm, but she was willing to accept such tokens as whiskey and food.

Modern investigators of her legend may suggest that Biddy, with or without her magic bottle, possessed a form of extrasensory perception. If so, it often took dramatic form, considering the number of persons she is supposed to have raised from their deathbeds. Certainly her prescriptions would be the envy of any modern practitioner of ESP. "As you near the Black Wood," she would tell one client, whom she had just given a herbal mixture, "your horse will take fright. Take care not to be thrown. And be extra careful that the bottle is not broken." She was amazingly precise in giving directions for locating lost or stolen livestock: "You'll find your cattle at Nanegh on the first fair day of next month" or "Your thoroughbred horse is grazing in a field five miles southeast of Dublin."

Many of those who consulted her had to walk the backcountry roads for four days to reach the cabin on a knoll outside the village of Feakle where Biddy maintained her clinic. Most of those who took her advice asserted that they were cured of their ills or found the solution to their various problems at the bottom of her miraculous bottle. Her intuition, or whatever it was, was sometimes alarmingly acute. A priest whom she had never seen before, one from a distant parish, came calling in the guise of a man who needed help. Presumably he wanted to determine what sort of witchery she was practicing. He had hardly sidled into the lean-to where she held her consultations when she asked, with a glance from the blue-green eyes which seemed to penetrate every earthly fallacy, "Where are your vestments, Father?"

Some of her insights would seem strange indeed to the modern mind but were accepted readily enough by people who still believed in the domination of an invisible world around them, in the manifestation of fairies and changelings and haunted woods.

William Butler Yeats, for one, seemed to give solemn credence to such goings-on when he wrote in *Irish Fairy and Folk Tales*:

> Sometimes the fairies fancy mortals, and carry them away into their own country, leaving instead some sickly fairy child, or a log of wood so bewitched that it seems to be a mortal pining away, and dying, and being buried. . . .
>
> If you overlook a child, that is look at it with envy, the fairies have it in their power. Many things can be done to find out if a child is a changeling, but there is one infallible thing—lay it on the fire with this formula, "Burn, burn, burn, if of the devil, burn; but if of God and the saints, be safe from harm." Then if it be a changeling it will rush up the chimney with a cry. . . .

A drastic means of determining whether you are dealing with the netherworld, perhaps, but the overwhelming influences of the unseen had to be combated by desperate measures. It was so easy to run afoul of them, to venture by mischance into their realm. One man, critically ill for no apparent reason, came to

Biddy (by then Biddy Flannery, her second marriage) as a last hope of recovery. Biddy determined the cause of his malaise immediately. "Throw your mind back," she told the sufferer. "One day you are cutting turf in the bog. Then came a fairy wind, whirling the straws as it moved across the bogland. You threw a sod of turf at it. You are the luckiest man in the world to be alive as you just missed hitting the Queen of the Fairies." A long and arduous formula for propitiating the fairies was then prescribed.

Biddy's fame spread across Ireland with the years. Her successive marriages indicated to women that her charms and spells worked with men as well as the "little people." The great Daniel O'Connell came to see her, whether or not to find a means of bewitching the English opposition in Parliament. The local lord named two of his racehorses for Biddy and her current husband.

When she lay on her deathbed in 1874, a neighbor named Pat Loughnane decided to arrange her reconciliation with the church. He summoned the parish priest, who heard her confession, gave her the last rites, and pronounced her shriven of her long apostasy. Before he left the dying woman's house, the priest searched through her possessions until he found Biddy's magic bottle. He took it to the nearby bog of Kilbarron and hurled it into the brown water. Nobody, it is said, has troubled to recover it, though the recent revival of witchcraft in Britain and America would seem to make it an object of considerable potency, always provided that one could find a changeling to restore its magic properties. Biddy's cabin has been restored by Dr. William Loughnane, the grandson of the man who brought the priest to Biddy's house in her last hours, but he can find no scientific explanation for her reputed talents.

The Irish, in any case, are more interested in intuitive rather than scientific answers to the riddle of the unknown. It cannot be said that they have entirely forsworn all the old beliefs which their priests have denounced as pagan superstitions. Only recently a youth in Aughnacliffe, County Longford, established himself as a faith healer whose reputation for cures and miracles, thanks to the swiftness of communication, already rivals that of Biddy Early. He has no magic bottle bequeathed by a changeling, but he is the seventh son of a seventh son. According to ancient Celtic belief, that endows him with magical powers.

The youth, Finbarr Nolan, discovered his ability to heal several years ago and began practicing in a modest, local way. Then he and his brothers—the less fortunate six—set up operations in a local dance hall. His method is what American faith healers call a laying on of hands, plus a dash of holy water. There is nothing picturesque, showmanly, or personally compelling about young Nolan; his manner is as unremarkable as a farmer disinfecting sheep. Deadpanned, rather commercial in his approach to the woes of mankind, he daily receives a standing-room-only crowd in a building in Arva, near Aughnacliffe, to which he transferred his headquarters because the Garda there are better able to handle the traffic his presence attracts. People come from all over Ireland and lately from America and Britain to be healed or comforted by Finbarr Nolan, seventh son of a seventh son. The other six sons constitute the administrative staff and collect cash donations at the door.

The clergy has frowned on him, as they did Biddy Early, but the crowds keep increasing. Clerical objections are based on his sprinkling the customers with holy water, thereby combining the ritual of the Catholic Church with the superstitions of the ancient Celts. Newspaper and magazine publicity, climaxed by an American television look-in on the enterprise, have multiplied his fame and increased his income so rapidly that in his first year of full-time healing young Nolan must have become one of the top moneymakers in Ireland. From February to September, 1970, he and his brothers collected about £40,000 ($96,000). Asked what he intended to do with all that money, the youth laconically replied, "Buy a pub, maybe."

Biddy Early was a practitioner of benign witchcraft, but there were predecessors of a more sinister mold who from time to time created a considerable stir in Ireland. Dame Alice Kyteller of a prominent Anglo-Norman family in Kilkenny and a number of her associates were examined in 1324 by an Inquisition panel made up of the Bishop of Ossory, five knights, and several other notables. Among the charges brought against her were that she poisoned her first three husbands and had addled the wits of her fourth by administering philters in which "entrails of cocks sacrificed to demons" were only one of the more savory ingredients.

The tribunal drew up an indictment against Dame Alice and her collaborators which also charged that they "offered in sacrifice to demons living animals, which they dismembered, and then distributed at crossroads to a certain evil spirit of low rank named the Son of Art. . . . They sought by their sorceries advice and responses from demons. . . . In their nightly meetings they blasphemously imitated the power of the Church by fulminating a sense of ex-communication, with lighted candles, even against their own husbands. . . . The Dame had a certain demon, an incubus named Art or Robin, Son of Art, who had carnal knowledge of her, and from whom she admitted she had received all her wealth. . . ."

Dame Alice fled to England, but the Inquisition rounded up her followers, some of them friends and others servants of the accused sorceress. Also implicated was her son, William Outlawe, who responded to charges that he was a heretic, a usurer, a clericide, and an adulterer by appearing in St. Mary's Church at the head of a band of armed men. Outlawe eventually, however, made his submission to the Bishop of Ossory and was ordered to show repentance by attending mass three times daily for a year, to feed a certain number of the poor, and to cover the chancel of St. Canice's Cathedral with lead sheeting. Of all of Dame Alice's other alleged accomplices, only a servant girl named Petronilla of Meath was made to suffer the consequences. After six floggings she confessed to summoning up demons, practicing black magic, and making certain female enemies appear to be wearing goat's horns. She was burned at the stake.

In the seventeenth century there was another uproar over witchcraft, this one breaking out in the town of Youghal, where there was a Puritan colony. An elderly woman named Florence Newton was summoned before the Cork assizes on charges of having bewitched a servant girl, Mary Longdon. She was sentenced to Cork Prison after some extraordinary testimony to her powers, including Mary Longdon's statement that "she saw a woman with a veil over her face standing by my bedside, and beside the figure was a little old man in silk clothes, and this man whom I took to be a spirit drew the veil off the woman's face and

I saw that it was Florence Newton." It was part of the assizes record that when Mary finished testifying against her, Mrs. Newton called down a curse on her, upon which "Mary went down like a stone" and a short time later was observed vomiting straw, wool, and crooked pins.

It was not recorded whether Florence Newton was convicted on that evidence or whether she was subjected to what was called the water experiment, a means of determining whether a person was a witch. The accused was trussed up by tying the right thumb to the left big toe and the left thumb to the right big toe, then thrown into a river or pond. If she floated, she was a witch, sure enough. If she drowned, it was all an unfortunate mistake, but at least she died with her good name intact. At any rate, Florence Newton was imprisoned but was not discouraged from her vocation. She kissed the hand of one of her jailers, thereby bewitching him, and he died a short time later.

About the same time there was a famous "white" magician known throughout the island as Mr. Greatrix, whose career was detailed by Joseph Glanvil in his lengthy treatise titled *Sadducismus Triumphatus, Or a Full and Plain Evidence Concerning Witches and Apparitions,* published in 1681. His real name was Valentine Greatrakes, a former soldier in the Puritan army, who discovered in 1662 that he had the gift of healing. The Irish called such a healer a stroker. His fame spread to England, and Mr. Greatrix followed it. "I was three weeks together with him at my Lord Conways' and saw him (I think) lay his hands upon a thousand persons," as Glanvil wrote. "There really is something in it more than ordinary. . . . I have seen pains strangely fly before his hand, till he had chased them out of the body; blindness cleared and deafness cured by his touch . . . running sores of the King's Evil dried up . . . grievous sores of many months date, in a few days healed . . . cancerous knots in the breast dissolved, etc. . . ."

The parenthetical "I think" was encouraging evidence of Joseph Glanvil's determination to be scholarly and properly skeptical, yet he also recorded cases of bewitched persons who, on being "cured" by various antiwitch remedies, vomited up needles, pins, feathers, straw, pieces of glass, nails, eggshells, and fish scales. Such cures were often effected by placing the victim in contact with a holy relic of some kind. Obviously it took a potent cure to relieve a person of evil spells. The unholy resources available to those in league with the demoniac world were all but inexhaustible. "The spells of the witch smell of the grave," Yeats wrote in *Irish Fairy and Folk Tales* during the period of his infatuation with the legendary Ireland. "One of the most powerful is the charm of the dead hand. With a hand cut from a corpse, they, muttering words of power, will stir a well and skim from its surface a neighbour's butter. A candle held between the fingers of the dead hand can never be blown out. This is useful to robbers, but they appeal for the suffrage of the lovers likewise, for they can make love-potions by drying and grinding into powder the liver of a black cat. Mixed with tea, and poured from a black teapot, it is infallible."

The last celebrated case of witchcraft occurred in 1894 after the discovery of the body of Bridget Cleary in a bog near her home outside Cloneen, County Tipperary. Her body had been badly burned in places. According to the testimony of the principal witness, Mrs. Cleary had been force-fed milk and herbs and held close to the kitchen fire by her husband, Michael, her father, and eight other relatives and neighbors, all of whom evidently were convinced that Mrs. Cleary was a witch and that it was their Christian duty to exorcise her. It was the Crown's contention that Mrs. Cleary died of the mistreatment at the hands of her well-wishers. Cleary was sentenced to twenty years in prison, his codefendants to lesser terms. At least the trial, which was widely publicized, discouraged any more home cures for witchcraft. Another result was a rhyme still occasionally recited in County Tipperary:

> Are you a witch, are you a fairy?
> Or are you the wife of Michael Cleary?

Throughout their history the Irish have placed great faith in the power of the word, in symbols, incantations, curses and exhortations, and if they rhymed, so much the better. Poets ranked above warriors at the court of the high kings. Even a warrior had to be articulate to qualify for renown; his wit was supposed to have as keen a cutting edge as his sword. Being punctured by a deadly shaft of wit without being able to supply an even more lethal riposte was worse than being decapitated.

In the long centuries when Ireland was under one form of subjugation or another, words were a defensive weapon, an armory any man could carry in his head. Doubtless they were the psychological mechanism of a conquered people, but at least it kept up morale to mock, to satirize, and symbolically to demolish an enemy too powerful to be cut down physically. It was no geographic accident that Ireland produced men of devastating wit like Swift, Shaw, and Wilde.

The power of suggestion, as opposed to physical force, has always been highly valued among the Irish. Their language rattles with curses, direly explicit, as often as it lilts with blessings. As a startling instance of the power of the word, even when pitted against naval guns and armor plate, they can cite the "battle" of Tory Island at which not a shot was fired. Tory Island is celebrated in Irish legend as the stronghold of the pre-Celtic Fomorians. The chief military asset of the Fomorians was their King Balor, a Cyclops who could destroy people simply by glowering at them; he lived in a glass castle which magnified the striking power of his single eye. Balor was finally destroyed when he was tricked into opening his baleful eye at the wrong moment.

Ever since Balor's time, the Tory islanders had regarded themselves as independent of the outside world. They refused to pay taxes to the British, who finally decided to teach them a lesson in the traditional nineteenth-century manner by sending the gunboat HMS *Wasp* and threatening to sink the island with broadsides. The people of Tory had their own way of dealing with unwelcome guests, a secret weapon known as the Cursing Stones which exercised a malignant power when the stones were placed in a certain way and turned counterclockwise. When directed against an enemy, they assured him of bad luck until he was persuaded to leave Tory Island and the nearby coast of Donegal. As it turned out, HMS *Wasp* ran aground on the rocks off Tory Island, and all but six of her crew were drowned.

The therapeutic value of impudence as a salve for the ego was also discovered early in the tribulations of the Irish. It ameliorated the frustrations of a people who could not help resenting having to tug the forelock continually before their mental inferiors. To be able figuratively to spit in the eye of the master and make him laugh at himself has a salutary effect on both parties. At this chancy game the wandering Irish scholar Erigena was an expert. He attached himself to the court of Charlemagne, who would serve as the butt of a joke if it was funny enough but was likely to summon the headsman if he was both bored and affronted. Once Charlemagne and Erigena were knocking back flagons of mead, and the ruler of Western Europe drunkenly decided that his Irish hanger-on was drinking too much. "How far is a Scot removed from a sot?" Charlemagne asked. (Irishmen were then known as Scots.) "The width of a table," replied Erigena.

To be witty under dire circumstances, in fact, was a much-prized attribute, the mark of an aristocrat. Any man, it was felt, could fire off a riposte when things were easy, but it took a real swordsman of the intellect to perform when the going was tough. As Edmund Burke once put it, "He that wrestles strengthens our nerves and sharpens our skill. Our antagonist is our helper." To be witty when the odds were against you was a guarantee of immortality, at least among the Irish. Thus when the short-tempered King Louis XIV complained to its officers that the Irish Brigade caused him more trouble than all the rest of his army put together, one of them replied, "Please, Your Majesty, your *enemies* make just the same complaint about us."

There was something in the atmosphere that made the ladies, whose sisters elsewhere were more likely to faint or have hysterics when confronted by disaster, as mettlesome as their menfolk. When Elizabeth Fitzgerald found herself surrounded in her castle by a neighboring tribe and was informed that her husband had been captured and would be killed if she didn't surrender the castle, she replied, "Mark these words, they may serve your own wives on some occasion. I'll keep my castle. For Elizabeth Fitzgerald may get another husband, but Elizabeth Fitzgerald may never get another castle."

And there was the comeuppance James II received from a female tongue after fleeing from the lost Battle of the Boyne and not halting his personal retreat until he reached Dublin. He burst in on Lady Tyrconnell complaining, "Those scoundrels of Irishmen ran!"

"Indeed," Lady Tyrconnell retorted. "I see Your Majesty won the race."

Equally treasured around Dublin is the memory of Father Healy, many of whose sallies were recorded by the American-born Mrs. T. P. O'Connor in her memoir *Herself Ireland.* Father Healy was especially adept at puncturing the self-esteem of the British, despite which he was popular with the garrison society and the Protestant peerage. Once he was playing cards at the viceregal lodge and took out a handful of coppers. "Ah, Father Healy," one of the peers at the table said, "I see you've been robbing the offertory box." Father Healy's reply was, "How clever of your Lordship to recognize his own contribution!" He once remarked of his parishioners at Bray: "An ideal crowd—the poor keep all the fasts and the rich keep all the feasts." His amiable rival, the Protestant rector at Bray, told him, "I have been sixty years in the world and I have not yet discovered the difference between a good Catholic and a good Protestant." Father Healy: "You won't be sixty seconds in the next world until you find out." It was too bad that Father Healy wasn't around when Susan Mitchell—noted in Dublin society for her adder's tongue—declared that the reason a Catholic wife could not be buried with her Protestant husband was that it "might mar the perfection of a Protestant resurrection."

There was another form of humor known as the Irish bull, specimens of which were especially prized by the British as evidence of Irish woolly-mindedness. It was a sort of unconscious humor, sometimes defined as a self-contradictory statement which is funny to those who hear it but not to the one who utters it. Irish authorities on the subject claim, however, that the humor is not necessarily unconscious. As Professor Mahaffy, a renowned Dublin wit himself, put it, "An Irish bull is always pregnant," which is a bull in itself. So there must have been two kinds of Irish bull, one consciously fabricated and the other a slip of the tongue.

Undoubtedly the champion producer of Irish bulls was Sir Boyle Roche, an elderly gentleman who was a member of the Irish Parliament until it was disbanded in 1801. One of his celebrated dictums was "Ireland's cup of misfortunes has been overflowing for centuries and it is not full yet." A soulmate to

Mrs. Malaprop—the creation of the Irish playwright Richard Brinsley Sheridan—he suffered short circuits in his thought processes which kept the Irish Parliament in uproarious laughter for years, and that institution might well have been preserved if only to provide an arena in which Sir Boyle's Irish bulls could chase each other around. He once delivered the most violently mixed metaphor in the English language: "Mr. Speaker, I smell a rat; I see him forming in the air and darkening the sky, but I'll nip him in the bud."

Self-intoxicated on his own oratory, he often fell into one verbal quagmire after another while trying to extricate himself. In one impassioned address to his colleagues, he demanded, "Why should we put ourselves out of our way to do anything for posterity? What has posterity done for us?" He sat down, satisfied that he had made a classic statement of the conservative position until he looked around and saw that his colleagues had turned puce trying to restrain an outburst of laughter. When the uproar died down, he struggled to his feet again to make his meaning clearer: "By posterity, I did not mean our ancestors but those who were to come immediately after them."

A French invasion in support of a rebellion in the west of Ireland rendered him incoherent, if not speechless. "Last Thursday notice was given that a gang of rebels were advancing here under the French standards. Fortunately the rebels had no guns, except pistols and pikes, and as we had plenty of muskets and ammunition we put them all to the sword. Not a soul of them escaped except some that were drowned in an adjacent bog; and in very short time there was nothing to be heard but silence."

On another occasion he was soaring into a denunciation of revolutionary movements, such as the one headed by Wolfe Tone, which he declared would "bring the foundation stones of the constitution down around our ears." Not content with having defied Newton's law, he roared on: "On that very table, honorable members might see their own destinies lying in heaps on top of one another. Here perhaps the murderers might break in, cut us to mincemeat and throw our bleeding heads upon that table to stare us in the face!"

As a specimen of the Irish bull, pregnant or otherwise, that would have been hard to equal, but Sir Boyle kept on trying.

"Oh, you're a precious blockhead," he wrote his bootmaker while suffering an attack of the gout, "to do directly the reverse of what I desired you. I told you to make one of the shoes larger than the other, and instead of that you have made one of them smaller than the other."

Or Sir Boyle in a moment of prophecy: "All along the untrodden paths of the future I can see the footprints of an unseen hand."

For the participants in the Irish literary revival which began in the nineties, there was a hidden treasure waiting to be unearthed, a wide and deep vein of myths, legends, word-of-mouth tales, ancient manuscripts, romances, and sagas to be recovered and recast in heroic form: a diorama of the proud and valorous past that would be used to inspire the finally successful revolution. The countryside teemed with a people rich in personality and endowed with originality; their only amusement for centuries had been sitting around their turf fires sharpening their wits on one another and outdoing one another in storytelling.

No other country offered so much lore just beneath the surface, waiting to be exploited, with the possible exception of the Aztec and Inca legends underlying many of the Latin American nations, whose literary talent has never come up to the Irish standard. The difference may lie in temperament, as well as talent. As Arland Ussher has observed, the Irish have a tendency to look upon life as a show from which they remain detached; they have an artistic temperament better suited to speculation and comment than to building industry; humanity interests them more than its ephemeral works. "No man is more realistic and cynical conversationally than the artist type of man," Ussher says, "but with all his sense of reality he is usually a failure in actual life, because he is not oriented toward a world of facts and duties; and the same is true of the Irishman—he is like the king who never said a foolish thing and never did a wise one."

The literary revivalists were favored by the fact that the ancients had always been as diligent in recording their history—not only military but social—as they were in making it. The Celts systematized the process with as much care as they gave to organizing their government. In Celtic times professional storytellers were classified as ollavs, shanachies, poets, and bards, all with the primary responsibility of memorizing the stories handed down to them, an oral literature and history combined, with the secondary duty of telling them for the entertainment of the kings and chiefs. "But even in the fictitious tales," P. W. Joyce observed in the introduction to *Old Celtic Romances* (1879), "the main characters were always historical. . . . The old ollaves wove their fictions around Conor MacNessa and his Red Branch Knights, or Finn and his Fena, or Lugh of the Long Arms and his Dedanns, or Conn the Hundred Fighter, or Cormac Mac Airt . . . like the Welsh legends of Arthur and his Round Table, or the Arabian romances of Haroun-al-Raschid and his court."

At a very early period these word-of-mouth legends were put into writing, before they could be lost in a breakdown of the memory process or warped beyond factual recognition in the retelling. A vast collection of manuscripts was assembled and then stored in monasteries or the houses of hereditary professors of learning. Much of the manuscript collections was destroyed in the Danish and Norman invasions, but the surviving material was collected and preserved in Trinity College and the Royal Irish Academy. The surviving manuscripts dated from no earlier than A.D. 1100, all of them copies of earlier books and manuscripts constituting a vast body of romantic literature, a highly colorful loom on which were woven poetry, legend, propaganda, all drenched in blood and ringing with the clash of long swords.

For all the efforts of the scribes in the monasteries an enormous amount of oral literature escaped their attentions, which necessarily were devoted largely to copying the Scriptures and various church documents. And they began the task of recapturing a millennium of thought only when the Celtic civilization began breaking up. As one indication of how much must have escaped them, an ollav or chronicler of the pre-Christian Celts had to spend about twenty years memorizing enough material to attain his rank, including 350 long narratives, the genealogies of the principal kings and chiefs, the structure of seven kinds of poetry.

Some of the quality of the tailings of that Celtic ore which was being recovered at the end of the nineteenth century may be assayed in the legend of the sons of Turenn recounted in P. W. Joyce's *Old Celtic Romances.*

Turenn's three sons slew his enemy, the father of Lugh of the Long Arms. They were captured by Lugh, who arraigned them in the hall of Micorta, the banqueting room of Tara. Lugh imposed an "eric-fine," a penalty, on the three young men, who were ordered to bring him three apples, the skin of a pig, a spear, two horses and a chariot, seven pigs, a hound puppy, a cooking spit, and three shouts on a hill. The three youths naturally thought they were being let off easy.

Then came the Celtic twist, the Catch-22, in Lugh's sentence. The apples, which were believed to cure any wound or illness, had to come from the Garden of Hesperides. The pig's skin belonged to King Tuis of Greece and would have to be forcibly detached from him. The spear was part of the personal armament of Pezar, King of the Persians. The two horses and chariot belonged to Dobar, King of the Sicilians; the seven pigs to Asal, King of the Golden Pillars. The hound puppy was the property of the King of Iroda (probably Norway)—every wild beast that saw the young hound fell dead in his tracks. The cooking spit would have to be liberated from the Amazonian women of the island of Fincara, numbering 150, each of them reputed to be a match for three warriors. The three shouts would have to be given on the hill of Midkena, which was guarded by a chief and his sons who were sworn not to allow anyone to shout on it.

The rest of "The Children of Turenn" concerns their hazardous quest, at the end of which Turenn's three sons were mortally wounded. Turenn begged Lugh for the apples of Hesperides to save their lives, but Lugh of the Long Arms refused. Not a happy ending, but that too was in the Celtic mode, in keeping with their dark view of life and of the stern necessities of justice.

Only those who experienced it can convey the exultation that the Irish literary revival aroused, the thrilling days when the Irish once again could catch a true reflection of themselves in their mirrored past, when the national spirit was expressed in the wild vocabulary of the west of Ireland, where the new poets and playwrights had journeyed as to a wellspring in which the purity of that spirit still bubbled up. That exhilaration has been vividly recaptured by Mary Colum in her classic memoir *Life and the Dream.* When she first went to Dublin as a convent-bred girl, she "nearly fell off the swaying jaunting car" when she caught sight of a poster reading: "Irish Plays for One Week. *Riders to the Sea,* by J. M. Synge, *Kathleen ni Houlihan,* by W. B. Yeats, *Spreading the News,* by Lady Gregory."

To her the classics which had been drilled into her were now part of a "long-dead world," while the works of Irish writers belonged to the present and the possibly glorious future:

> The voices who had spoken to my elders were English voices, only English voices—Tennyson, Swinburne, Meredith. These had spoken to my uncle's youth as he walked the streets of Dublin, and never an Irish voice. The new writers were especially ours; they wrote about our life, our history, our legends. But I pondered, as I have often done since, on why a country so proud of its nationalism was really intellectually and socially so Anglicized that when plays were produced by Irish writers they had to be labeled in Ireland's capital city "Irish plays," and the writers described in the local papers as "Irish poets."

The most spectacular thrust of the literary revival was in the dramatic field, perhaps because there was a market in both the Dublin theater and the enthusiasm of its audiences. Mrs. Colum wrote:

> I have seen young Dublin mechanics sit entranced at verse plays; their taste had not been spoiled by much theater-going, and in those days there were no movies. Besides, they loved to see the legends of the country and the people of the country put into plays. When Yeats' *Kathleen ni Houlihan* was performed they would rise to their feet in a display of emotion that was not perhaps more moving than Yeats' emotion when he came on the stage to acknowledge their calls. In fact the audience, though few, were such as to arouse any author to summon up his best powers. I have never anywhere seen such a responsive audience; they had an instinct for literature, whether they were students or workingmen in the pit, or the bourgeoisie or aristocracy in the stalls.

The great Irish writers who began producing just before and after the turn of the century would, consciously or not, be filling a void that existed between the hothouse lyricism of past decades and the realism of Ibsen, the naturalism of Zola (or in the United States, Jack London, Frank Norris, Stephen Crane, and Theodore Dreiser). From their native soil they drew a wild and quirky humor and a poetic sense tempered by hardheaded realism, both powered by a vigorous use of the language. They had not only a solid footing in their racial background but a mutual determination to make their works serve an overriding purpose: the liberation of Ireland.

Yeats, of course, was indispensable. Not only in what he produced himself but in what he inspired in others, he was the standard-bearer.

With AE and the widowed Lady Gregory, who was said to have served her apprenticeship as "an unpaid social worker on her father's estate," he discovered the mother lode of the Irish literary revival in a now-obscure work. Standish O'Grady's *The History of Ireland: The Heroic Period,* published in 1880, and to a lesser extent P. W. Joyce's *Old Celtic Romances,* published the year before.

O'Grady was a remarkable man, born in 1832, the son of a British admiral, educated at Rugby and Trinity. Like so many of the Anglo-Irish offshoots he inspired, he was possessed of a demoniac energy, more than his share of eccentricity and an insatiable interest in the Celtic heritage. Until he came along, Irish studies were largely the province of French and German philologists. His interest in the subject had been aroused at Trinity and resulted in his editing a new edition of *The Adventure of the Unfortunate Fellow,* a picaresque tale in verse written by Donncha Rua MacConmara in the previous century. For many years O'Grady's Irish studies were merely an avocation while he wandered around the world, mining for gold and skippering a coastal schooner in the United States and Australia, before he returned to Ireland and publishing his most notable work on the heroes of "the misty ages." A half dozen years later he was engaged to compile the catalogue of Irish manuscripts for the British Museum. This work was erudite, pungently witty, as much a commentary as a mere listing of manuscripts; its lack of pedantry disturbed his employers, and when they upbraided him, O'Grady clapped on his hat and walked out. On his own he produced translations of the ancient romances that were to prove so valuable to those who followed him. There was no library dust on his prose, but the mark of an astringent mind which could footnote the horrible death of a medieval warrior at the hands of his enemies: "Such burning of individuals (by no means rare) was not carried out deliberately at the stake, but was simply incidental to legitimate arson. . . ."

The realization of what had been lying under his feet, all but unnoticed until O'Grady's works nudged him, brought Yeats home from England, where he had been studying theosophy and the works of William Blake, back to County Sligo, where much of his youth had been spent, and the stormy isolation of the Aran Islands. The colorful language of the peasants, drawing on something as deep and mysterious as time itself, inspired the decision he related in lyric verse:

> I will arise now, and go to Innisfree,
> And a small cabin build there, of clay
> and wattles made;
> Nine bean rows will I have there, a hive
> for the honey bee,
> And live alone in a bee-loud glade.

He did not actually confine himself to a clay cabin in the west and abandon himself to a Thoreau-like existence among the bees; that was poetic license, urging Irish writers that their strength, like that of the mythical giant Antaeus, came from their native soil. Instead, he became a literary missionary while also producing the poems and plays which made his early reputation. He was a born poet, but not a dramatist. For the starring role in the new Irish theater he selected a diffident young man with a long, pale face and the waxen look of those destined for an early death: his fellow Anglo-Irishman John Millington Synge, the enduring genius of Irish drama.

Synge was in Paris studying Racine and other figures of the French theater who were then the accepted models for aspiring playwrights. If a date for the beginning of the Irish Renaissance had to be picked, it was the day Yeats looked up Synge in Paris, in 1896, and convinced him he would learn more from the people of the west of Ireland than from the polished and effete craftsmen of the French theater, that the everyday speech of the Aran islanders was cast in a poetic-literary form which needed only translation and refinement.

In discussing their plans for creating a nationalistic Irish theater which owed nothing to European classicism, Synge told Yeats, "We should unite stoicism, asceticism and ecstasy. Two of them have often come together, but the three never."

To Sean O'Faolain the inspiration of Synge by Yeats, their agreement in Parisian cafés and parks as they excitedly discussed their plans that they could make dramatic literature of the Aran islanders, was "the final stage of growth of the Irish mind." Long before Synge began writing, they had discovered a great new truth, that literature could be made of "the simplest life of the simplest people. . . . They had conquered their material by accepting it."

Years later Yeats would ruminate (in *The Autobiography of William Butler Yeats*) on the strangely self-sufficient and self-engrossed personality of the man he inspired. After Synge's death in 1909 Yeats wrote:

> He had that egotism of the man of genius which Nietzsche compares to the egotism of a woman with a child. Neither I nor Lady Gregory had ever a compliment from him. . . . He had under charming and modest manners, in almost all things of life, a complete absorption in his own dream. I have never heard him praise any writer, living or dead, but some old French farce-writer. For him nothing existed but his thought. He claimed nothing for it aloud. He never said any of those self-confident things I am enraged into saying, but one knew that he valued nothing else. He was too-confident for self-assertion. I once said to George Moore, 'Synge has always the better of you, for you have brief ghastly moments during which you admit the existence of other writers; Synge never has.' . . . I have often envied him his absorption as I have envied Verlaine his vice.

Another leading figure of the Renaissance, George Moore, asserted that "It is the land itself that makes the Celt," but that it was the Anglo-Irish who made something literary of the Celt. Yeats, Synge, Lady Gregory, and other leading figures were Protestants; so was the torchbearer of a newer generation, Sean O'Casey, and Moore was a lapsed Catholic. This was not due to any deficiency of talent or intelligence among the Catholic Irish, Yeats believed, but to the handicaps imposed by a Catholic education. To stand a chance intellectually, he said, a Catholic had to be educated outside Ireland. He noted that the secondary schools "substituted pedantry for taste," that Catholic boys and girls who had not gone on to secondary schools were, in fact, more imaginative than Protestants of their own age.

The Irish nation-in-being thus contracted a sizable debt to the caste it rightly resented for other reasons—one of those ironies that smudge over the human condition and make prejudice so much less viable or respectable. Yeats and his comrades were working for a national theater, the Abbey, and designing their works not for the world audiences they later achieved but to make the Irish see themselves in a different light. Not the charming, romantic, happy-go-lucky and clownish people who were so amusing to the outside world, but a people of sturdy character, a people once great who could achieve greatness again.

In its oblique way it was a revolutionary theater they established at the Abbey. The characters they brought to life were uniquely Irish; they could no more have been anything but Irish than Chekhov's Russians or Schiller's Germans. The remarkable thing was that they were conceived by persons of the upper or middle class, but without condescension. They and the plays which embodied them were created within the code formulated by Yeats himself in 1898 when the foundation of the Abbey Theater was announced: "We propose to have performed certain Celtic and Irish plays which, whatever their degree of excellence, shall be written with a high ambition, and so build a Celtic and Irish school of dramatic literature." The theater was to be a place of "intellectual excitement—a place where the mind goes to be liberated."

There was a we-happy-few atmosphere about the establishment of what became a national theater—Yeats, Synge, and Lady Gregory, as directors, attended almost every performance—that inevitably attracted a certain amount of malice and envy. It was said that Lady Gregory was a snob, that she was ambitious for her own career and a bad influence on Yeats and others whom she gathered around her at Coole House. Mary Colum dismissed such charges on the reasonable grounds that "her talents were her own, they were remarkable, and of the greatest value to Ireland and to Irish literature. If she had the talents without the ambition she would not have achieved much." To allegations that Lady Gregory wasn't nationalistic enough, that she had no real enthusiasm for a revolution that might sweep away Coole House, Mrs. Colum would point to the indubitable Irish patriotism of *The Rising of the Moon* and *Spreading the News* and to her literary aspirations: "What she wanted to do was to help re-create the spirit of the race, to waken its consciousness, with the help of literature and a revived racial tradition, which had once been potent in Europe and had produced so many trained and scholarly minds."

At any rate the Abbey probably would have been impossible without her executive abilities, her fund raising, and her equal role in its artistic direction with Yeats and Synge. The Abbey was the chief ingredient in the ferment which in a few years had turned Dublin into one of the more fascinating and intellectually lively of the world's cities. On a five-minute walk from Abbey Street to College Green and the gates of Trinity College, one could meet most of its creative talent late in the afternoon: AE with a brown beard that made him look like a Celtic sea-god; Yeats with his dark, hypnotic eyes; George Moore trailing wisps of scandal because it was known his English mistress had followed him to Dublin; even the eighteen-year-old James Joyce, whose critical essay on Ibsen had just been published by the most important literary review in England and who would flee the island for reasons set forth in doggerel which he titled "Gas from a Burner":

> This lovely land that always sent
> Her writers and artists to banishment
> and in a spirit of Irish fun
> Betrayed her own leaders, one by one.
> 'Twas Irish humour, wet and dry,
> Flung quicklime into Parnell's eye. . . .

But that was later when his collection of bitterly ironic short stories, *The Dubliners,* was refused publication. Now Dublin was an artistic and intellectual lodestar, bringing her expatriates home and attracting the attention and often the presence of scholars from all over Europe. Celticism was suddenly the rage among European culture hounds and tastemakers; the rediscovery of the Celtic mythology was studied, dissected, and propagated by the faculties of European universities, particularly in Germany with its Wagnerian obsession with old gods. The most famous of the German Celtic scholars, Kuno Meyer, was lecturing to large audiences at the School of Irish Learning—a German teaching the Irish about the Irish. At least he spoke in English; but "other devotees were always showing up," as one observer wrote, "and some of them knew the Irish language but not the English language, queer old scholars, all the romance of whose lives had somehow been connected with this conquered island in the North Atlantic. . . ."

Dublin also became the capital of a Celtic separatist movement (which has been revived in recent years), with Bretons coming over from France to make propaganda for the separation of Brittany, kilted Scotsmen and voluble Welshmen adding to the excitement over a new Celtic dawn. Naturally enough, all this romantic yearning over the past attracted satirical attention in England, where it was regarded as more Irish nonsense in keeping with the English belief that all the Paddies claimed to be the descendants of the high kings. Max Beerbohm got off one of his celebrated caricatures showing Yeats, as a limp elongated esthete, introducing George Moore to a crowned elfin creature who was supposed to be the queen of the Irish fairies; this, for the English, summed it all up beautifully.

Meanwhile, the Dubliners, a volatile and often raucously critical element, were creating a hubbub over the plays being presented at the Abbey. Many Proper Dubliners believed that the way the Irish were presented on that stage, in all their vitality and wild humor, was an insult to the race; it did not escape their attention that most of those connected with the Abbey were Protestants while the characters in their plays were Catholics. Soon the Abbey seemed like a citadel under siege. There were near-riotous complications when *The Playboy of the Western*

World opened on January 26, 1907. Much of the standing-room-only audience came with blood in their eye over advance reports that the word "shift"—a woman's undergarment—was to be uttered in the course of the play. One of the greatest plays in the English language was almost hissed out of existence on its opening night.

The reason wasn't simply Irish puritanism, pervasive as it was and is, but the fact that the Irish are strikingly image-conscious; they detested the idea of being presented to the world as a coarse peasant race; they abhorred the very qualities which the author, Synge, and his colleagues had seized upon as the enduring glory of the Irish, the Celtic difference which carried them undiminished through centuries of travail.

The Dubliners' reaction to *The Playboy of the Western World* is strikingly conveyed in Joseph Holloway's *Impressions of a Dublin Playgoer*:

> The theater was thronged in the evening to witness the first performance of *The Playboy of the Western World,* which ended in fiasco owing to the coarseness of the dialogue. The audience bore with it for two and a half acts and even laughed with the dramatist at times, but an unsuitably brutal coarse remark [evidently he referred to the word "shift"] set the house off into hooting and hissing amid counter applause, and the din kept up until the curtain closed in.
>
> On coming out, Lady Gregory asked me: "What was the cause of the disturbance?" And my monosyllabic answer was: "Blackguardism!" To which she queried: "On which side?" "The stage," came from me, pat, and I passed on, and the incident was closed. . . .

The reaction was so violent, the situation so menacing, that Lady Gregory telegraphed Yeats, who was lecturing in Scotland: "Audience broke up in disorder at word 'shift.' What should I do?"

"Leave it on," Yeats telegraphed in reply. He abandoned his lecture tour and hastened back to Dublin to take up the fight on behalf of Synge's play.

A large police detail had to be posted in the streets around the

Abbey Theater when Yeats appeared to defend the play. Mary Colum and another girl student were the only female members of the audience; they were ordered to go home, "if you are virtuous girls," but they stayed in their seats. "Yeats took the platform in full evening dress," she recalled. "Step by step he interpreted the play, delivering in the process some of his most complex theories of art, one moment cowing the audience, the next, shouted down by them. Synge, who was no fighter of this kind, stayed home. When the standard speech about freedom, patriotism, anti-Irish propaganda came from somebody in the stalls, the audience cheered. But even on the patriotics, Yeats was equal to them. . . . I never witnessed a human being fight as Yeats fought that night, nor ever knew another with so many weapons in his armory. . . ."

Yeats won his fight for *The Playboy of the Western World*; it became the centerpiece of the Abbey's repertory, and in a few years people wondered what all the fuss had been about. Yet he and Lady Gregory—the third member of the Abbey triumvirate, Synge, died at the age of thirty-seven—would have to fight the old battle all over again, against the even greater national sensitivity just after the struggle for independence, when Sean O'Casey appeared on the scene with *Shadow of a Gunman, Juno and the Paycock,* and *The Plough and the Stars.* O'Casey had brought the Abbey back to life and the Dublin theatergoers back to their easily outraged sensibilities. An extract from Lady Gregory's journal in July, 1926, provides a compressed version of the renewed struggle with the Irish feeling that the race was being vulgarized and defamed for dramaturgic convenience. "On Friday I left for Dublin to see 'The Plough and the Stars.' I got the post and papers in Gort, and when the train had started, opened the *Independent* and saw a heading right across the page: 'Riotous Scenes at the Abbey—Attempt to Stop O'Casey's Play'; and an account of wild women, especially, having raised a disturbance, blown whistles, etc., prevented second act from being heard and had then clambered on the stage—a young man had struck Miss Delany on the face, etc., etc. Then the police had been sent for. At Athenry I got *The Irish Times* which gave a fuller account. Yeats had spoken from the stage but the clamour had drowned his speech, but the reporters had got some of it.

(He said: 'You have disgraced yourselves again.')" Yeats met Lady Gregory at the station and suggested that they might invite protesters on the stage to debate with him, the method which had cooled off disturbances during the opening engagement of *Playboy of the Western World.* Lady Gregory disagreed, acidly remarking that "In *Playboy* time our opponents were men."

What outraged Dubliners about *The Plough and the Stars* was the presence of a prostitute among the characters. One critic declared it was well known there were no streetwalkers in Dublin, though it was even better known that certain districts were overrun with prostitutes. Dubliners might not rise in moral revulsion against their red-light district, it appeared to the directors of the Abbey, but the presence of a single whore in a play about Dubliners was outrageous. Obviously the hero of James Joyce's *A Portrait of the Artist as a Young Man* had his work cut out for him when he proclaimed his intention of forging the "uncreated conscience of my race."

Naturally enough in a small country which felt itself still menaced internally and externally, the nationalistic spirit of the twenties and subsequent decades provided an adverse climate for the second generation of the Irish Renaissance. A disgusted O'Casey expatriated himself to England for the rest of his life; Joyce wandered around Europe; the Nobel Prize-winning Samuel Beckett has spent most of his life in France and North Africa; the late Frank O'Connor sojourned frequently in America. The Abbey Theater went into a long decline and only recently, as the nationally subsidized theater, has started recovering some of the luster of its more venturesome early years. Only a few years ago a Dublin stage director was groaning that "Yeats would turn over in his grave if he could see what the Abbey is putting on. Mostly what Americans call soap operas, plays about nice middle-class families with the prodigal son returning to the Church and signing up with the Legion of Mary at the final curtain." Civil servants, he added, were poorly equipped to understand the problems of the modern theater. It was the Gate Theater, not the Abbey, which staged an adaptation of Joyce's *Portrait of the Artist as a Young Man* retitled *Stephen D.* and written by Hugh Leonard, who has returned to Ireland after many years in England. *Stephen D.* was a sublimated account of

Joyce's quarrel with the church, and its candor on the subject of religion made the fact it would be produced at all in Dublin a victory over what have been called the "secret censors," the Irish theatergoing public itself.

For the second generation of the Irish Renaissance, including such brilliant and internationally celebrated writers as Sean O'Faolain, Liam O'Flaherty, and Frank O'Connor, there was a less exhilarating atmosphere in which to create. The Yeats generation had benefited from an upsurge of hope and expectation, had been inspired by the dream of creating a new Gaelic Utopia. Instead, as Benedict Kiely grittily phrased it, a "grocer's republic" was established. The second generation's atmosphere was one of disillusion; its disenchantment was corrosively expressed by Oliver St. John Gogarty's *As I Was Walking Down Sackville Street* and in the latter-day foreboding of Yeats ("Mere anarchy is loosed upon the world/The blood-dimmed tide is loosed"), whose poetic power nevertheless seemed to expand with the years. And in O'Faolain's statement that "the greatest curse of Ireland has not been English invasions or English misgovernment; it has been the exaggeration of Irish virtues. . . . Ireland has clung to her youth, indeed her childhood, longer and more tenaciously than any other country in Europe."

Gone was the ebullience of the great days of the Celtic revival when the wit of the Olympians flashed over the scene, and a well-honed remark, often carefully thought out but always delivered as a throwaway, would be dropped in a Dublin salon or pub and a week later would echo in London, Budapest, and New York. Lethal belittlement was the style, AE defining a literary movement as "five or six people who live in the same town and hate each other." Joyce informing Yeats, with all the hauteur of "stately plump Buck Mulligan," that "We have met too late, Mr. Yeats, you are too old to be influenced by me." Or AE to Joyce, "I don't know whether you are a mountain or a cistern but I am afraid that you have not enough chaos in you to make a world." Or George Moore describing how Yeats coaxed dramatic genius out of Synge: "sweeping the strings of a harp of apple wood, rousing a masterpiece out of an abyss."

A siege mentality had replaced the old joyous heckling. Censorship, of course, was a dampening influence on literary spirits with government proscription of such Irish-born writers as Joyce, Shaw, O'Faolain, O'Flaherty, O'Casey, Frank O'Connor, Patrick Kavanagh, Moore, Gogarty, and Austin Clarke—not to mention an array of foreign authors—whose names would be repeated in this connection as a litany of intellectual disaster. Later they would be joined on the index by the late Brendan Behan and such young contemporary novelists as Edna O'Brien, John Broderick, and John McGahern.

Perhaps the most depressing instance of the Irish tendency toward repression occurred in the early forties with the publication of Eric Cross' *The Tailor and Anstey,* with an introduction by Frank O'Connor. The furor over that minor masterpiece, a gem of rural Irish humor and wisdom, eventually reached the front pages and the floor of the Irish Senate. It displayed the Irish at their worst, which is to say their narrowest and most xenophobic, yet it should be remarked that the brouhaha probably wouldn't have arisen at a time other than when Ireland was desperately striving to keep out of World War II and public opinion was more sensitive and inflamed than it had been since the Troubles.

Eric Cross is an Englishman, and that always helps. He had come to the Muskerry Mountains of West Cork during the thirties to seek refuge from a world which he, as a research scientist, was convinced was preparing to destroy itself in another world war. There he met a tailor named Tim Buckley and his wife, Anstey, and was enchanted by the old man's endless talk, so strongly in contrast with the sophisticated and suicidal nonsense he had heard in what the Irish always call the outside world.

Frank O'Connor, who knew the tailor and his wife from his own frequent sabbaticals in the Muskerrys, considered them people of natural genius. "She was thin, tragic, and sour; the Tailor was plump, wise, and sweet-tempered. He sat on a butter-box and blew the fire with his old hat, and carried on an unending dialogue with his wife. . . . He was one of the greatest talkers I have ever known; and if in the way of great talkers he did occasionally hold the floor too much, it was never because he was self-assertive, but because he had a sort of natural authority that asserted itself without assistance."

Cross recorded the old man's conversations and published

them with all their rural wit and occasional bawdiness intact. Immediately they were seized upon by William Magennis, a member of the Irish Senate and chairman of the Board of Censorship of Publications, as an insult to the Irish nation. The talkative tailor, in Magennis' opinion, was a "moron," the book itself blasphemous and obscene, the purpose of the enterprise an attempt to show the Irish people as foulmouthed and ludicrous.

The Tailor and Anstey was banned, but that was only the beginning of the persecution. Local hooligans, inflamed not by their own reading of the book but by press accounts of speeches denouncing it, made a misery of the last days of the tailor and his wife. Three priests invaded their cottage, forced the old man down on his knees, and made him burn a copy of the book in his fireplace. The elderly couple died a short time later, their end hastened and embittered by the scandal. Tim Buckley was buried under a headstone carved by his friend, the sculptor Seamus Murphy, with the epitaph composed by Frank O'Connor: "A star danced and under it I was born." Some years later an appeals board reviewed *The Tailor and Anstey* and decided it wasn't obscene or denigratory, after all. It stands as the real monument to Tim Buckley and all the great talkers of the Irish countryside. The story behind it also stands, as a parable of all that is fearful and repressive and life-denying in the Irish psyche.

Even more discouraging than the rigors of censorship is the fact that there are few publishers and bookstores. Irish genius usually must be discovered abroad; Irish writers must export or perish. Ireland is more of a country for talking than reading and, if one believes the pessimists, more for television viewing than talking. Yet the exiles, like Edna O'Brien and John McGahern, are bitterly regretted and the cause of a literary columnist's occasional complaint to the effect that "Irish literary blood is draining away into foreign gutters." A live author will have to make it on his own, but at least one safely dead one, James Joyce, has been canonized as a tourist attraction. The film adapted from *Ulysses* was banned, but Joyce scholars and admirers from all over the world are encouraged to gather in Dublin every June 16, Bloomsday, to commemorate their idol and listen to symposiums on the latest meanings extracted from his works. Less passionate *aficionados* are taken on bus tours around Joycean landmarks, with a long and reverent stop at the Martello Tower, Sandy Cove, where Buck Mulligan and Stephen Dedalus lived part of their fictional lives.

All this is not to suggest that Irish writing became desperately unwell in the last half century. Any period in which the roaring boy of O'Connell Street, Brendan Behan, was alive and producing could hardly be a fit candidate for the iron lung.

The wild humor and unfettered imagination which have always been part of Irish writing in prose, poetry, and the drama have evidenced themselves in the works of various writers, as well as the stark realism which often affronts both the secret and official censors of Ireland. There is also some truth in the old dictum that an Irish writer has to die or emigrate to achieve the recognition he deserves. A case in point is Brian O'Nolan, who died in 1966 and whose valuation on the literary market has been rising ever since. As Myles na gCopaleen he wrote a satirical column for the *Irish Times,* as Flann O'Brien he produced a novel titled *At Swim-Two-Birds* and three others published posthumously, and as Brian O'Nolan he worked as a civil servant. His career might serve as a cautionary for any Irishman contemplating a literary career. For all his considerable talent he had to make a living at a government job or choose the exile's route. He opted for Ireland and relieved some of his feelings, perhaps, by attacking the hypocrisies and pretensions of his contemporaries whose own talents were limited to exploiting the labor of others.

O'Nolan's first novel appeared in 1939, when he was still in his twenties, and revealed an offbeat, idiosyncratic humor which his admirers compared to Joyce's. For years he was a sort of secret celebrity, whose *At Swim-Two-Birds* was passed around the literary cognoscenti, was praised by Joyce himself, Graham Greene, and V. S. Pritchett, but it was strictly an underground, noncommercial success. One of his volunteer promoters was the young English novelist John Wain, who wrote of O'Nolan's novel as "just about the only real masterpiece in English that is far too little read and discussed . . . a Gargantuan comic novel which makes a simultaneous exploration, on four or five levels, of Irish civilization." O'Nolan, however, had to die, suddenly and at the age of fifty-four, before a Flann O'Brien cult sprang into life, and his three other novels were published posthumously. *The*

Hard Life, The Third Policeman, and *The Dalkey Archive* all have won the critical praise in England and America that O'Nolan could have used when he was alive.

Walter Macken achieved a more solid and visible success with his novels (*The Scorching Wind,* for one) of his native Galway, but for years he had to make his living as manager of the Gaelic Theater in Galway City and as an actor, director, and producer. His windfall, in the form of a film adaptation of one of his novels, came only after his recent death. Edna O'Brien migrated to England, where her sexual candor in *The Country Girls* and other novels, her disillusioned view of Irish life and its brutal repressions have been enthusiastically received. Benedict Kiely (*In a Harbour Green* and other first-rate novels) spends much of his time on American campuses. Possibly the best craftsman of the lot, the Belfast-born Brian Moore (*The Lonely Passion of Judith Hearne* and *The Feast of Lupercal* have Irish backgrounds), emigrated years ago, first to Montreal, then to New York and finally to Hollywood, where more than one fine Irish talent has desiccated under the California sun. Dr. Conor Cruise O'Brien is an educator, a highly controversial former diplomat, a member of the Dail, a Socialist propaganda maker, but above all a writer. Two of the better young writers are John McGahern and John Broderick, whose explorations of the Irish rural life are not totally cherished in Ireland. McGahern's *The Dark,* which records a troubled adolescence in a west of Ireland he pictures in a manner dismaying to the government tourist agency, was banned by the Irish censorship. He departed for England when his teaching contract was not renewed on the grounds that he had not only written a pornographic novel but had married a Finnish girl in a civil ceremony. Broderick hangs on, however, in spite of having described the secret sexuality and open greed of a small Irish town and having included a homosexual passage in *The Waking of Willie Ryan.*

As for the contemporary Irish theater, it seems to be stirring again with the New York acclaim for an adaptation of Brendan Behan's *Borstal Boy,* the success of Brian Friel's *Philadelphia, Here I Come!,* and the return to Ireland of Hugh Leonard. Everybody knows about the successful professionals, but there is an indigenous theatrical movement little known outside Ireland based upon the more than 800 amateur dramatic societies and the regional drama competitions leading to an all-Ireland competition, which has combined audiences and a burgeoning talent that the professional theater might well envy. A number of nativist playwrights, concentrating on rural Irish themes, supply this tributary theater; they receive only £5 ($12) a performance for their works, but they are produced so often that the writer can make a fair income.

The titan among these semiprofessional playwrights, little known outside Ireland but more famous in the countryside than most writers who have made good abroad, is John B. Keane. He runs a pub in his hometown of Listowel, County Kerry, which is rapidly becoming a tourist attraction (for Irish tourists, that is). Keane began writing plays after coaxing the last drunk to go home, and within a comparatively short time he has produced such works as *The Year of the Hiker, The Field, The Man from Clare* and *Many Young Men of Twenty*. They are written for the Irish, who are observed with a hard realistic eye; his work will probably not appeal to international audiences until he provides the sentiment and japery expected of an Irish playwright. That may never happen, because Keane is his own man and content to write for his own people. Some of his plays are given professional exposure in Cork and Dublin. At the Olympia in Dublin I saw a first-rate production of his *Big Maggie,* which revolves with antic humor and unabashed melodrama around the figure of a domineering Irish mother.

His work is designed for audiences which may be relatively unsophisticated but are knowing, every Irishman being a born critic if he isn't a creator. In his *Self-Portrait,* Keane takes note of the warning of Michael MacLiammoir, one of the present eminences of the Irish theater, that the "theater is an evil place for those who do not belong." Keane admits he doesn't belong to the metropolitan theater of which MacLiammoir speaks, but the rural theater, with its absence of commercial pressure and towering egos, is a different sort of place. It is open to everyone. It is also as international, he maintains, as Broadway or the West End because Yeats and Shakespeare were "country boys." The rural theater, he believes, should be kept free of "too much metropolitan influence" and be allowed to develop its own character. The theater, according to Keane, is experiencing a rebirth in the countryside, in the small-town dramatic societies, without any patronizing help or influence from Dublin or London. "It is taking a strange shape," he observed in his autobiography, "but the stranger the better, and the more independent of outside influence the better. . . . New plays by country boys are springing up like mushrooms all around us. Maybe some of them are crude and clumsy but it must be remembered that you cannot build a new native drama in a generation. The rising generation should bring the harvest of plays which the theatre needs to give it life and vitality and exuberance . . . because those are the things that a rising generation has in abundance."

If the work of Keane himself is an earnest of things to come, if the country-boy dramatists can take the direction he has indicated, independent of the faddish and fashionable trends of the metropolitan theater, then the next J. M. Synge may be driving the cows home or hoisting milk cans in a crossroads creamery.

12.

The Jackeens

How I love the old town where every man is a potential idler, poet or friend.

—OLIVER ST. JOHN GOGARTY

With cavalier hyperbole a recent *New Yorker* article by Jane Kramer described Dubliners as the residents of the world's largest village. "Everyone here knows everyone else, and is probably related to everyone else, too. The city is a little like a large and eccentric family in which father is a politician, mother is a saint, grandmother a terrorist, the two favorite uncles a bishop and an alcoholic, and the loving, bickering offspring include a poet, a policeman, a mad bomber, a union organizer, a Sister of Mercy, a Maoist, a socialist, a fascist, a beggar, a businessman and a moderately successful crook. It is a place where the local Bakunin is a daily communicant, and the maid at Parliament usually picks up the telephone."

Dubliners reacted to this description of themselves as they generally do to such journalistic bird-in-flight views, with rage and scorn and indignation. A Dublin columnist picked up excerpts from the article and demanded, "Recognize it, dear readers? No? Well, take a deep breath and think it over while you count to ten and then think again." On the other hand, they could have looked up a quotation from one of their native sons, James Joyce, who was even less flattering when he wrote that Dubliners numbered many of the "most hopeless, useless and inconsistent charlatans I have ever come across in the island or on the Continent."

To the rest of the country, Dubliners are pejoratively known as jackeens and are regarded as rude, overly energetic, dangerously sharp, and untrustworthy. Dubliners return the compliment by lumping the rest of their countrymen together as culchies, which, roughly translated, means country clods. The Dubliner venturing into the countryside is not unlike the New Yorker in his convictions of superiority. I once drove across Ireland to County Cork with a Dubliner, who whimsically commented along the way on the backwardness, stupidity, and knavishness of the culchies. When we arrived on the coast of Cork, he stared at the rude splendor about him with citified distaste and spoke of Corkmen as an English explorer of the mid-nineteenth century might speak of an obscure tribe of African jungle dwellers. To the Dubliner the culchies are tightfisted smallholders, the enemies of progress and culture, whose petty conservatism is holding the country back through the inordinate amount of political power they control.

If it seems like an overgrown village to the outsider, Dublin to its natives is a great capital, founded more than 1,000 years ago as a Viking naval base and once the second city in the British Empire. What makes it appear villagelike by comparison to any other metropolis is the prevailing gregariousness. You need strong buttonholes in Dublin because you will constantly be hauled into conversation unless you are quick on your feet; certainly it is the world capital of gasconade, its garrulous spirit embodied by the late Brendan Behan and captured in the plays of Sean O'Casey. "Dublin," V. S. Pritchett wrote, "likes the great evasion of the laugh; it relieves one of the dangers of having one's mind read and forwards the tricky business of keeping the big guns of polemic booming away while, under cover of the noise, one devotes one's continually sharpened intelligence to maneuver. The effort is self-consuming, for talkers are hermetically enclosed in their self-love. Yet, when the talk stops and the light goes out in the talker's face, one sees he is at once aware of his real situation. He is not so different from his sparring partners across the Channel—the day-dreaming English enclosed in their clichés, the startled Welsh, the conscience-stricken Scots, who all find themselves forced to live in one another's pockets, are alike in one thing: they are frontier dwellers. It is their curse and their advantage."

Buried deep in the modern Dubliner's psyche is that realization that he has always lived on a dangerous frontier since the days when Dublin was called Dark Pool after the waters of the Liffey, when the Danes made it their stronghold and later the English designated it as the Pale, beyond which the barbarians roamed. A garrison state of mind was formed early on. This mentality has been described in various ways by its eminent sons. Dr. Gogarty declared that Dublin was "stupefied by the Celtic chloroform," Joyce that it was "the centre of paralysis." When he wrote *The Dubliners* in 1905, Joyce struggled to explain to a publisher what he was trying to capture in the epiphanies (which he defined in *Stephen Hero* as "a sudden spiritual manifestation, whether in the vulgarity of speech or of gesture or in a memorable phase of the mind itself") to his native city: "I do not think that any writer has yet presented Dublin to the world. It has been a capital of Europe for thousands of years, it is supposed to be the second city of the British Empire and it is nearly three times as big as Venice. Moreover, on account of many circumstances which I cannot detail here, the expression Dubliner seems to me to bear some meaning and I doubt whether the same can be said for such words as 'Londoner' and 'Parisian.' . . ." He saw it as neither a conglomeration of people nor "a heap of broken images," as T. S. Eliot described it, but as a great capital populated by the ghosts of its history.

There was a haunted air then, and it can be sensed now in the older streets away from the city center, inside the ring of suburbs, on a foggy night when Molly Malone might be out crying the last of the wares in her barrow. It can also be sensed in a few lines from "Two Gallants" in *The Dubliners*:

> Not far from the porch of the club a harpist stood in the roadway, playing to a little ring of listeners. He plucked at the wires heedlessly, glancing quickly from time to time at the face of each newcomer and from time to time, also, at the sky. His harp, too, heedless that her coverings had fallen about her knees, seemed weary alike of the eyes of strangers and of her master's hands.

> One hand played in the bass the melody of *Silent, O Moyle,* while the other careered in the treble after each group of notes. The notes of the air sounded deep and full. . . .

Outwardly it is rather a melancholy gray mildewed old city, particularly to the eye half-blinded by the glass-box glitter of American cities, but it is populated by a lively, sharp-witted citizenry with a notoriously acerb sense of humor. Like the London Cockney, the native New Yorker, Parisian, or Berliner, the Dubliner is street-wise, nimble, and confident that no one can outsmart him. Unlike those other metropolites, he is friendly, approachable, curious about the stranger, and willing to form an undying friendship on the spot.

The gregarious quality is greatly expanded by the number and variety of bars, about 600 by the latest estimate. Close the pubs and Dublin socially would be a dead city. Dublin is the world capital of the drinking man as much as New York is the businessman's or Paris the sybarite's. Joyce once speculated on whether it was possible to map a route across Dublin without passing the door of a pub but had to concede the task was unthinkable. Tentaclelike malty fumes reach out for the passerby, especially when the light is fading and the weathered façades of the old city seemed to be closing in. Behind a pub's doors he can find instant and usually undemanding companionship.

Not that the Dubliner, "in drink taken," doesn't have his own rules of etiquette. The boozing may be hearty, but it is not unconfined. A stranger is ill advised to attempt monopolizing the conversation the moment he has lubricated his throat; he must wait for acceptance. Worse yet, he will start by talking about women, marital troubles, or sex; the pub is a refuge from all problems connected with women. Irishmen may be salty in speech but are generally averse to sexual discourse.

The talk may be wild as the evening progresses, but the establishment itself is always a model of discretion. If the telephone rings and the caller asks to speak to a patron, the publican asks, "Who?" in the most baffled tone, even though the subject of the inquiry hangs out there night and day. The house considers it a prime responsibility to erect a barrier between the drinker and the importunities of the outside world.

The discretion with which the pub enfolds its clients, even while functioning as a combination club, message center, escape hatch, and communications network, is illustrated by a cartoon which may be found framed on the walls of several Dublin pubs. It shows a barkeep leaning to whisper into the ear of a customer, "Mr. G. was in, Mr. O., but he said nothing about the other thing." Asking a direct question about any habitué is to be confronted by a blank wall of incomprehension. A passing stranger might get the idea that the establishment is frequented entirely by fugitives, spies, and IRA men on the run, even though its clientele is composed of civil servants and bank clerks.

It is astonishing how the mood of a pub revs up as the night falls and the alcoholic tide rises. Observing the Dublin drinking man with scholarly detachment, Conor O'Brien has described the tidal effect on his subject:

> More often than not the Dublin drinker is predictable—solemn, silent, and sometimes solitary in the afternoon, garrulous and declamatory in the evening as he surrounds himself with a constantly increasing circle of friends. Is it so different in bars anywhere else in the world? My experience in this context is obviously limited, but it is a fact that we Dubliners talk far more than, say, New York bar lizards. Our improvidence with words usually varies proportionately with the consumption of fuel. For the outsider the challenge is to select with precise accuracy the optimum moment for joining one of these highly charged groups; too soon (before two pints of stout have settled into the blood stream) and one runs the risk of being treated merely as an outsider; too late (after the square root of two pints to the power of four) and one is certain to be overwhelmed by a tide of amicable near-incoherence.

There are a number of the most attractive drinking places anywhere in the world to be found in Dublin. Ryan's, near the Heuston railroad station, is a perfect preservation of the pub of mid-Victorian times. It includes four snugs, small areas partitioned off from the rest of the establishment in which women are permitted. Not long ago a woman who entered a pub, even in Dublin, was suspected of being a streetwalker. The snugs are the equivalent of the ladies' entrance of the American saloon, in which men unconventional enough to prefer their wives' company, occasionally, may entertain the ladies. They are not scenes of extramarital hanky-panky, as the furnishings are designed only for the sober business of drinking. The Long Hall, in South Great George's Street (reading Dublin street signs and studying its outdoor statuary are a means of tracing the British occupation), is another Victorian survival: a magnificently carved oak bar with brass fittings, ornate mirrors, and candelabra. The Antique Bar in Jury's Hotel is a more self-conscious study in recapturing an era when drinking was done by solid men in an atmosphere of immense dignity and decorum.

It is a tribute to the taste of Dubliners that, like Londoners, they have maintained so much of the ritual of John Barleycorn's past—inglorious though it is to a large segment of the population which wears the insignia of the Pioneers. One of the ceremonies preserved is that of buying rounds, it being a matter of honor in Dublin pubs to take your turn at buying a drink for each of the persons you're drinking with. A nice display of drinking manners—not unknown in the United States—but it can result in your having eight drinks, accidentally, when you'd just dropped in for a quick one. The dangers of this tradition are made manifest in several pubs where writers and journalists gather to bedazzle one another, in the Silver Swan on one of the Liffey quays, and in the Pearl Bar in Fleet Street, in which more unwritten novels and plays have spun into the smoky air than have ever reached publication.

The singing pubs, reverberating with balladry amateur and professional, are an Irish tradition of sorts, heavily played up in tourist advertising but not an unmitigated blessing to music lovers. I have heard one Irishman say that none of his countrymen, with the possible exception of the late John McCormack, should ever have been allowed to sing in public. It all depends on how much enthusiasm you can muster for folk singing and for fellow patrons taking their turn at being electronically amplified, the lady from Wolverhampton expanding on the glories of the biggest aspidistra in the world, or an alcoholized American rendering a homesick version of "The Eyes of Texas Are Upon You."

Most of the singing pubs are tourist-oriented, but the more authentic style may be sampled at Howth, the tiny peninsula jutting from the north side of Dublin Bay. The singing at the Abbey Tavern in Howth Village leans heavily toward the come-all-yes of revolutionary times, a night-long recitative of British crimes and Irish martyrdoms. One of the more popular ballads sung at the Abbey Tavern commemorates the futile death of Sean South of County Limerick, who was killed in an IRA raid on a police barracks in Northern Ireland in 1957. That the raid fatal to Sean South contravened the official policy of the Irish Republic is beside the point; the important thing is that his death demonstrated that Irishmen are still willing to die for an ideal. "A cynic would say," as Conor Cruise O'Brien commented on the ballad, "that his only real service to his country has been the posthumous one of contributing to Ireland's external assets by adding local colour to places of entertainment: his bones have become bait in a tourist trap."

There are indeed somber undercurrents to be sensed in the ballad singing of Howth's pubs, which awaken one to the realization that Dublin is not entirely engrossed by its new material prosperity and the pursuit of its ancient pleasures. In a flash the mood can turn searingly nationalistic. One of the performers will be telling a joke about the drunken Irishman who has appeared at the gates of heaven and is having a lighthearted conversation with St. Peter. Suddenly the joke turns itself inside out, in one of those lightning switchbacks characteristic of Irish humor, and the Irishman demands: "But give us back our Six Counties of the North!" And the house, largely composed of natives, until now in a carefree mood, explodes with vehement applause and cheering.

There is more to Dublin, of course, than genial tippling. Underlying the bustle of its commerce, the magpie coveys of shoppers in O'Connell and Upper Grafton streets, is the anxiety of nations recently introduced to the tensions of development. Dublin is halfway between an old way of life and a new one that thrusts aside Georgian houses as briskly as it destroys the former graces of human conduct.

There are tension and misery, for instance, in the conflict between town and country. Dublin swarms with thousands of people recently migrated from the farmlands to work in offices and shops and the production lines of the Volkswagen assembly plant on the outskirts, most of them still bearing that lost and wondering look of country people thrown into an urban environment. For the first time in their lives they have money to go to the films or buy a new dress when the urge strikes them, but they are still homesick for the mountains and boreens. They are delighted to be freed of the watchful eyes of parents and neighbors and the strictures of parish priests, but they are distressed by the anonymity of living in an uncaring and often inimical mass. The lost joys of neighborliness, even the monitoring and bad mouthing that go with it, are eternally mourned. That feeling of reaching out for human contact was touchingly conveyed by V. S. Pritchett when he noted that as you walk down any Dublin street, "you see the man or woman who is coming toward you pause for a second. They gaze at you perplexedly, search your face, even smile to convey that they wished they knew you, and not knowing you, are puzzled by this break in the natural order. They ache for acquaintance; and if they don't find out who you are they will invent it." The same disorientation is visible in the shops, now largely staffed by country girls, when a customer strolls in to find them chattering in a corner and raps on the counter for service. The girls are shocked by the peremptory summons because in the country the shops are meeting places, where gossip and tapping the rural grapevine are as important as any paltry business that might be transacted.

In such moments you can sympathize with President De Valera's little sermon of more than thirty years ago: "Let us resolve never to become a cosmopolitan people."

The new citizens of Dublin are packed into what has been called the bed-sitter civilization, a world of rented rooms in which, as Brendan Behan warned, they find conviviality, but not friendship; loneliness, but not solitude. This rooming-house culture was achingly recalled by Edna O'Brien, the heroine of restless Irish womanhood, the country girl who made it not only in Dublin but on the literary and cinematic heights of London. She came to Dublin from a farm in the west as a girl of seventeen to study pharmacy. Since that wasn't too many years ago, such novels as *The Lonely Girl,* strikingly filmed as *The Girl with the*

Green Eyes with the English actress Rita Tushingham as the Irish heroine, convey with compassionate exactitude the plight of the young rural females plunged into the bed-sitter ambience of Dublin.

"It was a terraced brick house, linoleumed from top to bottom," Miss O'Brien described her heroine's rooming house. "She [the landlady] had a strip of matting, which she had got cheap, on the downstairs hall. The furniture was dark and heavy, and the front room was stuffed with china dogs and ornaments and knickknacks. There was a green rubber plant in a pot on the piano." The heroine and her roommate look for adventure in the dance halls, though not without trepidation. "There was a rumour that two girls were doped and brought up the Dublin mountains the week before. Doped cigarettes! We didn't even get asked for one dance; there weren't enough men. We could have danced with each other, but Babs said that was the end. So we just sat there, rubbing the goose flesh off our arms and passing remarks about the men who stood at one end of the hall, sizing up the various girls who sat, waiting, on long stools. They never asked a girl to dance until the music started up, and then they seemed to pick the girls who were near. We moved down to that end of the hall, but had no luck there either. . . ."

The girls are obsessed by the hope of meeting someone handsome, distinguished, or at least interesting, like a diplomat, but they run into squalid misadventure with fellow culchies instead. Once they have to hire a taxi to take a drunken young man home, a vexation which points up the apartness and dislocation of city life for the country girls. "We had no idea where he lived. It's funny that we should have known him for a year but did not know where he lived. Dublin is like that. We knew his local pub but not his house."

For many young women, like the Edna O'Brien they look up to, Dublin becomes only a stepping-stone to England, which seems the most worldly and attractive place they can hope to reach, and never mind that their grandfathers have described it as the source of all of Ireland's troubles. They become bored with roommates, fed up with wandering the streets with two or three of their girlfriends and looking into shopwindows, annoyed by the shyness of the Irish boys who cluster around street corners eyeing them warily or cling together in pubs, depressed by statistics showing that women outnumber men in Dublin.

The country boys, on the other hand, are disenchanted by the steely insistence of Irish girls on sex as a fringe benefit of marriage; the contraceptive pill hasn't changed *that*. Queuing up for the movie theaters becomes tiresome, there are no nightclubs, and Dublin is asleep by midnight except for a few people catching the last buses home. Hasn't the word got around that English girls are free and easy? So they take the night mailboat for Holyhead and England and often wind up marrying an Irish girl anyway.

In Dublin, too, the thousands of rural Irish who come annually in search of a job and a new life are confronted by an intramural hostility, a sectional prejudice, that seems a throwback to the days when a villager regarded anyone coming from farther than the next village as a species of Martian. Corkmen tend to think of Donegal as the other side of the moon. And when a Dublin solicitor complains that the "real Dublin" is being swamped by "foreign influences," he isn't referring to a phalanx of Germans carrying their lunches in briefcases or a new influx of Japanese businessmen with cameras that seem attached to their umbilical cords. No, he is bemoaning the incursion of the "bogmen," his fellow citizens from the rural areas. "You don't hear the old Dublin accent anymore," he will complain. "We're being pushed under by the bogtrotters from County Mayo." The newcomer runs up against the hard edge of the Irish city dweller's mentality, which has been characterized as "a cold, hard, detonating impartiality."

The Dublin argot will also be confusing. Dubliners appear to the countryman to be speaking neither English nor Irish, but some metropolitan tongue of their own devising or in a code which excludes the unitiated. True enough, much of the slang used by Dubliners, particularly those of the lower orders, not Trinity graduates, requires interpretation. Some of it is rhyming slang, a device they have borrowed from the Cockneys across the water or vice versa. Some of the commoner expressions which would require translation include:

Brass, meaning money.

Buckshee (adapted from baksheesh), something given as a bribe or gratuity.

Bundle, a fight, a free-for-all.

China, a friend or mate (rhyming slang for "china plate").

Craw-thumper, a religious fanatic, a breast-beater.

Dicky-bird, rhyming slang for "word."

Frit, frightened.

German band, rhyming slang for "hand."

Grass, an informer, a stool pigeon.

Half-inching, stealing (rhyming slang for "pinching").

Hooley, a party, a rout.

Jarred, drunk (having a jar means having a drink.)

King Lear, a homosexual (rhyming slang for "queer").

Lag, a convict.

Lumpers, the lumpenproletariat.

Mince pies, rhyming slang for "eyes."

Nark, an informer.

Rosy Lee, rhyming slang for "tea."

Scarper, to break out of prison.

Scouse, native of Liverpool, named for a stew popular there.

Smoke, the city of London ("the Big Smoke").

Snout, tobacco.

Squaddy, a soldier.

Spiv, small-time crook (stolen from the English).

Tea leaf, rhyming slang for "thief."

Topping, execution by hanging.

Aside from the initial language barrier, the countryman come to Dublin has to deal with his own prejudices against the capital, which are deeper than most of that sort because of historic complications. Until a half century ago, the rest of the Irish regarded Dubliners living within the Pale, cheek by jowl with British garrisons, consorting in the case of the Castle Irish with the overlords of the Ascendancy, as quislings and collaborators—and such prejudices are a long time dying in Ireland. And there is the problem of moving from one secret society, that of their native village or townland, to a much larger but no less exclusive one. The Irish were a race long before they were a nation, and a secret society before that; to be Irish is to be part of a conspiracy.

Even in the most banal matters they adopt the conspiratorial manner, look around carefully, and speak in a whisper. A man goes into a bank and whispers to one of the officials. A disastrous overdraft, a plea for an extension on a loan? No, he is probably discussing the weather. A woman murmurs into the ear of a clerk at the General Post Office. A bit of scandalous gossip, perhaps? No, she is saying, "Would you be having an airmail stamp for America?" If you ask the whereabouts of someone, you are likely to be told, with a confederate smile, "I have no treasonable information on that subject."

Seen in a certain light and perhaps in a certain mood, Dublin can assume a slightly sinister aspect, like something glimpsed out of the corner of the eye which vanishes the moment you turn to look squarely at it. This may be the trick of an imagination overstimulated by a measure of historical knowledge, for there is hardly a street or elderly façade which does not have its place in the record of violent retribution, blood guilt, armed revolt. If streets can be haunted by such events, it is easy to believe that Dublin's are. Even the more squalid streets have a sort of dingy glamor, a suggestion of menace. It was no accident that when the East Berlin scenes of *The Spy Who Came In from the Cold* were filmed, the company went on location in Dublin. When the latest film version of *Of Human Bondage* was made, likewise, Dublin provided a representation of the more sinister streets of Victorian London.

Nor was it any mischance that Sheridan Le Fanu drew on his native Dublin as the background for some of his masterly horror stories. Le Fanu usually made guilt the main theme of his ghost stories; his characters were haunted, as a form of revenge, by ghosts representing the evil they had done, thus giving his stories a moral and psychological cutting edge not often found in that genre. One was the celebrated story of Mr. Justice Harbottle, one of those lamentable hanging judges who figure so often in English and Irish fiction. Justice Harbottle is haunted by the ghost of a man he unjustly sent to the gallows, and at the end is hanged by the ghost. The things in Le Fanu's stories that manifest themselves in the night or wander the Dublin streets are not ordinary revenants whose main purpose seems to be frightening innocent people, but the wraiths of our guilts demanding that their price be paid.

The retributive atmosphere of Dublin's streets also invaded the home of Sir William Wilde a few doors down Merrion Square from the Le Fanu residence. Not merely because the vigorously, even scandalously heterosexual physician, writer, and antiquarian fathered a son named Oscar, whose sexual proclivities took a lamentably different turn, but because of a deathbed scene that might have been concocted by Le Fanu.

Aside from operating a clinic which provided free medical services for the poor and handling a practice which included some of Dublin's wealthiest citizens, who indirectly paid for the clinic, Dr. Wilde managed to find time for a succession of mistresses. He was also a four-star drinking man. Later in life, the whiskey raddling him as absinthe would his son, he grew so careless about antisepsis and personal hygiene that there was a medical student joke making the rounds of College Green: "Why are Dr. Wilde's fingernails always black? Because he scratches himself."

One of his ex-mistresses served as Dr. Wilde's all too solidly fleshed wraith, one with a Le Fanu-like persistence. When he cast her off, she went around wailing that Dr. Wilde had seduced her after surreptitiously drugging her. She published a pamphlet containing that charge, and Dr. Wilde was forced to sue for libel. The lady was awarded one farthing damages by a jury which may have underestimated the value of a woman's virtue.

Many years later, when Dr. Wilde lay dying in his house on Merrion Square, his accuser, for reasons no one ever discovered, came to sit at his deathbed day after day. The Wilde family did not attempt to exclude her; perhaps they felt she had some obscure but legitimate claim to sharing the death watch; it was quite in keeping with the Dublin spirit that his most implacable enemy should be given her place. As the family's living ghost, she was entitled to respectful treatment. Every day "swathed in black and heavily veiled," as Patrick Byrne wrote in *The Wildes of Merrion Square,* "she would enter silently and make her way upstairs. None interfered with her. There she would sit for hours, nearly the entire day, like a Buddha, without speaking, almost without moving. Through the thick veil the eyes rested unceasingly on the features of the dying man, whose half glazed glance returned hers uncomprehendingly."

She kept watch until he died and was placed in his coffin. Then she disappeared and was never seen again. But what a small hell she must have created for Dr. Wilde as he lay dying, helpless to escape from that unending speculative stare, haunted by the live ghost of his green and licentious years.

The aspect of the city has changed considerably, of course, since Dr. William Wilde thankfully breathed his last. Many of the old houses have been knocked down to be replaced by apartment blocks, much of its leisurely pace and dignity is being trampled by the onrush of progress, there are a couple of mini-skyscrapers on O'Connell Street and more coming, the population will reach the million mark within a generation; but it is still a city in which workers go home for dinner at noon, the pubs close for the Holy Hour in midafternoon, and hardly anyone punches a time clock. Le Fanu's ghosts would find the traffic bothersome and their former haunts taken over by bed-sitters, but it is still a place where the rebellious can raise their voices.

Progress can't jackhammer its priceless location between the sea and the hills or the "sweet and stately order" of its landmarks, which Brendan Behan recited as a litany when he returned home from a British reformatory. As his ship entered Dublin Bay he counted them off like a miser checking his accounts: "Bray Head, the Sugarloaf, the Two Rock, the Three Rock, Kippure, the king of them all, rising his threatening head behind and over their shoulders till they sloped down to the city. I counted the spires, from Rathmines fat dome on one side to St. George's spire on the north, and in the centre, Christ-church. Among the smaller ones, just on the docks, I could pick out, even in the haze of morning, the ones I knew best, St. Laurence O'Toole's and St. Barnabas; I had them all counted, present and correct and the chimneys of the Pigeon House, and the framing circle of the road along the edge of the Bay, Dun Laoghaire, Blackrock, Sandymount Tower, Ringsend and the city; then on the other half circle, Fairview, Marino, Clontarf, Raheny, Kilnarrack, Baldoyle, to the height of Howth Head. . . ." It is the same reassuring presences that so many returning Irishmen count off to themselves as though, pessimistic as only Celts can be, they might have been swept away in their absence.

The real enduring thing is the Dublin spirit, which is not diminished but reinforced by the thousands of annual newcomers. The spirit that rose against the British while the rest of the country looked idly on. The spirit, generous or eccentric, that cheered on the Dublin fire brigades, during World War II, when they were sent roaring north to help put out the fires started by German bombers in Belfast. The spirit that informs the old Dublin saying in times of trouble that "God never closes one door that He doesn't open another."

That spirit is partly retained by the unchanging aspect of the narrow and crooked streets of the inner city, the thoroughfares leading from the quays on both sides of the Liffey within the boundaries of the North Circular Road to the north of the river and the Grand Canal to the south. They provide a small-town feeling even within sound of the traffic on the main commercial avenues, and in an hour's walk you might brush past Peadar O'Donnell, the firebrand writer, still a fiery radical, or Liam O'Flaherty, erect and white-haired and also in his seventies, or Sean O'Faolain in from his suburban home.

Dublin is a city of strange, sometimes perverse and unfortuitous encounters. It seems unavoidable that you will run into enemies, creditors, bores, and cranks the moment you set foot in the street. Of such untoward encounters, Honor Tracy has written:

> . . . they perhaps explain the wary look in the eyes of Dubliners and the strange crab-like sidle of the more nervous among them. The streets bristle with danger. You may be mooching along, intending no harm to a soul. . . . Towards you comes a lank figure in hairy tweeds and battered hat, one of Dublin's innumerable geniuses. From the air of purpose in his bearing it is clear that he means to borrow a pound. . . . Just in time you pull up, slap your forehead histrionically as if remembering the milk on the stove, wheel about and make down a side-turning as fast as your legs will carry you. A tall, distinguished man coming out of a shop raises his hat and looks daggers. Up to that moment you were not conscious of having offended in any way, had cher-

> ished the belief that you were rather a favourite, but no sooner do you get that steely look than you realize what is behind it. It flashes across your mind that when you were last in Dublin you never went to see this person. . . .

All the resilience, self-mockery, hoydenish humor, and resourcefulness of the quintessential Dubliner could be studied under laboratory conditions during the most recent of the bank strikes, which lasted six months. This calamity, which would have paralyzed the nerve of any other capital, was met with the same bland confidence as the Viennese who shrugs and says, "The situation is critical, but not serious." Not serious at all was the demeanor of many Dubliners who regarded the closing of the banks as an extended holiday from fiscal responsibility, proceeded to have their own checks printed (whether or not backed by accounts), and capered off on a paper chase that ended only with the news that the strike had been settled.

Irish bank officials estimated that 10,000,000 checks representing a total of $6 billion had accumulated, many of which were rubberoid in texture. Pubs had largely taken over the banking functions, and their owners appeared at the reopened banks with suitcases stuffed with checks even as a number of their customers left town for a cooling-off period. They would return and pay the piper, of course, because no one gets away with anything on a small island.

When the strike started, such people did everything they could to encourage a long strike. They wrote letters to the newspapers urging the bank employees to stand firm in their search for justice. Curious scenes were enacted in the pubs of the Dublin port suburb, Dun Laoghaire, where the steamers leave for Britain. Immediately after the strike started, the strikers, instead of drearily shouldering picket signs, headed for the English job market. They gathered for drinks in the pubs of Dun Laoghaire before the departure of the 8 P.M. mailboat for Holyhead and were amazed at the number of well-wishers and advice givers, though strangers, who came down to see them off. They were also surprised at how popular they had become until they reflected later, on the mailboat, on how emphatically they had been advised by their well-wishers to seek permanent employment in

England and to hell with the penny-pinching Irish banks. Then they realized what the jackeens were up to: "God never closes one door that He doesn't open another one."

Newspaper headlines kept referring to what they cautioned would be a "Day of Reckoning," but that didn't inhibit large numbers of Dubliners from floating checks without visible means of support. The Dublin print shops did a roaring business, running off checkbooks for all comers, a practice which may come up for review by the Irish Parliament.

One publican turned banker thumbed through stacks of checks representing, he hoped, about $48,000 and admitted, "I know that a few of them are losers. Maybe more than a few. The trouble is that some of the printers turning out checkbooks will sell them to whoever comes in the door, whether they have credentials or not. They are being bought by men who never had a bank account in their lives. I would say there will be a lot of people leaving the country for health reasons when the day of reckoning comes."

When judgment day did come, one man who had checks printed on a purely fictional account and had cashed $480 worth of them called the bank he had informally patronized and, with all the gall which the rest of the Irish attribute to Dubliners, said, "I hope you'll have me as a customer now."

Dublin's underpinnings, which were once a bog stretching along the Liffey, may eventually support a high-rise city of glass towers and belching smokestacks, but it is hard to believe that the quick, quirky, and volatile spirit of the Dubliners will be crushed into conformity.

13.

The Emerging Classes

Top Society is a mixum-gatherum . . . a conspired association . . . the ruling set that Dublin peculiarly required and peculiarly got.

—KATE O'BRIEN, *My Ireland*

☘ A half century ago, when the Irish Republic was emerging from the turbulence of the Revolution, there was a widespread hope that a less class-conscious society would replace the intricately exclusive structure willed by the British. Everyone, it seemed, had experienced a surfeit of the social and economic barriers erected by the Anglo-Irish and their English sponsors. As for the more radical yearnings for a workers' Socialist republic in which everyone would wear a cloth cap and memorize Marxist slogans, they never came close to fulfillment. For every James Connolly there was at least one William Murphy, the traction magnate and newspaper publisher, to apply the truncheon to such extreme aspirations.

So a class structure has developed, not entirely against the grain of Celtic traditions. The ancient Irish preached equality, legislated for it, and in part practiced it earnestly, yet Ireland before the invasions had its high kings, regional chieftains, its Druidic caste, and its lawyers huddled close to the seat of power at Tara, and its knights, all of them no doubt considering themselves superior to the peasants and herdsmen. Today the kings and chiefs are politicians; the Druids have been replaced by the Catholic hierarchy, which in many ways is the real aristocracy now; and the knightly ones are the entrepreneurs who armor themselves in Mercedes limousines.

The underclass may be observed in the Dublin tenement districts, in the police courts, or in the countryside where the tinkers (more politely known as itinerants) live in a state of vagabondage which the government's social agencies are trying to end. Almost any day in Dublin's Children's Court you can watch a juvenile charged with theft being sentenced to six months in the reformatory at Daingean; the process takes no more than ten minutes; the boy is unrepresented by counsel, unaccompanied by any member of his family or anyone else. And you can trace that lonely, abandoned figure of a boy to where he came from—a slum called the Cage, an accurate designation. The Cage is made of concrete, a narrow canyon formed by tall structures divided into flats reached by catwalks on which lines of laundry are hung in defiance of the soft gray rain, a human honeycomb almost as dismal as anything to be found in East Harlem or the Lower East Side of New York. The stairways and the thirty-foot divide between the buildings are cluttered with garbage and littered with rubbish; the only playground in sight is an abandoned, wheelless van which a number of children are using as an Irish version of a jungle gym. Behind the Cage is a row of cottages occupied by pensioners, at least one of whom, an old man with a club in his hand, is standing guard over his property against the destructive impulses of kids spilling out of the Cage.

If theoretically it is possible for a boy or girl born and raised in the Cage or on the quays of Cork City to work and fight his way into the upper echelons of Irish society, the odds against it are close to insuperable. The best they can hope for is a marginal existence, often eked out by help from the state. At the same time there is a growing resistance from the smaller towns and rural areas against government support of "layabouts." The cost of such programs is indicated by the fact that in Ireland 100 people of working age have to support 74 of dependent age, compared with 48 in West Germany, 53 in England, and that this same working class, earning less than $2,880 a year, is carrying the major share of the social-welfare burden. "Those over the £1,200 [$2,880] mark who can best afford to pay," a West Cork newspaper (*The Southern Star* of Skibbereen) protests, "including, of course, numerous professional classes already dodging income tax, are escaping altogether. . . . This is layaboutland gone mad. . . . We talk about unemployment and emigration, but as is well-known, job opportunities are allowed to go a-begging even in provincial areas while potential employees draw the dole." The result of "cradle to grave welfare statism," the newspaper warned, would be "a race of vegetable-like parasites."

Even below the chronic dependents of the dole and the permanent residents of "layaboutland," there is a segment of the population which constitutes Ireland's own "peculiar institution," though it is not formally enslaved. At the bottom of the social and economic system is a despised and ill-used minority numbering perhaps 10,000 men and women and children who make up the estimated 1,200 tinker families: Ireland's untouchables. To the Irish, there is nothing romantic about their native gypsy tradition. The tinkers, or itinerants, as sociologists and other enlightened persons call them, or the traveling people, as they were once known, haven't a drop of Romany blood but are as pureblooded Irish as anyone. Some are members of families that took to the road during the famines and have never settled down; others are descendants of tinsmiths (hence tinkers) and horse traders who roved the island for generations.

Many wouldn't take to a settled life if they had the chance, preferring to live as far beyond the purview of social workers and educational reformers as possible, roaming the byways in their caravans, trailed by horses, dogs, and children, sleeping in or under their wagons (on a cold night a row of chilblained feet may be seen sticking out of their sides), with nothing but the hedgerows between them and the often-dripping sky. Indubitably they beg from door to door; they show up at market-town fairs, where the women insist on telling fortunes; occasionally, it is alleged, they steal.

Altogether, in a modern society inhospitable to variants, they are a sociological problem of some magnitude. Government officials and high-minded people generally insist that they must be settled, jobs found for the men, schools for the children, washing machines for the women. Their plight—notwithstanding their ruddy physical health—is regarded with horror by liberal journalists, such as one who recently wrote:

> Ireland's itinerants live in a sort of prison-in-reverse. Just as surely as if there were iron bars between them and the "settled" community, they cannot break through. The freedom that they are deprived of in this cultural prison is acceptance by their fellow human beings, their fellow Irishmen. . . . New sociological work is showing that itinerant children have nightmare fantasies of persecution by the "quality people"—their name for the settled population. They imagine that people are plotting to kill them or injure them.

Ordinary people, however, have a deep-rooted objection to itinerants' being settled in their neighborhoods, claiming they simply don't fit in with decent respectable people. Obviously, fitting in is a process that will take some time. In Skibbereen, County Cork, several tinker families were given council houses —that is, public housing—which were soon stripped of their beams and other wooden fittings used as firewood. One tinker woman with six children lives in Skibbereen, where she puts the child-welfare allotments in postal savings and lives off the proceeds of begging in Ballydehob, twelve miles away. Almost everyone of the "quality" has some horror tale of how the tinkers fiddle their accounts with respectable society.

There have been riots over attempts to provide permanent campsites in some localities and civil disobedience, to put it mildly, over other efforts to find homes for itinerants who have signified their intention of settling down. The government began taking a paternal interest in 1963, when the Commission on Itinerancy reported that the tinkers had been on the road, often for six or more generations, too long to be able to help themselves. "The arguments that itinerants are free to leave the road of their own volition and that their plight is of their own making," the report emphasized, "does not bear examination. Little heed is given to the virtually insuperable difficulties which face the unaided efforts of an itinerant family to settle down." The stigma of having been a tinker, the commission learned, was all but ineradicable; there were cases of tinker families which had been settled in one house for twenty-five years and were still ostracized, thanks to the unforgiving length of the Irish memory.

The Irish often take a highly idealistic attitude toward American and British racial problems, point to the presence of several hundred African students peacefully in their midst, and will vocalize at length on the injustices and prejudices of other countries. The same people will fall strangely silent when the matter of the itinerants is raised, or they will point out that the tinkers are of the same race. Often blond and blue-eyed, they are Ireland's blacks, and they arouse the same sort of liberal hypocrisy as black Americans in the United States. Whenever there is a furious controversy over the resettlement problem—often with outbreaks of communal violence—the letters columns of the national dailies are filled with righteous indignation. Everyone, it seems, wants social justice for the itinerants, provided they are settled in someone else's neighborhood. If all this has a familiar ring for Americans, it only suggests that such problems are universal and not necessarily linked to the color of the minority's skin.

During a recent outbreak of antitinker sentiment in Galway, where an attempt was being made to find housing for a middle-aged woman and her children, a letter was published in the Dublin *Evening Press* which stated the moral problem with a riveting emphasis:

> It was with great pleasure I read of the action taken by the people of Galway towards this tinker woman and her undernourished, uneducated children. It is about time these lower-classed Christians were eliminated from our society altogether. Therefore I would suggest that the good people of Galway should congregate after Mass tomorrow morning and hold a protest march to their government representative, demanding that gas chambers be built to insure that these conscience-pricking elements be driven from Holy Catholic Ireland once and for all.
>
> Once we have got the tinkers out of the way, we can then progress a little further. Why, the magnitude of elimination is overwhelming. There are the deformed, mentally handicapped, the

Protestants, Jews and Orangemen, the uneducated, unemployed and the coloured students. Why there is no end; we could go on and on. There could even be the people of Galway. Then when we have succeeded in our task we can go to Mass and Holy Communion and thank God for His blessed guidance. They say John F. Kennedy's grandparents came from Wexford. I wonder where Adolf Hitler's came from. Galway, perhaps.

One of the more reasoned replies to that Swiftian thrust, echoing the resentment of wage earners toward the dole and other forms of government subsidy, suggested that "the paragons of virtue among us should hesitate to pick up stones. Those of us spending twenty to thirty percent of our incomes repaying mortgages . . . are understandably awed at the prospect of our investment depreciating by £1,000 [$2,400] overnight. That this actually happened in our Christian society is one of the hard facts of life."

During the spring and summer of 1970 the government made resettlement of tinkers a matter of urgent priority and managed to find homes or caravan sites for about 450 families, sometimes with little trouble or social distress, but often with near-riotous complications. The problem, as those most intimately concerned with the program saw it, was one of simple goodwill—an element never very simply extracted from human nature. In discussing the public's attitude toward integration of the tinker families, Victor Bewley of the Dublin Itinerant Settlement Committee remarked, "It is fear which makes many people oppose the provision of camping sites. Our present responsibility is to see that those who want it have a place in which to live. It is a reasonable request in their own country. It is their right. There are difficulties to be faced in helping travellers to settle but none that can't be solved, if we have good will in our hearts."

Bewley and his colleagues claim that the itinerant sites established around Dublin beginning in 1967 are proving successful. At Ballyfermot there are prefabricated houses; at Avila Park, Finglas, similar boxlike structures, where the rent is 15 shillings ($1.70) a week. "Street-begging is on the decline where families have settled," Bewley reports. "When families settle, things go ahead. They have a place for the scrap they collect. And remember it is our scrap, our rubbish, and that in this way they do a certain public service. Their standard of living is rising. A few have gone to work. About a dozen men and women [of the thirty-nine families settled at Ballyformot] have steady jobs now. The children are getting schooling, becoming literate."

In the autumn of 1970 there was a textbook example of the problems faced by the government, the church and the socially conscious in finding homes for the outcasts. I happened to be in Galway City when the uproar broke out over establishing a home for Mrs. Annie Furey, a matter which subsequently was subjected to full exposure in all the Irish media but without arriving at any solutions. To some commentators the ferocity of the opposition to relocating Mrs. Furey and her children demonstrated that there are serious flaws in the Irish character. "Of course," wrote Gabriel Fallon in the *Catholic Standard,* "if you insist on cherishing an educational system which teaches its pupils to do rather than to be, which instils the principle that success at all costs should be one's life goal, you must expect the consequences. Self-interest becomes the lode-star of living. God is not necessarily thrust aside; He is simply put in His place."

Mrs. Furey is a sturdy, cheerful, well-spoken woman of fifty years, one of those Junoesque Irish earth-mothers who have known more than their share of hardship and sorrow. To call her a tinker, as her fellow citizens did, would seem to be a misnomer; she has been established in one wretched place for the past ten years. Living on the £3 10s ($8.40) a week they receive from social welfare, she and the two children still with her have been squatting in a condemned house on the Spanish Parade, an area all but cleared now for urban renewal, a block from the quays over which the trade with Spain was conducted several centuries ago. The Spanish Parade was the promenade where Spanish merchants, captains, and dandies strolled with the Galway girls. It is no longer glamorous, except for the splendid remains of the Spanish Arch. For ten years Mrs. Furey had been making her home in one of the less dilapidated rooms of an abandoned three-story house with half the slates missing from the roof, the windows covered with corrugated iron sheets, the chimney pots tumbling, the masonry crumbling. Her only light comes from a candle, her heat from a tiny fireplace. There are rats in the building. The cold winter winds off Galway Bay search for openings.

As the town clerk, P. J. Watters, tells the story, "Mrs. Furey has been on the housing list for ten years. Herself, her husband and their children used to live in the usual canvas caravan in Knocknacarra. From there they went to the place she is now in, in Spanish Parade, and squatted there. They then applied to be put on the Corporation Housing List. Each year when the housing list came up for review there was no objection to their being put on. So therefore, they have been on the Galway housing list since January, 1959.

"In October, 1968 we allocated the Fureys a house in the Claddagh [a section of the city adjoining the Spanish Parade]. Unfortunately some nice charitable person brought them from Spanish Parade on the day they were to occupy the house in the Claddagh and brought them to their own house to be bathed. This person kept them away for three days in her own house. This was a mistake, for by the time Mrs. Furey got to the house in the Claddagh she could not get in, for it was being picketed so she could not establish tenancy. So she went back to the Spanish Parade. The Corporation later called on the County Manager not to allow Mrs. Furey and her family to take up tenancy of the house."

Her husband left her several years ago, "a fine man who just got overcome by the depression of their situation," Town Clerk Watters says, "and went to England." One of their grown daughters is married and living in nearby Ballinasloe; another child is going to school in County Westmeath, and others are scattered around the country. The two children still living with her are an eight-year-old girl attending the national school in Galway and a five-year-old girl who is mentally retarded.

Considering her circumstances, her misfortunes heroically and cheerfully borne, Mrs. Furey would have seemed an excellent opportunity for a display of Christian charity. But the people of Galway, like those of Ireland as a whole, are strongly prejudiced against the tinker class, whom they assert to be "different," to live by their own moral code, to be incurable liars, beggars, and thieves. They will not admit that one tinker can be different from, or better than, another.

Early in September, 1970, another house was found for Mrs. Furey and her two children at 23 Fursey Road in the Shantalla district. This time, she said, she was determined not to be "tricked out of it again." She moved a few possessions into the designated house to establish tenancy. As soon as the news got around the Shantalla district that the "tinker woman" was moving into their midst, there was a strong and organized reaction from the Shantalla Residents Association. The day she tried to move in with her children, 300 of her prospective neighbors massed in front of 23 Fursey Road and prevented her from entering. By then someone had broken the windows and nailed up the door.

The Galway police offered to enforce the edict of the Galway Corporation—that is, the city government—but Mrs. Furey refused. "I would be afraid to go to Shantalla," she said. "I would not be afraid for myself, but for my children, for fear they might be hurt at night or when I was away."

It was pointed out by officials of the Galway Corporation that if an itinerant family does not abide by the regulations, it will be evicted. Any tenant provided with such housing must not use his home for work or business purposes, must keep the garden, yard, and windows in repair, cannot keep livestock, cannot conduct himself in a way "calculated to cause annoyance or give scandal to adjoining owners and occupiers."

Local officials and the clergy pleaded for tolerance from the Shantalla Residents Association. Dr. Michael Browne, the Bishop of Galway, declared their actions were strikingly un-Christian. It was their duty to accept Mrs. Furey as a neighbor, he said. "If we were to refuse shelter to people because they were of a different race, colour or religion it would be regarded in every country today as shameful and criminal. To refuse shelter to one of our own people is contrary to the noblest traditions of the Irish Catholic people."

In Dublin, the Minister for Local Government, Robert Molloy, himself a Galwayman and former mayor of Galway, condemned the mob action in even stronger language as "monstrous, criminal, comparable to the apartheid policy of South Africa." He pointed out that several months before, he had increased subsidies for campsites on which itinerant families might settle and for more social workers to help them in the process. "Some itinerants," he noted, "need to be settled for a period in camping sites as a preparation for normal living. Others can be housed forthwith. Since becoming Minister I have taken advantage of every suitable opportunity to encourage local authorities to implement Government policy."

The answer of the Shantalla residents to both clerical and secular pleas was to stage a protest march on the offices of the Galway Corporation against any continued effort to establish Mrs. Furey and her children on Fursey Road. One of its leaders, ironically, was Gay Cooke, a twenty-two-year-old sociology student at the University of Galway, who said the objections were based on the fact one itinerant family had already been located in Shantalla; that contrary to the claims of government officials and social workers, integration did not work out; and that Shantalla felt it was being "bulldozed" by the local bureaucracy.

Suddenly there was a gleam of hope for Mrs. Furey: A seventy-seven-year-old woman and her forty-year-old son who lived in another neighborhood, on Liam Mellows Terrace, announced they were willing to trade houses with Mrs. Furey. The moment the plan was announced their neighbors circulated a petition around Liam Mellows Terrace strongly objecting to Mrs. Furey and her children as prospective tenants, and the idea had to be dropped.

Mrs. Furey and her plight had become a *cause célèbre,* with press, television, and radio focusing much of their attention on the controversy. Ten days later the media had lost interest and turned to other momentary sensations; Mrs. Furey was back on square one . . . back in the sodden, drafty room on the Spanish Parade. A builder with offices nearby announced that he would, on his own, make her hovel more habitable. Officialdom swore it would find more suitable accommodations somehow, somewhere.

Annie Furey, of course, is only one of hundreds trapped in a similar vicious circle. If they cling to the old ways, they are driven from place to place by communities outraged at the first glimpse of their canvas-covered wagons. If they yield to the social workers, they find themselves unwanted, scorned, and ostracized by the people among whom they have been resettled. "Ultimately," as Father Thomas Felihy, chairman of the Irish Council for Itinerant Settlement, says, "it's the community as a whole, and only the community, that can solve the problem. It's not just ill-will that is in the people. It's lack of knowledge; it's fear of the unknown." He believes that less than one percent of the itinerant class really wants to stay on the road, that "they almost all now avidly want education for their children and permanent roofs over their heads."

About the same time Mrs. Furey was being shunted around Galway City, twenty-nine of the thirty-six tenants in a council estate (housing project) at Castlebar, County Mayo, were refusing to pay their rent because an itinerant and his family, including ten children, had been allocated a house in the tract. "The itinerants will never be accepted here," declared the chairman of the tenants' association, "because they were allocated a house before nineteen other qualified families in the town."

Even those itinerants who have saved up enough money to buy a house run into the same intransigence as those allotted public housing. In Mullingar, County Westmeath, Hugh Nevin, an itinerant with a wife and six children, scraped up £1,700 [$4,080] to buy a house, but his prospective neighbors at Cathedral View Terrace immediately organized to protest the sale. Nevin and his family were then camped on a roadside outside Mullingar, they and the children sleeping on a bed of straw under the canvas roof of their caravan. "We were flooded out of here two nights ago with the heavy rain," Mrs. Nevin said, "and had to get up at four o'clock in the morning. If those people who are objecting could only live in conditions like that they would not be objecting. It's not as if we were getting the house for nothing. . . . My husband and I have been on the roads of County Westmeath all of our lives. Now we have saved a few pounds and bought this house, to give our children a home and a start in life better than we ever knew—and people want to deny us that opportunity."

In Mullingar the local officials stood up to public opinion and ruled that the people of Cathedral View Terrace could not legally oppose the presence of the Nevin family.

Elsewhere in the west, where the problem of taking itinerants off the roads is especially aggravated by a high regional rate of unemployment and a severe shortage of housing, a different sort of communal spirit seems to prevail. For no discernible reason an atmosphere of tolerance, if not wholehearted welcome, has developed. That, too, is part of the picture; contradictions are never hard to find in Ireland.

County Kerry has been working hard to resettle the floating population, even though it is not one of the more prosperous regions. It has provided forty families with hard surface for their caravans, water, and sanitation facilities in scattered locations. It is now building cottages for more permanent settlement. An even more encouraging example of how the resettlement program can be made to work smoothly in a community determined to display a measure of humanity may be found in Ballinrobe, County Mayo. Fifteen families have been integrated in the life of a town of 1,165 population, much smaller and much less prosperous than Galway City or Castlebar.

The itinerants who have settled in Ballinrobe tell you that they had less trouble winning the confidence of the residents than they had in shaking off their own traditions, in accustoming themselves to a more conventional way of life and staying in one place. Their children, most of them born under roofs rather than canvas, could never be persuaded to take up the life on the roadways their antecedents had known for generations. They attend the national schools, the Christian Brothers operating the one for the boys, the Sisters of Mercy the one for the girls. Some of the older ones are being trained for apprenticeship in the trades at the Ballinrobe vocational school.

Within a few years the itinerants settled in Ballinrobe found they had lost the stigma attached to their former way of life and were accepted as fellow citizens. Perhaps their acceptance was facilitated by the fact they were eased into the community, one family at a time, over a period of eighteen years—admittedly a long time considering the urgency of demands for social change. The only other explanation is that there is some special emolument in the air of Ballinrobe that makes people more tolerant of one another.

It isn't that the itinerants have been introduced to a life of ease and affluence or anything beyond a minimum of comfort and opportunity. A number of the former tinkers are employed by the local bakery and have managed to demolish the shibboleth that all tinkers are incurably lazy. One group of teen-aged girls takes the bus daily to and from Westport, where they are employed in a thread-making factory. Like many of their fellow townspeople, some of the former itinerants are forced to undertake an annual migration in order to supplement their seasonal employment. They pack up their possessions, lock their houses, and go over to Scotland for the "taty hokin," the potato harvest, then return to their homes in Ballinrobe when the harvesting is finished.

Ballinrobe and other places where the traveling people have been made welcome, where they live in houses, send their children to the national schools, and find jobs for the first time in many generations—without discrimination from their fellow citizens so long as they conform to the prevailing values and standards—suggest that the tinker problem may soon be solved. Then the tinkers will be only a memory. One more picturesque element in Irish life will have been removed, but that presumably would be a matter of regret only to tourists in search of the little quaintness left in the modern world.

For more than a century, outlanders, particularly the doggedly instructive English, kept advising the Irish that what their country needed for economic growth and social stability was a strong and expanding middle class. Back in 1842, William Makepeace Thackeray observed:

> The country is steadily advancing, not nearly so wretched now as it was a score of years since; and let us hope that the *middle class,* which this increase of prosperity must generate (and of which our laws have hitherto forbidden the existence in Ireland, making there a population of Protestant aristocracy and Catholic peasantry), will exercise the greatest and most beneficial influence over the country. Too independent to be bullied by priest and squire—having their interest in quiet, and alike indisposed to servility or to rebellion; may not as much be hoped from the gradual formation of such a class as from any legislative meddling?

Conventional wisdom has always stressed the need of a fulcrumlike middle class in a democracy, but Ireland was a long time in developing one. It was not only the historic effects of long subjugation, by which Mr. Thackeray's countrymen kept a swollen peasantry fully occupied by the task of filling the British larder at the lowest possible price for its labor, or Eamon De Valera's nostalgia for "the simple life I knew as a boy" translated into an economic isolationism for several decades, but the slow pace of industrialization and the slackness of the export trade that delayed the process. Then, too, there was a rooted prejudice against the tiny middle class of prerevolutionary times, including the Castle Catholics and the "hybrid Irish" denounced by James Connolly, because they perforce were economic collaborators with the British.

When the middle class finally began evolving, it was not greeted with any excessive enthusiasm. It seemed to bear the germs of the acquisitive society elsewhere, a suggestion of grossness and overweening self-importance. A number of businessmen were enriched during and just after World War II when most of Europe was on near-starvation rations and there was a booming market for Irish agricultural products. As an act of grace, they got together and approached Benedict Kiely, then a young Dublin journalist, to publicize their scheme: the construction of a gigantic statue of the Sacred Heart on the summit of Howth, overlooking Dublin Bay, which would be larger and therefore supposedly more pious than the Christ of the Andes and, like the Statue of Liberty, could be seen by ships approaching the port. "My immediate thought, fortunately unexpressed, was that it was high time Howth redeemed its reputation," Mr. Kiely recalls, "for there had been recently around Howth Harbour a most unholy outbreak of homosexuality that had given rise to a bookful of Dublin jokes, like the one about the man who dropped the half-crown in Howth and had to kick it all the way to Sutton Cross before he had the nerve to stoop to pick it up." He reflected that "the Sacred Heart, too, had had his own sad experience of power politics, and might find it against his principles to have much to do with a group of well-to-do merchants and money-changers congratulating themselves on their own comfort while the rest of the world, including a lot of their own countrymen, were hip-deep in chaos." Kiely would have nothing to do with the project, and the businessmen kept the profits sweated out of Irish neutrality in their well-lined pockets.

Perhaps it was excesses of that sort that Sean O'Faolain had in mind a few years later when he condemned the new middle class as a "combination of vulgarity and insincerity." Yet, he asked, "How could we expect a stock so long suppressed to blossom into a class of cultured men? For in the feverish pursuit of wealth this class seems to have thrown aside all their old, fine rural traditions and every standard but Success." The hopes of Sinn Fein's first ideologue, Arthur Griffith, that Ireland would find spiritual freedom and cultural independence through economic self-sufficiency were never realized. Necessarily more concerned with profit margins than vague patriotic aspirations, the Irish middle class could no more resist the magnetic force of the British marketplace than Canada can help succumbing to the tidal pull of the American economy.

Only a few years ago John Healy, in *The Death of an Irish Town,* was condemning a form of Americanization, which seemingly has become the pejorative label for all unwelcome outside influences, as "Koka-Kola-Kulture." To those Irish and all others who resent being Americanized, to use the portmanteau word, imprecise as it is, it is all the more annoying that they are subjected to a form of cultural aggression borne on television frequencies and other media before which any modern nation is defenseless: a form of nonviolent conquest, of haphazard colonialism. Healy feels that homogenization is ruining the Irish spirit, that "the age of honest indignation is dead in Ireland . . . one is supposed to wrap an honest protest in the unctuous language of a doubtful compliment. . . . Holy economic writ is all."

The emphasis on economic growth which was the main feature of Sean Lemass' years as Prime Minister and naturally resulted in an expansion of the middle class and a spread of affluence is endangering something intrinsic and irreplaceable in Irish life: its sense of individuality. The Irish always scorned what they called the West Britons, Irishmen who had been subverted by English manners and customs, but the perceptive Irishman now feels that an even more pervasive sort of homogenization is corrupting his society.

One of the veterans of the Old IRA up from County Tipperary for a day in the capital might wonder why he risked his neck during the Troubles merely to establish a new system of overlordship all the more detestable because it has been constructed by a species of hustling, hard-eyed, mid-Atlantic New Irishman. In his black Sunday suit and heavy brogans, he is made to feel unwanted and out of place. He wonders how much he has in common with the well-fleshed citizens flashing by in Mercedes limousines. The aged veteran of Sean Treacy's Third Tipperary Brigade, which went up against the British armored cars with an antique shotgun, also wonders whatever happened to the ancient Celtic law of Gravelkind, which replaced the law of primogeniture and established in Ireland the principle of individualism and equality. "As this law of precious equality," commented the French historian Jules Michelet, "has been the ruin of the Celtic races, let it be their glory also, and secure to them at least the pity and respect of the nations to whom they so early showed so fine an ideal."

In the glossier precincts of Dublin the law of Gravelkind has been replaced by the pseudo-equality of Orwell's *Animal Farm*. As a part-time social historian Kate O'Brien has studied this new class of postrevolutionary thrusters and concluded that Balzac, in his fascination with the "money power," would have found today's Dublin as familiar as Paris during the Orléans restoration. "Top Society is a mixum-gatherum . . . a conspired association . . . the ruling set that Dublin peculiarly required and peculiarly got." Everyone from duke to jockey is eligible. Obviously there is a saving grace about such a haphazardly formed elite to fill the vacuum when the British packed their shooting sticks and ancestral portraits and quit Dublin Castle. At least its recruitment is based, if not on sheer merit, then on achievement, on success gained by personal effort rather than inherited money or position. To that extent it pays just tribute to the law of Gravelkind.

In Dublin and other cities there are all the signs of a burgeoning, luxury-craving middle class: new department stores, supermarkets, streams of new cars, Irishmen going abroad for their holidays, smarter clothing, all the wares of the hire-purchase world laid out for inspection. Yet, if statistics are any firm indication, the size of the middle class enjoying the good things is more apparent than real. Certainly the upper middle class, financially speaking, rests on a rather narrow base. In 1966 there were only 119 persons with incomes over £10,000 ($24,000); 58 earning between £9,000 and £10,000; 90 between £8,000 and £9,000; 125 between £7,000 and £8,000; 226 between £6,000 and £7,000; 443 between £5,000 and £6,000. In all there were only 3,728 persons who had to pay the surtax, which was assessed on incomes over £3,000 annually.

That many Dubliners and others had joined the middle-class display of affluence through the back door and were doing it by stretching their credit was the guess of Alan Bestic, the Dublin-born correspondent for a London newspaper, who wrote that he suspected "there are quite a few people who are living at a surtax level without the income to meet it . . . blurred carbons of English suburbans from the mock-stockbroker belt. They keep up with the Murphys and so they are afraid most of the time. They live high, but that is not prosperity."

During the past twenty years a fairly venturesome group of entrepreneurs has sprung up to take advantage of possibilities unique in the Irish market. These upward-thrusting industrialists and purveyors of services, along with the politicians and the hierarchy, form the loosely defined Irish Establishment. One of the pioneers in catering to the specific requirements of the Irish market is Stephen O'Flaherty, whose endeavors in the automobile assembly field have provided him with the largest fiber-glass yacht ever built in Britain. The first assembly plant was established by Henry Ford in Cork City more than half a century ago. O'Flaherty saw that there was a need for a small car, easy and inexpensive to maintain on the rudimentary Irish road system, and acquired the Volkswagen concession. In a plant outside Dublin he assembles Volkswagens and also the Mercedes, which is the number one status symbol. Another such entrepreneur is Joe Murphy, who was inspired to go into the potato chip (or crisp, as they are called in Ireland) business. He began processing the potatoes in a back-street shop in Dublin on borrowed money, invented the onion and cheese-flavored potato chip, and was soon producing 5,000 tons a year.

One of the more spectacular careers is that of Dermot A.

Ryan, who went into the car-rental business back in 1948 before he had reached voting age. The seed money for his subsequent fortune was $225 he had saved from selling advertisements in a university magazine. With that he bought a battered 1935 Ford and opened an office over his father's Portobello pub. When English visitors insisted on a chauffeur-driven car, he clapped on a chauffeur's cap and did the driving himself. After years of struggle, his business expanded enormously with the boom in tourism.

At the age of forty-one, at the cost of an ulcer, the tall and gaunt Ryan is pretty close to the summit. He is not only board chairman of the island's largest car-rental firm but the operator of the largest privately owned hotel chain, the biggest retail gasoline company, the number one taxi company, and a concern which rents caravans to the more leisurely tourists.

Along with his millionaire status Ryan acquired a taste for crusading politics, with more than a touch of the idealism which he believes motivated the Kennedys of America. That impulse toward the humanitarian, rather than the considerable wealth evidenced by his Edwardian mansion and his Rolls-Royce limousine, resulted recently in threats against his life, in telephoned warnings that his French wife and nine children might be harmed. His mansion, with its magnificent gardens and its stables full of thoroughbred horses, was placed under constant guard by relays of Special Branch detectives.

As he recalls, he entered politics in 1964, joining the Fianna Fail Party, because he wanted to do good. "After all, President Kennedy was a millionaire, too, his family verging on a political dynasty, and he turned out to be all right. I don't see why they should be against me so that I can't do something decently."

Greatly distressed by the rioting in Ulster, he organized the Northern Interdenominational Distress Fund for the relief of those made homeless during the disorders. Even that gesture, he says, was misunderstood or misinterpreted. His enemies charged that he was using the relief organization as the stepping-stone to a larger political career, which he claims is "bellywash for jealous politicians who were never behind a barricade in their lives. . . . In the first place, all the cash and provisions has come out of my personal pocket and not from the company's. In the second place, the company would not allow me so much money for such a venture."

His troubles came about, he says, because he was searching for a peaceful solution to the Ulster problem. "We do not want to destroy an enemy. We want to unite a people." When he resigned from the Fianna Fail party executive in the summer of 1970, he remarked on the fact that during Cabinet meetings to decide what action the Republic should take during the fighting in and near Belfast, "the hawks were there in force in the form of at least four Ministers, who sincerely believed that the Irish people in the South should physically support their brethren in Derry." Obviously his venture into the near-cannibalistic atmosphere of nationalistic politics has disillusioned him to the point where he can only say, "People don't understand me."

Another Dubliner who went into business the same time as Dermot Ryan was Leslie Dacus, who in ten years built up Gateaux Ltd., the world's largest cake-exporting firm. Back in 1949 Dacus, who had previously dabbled in the perfume business, decided that cake baking was ideally suited to Ireland because it had all the raw materials available and it was an untested market. He established his bakery in a ten-acre field in the Dublin suburb of Finglas. Expertise in the actual baking was provided by Eugene Hohn, a Swiss-born baker who had come over to Ireland to play in a soccer match in the 1920's and liked it so well he never returned to Switzerland. Gateaux cakes, vigorously promoted and advertised, were an almost instant success in both the foreign and the domestic markets, and began bringing more money into the country than Irish whiskey. To overcome the traditional resistance of Irish workers to assembly-line methods —Stakhanov would have been run out of the country if he had tried his hurry-up schemes on Irish workers—Dacus introduced a program of incentives under which his employees can earn up to 30 percent over the union scale.

With hundreds of light industries and service enterprises springing up in the past twenty years, Ireland can no longer boast of an entirely smokeless atmosphere for tourists. Many of them are sensibly geared to the raw materials and skills available on the island, such as the fashion designers Clodagh, Irene Gilbert, and Sybil Connolly and others who base their designs on the native fabrics. In such haunts as the Shelbourne, the Gresham, and the Royal Hibernian, formerly the preserve of the Anglo-Irish aristocracy and its imitators, brisk young businessmen and a few lady executives have brought a middle-class accent unmarked by Oxbridge or Trinity.

In the smaller cities and towns, too, middle-class affluence is widely apparent among the shopkeepers who have always composed the bourgeois element, even during the centuries of British rule. The Irish Babbitts, like those of America, are concentrated on the Main Streets, the designation of the principal thoroughfare in most Irish towns. Behind the pastel-tinted stucco of their shopfronts, they are as keenly opportunistic as any Dublin or Cork businessman. Often they operate mini-conglomerates; one man will own, say, a hardware store, with sidelines in furniture, coal, and electric appliances, and will also have a pub or two and a farm nearby. Formerly he was pejoratively known as the gombeen man and was often the rapacious local moneylender. Frequently he was accused of sucking up to the gentry, of imitating the Anglo-Irish grand manner as best he could, and speaking in a "Protestant accent" to please his more important customers. Notably he is one of the more conservative elements in the national life and has never as a totality been considered one of those who risked his life and property to turn out the British or take sides during the civil war.

Nowadays the market-town or village businessman, creamery operator, grocer, or hotel owner is often a figure of consequence. He may watch the till closely, live with his family over his shop, but he may also own a racehorse or two and ride with the hounds of the local Blazers. To the envy of the countryside, he may own a villa used for weekends, a cabin cruiser, and an English or German luxury car. His holidays are spent on the Continent; his daughters go to a convent school. But no matter how prosperous and worldly he becomes, the people he went to school with still call him by his first name, thanks to the vigorous equalizing tendency of Irish society.

The materialism of the small-town middle class is delineated, perhaps with a little unfriendly exaggeration, by John Broderick in his novel *The Waking of Willie Ryan,* which explores the shopkeeping class with scant sympathy. Broderick pictures two matrons luxuriating in their affluence: "Side by side they moved about the stifling room, fingering silver, stroking satin and velvet, and praising pieces of auction china. . . . They inhaled again and again the incense of each other's expensive scent; they lingered with caressing hands beside the smooth surfaces of tables loaded with the loot of crumbling mansion houses. They put their heads together, comparing consecrated possessions in low tremulous voices." Broderick creates an almost suffocating sense of materialism as he pictures the two matrons worshiping before a Jack B. Yeats painting acquired for a few pounds from one of the Anglo-Irish estates, which to them represents not only the work of Ireland's greatest painter but a profit of 200 percent. "Like pilgrims, humbly proud and grateful at a shrine loaded with images that glorified and proclaimed their own pursuit of revelation," they drew comfort from "things that do not wilt or fall away with the apostate years. . . ."

The Anglo-Irish aristocracy survives, in diminished form and with little of its former arrogance, grateful perhaps that it did not suffer the terrors of the Russian aristocracy. It coexists, more easily than might be expected, with the prevalent republicanism. A certain amount of deracination occurred as one by one most of the great estates were taken over by the Republic and parceled out in small farmer's holdings.

Yet there are a number of the former Ascendants who still own castles, stables for fifty or sixty horses, packs of hunting dogs, and enough acres of rolling hills and parkland not to feel hemmed in by their neighbors. On the pages of the eighty-year-old *Irish Tatler & Sketch* there is a curious mélange of photographs of trout-faced gentry posed in front of manorial façades or with their flower-bedecked horses at the Curragh or in bridal couples, juxtaposed with more reassuring layouts showing various freeloaders herded before the cameras at receptions and the openings of commercial enterprises. At the top level a hesitant process of integrating the old nabobs and the new money has been observed. Sean T. O'Kelly, former President of the Republic, and his wife, both of whom were members of the force under siege at the General Post Office during the Easter rebellion, often entertain mixed gatherings of the Irish-Irish and the Anglo-Irish who, after all, to the detriment of their class interests, provided much of the impetus and leadership for the revolution.

The Anglo-Irish may have dwindled in number; there may be fewer choleric brigadiers roaring tally-ho over the wet green fields of Ireland, but they still amount to something more than Brendan Behan's cavalier description of them as "Protestants with horses." They lend tone to race meetings, presence to committees, dignified continuity to ceremonial occasions, and they rejoice in harmless titles which faintly echo with the trumpery of a defunct empire. Not that the ordinary Irish mind a bit of pageantry so long as the sabers are simply part of the costuming. Not too long ago their taxes paid for a troop of Blue Hussars which was turned out in full panoply for the President on the more solemn occasions.

You may get no closer than the gatehouse of those surviving manorial estates which lord it over the countryside, but you can still be aware of the fact that a Marquess and Marchioness of Waterford, an Earl and Countess of Rosse, a Viscount Powerscourt, an Earl of Iveagh, and other resounding titles are still active: the society pages of the newspapers and magazines are full of their activities. Or that there are long-established enclaves where polo and cricket are still played, hunt balls draw the elect from all over Ireland and England, and hunt clubs take the field from manorial courtyards, including the celebrated Galway Blazers, of which the American-born film director John Huston, now an Irish citizen, is joint master.

And you can take the word of Mark Bence-Jones, himself a member of the old landowning caste and a first-rate writer, that something of the harum-scarum quality of Anglo-Irish society survives as a grace note from the storied past. Jaded members of the international jet-borne society, always in transit, come to Ireland to refresh themselves among the tweedy, outdoors-loving Anglo-Irish, with whom as Mr. Bence-Jones remarks "Dior and dogs' dinners go hand in hand." A house party in Ireland is still an occasion at which anything can happen, at which characters of ripened eccentricity may be encountered. He cites a dinner party in one of the more remote sections of County Galway at which Jean-Paul Sartre could be found losing a theological argument with the parish priest; an Italian princess gracefully posed in a doorway among the dogs' bowls. Social barriers have been taken down, and to some extent the Anglo-Irish were liberated along with the rest of their countrymen by independence.

Even the traditional hunt balls, according to Mr. Bence-Jones, have become occasions for a classless intermingling, "the daughter of a marquess, the wife of a millionaire, a World War II admiral, an Italian playwright, the local veterinary surgeon, a jockey, a local farmer, and the local sergeant of the Gardai all clasped together in a riotous and democratic huddle."

For all the literature on the subject, both that created by sympathetic insiders and the usually satiric view of them taken by outsiders, the Anglo-Irish do not in reality seem to be so easily stereotyped. The only unifying characteristic appears to be unpredictability. Take, if you will, a humorous-looking man of fifty who was christened John Godley and who looks approachable enough, despite the innate authority with which he handles a glass of brandy and wields a Churchillian cigar. He was a naval bomber pilot during World War II and survived to become a reporter on the Labour tabloid, the London *Daily Mirror,* and to spend a half dozen years in the rough and tumble of Fleet Street.

In 1951, John Godley's father died, and the journalist succeeded to the title of Lord Kilbracken and the estate of Killegar in County Leitrim. His inheritance consisted of a Georgian house in a state of acute disrepair, without electricity, 220 acres of grazing land, 80 acres of woodland, and a dairy herd which had dwindled to one cow named Mary. Rather than go back to Fleet Street, the new Lord Kilbracken decided to rehabilitate Killegar through his earnings as a free-lance writer, a quixotic program that only another free-lance could appreciate. "I hadn't a bean," he recalls, "and the farm was up for sale with £8,000 [$19,200] the highest offer. I withdrew it from the market. I hadn't a clue about running a farm; but I gave it a try, and now it ticks over and I have a hundred cows."

Lord Kilbracken regards himself as a left-wing Socialist with a strong anticolonial bent. He recalls that his grandfather was Liberal Prime Minister Herbert Asquith's secretary and the first of the Anglo-Irish gentry to sell most of his holdings under the Land Act. He works for the Committee for the Liberation of Mozambique and has taken up another exotic cause, the aspirations of the Kurds to carve their own country out of Iraq, Iran, and Turkey. The campaign for Kurdish autonomy, he says, is "exactly like Irish history messed about by the British and the Boundary Commission of fifty years ago." He stands aloof from the fratricidal huggermugger of Irish politics. "They are getting nowhere," he remarks, "all lineal descendants of the civil war, fighting about the treaty, which is a dead letter because no one wants partition now. There must be a new party which won't look back to the Easter Rising of 1916, but I don't see any coming. There is the Labour Party, but they can't make much headway because agricultural Ireland is reactionary."

Obviously Lord Kilbracken bears little resemblance to the huntin', ridin' Anglo-Irish aristocrat of literary legend.

Another genial exception is Lord Dunboyne, a London barrister, recorder of Hastings, and a member of Kings Inn, Dublin (the equivalent of an American bar association), as well. His family seat at Knappaogue, County Clare, is leased to Shannon Airport and forms part of the Bunratty Castle tourist complex.

Lord Dunboyne, too, is passionately involved in a cause. Ten years ago he founded the Irish Peers Association, with the objective of bringing the disestablished Irish peers "in out of the cold." Under the Act of Union, they had relinquished their right to sit in the House of Lords in return for life tenure for twenty-eight of their number. Now Lord Dunboyne campaigns for the return of the Irish peers for whom no provision was made in the 1922 treaty and who were not replaced when the twenty-eight with life tenure died off. "It would do Ireland no harm at all," he explains, "to have 28 friends in Parliament. I have spoken about this on television and radio in Dublin, and was told that Ireland can perfectly well manage her own affairs. But we do not want to interfere in Irish politics. There is enough prejudice in England anyway against the Republic. But we could be very useful in the House of Lords now that Ireland keeps coming into the Parliamentary agenda."

So many of the Anglo-Irish aristocracy migrated during and after the Revolution that it no longer causes a clucking of tongues when the news gets around that the younger son of a Waterford landowner is selling vacuum cleaners door to door in Kuala Lumpur or that a small rancher in California, who has never set foot in Ireland, has fallen heir to the remnants of an Irish estate and the title that goes with it.

There is no longer a real, tradition-bound upper class in the Irish Republic, only the surviving fragments of Anglo-Irish society, with the Kildare Street Club in Dublin as its last stronghold, and those Irish who have made the top drawer in business and industry but who have not coalesced or established a pecking order, created unique snobberies, erected barriers against newcomers, published a social register or blue book. Efforts to combine the old Anglo-Irish survivors with the new order have been desultory, a matter of individual taste. There is no longer any great animus between them, merely the lack of any strong impulse toward coalition.

Besides, social frivolity and extravagance in style have always been frowned upon as unseemly, unrepublican by the ruling Fianna Fail, who are, after all, Soldiers of Destiny, not fops or dandies or wealthy clubmen. Unlike the first Free State government of William T. Cosgrave, which the Anglo-Irish largely supported for its moderation, Fianna Fail decreed an austere style, an avoidance of flash in dress or deportment, in the manner displayed by Eamon De Valera. The top hat was discarded; champagne drinking was regarded as a sign of decadence.

There are neutral meeting places for the old top dogs and the new at diplomatic receptions, fashion shows, and charity fund raisings, and they are linked by a mutual passion, if that isn't too mild a word, for horse racing. Even the austere Mr. De Valera goes to the races and owns some racing stock. At Punchestown those whose fathers wore cloth caps mingle easily enough with those whose fathers wore gray toppers.

But it will be a long time, if ever it happens, that Dublin will be the social capital it was when Dublin Castle and Phoenix Park were the seats of British power. Inevitably there are classes, graduated according to money and achievement, but the Irish are more adept at forming cliques, conspiracies, and juntas than at molding themselves into social castes and are willing to leave the aristocratic style to the churchmen.

Pretentiousness just doesn't come naturally to them. A year or two ago the Minister for External Affairs returned from an important speech before the United Nations, traveling on one of the all-tourist-class Aer Lingus flights. He was unaccompanied by the aides, advisers, luggage bearers, and valets who attend even lesser statesmen on such missions. None of his fellow passengers knew he was a dignitary named Dr. Hillery until the plane landed in Dublin and he was greeted by a barrage of strobe lights and photographic flashes.

14.

A Frieze of Spear-Carrying Warriors

The race is at the same time inferior and superior to the rest of humanity. . . . Placed between memory and hope, the race will never conquer what it desires, and it will never discover what it regrets.

—ÉMILE MONTEGUT

Within a few years Ireland's celebrated "backwardness" may be her greatest asset. As smog, urban congestion, strangulated traffic, and all the other evils attendant on total industrialization multiply, Ireland will relatively be an oasis of pure air and water, of an uncluttered countryside and cities with a controlled growth . . . if she is careful. And in many ways she is a cautious old lady. From the tales of her sons and daughters who have emigrated she knows that "progress" can entail more than high wages and easy access to consumer goods.

It seems likely that the Irish, with their innate resistance to change, will retain their special qualities longer than most peoples. The homogenization which has made young Frenchmen, Germans, Italians, Danes, Belgians, and Dutch all but indistinguishable except for a few physical characteristics and language differences has not yet reached Ireland in full force. Nor has she been infected with any great enthusiasm for the hectic joys and manic frustrations of the rat race. Television and the other media have created a certain tendency toward materialism, but it is qualified by reflections that the world is only an inconvenient way station on the road to the afterlife in which the

Irish, more than any other Western people, invest their hope and faith.

They have of course advanced from the condition which Giraldus Cambrensis, the twelfth-century English scholar, scathingly described in his *Topography of Ireland.* Cambrensis found that "their greatest delight is to be exempt from toil," that they were "immersed in sloth," that "whatever natural gifts they possess are excellent, in whatever requires industry they are worthless," that they were "truly barbarous" in their avoidance of a settled life and their aversion for living in towns and busying themselves with "any kind of trade or mechanical art."

Ireland still treasures its own peculiar civilization formed partly by its geographic isolation, its determined aloofness from what it regards as the paganism of Western Europe, its strong sense of national identity. To the outsider its surface may seem a trifle shabby and old-fashioned, the pace of life outside Dublin slowed to a saunter, but on the whole the Irish believe there's no sense rushing after things that aren't all that important. They seek contentment more than hectic pleasures; they are not prey to overexpectation because nothing in their history has encouraged anything more than a guarded pessimism.

Undoubtedly some sociologists, publicists, and politicians would assert that the Irish want all the color television sets, refrigerators, electric toothbrushes, and mink coats that obsess other peoples, that they are just as vulnerable to the lures of advertising as anyone else. This argument is belied by the statistics on emigration. The more ambitious Irishman will always emigrate, probably, but the majority prefers to stay at home if there is sufficient employment. An Irishman can earn higher wages and obtain a more expansive standard of living simply by taking the boat to England, yet he will stay in Ireland if there's any hope at all of making a decent living.

The latest government statistics indicate there is now a solid basis for such hopes: the industrialization program of the past decade burgeons with achievement, the scope of which is indicated by the 350 foreign industrial plants established in Ireland since 1960. In that ten-year period Ireland's gross national product has risen from $1.62 billion to $3.47 billion, a 125 percent increase.

For the first time in history the value of Ireland's industrial exports, $514,000,000 or 53 percent of the total, exceeded that of its agricultural exports. The political and economic importance of the relationship with Great Britain, however irksome to diehards, is emphasized by the fact that 62 percent of those exports went to Britain, against 13 percent to the United States.

Why the industrial interest in Ireland? Two state enterprises, the Industrial Development Authority Ireland and the Shannon Free Airport Development Company, offer considerable inducements to foreign capital, which in turn has provided an estimated 50,000 jobs for Irishmen. There is a fifteen-year tax holiday on all export profits and five years of partial tax exemption. The government-sponsored schemes also provide 50 percent of the cash for purchase of fixed assets (machinery, plant site, and plant) and all the cost of training workers. There are low rents at the Galway and Waterford industrial parks, duty-free access to Britain's 55,000,000 consumers and the prospect of similar access to another 355,000,000 European consumers if Ireland is admitted to the Common Market. Another attraction is the plentiful labor supply, not as militant or organized as in Britain and the United States, and relatively low wages. The Irish wage scale may be the greatest inducement of all. As an example, workers at the Kerry Precision Ball Bearing plant in Tralee start at $22 a week, advance to $26 when fully trained, to $36 after one year, and can earn as much as $45 a week only by putting in a lot of overtime.

There has been a dramatic decline in emigration since Ireland attained a modest degree of prosperity in the sixties. According to a recently published survey compiled by R. C. Geary and J. C. Hughes, net emigration from 1961 to 1966 dropped off to 16,000 annually compared with an average of 42,000 annually for the 1956-61 period. The hemorrhage has been stopped, not only by greater opportunities for employment in Ireland but the experience of those who migrated and return at every opportunity with stories of the crushed and harassed lives they must lead in the industrial cities of England and America. Many, having learned trades and acquired skills abroad, are returning to make further use of them in Ireland.

In their survey *Internal Migration in Ireland,* Geary and Hughes have also plucked out the fact that the country is rapidly becoming urbanized. In five years, from 1961 to 1966, the percentage of the population living in towns of over 1,500 had increased from 46.1 to 49.2. The 1971 census, it was predicted, will show that the number of urban dwellers has finally become a majority for the first time in Irish history. Young people from the rural areas, instead of migrating, are moving to the Irish cities.

That tendency, in the predictable future, still won't turn Dublin into another London or Limerick into another Manchester. Probably a greater impact will be registered if Ireland joins the Common Market; that would accelerate the movement from rural to urban areas. There are widespread fears that Ireland will be economically submerged in a Common Market dominated by highly industrialized West Germany, that it will become a Celtic slave bounded to the wheels of the Teutonic chariot, that the freewheeling Irishman will be turned into a good gray burgher with all his individualism leached out at the far end of a German production line.

But joining the Common Market, following dutifully in Britain's footsteps, is the policy of the ruling party, the Fianna Fail. It is opposed mainly from the left, its position defined in the Marxist *United Irishman*:

> Most farmers do not want to leave the land. But they may think that if they are forced by economic circumstances to leave their farms that the policies of the Fianna Fail Government and the Common Market will ensure that there are adequate jobs for them in Ireland. But this is nothing but false hope. The main economic resources needed for any type of economic or industrial activity are capital and labour. An elementary knowledge of Irish history is enough to show that the main movement of capital and labour in Ireland since Famine times has been out of the country. . . . The tendency in any Free Trade area is for resources to move away from the periphery towards the centre rather than vice versa, and Ireland will certainly be on the periphery. . . . The decline in the farm population, which will inevitably come with Common Market entry, involves the destruction of all in-

> dustry at present supplying the home market. Without the farmers there will be no market, no industry, and no work in Ireland for Irish farmers forced off their farms. . . .

A government white paper defending the decision to seek Common Market membership has claimed that Irish agriculture will actually be bolstered by a more profitable market for its products in Western Europe, that cattle and sheep prices will rise by 40 to 50 percent. The leftward counterclaim is that those profits will go to larger farms, combined out of small holdings, using industrial methods and causing a decline in farm employment from the present 300,000 to 45,000. "The reality is that the agricultural policies of the Common Market are geared toward the needs of the vast industrial monopolies of Germany and France where industrial workers are in constant demand. Ireland just does not have the industry to give work to those 250,000 people who are going to have to leave the land." *

There is an uneasy feeling, apart from such warnings, that somehow Ireland will be squeezed out of its traditional shape, will lose its cultural identity by linking its economic destiny to that of the larger powers, by converting itself from an Atlantic outpost to an appendix of Western Europe.

Other changes, more or less in keeping with the decision to become an economic segment of Europe, are forecast in the lengthy and exhaustive Buchanan Report. This was a survey of Ireland's prospects, including recommendations for its future course, undertaken on behalf of the government by Colin Buchanan and Partners and Economic Consultants Ltd. with the assistance of the United Nations. Government planning of a fairly rigorous order would result in a transformation of the island if most of the recommendations are carried out.

Essentially the Buchanan Report calls for regional development of growth centers which would further concentrate the population. The objective is a full employment society, bringing

* The fears of Irish farmers for their future as producers for Western Europe were heightened by the recent proposal of the Common Market Executive Commission in Brussels for a large reduction in the European community's dairy herd, which now totals 22,000,000 cows. Dairying is the backbone of Irish agriculture. The possibility that Irish farmers, too, would be required to thin out their herds was naturally alarming.

the unemployment rate down from 5 to 2 percent and paring emigration to 5,000 annually.

Its summary of the Irish problem is: "The main reason that in Ireland the towns have not grown as fast as in other countries, so that people have had to seek work overseas, is that industry has not developed fast enough to offset the decline in employment in agriculture." The reason for industrial backwardness, the report suggests, is a declining population and the country's lack of cheap fuel, power, and other resources. The slenderness of the population base provides a home market too small to support wide range of modern industries. The report also took note of a lack of "buoyancy and optimism" as militating against industrial expansion.

The goal of the Buchanan Report is 330,000 industrial jobs by 1986. Achievement of that objective would be facilitated by designating nine different main growth centers. Under that scheme the population of the various cities would be increased as follows: Dublin, 795,047 by the 1966 census to a 1986 forecast of 1,125,000; Cork from 122,146 to 250,000; Limerick from 57,570 to 175,000; Waterford from 29,842 to 55,000; Galway from 26,295 to 47,000; Dundalk from 21,687 to 44,000; Drogheda from 17,908 to 35,000; Sligo from 13,424 to 25,000; and Athlone from 10,987 to 18,000. The expansion of Dublin's population would be circumscribed because of "congestion problems," which have already made their appearance, while Cork and Limerick would expand the most, by 105 and 204 percent respectively.

The report faces the fact that such changes as it envisions would be more than a mere face-lifting, that they might be socially traumatic, that "such a programme of construction, such a scale of public spending, such a reorganization of planning machinery, are bound to present problems." That is more an English than an Irish understatement.

Something a lot more complicated than an economic blueprint, calling for much more Christian charity and understanding than has ever been summoned up in the past, will be required to solve Ireland's oldest, most painful, and most regressive problem. Without a miraculous solution that would end partition or, even less likely, make it tolerable, Ireland will never escape from its quandary, its special dilemma, its historic impasse. Nor will it shake off that Celtic morbidity which prevents the Irishman from feeling at home in the world. A long time ago an astute Frenchman, Émile Montegut, summed up that feeling of displacement: "This race is at the same time inferior and superior to the rest of humanity. One may say of the Irish that they find themselves in a false situation here below. Placed between memory and hope, the race will never conquer what it desires, and it will never discover what it regrets."

Ulster is the "other Ireland," Southern Ireland's Alsace-Lorraine, the lost province it will never give up hope of recovering. About the best thing that can be said of the 200-mile frontier between the two Irelands is that it has not yet seen the erection of a Berlin Wall.

Belfast is an easy morning's journey by rail or road from Dublin, less than an hour by air, but the difference between the two capitals is as great as if they were on separate islands. Dublin may not be cosmopolitan, but it has style and architectural grace and an easygoing atmosphere. Belfast is provincial, dour, hard-working, and looks like a northern industrial city in England. The Belfast-born novelist Brian Moore who returned there on a visit recently found the city almost as neglected architecturally as during the war years when the Nazi bomber fleets laid waste to whole sections. It seemed to Moore that Belfast is suffering from an old and incurable sickness, the most disfiguring element of which is the religious riots: "Mobs of rampaging Protestant *lumpenproletariat* trying to terrorize their equally ignorant Catholic *lumpenproletariat* neighbors. . . ." He believes there is something "old and rotten" still alive in Belfast. That something just might be the fact that ancient wrongs, no matter what hopeful liberals may believe, can never be laid to rest. Gestures of reconciliation are made, but forgiveness never comes from the inmost chamber of the psyche.

The moment you get off the train you realize you are in a different country, even if it's on the same island: the pillar-boxes are painted red instead of green, the Union Jack waves over public and many private buildings, there are British troops in the streets, and the architecture has a "forted-up" look. There is a briskness seldom observed in the South, the hard-driving spirit of a city whose function is to make and build things and earn a profit. Outside the city center you discover why it is called the "black city"—the shipyards and linen mills, the endless terraces of dingy streets, the great white pile of Portland stone on the edge of the city called the Stormont, the Ulster Parliament, the Catholic quarters where walls are chalked with aggressive slogans ("Up the Republic!") and just across a narrow no-man's-land the Shankhill Road behind which are the Protestant streets and other walls chalked ("Kick the Pope," "No Surrender!").

Behind these hotly competing slogans lie more than four centuries of history so infused with hatred and fear, so tangled in prejudice and misunderstanding that it seems like a cancerous growth which time makes only more deadly and ineradicable. The province of Ulster, which once included Counties Donegal, Cavan, and Monaghan (now part of the Irish Republic), as well as Antrim, Down, Tyrone, Derry, Armagh, and Fermanagh, was once the most Celtic and Catholic part of the island.

Then came Henry VIII's proclamation of himself as King of Ireland, the struggle of the Northern Catholics to keep out the Protestant planters imported to Anglicize and occupy large sections of Ulster, the doomed resistance of Hugh O'Neill, the Earl of Tyrone, and the flight of the earls to the Continent. Their vast estates were broken up and handed over to English and Scottish Protestants. The new settlers, surrounded by a hostile Catholic peasantry, could never achieve the eccentric charm of the Anglo-Irish to the south; they always felt themselves besieged, and with good reason. During the uprising encouraged by the deposed Catholic King James II of England, 7,000 Protestant citizens of Londonderry were killed or died of starvation and disease before William of Orange lifted the 105-day siege and pursued James II and his Catholic army to their doom at the Battle of the Boyne. In the following centuries, the Orangemen prospered, took over more land, and were reinforced by Lowland Scots while the Catholics sank to a state bordering on serfdom.

During the mid-eighteenth century many Orangemen, largely those oppressed by landlords of their own faith, migrated to the American colonies. The iron in the character of what became known in America as the Scotch-Irish was demonstrated by their aggressive settlement of the colonies; their pioneering in Ulster had molded them for the task of colonizing the early frontiers of the New World and produced such characters as Davy Crockett, Sam Houston, Stonewall Jackson, and ten Presidents of the United States, although Woodrow Wilson as one of their number may have been going too far when he said, "No one who amounts to anything is without some Scotch-Irish blood."

Then and always those Ulstermen who stayed in Ulster have wrapped themselves in the Union Jack and endlessly reiterated their allegiance to the Crown as their only protection against the "Papists." A pamphlet published by the Ulster government, titled *How Northern Ireland Is Governed,* vibrates with a monarchial spirit which has not manifested itself elsewhere since the reign of the Sun King: "In our constitution the Sovereign is thought of as being what we might call an ideal human being. He or she is, in theory, perfect in all human attributes, has almost unlimited power, and is endowed with perfect goodness, wisdom and justice. . . . Those attributes, in turn, are considered to be derived from God. Thus the centre of the British constitution is a great religious ideal, an aspiration towards perfection."

When the British Parliament passed a Home Rule bill in 1913, Ulster, despite its often proclaimed fealty to the Crown, objected to the point of rebellion. The bill provided that a Parliament be established in Dublin to deal with all Irish domestic affairs. The leader of the dominant Unionist Party of Ulster, Sir Edward Carson, drew up a covenant signed by 220,000 Ulstermen, some of them in their own blood, in which they affirmed they would never recognize an Irish Parliament. Ready to fight anyone, including their protectors, to forestall Home Rule, Carson and his collaborators organized the Ulster Volunteers and smuggled in boatloads of weapons to arm them. The British Conservatives, always opposed to Home Rule on principle and in practice (Lord Randolph Churchill, father of Winston, had given the Ulstermen their slogan, "Ulster will fight and Ulster will be right"), supported Carson and his Volunteers. One result of that intransigence was that when the southern twenty-six counties gained their independence, Ulster was permitted to establish its own Parliament, the only one in the United Kingdom, a privilege which has always been denied the nationalist movements of Wales and Scotland.

The Unionist Party remains supreme. It has always succeeded in fighting off any challenges from the one-third minority of Irish Catholics, though at times the latter have posed an even greater threat to the established order in the Stormont Parliament than the civil rights movement's demonstrations of force in 1969-70. In 1922, when a determined effort was made to unite both green and orange Ireland, 232 persons were killed in the disorders, almost 1,000 were wounded and more than $3,000,000 worth of property was destroyed. The backbone in the Unionist Party then and now is the Orange Order, which was founded in 1795 to protect the Protestant faith from the threat of "Popery." A Unionist candidate, if he does not belong to the Orange Order, at least needs its approval if he hopes to be elected.

In recent years, defying all trends elsewhere at least to attempt to achieve a measure of tolerance toward minorities, Protestant Ulster has maintained and possibly strengthened its anti-Catholicism. Not one instance can be produced in Ulster of the sort of tolerance pervading the Irish Republic when it chose a Protestant, Dr. Douglas Hyde, to be its first president, and elected a Jew, Robert Briscoe, to be lord mayor of Dublin. Catholic citizens' unemployment rates are higher; their housing is poorer. The Unionist Party denies them proportionate political power by gerrymandering certain electoral districts; until recently Unionists occupied all twelve of the Northern Ireland seats in the British Parliament. Any Unionist politician suspected of being too sympathetic toward the Catholic minority finds his career endangered. A moderate Prime Minister, Captain Terence O'Neill, was forced out of office not long after he and Prime Minister Sean Lemass of the Irish Republic held the first meeting of the leaders of both Irelands to discuss economic cooperation.

If Northern and Southern Ireland are two separate nations, so in effect are the Protestants and Catholics of Ulster. Not only are their communities barricaded against each other, but the children go to different schools, Catholic and Protestant, and when they grow up, they drink in separate pubs and mingle only on the job, never socially. Intermarriage is rare and often turns the families involved into Montagues and Capulets. In the rare case of Catholics and Protestants living in adjoining houses, there is an invisible wall between them.

When the majority and minority do meet, it is usually in riotous streets, the black city's battlefield. The Catholics are provoked to violence when an Orange Order parade, celebrating the Battle of the Boyne, is perversely scheduled to take a route through or impinging on Catholic neighborhoods. Both sides cling to ancient history and long-smoldering grievances with a recidivist passion. During the violent summer of 1970, there was a particularly pathetic incident involving the death of a seventy-six-year-old Catholic from County Tyrone, pathetic not only for the man's death but because of its demonstration of the bitterness and tragedy that dog individual lives. The victim, John Haughey, had served in the IRA and spent much of his life in prison or internment as a result of his activities, yet he managed to raise a family that includes two solicitors and an insurance broker. He was struck down in a police baton charge during disturbances in his home town of Coalisland, which erupted during an Orange Order parade, and died of his injuries two months later.

It is a matter of ironic reflection that when Protestants and Catholics do meet and mingle on fairly easy terms, it is on the campus of Queen's University, Belfast. It was there that Bernadette Devlin, one of six children in an impoverished Catholic family, one of whose earliest memories is of watching the B Specials (an armed Protestant militia, or police auxiliary, which has recently been disbanded) hunt down IRA men in the Black Bog near her Cookstown home, was educated and radicalized. There, too, that People's Democracy—which she serves as a sort of La Pasionara—was born and the civil rights movement took shape.

As a student Miss Devlin became what she calls in her autobiography, *The Price of My Soul,* a "theoretical terrorist." She once planned to set fire to Gortin Forest Park as a diversion while lobbing hand grenades over the fence of the American communications base outside Derry and desisted only because of the fear somebody might be killed or injured in the forest fire. She is candid about her radicalization, recalling that the People's Democracy started out with "very little political awareness" but "a big contribution to our political education was made by the Young Socialists' Alliance . . . just young lefties, basic Marxists."

Oddly enough she identifies herself, not with her ideological hero James Connolly but with Michael Collins, even though she considers him "basically an aggressive, bullying type of personality, almost a dictator . . . totally undiplomatic, so arrogantly honest that he was annoying. . . . I feel a kindred spirit with the arrogant personality of Michael Collins, and I believe that I'm in much the same situation as he. Basically I have no place in organized politics. By coming to the British Parliament [having been elected to one of the twelve seats allotted Northern Ireland], I've allowed the people to sacrifice me at the top and let go the more effective job I should be doing at the bottom."

Though viewing herself as a "sacrifice," Miss Devlin stood for Parliament again and was reelected. Such personal successes have not tempered her aggressive personality, nor have several months in jail for her participation on the barricades modified her amibitions to stand all Ireland on its ear. First, as she sees it, she and the People's Democracy will have to move the Protestant working class in the North leftward, at least far enough so they'll forget religious differences and join up with the Catholics. The next task will be to shake things up in the Irish Republic. During the battle of the Bogside she appealed by telephone to Prime Minister Lynch in the Republic for a thousand gas masks but was refused and thereby considerably irked. Lynch, she said, was "making grand-sounding statements from Dublin about his readiness to march to our defense. But he was only playing politics; such a march would have been tantamount to a declaration of war on England, and Mr. Lynch is economically tied to Mother England's apron strings and his army is no match for the British."

North and South, the Catholics of Ireland admire her but are a little puzzled by her. Her radical-youth style, her toughness, her enigmatic smile—all tend to make older and more conservative people wary of her somewhat simplistic program for healing ancient wounds. During her 1970 reelection campaign she forthrightly announced that she was working for an "All-Ireland Socialist Workers' Republic." There is not really much visible sentiment for turning Ireland into something like another Cuba.

Miss Devlin is not the leader of all the Catholics in Northern Ireland, nor is the Reverend Ian Paisley the Protestant Führer he often pretends to be. Tall, beefy, and blustering, the Reverend Mr. Paisley is head of the Free Presbyterian Movement, a member of the Ulster Parliament and the hardest of hard liners against the country's 500,000 Catholics. He also leads the resistance to reforms promised by the government of Prime Minister James Chichester-Clark, including those of proportionate representation, new housing for the Catholic ghettos, fuller employment for Catholics. One of his election slogans: "You cannot talk peace until the enemy surrenders, and the enemy is the Catholic Church." If his blustery, humorless, loudly self-righteous personality possesses any element of the charismatic, it is visible only to those thousands of followers of his who are stricken by the fear that when the Catholic Irish become first-class citizens, they will become even more troublesome, that even farther into the future the Catholics will outbreed the Protestants.

(The demographic threat may be more real than the other fears upon which Paisley plays with ham-handed zeal. Equality of opportunity in the North could arrest the high rate of emigration. Because of a higher birth rate, according to Brendan M. Walsh's *Religion and Demographic Behaviour in Ireland,* recently published by the Economic and Social Research Institute, the Catholic minority in North Ireland could become a majority in fifty years. In the Republic and Northern Ireland combined, Walsh found, the fertility rate among Catholics is 50 percent higher than Protestants. Among the professional classes in North Ireland, for instance, Protestant families have an average of 1.98 children to 3.61 for Catholics. In both the North and the South, however, the birthrate may fall with growing prosperity. "It is not unimaginable," as Walsh says, "that in a situation of equal economic opportunity, a sharp fall in fertility, experienced in such countries as Italy and Spain since the war, could be duplicated among the Catholic population of Ireland in the not-too-distant future.")

The reality of the situation in Belfast, Londonderry, and other places where Catholics and Protestants confront each other is so edged with fear and hate it all seems like a throwback to another century when religious conflict was the norm. The intransigence on both sides is all but incredible. Emotions run even higher than usual when there are television cameras on the scene; at times in Belfast, as in other places, they seem to be the agitprop instrument of modern revolution. There was the day early in the summer of 1970, for instance, when television crews and the press were out in full force to cover two funerals resulting from a riot in which six Protestants and one Catholic had been killed. Belfast and Londonderry were being patrolled by 11,000 British troops, whose presence alone prevented a massacre. Down one street near the Newtownards Road came the cortege of James McCurrie, a Protestant, with hundreds in the grim-faced procession. Down an intersecting street came the coffin of Henry McIlhone, the Catholic riot victim, borne on the shoulders of a half dozen young men and followed by the weeping widow and other relatives. The two processions came within sight of each other; there were shouts of "Dirty Papists" from the Protestant mourners and "Bloody Prods" from the Catholic, and just before the two bands of mourners could come to blows a British army patrol hurried up and diverted the McCurrie funeral. The riot which caused the swift transfer of fresh regiments from England had resulted from the jailing of Bernadette Devlin on charges of rioting and inciting to riot.

About eight months later, in February, 1971, those peacekeeping troops from Britain themselves came under heavy attack. The pretext was the death of a five-year-old Catholic girl in Belfast, who was run over by a British scout car. Rioting quickly broke out, in which scores of children, many of them under twelve years old, led attacks on the British troops with stones and gasoline bombs. Lurking in the background, according to neutral observers, were members of the ultramilitant IRA provisionals, two members of which faction were given "military" funerals by their comrades provocatively uniformed in black berets and khaki jackets. (The black-and-tan motif was odd, considering the same color scheme was used by the most hated of British auxiliaries fifty years before.) Before that February riot was ended, eleven persons were killed; they included a British soldier, the first fatality suffered by the peace-keeping troops, and five men who were riding in a Land Rover which struck a land mine evidently planted by terrorists in County Tyrone.

The use of children in the front ranks of attacking mobs has not increased the popularity of the IRA extremists with Catholic moderates in either the North or the South, but it suggests the development of a new strategy of terror operating against both the young British soldiers reluctant to fire on children and public opinion in the Republic. It is aimed, first of all, at forcing the withdrawal of the British troops, an objective well in sight, considering the abhorrence of the British public for any more refereeing among the Irish. That, of course, could result in a resurgence of Protestant militancy. The outnumbered Catholics of Ulster might be overwhelmed, but that could force the cautious government in Dublin to send up its army and reclaim the six northern counties, with a "workers' republic" the eventual result.

On both sides a siege mentality has developed that would seem likely to endure, short of a Second Coming of Christ. It is strengthened with each new martyrdom, and there are no people who place a higher emotional value on martyrdom than the Irish; there is hardly a place in the island where some past bloodletting is not marked by a Celtic cross, a plaque or marker, hardly a Sunday that passes without the commemoration of a long-dead hero or victim of past misunderstanding and injustice. "If this goes on," a minister in the Ulster government said recently, "this province will be reduced to a dunghill with only Ian Paisley crowing on its summit and Bernadette Devlin scuttling like a hen around its foot."

The dead-end bitterness may be studied on both sides of the barbed wire strung up and patrolled by British troops on the "peace line" in Belfast which was established after the 1970 riots.

It cuts across Percy Street, where a young Protestant man and his family live on their side of the barbed wire, and Hugh Davey and his two sisters, Catholics, live on the other. Desmond Ball, a twenty-two-year-old machinery repairman, his wife, and his children live at 78 Percy among houses and storefronts displaying the Union Jack and shields bearing the Red Hand of Ulster. Across the barricade he can see the house of eighty-year-old

Hugh Davey and his sisters at 112 Percy, but the two men have never met and probably never will.

Ball acquired his red-brick house after a Protestant gang had given the Catholic family which occupied it a half hour to clear out with all their possessions. "Mr. Davey?" he says. "Don't know him. We don't know any Catholics. Individually a Catholic can be all right, but as a group they're dangerous. I'd never turn my back on a Catholic. If we wanted Catholic friends and the word got around the neighborhood, we'd get our windows broken in. People feel that strongly."

Ball insists that he has no ingrained prejudice, that "my parents didn't bring me up to hate. I wouldn't bring my son up that way either. But my father wouldn't've let me marry a Catholic and I'd never let my son marry one."

His fears aren't centered on being outnumbered, but on his conviction that Ulster's Catholics are determined to achieve a union with the Republic. The fighting will go on for years, he believes, riot after riot, death after death, and there's no way of stopping it. Eventually he—and many Ulstermen—think there will be a civil war involving both Irelands and eventually England. "The Irish army will come up and support the Catholics; the British army will intervene to support us." In less than forty years, he believes, "there will be no Northern Ireland." Yet he sees no value in concessions, in trying to arrive at a working arrangement with the Catholics. Instead, he clings fiercely to his Orange Order sash, which has been handed down to him by his forefathers, and all it stands for.

Down the street the aged Hugh Davey feels equally threatened in the small house where he has lived since 1958 with his unmarried sisters. Fifty years ago, when they lived in Crumlin Road, they were dispossessed by a Protestant mob. "The soldiers saved us then," Davey recalls. "This last summer I was almost burned out again. There were fourteen other Catholic homes destroyed on this street by the Protestants with Molotov cocktails and paving stones. I managed to save my house only by having buckets of water ready in every room. Every time a fire would start I put it out. It kept up for three hours, and my sisters and I said more prayers in that time than we'd said in a lifetime. We didn't think we'd live to see daylight again."

A retired publican, Davey recalls that sectarian bitterness was a part of his earliest memories. "When I was seven years old, the Protestants used to put up orange arches over the street. We had to walk through a small brook to avoid walking under them. Sheer bloody-mindedness. And things aren't getting any better. I don't dare go out on the streets after three o'clock in the afternoon. If the British pulled their troops out, we wouldn't last here for one week. They'd come down that street and firebomb us out."

The main difficulty aside from religion is the inequality of opportunity, Davey believes. (The statistics seem to bear him out. A 1967 survey showed that only 3 Catholics held the 106 civil service positions which paid more than £4,000 ($9,600). The same holds true of other occupations, partly because the Protestants are generally better educated.) "The ruling Protestants have always had the good jobs," he says. "We've always been hewers of wood and drawers of water. If I'd been a Protestant, I'd probably have had a better job than pulling pints for twenty-seven years."

Like his Protestant neighbor up the street, he sees no end to the struggle. "It's a tradition," he says with a shrug. "There isn't any way out."

So both Catholics and Protestants are trapped in medieval attitudes, like a frieze of spear-carrying warriors eternally marching toward each other. The youth of both persuasions are as fanatical as, and physically a lot more active than, their elders; it's no good waiting for a new generation so long as Ulster boys and girls are educated and indoctrinated in separate school systems.

Brian Moore was so despairing after his visit to Belfast that he believed "Ulster people must die like dogs. Unless they do, nothing will change. The British public cares deeply about dogs. It does not want to think about the Irish who are a centuries-old nuisance." Though Moore describes himself as "a Catholic who is no longer a Catholic," he considers the British the only possible saviors. "We must now become wards of the English state. England must, at last, accept its responsibility toward us, which is to rule us, directly, totally, as part of that 'United Kingdom of Great Britain and Northern Ireland' which our passports proclaim us to be. Forever and ever, amen."

Mr. Moore's prescription would undoubtedly be palatable to the Protestant majority, except for the fact it would probably entail the abolition of the Ulster Parliament. The Catholics, however, would prefer union with the Irish Republic, though they do resent the English less than the Orangemen. The question is whether the British government and people, having unshouldered the burden of empire everywhere else, would be willing to take on the additional responsibility of directly administering Northern Ireland. There's little or nothing in it for the British; they are already subsidizing Northern Ireland at the rate of £170,000,000 annually, aside from the cost of maintaining thousands of troops there. The state of the British economy, the failure of the Belfast shipyards to approximate the productivity of the West German and Japanese competition, the distaste of the British electorate for heavily financing profitless ventures abroad —all argue against Britain's assuming direct rule over Northern Ireland.

The only sensible solution is union with the Republic, which has more than amply demonstrated its tolerance toward the Protestant minority within its own borders. The only losers would be the Ulster magnates and the fanatics like the Reverend Ian Paisley. The hard task of the future is to convince the 1,000,000 Protestants of Northern Ireland that they have little to lose but the paralysis of ancient attitudes and much to gain in the form of civil peace. Many of the more thoughtful people in the South believe that it is principally the task of the southern Irish to make concrete proposals which would reassure the northern Protestants; that the Ulstermen must be convinced that neither they nor their religion would be endangered by a union of the two Irelands; that the Prime Minister of a united Ireland would not necessarily be Miss Bernadette Devlin or some other firebrand.

A visit to the "black city," even a few hours in the streets where Catholic and Protestant neighborhoods confront each other as armed camps, and a blurred glimpse of boys no more than twelve or thirteen engaged in street fighting, is more likely to convince one that the heraldic Red Hand of Ulster was a symbol well chosen, and that this may be one of the world's many insoluble problems.

15.

A Sense of Destiny

Ireland, like Israel, has a sense of some special destiny, which enables her to bear her discomfitures with fatalism and secret pride.

—Arland Ussher

☘ There are plentiful shorthand symbols for the transition the Irish are experiencing in their passage from a largely pastoral life to that of a modern nation. One of the more graphic is Druid Hill on the outskirts of Dublin: a ring of trees once regarded as sacred enclosing an arrangement of stones on which sacrifices were once made and prayers offered. It is still regarded as a place to make wishes, not necessarily to the old deities, and most people silently do. The glade is now surrounded by a housing project. The important thing, of course, is that bulldozers did not simply level what is, after all, only a ring of trees and a pile of stones as a matter of convenience, as American progress has trampled over everything from Indian burial mounds to three centuries of some lovely architecture. The Irish respect their past and draw strength from it. That is why any book about the Irish can hardly avoid a recitation of political history and ancient wrongs; this is not merely waving the bloody shirt. The Irish are incomprehensible without an understanding of what has been done to them in the past. Having survived so much, having triumphed over their bitter history, they are equipped with a certainty that fate, somehow, has reserved something special, something morally and spiritually significant for them.

That secret assurance, perhaps, is why the Irish spirit remains buoyant. You may find plenty of gloomy, cynical, and pessimistic Irishmen; you may find many who are living below what has been established as the poverty line in more prosperous countries, but the Irishman has a mysterious faith that everything will come out right in the end. Nothing but the most outrageous manifestation of that spirit could have prompted a few hundred men to set out one Easter with pikes and shotguns to drive out a modern British army.

The gloom, cynicism, and pessimism you find are largely traceable to the years following that Easter Rising. Just as Ireland was the pilot model for the British in extending an empire around the world, the Irish liberation served as a standard for subsequent lowerings of the Union Jack in India, elsewhere in Asia and in Africa. Thus the Irish were the first in the modern world to know the sharpest pang of decolonization: the reluctant recognition that not all their earthly troubles could be blamed on the British. Those withdrawal symptoms, those frustrations paradoxically born of political freedom, have lasted for decades, as they will in all former colonies.

Perhaps the hangover would not have been so long and painful if the Irish, like the American colonies, had simply fought to rid themselves of the British presence. But the Irish are an ancient race while the Americans were and are a new one with constantly changing multiracial components; they were not struggling merely for a visible, material objective, but for their vision of what Ireland should be. They were gripped by a mystique, and their aims were hard to define. Some leaders (like De Valera) looked to the past for inspiration, others (like Cosgrave) looked to the future, and others (like Collins) hoped for a practical fusion of elements which could not be fused. No more than any other nation can Ireland be both modern industrial and preserve such ancient forms as are represented by the Irish language and the urge to seek a mid-Atlantic isolation.

Many Irish, being intellectual introverts, understand that what seemed to be a political movement, which achieved their independence, was actually a sort of religious cult. Its real objective was to restore Irishness to Ireland and delve deep in legend, if necessary, to find the clue to that restoration. In the course of that effort the Irish suffered all the afflictions of a religious emergence, complete with schisms, martyrs, saints, heretics, doctrinal quarrels. It is that cultish atmosphere in which the modern Irish spirit was formed. And thus the image is all-important, and reality is something to be brooded over in private. As President De Valera once shrewdly remarked, "In England you can say anything as long as you do the right thing; in Ireland you can do anything as long as you say the right thing." It was not necessary for him to add that the most successful of Irish careers, his own, was solidly based on that principle.

What, then, is so precious about this Irishness the Irish are bent on preserving? Or is it precious at all? You could no more ask that question in Ireland and expect a mild answer than you could ask an Israeli what is so valuable about Jewishness.

Perhaps the most valuable thing about Irishness is its dogged defense of individualism, its tolerance of the individual no matter how far he may stray from conventional norms. Its racial tolerance has been tested and, on the whole, found durable. Its religious tolerance, considering how intolerantly the Irish themselves were treated by their conquerors, can serve as a model at least until utopian ideals have been realized elsewhere. The Irish have retained their ability to make up their own minds about the human condition and stubbornly refuse to be greatly influenced by outside currents of propaganda washing against their shores. Ireland, after all, is the only independent Celtic community left in the world.

What the Irish and their fellow Celts have to offer a world which has largely absorbed and deracinated them is the spiritual and cultural qualities which have allowed them—Scots, Welsh, Bretons, Cornish, Irish—to make an impact on Western civilization greatly out of proportion to their numbers. They have a deep sense of humanity which has never desiccated into an automatic or dogmatic humanitarianism. That is what makes living among the Irish a vivid and reviving experience for refugees from a more standardized outside world. It is true that the Irish, in taking a highly personal view of you, may occasionally succumb to gossip and malice. Their intense curiosity about what makes you tick may become annoying. But there is considerable virtue in a society that refuses to judge you solely on such criteria as the kind of car you drive, the size of your income, the scope of your business or social accomplishments. The Irish are better equipped on the whole than most peoples to resist what Matthew Arnold defined as the worst results of the Industrial Revolution in England, the materialism that took over the upper class, the vulgarity of the middle class, and the brutalization of the lower class.

Several years before he was appointed President Nixon's ambassador to Ireland, John D. J. Moore, then a vice-president of W. R. Grace & Company who had spent much time in Ireland, told me that even an Irish-American considering a move to Ireland should "keep one foot" in the United States. Why? "The sociology," he replied, "is different." With a reticence that prefigured his ambassadorial role, he did not elaborate, but one can guess at what he meant. Ireland is anything but a closed society—its hospitality may be a tourist-pamphlet cliche but is nevertheless a solid reality—but it is a nation of conspirators. The nonnative will rarely find any doors closed in his face, but with equal rarity will he be admitted to the inmost recess of Irish life.

It does not take any great amount of perception, however, to observe that next to their jealously guarded individualism, the most pervasive Irish trait is a consuming zest for life. The Irishman is the least indifferent, the least disinterested, the least aloof member of his species. He will stop to talk to you in the middle of a cloudburst; he will come out of a field and engage in lengthy discourse while his crop of hay is endangered by the onset of a northwest gale. The commonest sight along an Irish thoroughfare is a roadblock constituted by two cars parked together while their drivers converse. The oddities and small dramas of daily life are simply more important than matters other peoples find more urgent. Work is not an obstacle to be surmounted or cleared away with a puritan relish; it can be reconnoitered, considered, and deferred without loss of self-esteem, and it will be done with a leisurely grace that contains an element of efficiency which outsiders can only regard as mysterious. The Irish may not have solved all the problems of industrializing themselves, but leisure, the constructive use of time, which is one of the least-considered problems of a mechanized society, is something they can cope with, with an innate authority. Give a man a pint of stout and a few companions, and he will make an afternoon vanish without effort. A soccer ball and an empty pitch will keep a sizable throng of Irish men and boys out of mischief until twilight. This talent for making something out of the thinnest materials—a cup of tea, a walk down the road, a Saturday in the nearest market town—is not to be underrated by other peoples who flay their senses with more destructive pleasures. Of course, they live in a country which is a constant sensual delight: There is no need for a greening of Ireland, there are tastes (gooseberries crusted with sugar) and smells (burning turf, flowering hillsides) and sounds (the eternal wind warping the trees and hedgerows) and sights (a whole panorama with nothing in movement but the slow drift of a dairy herd) which have long vanished from most parts of the world. Perhaps the greatest blessing of history, otherwise so harsh for the Irish, is that they have had time to consider what "progress" has done to more "advanced" nations, and it is the greatest blessing of the Irish character that, probably, one hopes, they will not allow their gemlike island to be similarly treated, that there will always be a "bee-loud glade" in which a future William Butler Yeats can restore himself.

That sturdy sense of independence, which is their Celtic heritage, and their determination to go their own way, which (again hopefully) will prevent them from being converted into a slavish appendage of the European assembly line or a mirror image of American popularization, may guide the Irish toward that special destiny which is their secret national hope.

Ireland's search for a role on the international stage, without succumbing to the pretentiousness of a neo-De Gaullism, is not as ridiculous as it may seem.

In the past decade Ireland has exercised an influence in the United Nations out of proportion to its size and power. It was a chief sponsor of the concept of nonproliferation of nuclear weapons; it kept out of NATO in preference to increasing its influence among the neutral nations, and undersized as its armed forces are, it provided peace-keeping troops for the Congo, the Gaza Strip, and Cyprus. For some years it seemed to be vaguely aspiring to a leading role in the Third World, for which it was specially equipped by its own lengthy colonial experience and by its long-standing missionary efforts among the African and Asian peoples. (The gruff Irish priest stationed in some African water hole or Chinese village was as much a part of the colonial era as such stock characters as Sanders of the River, Yank adventurers, or Maughamesque planters.) Race and geography, however, seemed to rule out any great affinity of Ireland with such nations as Indonesia, Algeria, and Ghana. Whatever other credentials he may have, and no doubt to his enormous disgust, the Irishman in the colored Third World is hardly distinguishable in speech or appearance from an Englishman or American. This is not to say the Irish have lost all interest in the struggles of the emerging nations, with which they can sympathize more than most other Westerners.

There is a Fourth World, hitherto the province of dreamers and mystics and perhaps a few madmen, which is in the process of rebirth. That is the fragmented world of the surviving Celts, as nebulous and problematical as Cockaigne. Before the Irish Revolution, during the literary renaissance, Dublin was the capital of a Celtic revival movement that drew partisans, some rather hairy and wild-eyed, from all over Western Europe. Dublin once again is the headquarters of those various separatist movements, with a sprouting of strange flags and aggressive slogans, which serve at the moment as easy satirical targets for visiting English journalists.

Yet the Celtic nationalist movements in France and Britain are not merely the product of a lunatic fringe boozily projecting a Celtic Dawn. A short visit to Wales will demonstrate to the disbeliever that Celtic-consciousness is very much alive, with almost a million Welshmen speaking their ancient tongue (more fluently and enthusiastically, perhaps because voluntarily, than most Irish can speak Irish), hearing it on their own radio and television stations and reading it in their own books, magazines, and newspapers. In recent years the Scots have been particularly active in promoting their own political cause and are sending more and more Scottish nationalists to Parliament; they are more inclined to politicking as the Welsh and Irish are adept at the various forms of propaganda. In Brittany, the Celtic Bretons have been stirring up considerable resistance to the central government in Paris, ostensibly over agricultural disputes, actually as a confrontation of Celt versus Gaul.

It would be overstating the case for Celtic unity to suggest that one day soon there will be independent republics of Scotland, Wales, and Brittany allied to the Republic of Ireland, though there is a worldwide tendency toward such breakaways. There does not have to be a violent exercise in separatism to bring the Irish and the other Celtic remnants together in a cultural and spiritual association. Individually, scattered far and wide, the Celts have made good in the world; reunited in some form, they could have a tremendous impact on the world's affairs. Ireland, instead of an outpost, might become a centrifugal force, the headquarters of an All-Gaelic Parliament and a great Celtic university without a nuclear physicist or a computer scientist in sight.

Worse things could happen.

Even without the culmination of such romantic aspirations, Ireland and its people stand for something unique and humanly valuable. More than any other nation, they have proved that it is possible to survive in the modern world through powers as insubstantial as thought and as invisible as an idea.

Appendix I

Paddywhackery

☘ Paddywhackery is a uniquely Irish endeavor as the word suggests. The English would call it a send-up, the Americans a put-on, but it goes further than that. It might be defined as exaggerating Irish characteristics to the point of self-caricature, though generally the distortion gently ridicules the beholder rather than the subject. It might also be defined as an offshoot of blarneying, with a slightly bitter aftertaste.

You may be certain that you are being paddywhacked if a native uses the words "begorra" or "bejabbers" in your presence. Walter Bryan holds that the Irish are culpable as far as their rather colorful image abroad is concerned. "The Irish are to blame for their reputation because some of them retell these stories themselves and others even act them out for the benefit of strangers. One of the great Irish faults is that they can never resist a joke, a failing which lands them in endless trouble. . . . If a visitor to Ireland happens to be the sort of person who throws his weight about, he will come home with enough stories of Irish incompetence to last him a lifetime."

A sterling example of paddywhackery could be found in the propaganda surrounding the 1970 visit of President Nixon, who was supposedly bent on tracking down some of his remote ancestors during a stopover on his return from a tour of the Mediterranean. Obviously it takes more than a few hours to discover the spoor of a great-great-grandfather who lived obscurely in an Irish village, the annals of the poor being notoriously scant and elusive.

The Irish could view the Presidential project, undertaken a short time before an election in which Irish-Americans were being wooed away (successfully in many cases) from their traditional allegiance to the Democratic Party, only with a certain amount of skepticism. Thus, when the propaganda makers descended, there was a veritable carnival of paddywhackery: an elderly woman persuaded to pose for photographers while smoking a clay pipe, a lineup of merry villagers each solemnly clutching a pint of Guinness in the local pub, and other sardonically staged views of the Irish as they believed the outside world thinks of them.

You had only to hear of a clay pipe being trotted out to know the paddywhackers were at work. If they chose a symbol for their avocation, it might be a green derby, sprigged with shamrocks, rampant on a field of empty stout bottles.

Paddywhackery of a scientific type is, of course, the special province of the Irish Tourist Board, the resort hotels, travel agents, and others concerned with tourism. It's only part of their job, like that of their counterparts elsewhere who attempt to persuade you that Bavaria is rife with jovial peasants in short leather pants and that the female population of Sweden is entirely composed of long-legged concupiscent blondes. This is commercial paddywhackery, the work of professionals who become jaded in their pursuit of salable folkways and picturesque survivals.

The more authentic sort of paddywhackery is produced by amateurs. If you fall into the hands of an expert, you are likely to feel as though you have been psychologically bushwhacked; there is a real as well as etymological kinship between paddywhacking and bushwhacking. If you were a sheepherder out in the American West in the days of the open range, for instance, you might be bushwhacked for invading cattle country. If you come to Ireland brimming with misconceptions—many of them, perhaps, stemming from overindulgence in Irish literature, or whiskey, or motion pictures made by sentimental Irish-Americans—you greatly risk being paddywhacked. "We welcome strangers—no place more—and they accept willingly our blatant hypnotism and our narcotic charm," the knowing Tony Butler has observed. "Brainwashed in a million shades of shamrock, they stagger back to the world refreshed in living and with green-laughtered blood going in and out with the tides of Ulster, Leinster, Munster and Connaught."

Paddywhackery

The Irish have suffered for centuries from outlanders determined to misunderstand them, particularly the Anglo-Saxons, who persisted in viewing the Irish as mischievous children and thus justified their stern parental presence on the island. They resent the legendary picture of themselves as a race of dreamers and drunkards and superstition mongers, yet that picture has not been entirely erased, if only because, like most caricatures, it contains an unpalatable element of truth. There is only one way of combating it: exaggerating the exaggeration so that anyone foolish enough to accept it is the real butt of the joke.

Appendix II

Traveler's Warnings

☘ Never buy poteen (the mountain dew distilled from anything available and possessing the kick of white mule made by Appalachian distillers) from a stranger. Better yet, never drink poteen.

Never agree with an Irishman when he is criticizing himself; he can do a far better job on his own and resents any footnotes to his self-destructive soliloquies.

Don't expect any special favors because you're an Irish-American. They'll be all the gladder to see you if you don't fulfill the libelous stereotype by brandishing a large cigar, driving a large automobile on the narrow Irish roads, and talking in a large voice. The Irish, mostly, are a quiet people. Lower your voice a few decibels, and this goes double for a female American.

Never underestimate the efficiency of the Irish grapevine or bush telegraph, which is swifter and better organized than the Associated Press.

If you buy property, don't build a fence around a beach or field. The Irish are still nomads at heart and like to wander where they will. They purple with rage at the sight of barbed wire. Nothing offended them more since Cromwell's invasion than the Germans who bought coastal property and proceeded to fence off their beaches until dissuaded.

Fast service anywhere is not in the Irish tradition and, if encountered, must be regarded as a happy accident.

Don't be surprised if the young porter or chambermaid in a

country hotel takes flight when you try to tip them. In most parts of the countryside, tipping is still regarded as a little shameful and degrading. It is probably the last civilized country in the world where you will have to pursue a hotel employee, who has just coped with a mound of your luggage, down the corridor and force money on him. If you are as embarrassed as he is by the transaction, you can reflect that he needs the money a lot more than you do.

Sources

In a lifetime of reading about Ireland and the Irish I have found two books by and about the modern Irish to be invaluable for their wit, perception, objectivity and penetration. They are Sean O'Faolain's *The Irish* and Arland Ussher's *The Face and Mind of Ireland.* Coincidentally both were published in 1949. For straight history, political and social, the outstanding are Timothy Patrick Coogan's *Ireland Since the Rising* and Dorothy Macardle's *The Irish Republic.* Strongly recommended as the wittiest of surveys, one which has not received sufficient notice, is Walter Bryan's *The Improbable Irish.* Listed below are many of the authors I have quoted in the preceding pages and the works on which I have leaned:

BARRY, TOM, *Guerilla Days in Ireland.* New York, 1956.
BEHAN, BRENDAN, *Borstal Boy.* New York, 1958.
BENCE-JONES, MARK, *The Remarkable Irish.* New York, 1966.
BESTIC, ALAN, *The Importance of Being Irish.* London, 1969.
BLANSHARD, PAUL, *The Irish and Catholic Power.* New York, 1954.
BREEN, DAN, *My Fight for Irish Freedom.* Dublin, 1924.
BRISCOE, ROBERT, and HATCH, ALDEN, *For the Life of Me.* Boston, 1960.
BRYAN, WALTER, *The Improbable Irish.* New York, 1969.
BUTLER, TONY, *The Book of Blarney.* Dublin, 1969.
BYRNE, PATRICK F., *Witchcraft in Ireland.* Cork, 1968.
COLUM, MARY, *Life and the Dream.* New York, 1947.
CONNERY, DONALD S., *The Irish.* New York, 1968.
COOGAN, TIMOTHY PATRICK, *Ireland Since the Rising.* New York, 1966.
———, *The IRA.* London, 1970.
DANAHER, KEVIN, *Ireland Long Ago.* Cork, 1962.
DEVLIN, BERNADETTE, *The Price of My Soul.* New York, 1970.

DOWLING, P. J., *The Hedge Schools of Ireland.* Cork, 1968.
EDWARDS, OWEN DUDLEY, ed., *Conor Cruise O'Brien Introduces Ireland.* London, 1969.
GOGARTY, OLIVER ST. JOHN, *As I Was Walking Down Sackville Street.* London, 1958.
GRAY, TONY, *The Irish Answer.* Boston, 1966.
HEALY, JOHN, *The Death of an Irish Town.* Cork, 1968.
JOYCE, JAMES, *The Dubliners.* New York, 1958.
JOYCE, P. W., *Old Celtic Romances.* London, 1879.
KEANE, JOHN B., *Letters of a Successful T. D.* Cork, 1967.
———, *Self-Portrait.* Cork, 1964.
LUCEY, CHARLES, *Ireland and the Irish.* New York, 1970.
MACARDLE, DOROTHY, *The Irish Republic.* Dublin, 1951.
O'BRIEN, KATE, *My Ireland.* New York, 1962.
O'CONNOR, FRANK, *An Only Child.* New York, 1961.
O'FAOLAIN, SEAN, *The Irish.* New York, 1949.
O'SUILLEABHAIN, MICHAEL, *Where Mountainy Men Have Sown.* Tralee, 1965.
POWELL, T. E. G., *The Celts.* New York, 1956.
PRITCHETT, V. S., *Dublin: A Portrait.* New York, 1967.
ROHAN, DORINE, *Marriage Irish Style.* Cork, 1969.
ROLLESTON, T. W., *Myths and Legends of the Celtic Races.* London, 1911.
RYAN, DESMOND, *Michael Collins and the Invisible Army.* Dublin, 1968.
SHERIDAN, JOHN D., *The Right Time.* Dublin, 1951.
SOMERVILLE, EDITH, *Irish Memories.* London, 1919.
TAYLOR, REX, *Michael Collins.* London, 1961.
TRACY, HONOR, *Mind You, I've Said Nothing!* New York, 1950.
USSHER, ARLAND, *The Face and Mind of Ireland.* London, 1949.
WHITE, TERENCE DE VERE, *Kevin O'Higgins.* Tralee, 1966.
YEATS, WILLIAM BUTLER, *The Autobiography of William Butler Yeats.* New York, 1916.
YOUNGER, CALTON, *Ireland's Civil War.* London, 1968.

Index

Index

Index

Index

Index

Index

Index